Cajun and Creole Folktales

Cajun and Creole Folktales

The French Oral Tradition of South Louisiana

Collected and annotated by
Barry Jean Ancelet

University Press of Mississippi
Jackson

The paper in this book meets the guidelines for permanence and durability of the
Committee on Production Guidelines for Book Longevity of the Council on Library
Resources.

Library of Congress Cataloging-in-Publication Data

Cajun and Creole folktales: The French oral tradition of South Louisiana / collected and
    annotated by Barry Jean Ancelet.
        p. cm. —
    Originally published: New York: Garland, 1994, in series: World Folktale library; v. 1.
    Includes bibliographical references and index.
    ISBN 0-87805-709-9 (alk paper)
        1.Cajuns—Folklore. 2.Tales—Louisiana. 3.Folklore—Louisiana. 4. Cajun French
dialect — Texts. I.Ancelet, Barry Jean.
    GR111.F73C35 1994   93–48885
    398'.089410783—dc20   CIP

For my grandmothers, Elia Arceneaux Ancelet and Ida Chautin Mayer, and my parents, Maude and Elmo Ancelet

---

"Si c'est beau, ça a pas besoin d'être vrai; et si c'est vrai, ça a pas besoin d'être beau."
— Jean Arceneaux

Contents

Foreword

Barry Jean Ancelet is best known among folklorists as the foremost interpreter of Cajun musical traditions. His book, *The Makers of Cajun Music* (1984), is both a perceptive analysis of Cajun musical styles and a vehicle for the musicians to express, in their own words and on their own terms, their life experiences with and deepest feelings about their art. In this book, as in all his other work, Barry does not steal the stage, but yields it to the performers.

As a scholar, Ancelet takes pride in his folkloric studies. But as a Cajun, he takes equal or greater pride in his role as a leading figure in the Cajun musical renaissance which has deeply affected musicians and music lovers throughout South Louisiana as well as far beyond the borders of the state. In 1974, he co-founded the Tribute to Cajun Music, which has evolved into a two-day "self-celebration" of Cajun culture that Ancelet directs each September. He also helped originate and now serves as master of ceremonies for the *Rendez-Vous des Acadiens*, a weekly live broadcast of Cajun music narrated in French. He played an instrumental part in having musicians Dennis McGee, Canray Fontenot, and Dewey Balfa named Honorary Professors of Cajun Music at the University of Southwestern Louisiana. All too often, folklorists have assembled stables of great performers whom they've exploited and treated in condescending fashion. Ancelet's approach has been the opposite: it has been his goal to gain recognition for the artists rather than for himself and to see that they were recognized by their fellow Cajuns, and even by the academy, as the true heroes of the Cajun cultural revival.

Cajun and Creole Folktales reveals another important facet of Ancelet's engagement with Louisiana French folklore. When he first introduced me to his work with Cajun narrative he told me, "Most people don't know it, but I love the stories as much as the music." I suspect that his regard for these tales runs even deeper than his love of the music, be-cause—while the Cajun musical revival is now running on its own steam, carrying with it even the younger Cajuns who know little or no French—the complex taletelling tradition, far more intimate and language-bound, persists hidden from those who are not fluent in French. For most of the last twenty years, Ancelet has worked nearly alone in recording Louisiana French oral narrative and in gaining recognition for the great narrators who have fashioned it.

Since he began collecting folktales in 1973, Ancelet has published numerous tales with commentary in journals and books (1974, 1975, 1980a, 1981, 1982, 1991); con-ducted specific studies of Cajun anti-clerical humor (1985), oral historical accounts (1983),

jokes about Cajuns (1989), and violence in Cajun and Creole folk narrative (1988); and produced a brilliant contextual analysis of a Cajun tall tale telling community (1980b). But the present collection is by far his most comprehensive work; indeed, it is easily the most thorough compendium of Cajun and Creole oral traditions yet published.

Perhaps the most important aspect of *Cajun and Creole Folktales* is its refusal to submit to the arbitrary restrictions of traditional scholarly boundaries. Ancelet effectively demolishes some of the compartmentalizing stereotypes which dominated early research. First, previous treatments of Louisiana French folktales have dealt exclusively either with black Creoles (e.g., Fortier 1895) or white Cajuns (Saucier 1962). Ancelet, however, treats the two groups as a continuum, an approach which he fully justifies by documenting powerful connections between Cajun and Creole tales. Second, earlier collections were limited in generic breadth: Fortier dealt almost exclusively with animal tales, Saucier, with magic tales; Bergeron (1980), with personal narratives—each conveyed at best a fragmentary impression of French Louisiana oral art. But *Cajun and Creole Folktales* presents all of these folk forms, and many more as well, in an expressive span ranging from somber, often-repeated belief legends to fanciful, extemporaneously composed adventures featuring the imaginary tall tale hero Pascal. Finally, earlier collections of Cajun folktales—Calvin Claudel (1948) and Saucier—concentrated on Old World survivals and only included those tales that most strongly reflected the vestiges of seventeenth-century French tradition still alive in Louisiana. Ancelet's work presents a much fuller and more accurate account of Cajun taletelling, because he has collected the full repertoire of narrative genres developed by French speakers in the region. As the tales themselves demonstrate, and as Ancelet documents in his copious comparative notes, Cajun and Creole oral traditions are not simply French, but rather unique to French Louisiana, where African, African American, British American, Native American, and Spanish American populations have created a complex cultural mix, and where the once-dominant French-speaking cultures have created artful narrative combinations conditioned by a unique environment and reshaped to meet the distinctive needs and values of the new societies that came into being on the southern Louisiana prairies and bayous.

To transcend the scholarly stereotype that these Louisiana folktales were simply survivals of French originals, Ancelet immersed himself in comparative narrative scholarship, examining parallels from the African, African American, British American, French, French American, French Canadian, Native American, and Spanish American traditions whose mingled presence is reflected in the Cajun and Creole corpus. More importantly, he drew upon his personal experience as a Cajun, a lover of oral historical traditions, and a fluent speaker of Cajun French: only such knowledge could make this collection possible. Most of the narrators whose tales appear here would not have told their tales so richly without the presence of a listener who shared their frame of reference as deeply as did Ancelet. In telling "La jument verte," master narrator Félix Richard adorns his tales with subtle cultural cues. For example, the giant hairy-chested bully who confronts the little bachelor has a handkerchief protruding from one of his pockets—a detail that seems ab-

surdly delicate, completely out of place for those who don't know that such handkerchiefs were used in knife fights in Cajun dancehalls. Each fighter would hold one end of the handkerchief in one hand and his knife in the other; this ensured that the two would fight at close quarters. Without a listener who shared his knowledge of Cajun tradition, Félix Richard would not have bothered to add this detail to his tale—if he had bothered to tell the tale at all.

One reason why no book of Cajun folktales has ever before appeared in French is that, until very recently in Cajun country, French has not been a literary language. Banned from the classroom, French stayed at home, thriving as the medium for the most important family and community communications. Some Cajun taletellers are exquisitely literate in English, but have never learned to read or write their native speech. Thus, such indigenous collections as John Bergeron's *Cajun Folklore* (1980) present in English stories that were actually told more often in French; otherwise the tellers would not be able to read the stories that they told.[1] One positive aspect of this linguistic irony is that Cajun storytellers have been forced to rely exclusively on their oral skills to keep these tales alive, a challenge to which they have responded vigorously and artfully.

In his introduction, Ancelet calls attention to the great range of narrative genres represented in this collection. *Cajun and Creole Folktales* serves as a record of the extraordinary breadth of Louisiana French narrative traditions, but it is, more specifically, the record of a particular transitional moment for those traditions. As Ancelet notes, the animal tales and magic tales presented here are no longer active in the repertoires of present-day Louisiana narrators, and many of the legends and historical tales are viewed by their tellers as messages from a vanished world. Yet the jokes and tall tales, some of the legends, and most of the historical narratives are told just as often as they ever were. There is no doubt whatever that Cajun men and women will continue telling masterful tales, but the particular range of tales, styles, and topics embraced here will never be present again. Stanislaus "Tanisse" Faul—who contributes to this collection a magic tale, an animal tale, a tall tale, and many jokes, legends, and historical narratives—represents a cultural context in which all of these genres thrived side by side. Tanisse is now dead, like many of the other great narrators— Frank Couppel, Elby Deshotels, Burke Guillory, Ben Guiné, Martin Latiolais—whose stories follow. And Tanisse's descendants have not continued telling the more old-fashioned tales.

Thus, although *Cajun and Creole Folktales* reflects many environments, it is above all the product of the crucial years before 1950, when cars and horses mingled in equal numbers on the streets of Cajun towns, when French-language waltzes and English-language adaptations of Western Swing were sung on dancehall stages, when most families worked farms but some were being lured to town by growing industries, when adults spoke almost exclusively French but their children were being whipped in the schools for doing so.

I have had the great privilege of being present when Barry collected some of the tales published here, and of witnessing firsthand the exchange of human warmth and artis-

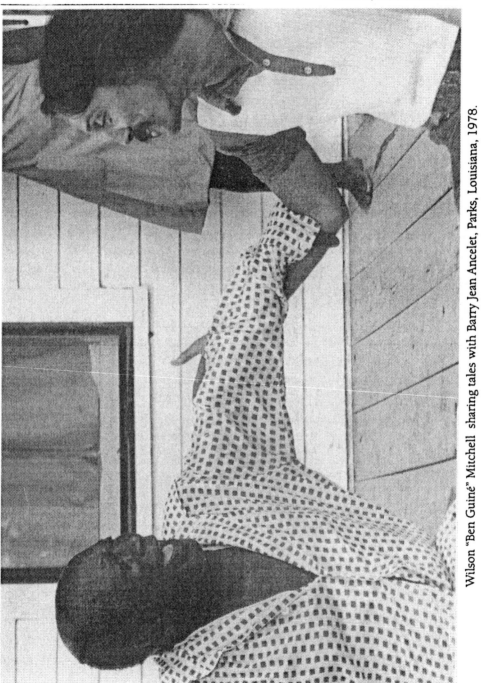

Wilson "Ben Guiné" Mitchell sharing tales with Barry Jean Ancelet, Parks, Louisiana, 1978.

tic energy by which they were transformed from memories to living works of oral art. Except for the Pascal tales and some of the jokes and tall tales, all of the performances rendered here are products of what from a distance may seem to be "artificial contexts." Generally, the tales emerged from one-on-one interviews. Barry sometimes coaxed stories from tellers whose original audience had died and whose children and grandchildren did not understand the language in which they were so artfully told.

Thus, perhaps, it could be said that the tales did not arise from "natural contexts." But such an overhasty assessment would not factor in the strong personal bond forged—sometimes instantaneously—between Barry and the taletellers. The essence of this bond is respect, a respect for the depth of the tellers' experience and the subtlety and intensity of their artistry that Barry extended to the tellers, a respect that they happily extended back to him. This mutual esteem was anything but somber and often marked with the laughter of both narrator and listener on the original tapes.

The collecting process was often so pleasurable for the tellers that they refused to let the storytelling end. One excellent narrator, Évélia Boudreaux, would withhold tales from Barry to ensure that he would visit again. Every few months she would call him and say, "I have some more tales for you"—and Barry would return to listen to her tales, as he has now done for nineteen years.

One performance by Ben Guiné crystallizes Barry's roles as collector, audience, fan, and close friend of these Creole and Cajun artists. In 1978, in recognition of Ben's enormous narrative talents, the French Department of the University of Southwestern Louisiana invited him to tell stories at a gathering in their spacious French House. Barry was apprehensive about taking Ben to such a formal setting, but Ben's interest and curiosity won out in the end. Ben, a natural storyteller who had performed with ease—even for strangers who did not understand his rich Creole dialect—on the *galerie* of his home in Parks, was visibly unnerved by the size of the crowd—some eighty listeners—and the unfamiliarity of his surroundings. Barry introduced Ben and then took a seat next to him on stage. Nothing in Ben's eighty years had prepared him for such an environment. Midway through the first story it was obvious to Barry that Ben was straining to reach many more listeners than he had ever faced at one time. In the midst of a broad gesture, he touched Barry and then instinctively swivelled his chair to face a more familiar audience. In this intimate posture, Ben regained his footing and salvaged his art from dauntingly strange surroundings. The stories flowed, powerfully and naturally, as eighty strangers were treated to the experience of a great narrator sharing tales with his friend.

Now many more strangers will share a similar experience. Invisible hands and unheard voices lie behind the masterful stories that appear here palely on the page. But intent readers will *hear* the tales, thanks to the respect and affection which Barry brought to the tellers, and which they reciprocated with some of the finest performances of their lives. Painstakingly transcribed, sensitively introduced and translated—somehow still vibrantly alive even when written in the Cajun French that their tellers spoke from birth but never read—*Cajun and Creole Folktales* is the product of the nearly miraculous process through

which one man's love of his tradition has created an enduring justification of that love, a freeze-frame record of that most perishable and delicate art of Louisiana French storytelling.[2]

Carl Lindahl,
General Editor,
World Folktale Library

Notes

1. Actually, Bergeron presents French-language versions of four of his tales, but certain textual details of these texts indicate that he does not expect his fellow Cajuns to read them. For example, his French text of "La boucan des Cajuns" explains what a barbecue is, while the English version ("Cajun Smoke Signals") does not. None of Bergeron's Cajun readers would need such an explanation, but readers from France conceivably would.
2. I thank the University of Houston for awarding me a Limited Grant in Aid to support editorial work on this volume, and Katherine Oldmixon for her expert editing.

Works Cited

Ancelet, Barry Jean. 1974. "Three Acadian Folktales." *Revue de Louisiane / Louisiana Review* 3: 39–42.

———.1975. "Louisiana Acadian Joke-Lore." *Revue de Louisiane / Louisiana Review* 4: 53–54.

———.1980a. "Talking Pascal in Mamou: A Study in Folkloric Competence." *Journal of the Folklore Institute* 17: 1–24.

———. 1980b. "Creole Folktales from Louisiana." *Revue de Louisiane / Louisiana Review* 9: 61–68.

———. 1981. "La littérature orale de la Louisiane." In *Littérature française de la Louisiane: Anthologie.* Ed. Mathé Allain and Barry Jean Ancelet. New Bedford, NH: National Materials Development Center for French. Pp. 201–250.

———. 1982. "Louisiana French Oral Literature: An Overview." In *Louisiana Tapestry: The Ethnic Weave of Saint Landry Parish.* Ed. Vaughan B. Baker and Jean T. Kreamer. Pp. 49–69.

———. 1983. "And This Is No Damn Lie: Oral History in Story Form." *International Journal of Oral History* 4:99–111.

———. 1984. *The Makers of Cajun Music.* With photographs by Elemore Morgan. Austin: University of Texas Press.

———. 1985. "Ote voir ta sacrée soutane: Clerical Humor in Louisiana Oral Tradition." *Louisiana Folklore Miscellany* 7: 26–33.

———. 1988. "My duck! My Land!: Strains of Violence in Louisiana French Oral Tradition." Paper presented to the American Folklore Society, Boston, 1988.

———. 1989. "The Cajun Who Went to Harvard: Identity in the Oral Tradition of South

Louisiana." *Journal of Popular Culture* 23: 101–114.

———. 1991. "Oral Traditions." In *Cajun Country*. By Barry J. Ancelet, Jay Edwards, and Glen Pitre. Jackson: University Press of Mississippi. Pp. 183–223.

Bergeron, John W. 1980. *Cajun Folklore: Real Stories about Louisiana Cajuns*. Esther, LA: John's Trading Post.

Claudel, Calvin. 1948. "A Study of Louisiana French Folktales in Avoyelles Parish." Diss., University of North Carolina, Chapel Hill.

Fortier, Alcée. 1895. *Louisiana Folktales in French Dialect and English Translation*. Memoirs of the American Folklore Society, no. 2. Boston: Houghton-Mifflin.

Saucier, Corinne. 1962. *Folk Tales from French Louisiana*. New York: Exposition Press.

Preface

This study began in January, 1974, when I first collected Louisiana French folktales with Barbara F. Ryder, who used the recordings we made as the basis for a mid-year research project at Colby College. I had just finished my coursework for the B.A. degree in French at the University of Southwestern Louisiana and I was already enrolled in the M.A. program in French at Indiana University. During an academic year abroad at the University of Nice (1972–73), I had begun to understand that I was less interested in the study of the French language itself than of what it served to transmit. For me, French was not an end in itself, but a tool to help understand the cultural context of French Louisiana. That first modest collection from 1974 revealed new and interesting possibilities for me. At the same time, I started graduate studies in French at Indiana, but I soon transferred to the folklore program. My master's thesis, an annotated collection of Louisiana French folktales, was an intermediate step toward the present study, which seeks to explore the relationship between culture and language and to place the oral tradition of French Louisiana in a variety of contexts: historical, geographical and linguistic, regional, national and international.

I would like to take this opportunity to thank some of my colleagues who contributed to the preparation of this book: Mathé Allain, who showed me the difference between the student and the study as well as the importance of communicating beyond cultural boundaries; Carl Brasseaux and Glenn Conrad, my colleagues in the Center for Louisiana Studies, who taught me much about the history of the French presence in Louisiana during many informal discussions; Isabelle Deutch, who helped to prepare the preliminary typescript; Carl Lindahl, who challenged me to recognize connections between variants, between genres, and between cultures; Richard Dorson, who encouraged me to begin this journey; and Robert Chaudenson, who encouraged me to complete it. As always, the University of Southwestern Louisiana provided a solid base from which to work. The Government of Québec subsidized a research trip to the Centre d'études sur la langue et les traditions populaires (CÉLAT) at the Université Laval where I discovered many correspondences among the French-speaking cultures of North America, especially during long sessions with Luc Lacourcière and Margaret Low. My wife, Caroline, and my five children, Jean, François, Louis, Emile, and Clélie, not only tolerated my sometimes obstinate pursuit of this goal, they even sometimes encouraged it. Finally, I would like to thank the storytellers whose tales are included in this study. They shared their knowledge with enthusiasm, even when they did not understand how a supposedly serious college student could possibly be interested in "all that nonsense."

The Context

On April 9, 1682, a French Canadian explorer named Robert Cavalier de la Salle claimed the lands drained by the Mississippi River and named this new territory Louisiana in honor of his king, Louis XIV of France. After an abortive effort to develop the region, the French monarch neglected his new possession until May 1699, when he sent Pierre Lemoyne d'Iberville to establish a small fort on the shores of the Gulf of Mexico. The colonization of Louisiana was slow and difficult at first, conducted primarily by Iberville's brother, Jean-Baptiste Lemoyne de Bienville, who served on several occasions as the colony's governor. The first French colonists managed to overcome the heat, torrential rains, diseases, mosquitoes, and loneliness of the sub-tropical environment to establish a few settlements along the rivers, notably the Poste des Natchitoches in 1714 and New Orleans in 1717.

In 1717, France granted John Law and his Compagnie des Indes a monopoly to exploit the colony. Despite the spectacular failure of Law's "System" in 1720, the Compagnie des Indes continued to control the colony until 1731. During this period, Louisiana's population grew considerably, as Frenchmen, Germans, and Swiss established farms along the Mississippi. African slaves brought to work on the colony's plantations also added to the colony's numbers. Such growth, however, should not be misinterpreted. Louisiana was not considered a priority of the French crown, as it produced nothing of real value for the French economy. At best, France only reluctantly maintained its colony and heaved a sigh of relief when it was ceded to Spain by the Treaty of Fountainbleau in 1762.

For Spain, Louisiana functioned as a buffer zone between its colonial empire and the English colonies which threatened to expand toward the west. The Spanish crown took the development of the colony seriously, knowing full well that Louisiana needed to be populated if it was to serve as an obstacle to English expansion. Thus, the population grew under the new regime, but though the most important adminstrative posts were filled with Spaniards, French remained the language of daily life and Frenchmen continued to form the majority of the population. The descendants of Europeans born in the colony distinguished themselves from immigrants by calling themselves Creoles (from the Spanish *criollo*). Creole also served to distinguish that which was native from that which was imported, both products (food, animals, furniture) and styles (architecture, literature, music). African slaves were distinguished from Creole slaves who were born into slavery with no memories of freedom, already acculturated and acclimatized, and thus were more valuable than those that were brought from Africa. Later the term served to distinguish French-speaking black people, called black Creoles or Creoles of color, from English-speaking African Americans.

White and black Creoles alike are very conscious of their French heritage, but the majority of French-speakers in Louisiana are descendants of the Acadians, French colonists who first settled along the Bay of Fundy in 1604. For more than a century, they prospered in their new homeland, adapting to the environment with the aide of the region's native American Indian tribes. Long before the English colonists called themselves Americans, the Acadians insisted they were no longer French. They lived outside the main lines of communication between France and New France, though their isolation was often disturbed by the wars between England and France. Acadia changed hands back and forth between the two until 1713 when the Treaty of Utrecht granted permanent possession of the colony to England, which renamed it Nova Scotia.

In 1755, English Governor Charles Lawrence ordered the deportation of the Acadians in an effort to disintegrate their society which he considered hostile to English rule. Some exiles were dispersed throughout the English colonies along the Atlantic coast, others were sent to England and later repatriated to France. Some of these were later sent to the West Indies, and still others found themselves in such faraway places as the Falkland Islands and Guyana. Between 1765 and 1785, nearly six thousand exiles arrived in Louisiana, determined to create a New Acadian society. Within one generation, they firmly reestablished themselves in southern Louisiana, first along the rivers and bayous on both sides of the Atchafalaya Basin, then in the prairies to the west. By far the largest group of immigrants to come to Louisiana, the Acadians recreated the cohesive society they had known in Acadia and quickly became the area's dominant cultural and ethnic group. Creoles, Spaniards, Germans, Scotch and Irish, West Indians and Anglo Americans eventually adopted the traditions and language of the Acadians who in turn adopted certain traits of their new neighbors. This cultural and linguistic blend produced a new Louisiana-based ethnic community called the Cajuns (Brasseaux 1987 and 1992; Dormon 1983).

France reacquired Louisiana in 1803 and just as quickly sold it to the new United States. Yet even when the Territory of Louisiana became a state in 1812, life changed little in the south where French remained the dominant language. Throughout the nineteenth century, Louisiana's French community grew in its own terms. Immigrants continued to come to the region but the flow was manageable and the Cajuns and Creoles eventually absorbed them.

The beginning of the twentieth century quickened the pace of immigration and began to reverse the currents of cultural influence. French Creoles in urban centers like New Orleans were almost completely Americanized. It was just a matter of time before the southern parishes headed in the same direction. In 1901, oil was discovered in what became known as the Evangeline field near Jennings, and the trickle of Anglo American immigration became a flood. At about the same time, the rise of American nationalism began to affect the region. Local school board policies reflected the State Department of Education's desire to impose mandatory education exclusively in English, banning French from the schools. The First World War and the Great Depression combined to fuel the melting pot's fire, and ethnic groups across the country came to understand that they were minorities in the new context of a homogenous America. The development of mass media and modern

Cajun storytellers, Lafayette, photographed in 1938 by Russell Lee for the Farm Securities Administration.

transportation opened previously isolated regions while crowding local cultures into the corner. For the Cajuns and the black Creoles of the rural parishes in the 1930s and '40s, the French language became the symbol of a cultural stigma they were trying to overcome. They made every effort to Americanize their culture, imitating styles and customs imported from the outside and stripping themselves of their traditions. Even the musicians began to perform western swing and country music, singing in English as soon as they had learned enough (Ancelet 1984 and 1989).

By the end of the Second World War, however, Cajuns began to show signs of learning to better negotiate the American mainstream in a way that would allow them to preserve their own cultural identity. Musicians were among the first to announce the change by returning to traditional sounds. In 1955, politicians like Dudley J. LeBlanc and Roy Theriot saw to it that the bicentennial of the Acadian exile was celebrated with due pomp and fostered an interest in the survival of the culture as Cajun ethnicity was mildly politicized. The establishment of the Council for the Development of French in Louisiana (CODOFIL) in 1968 focused the rather diffuse activities of the late '50s and early '60s. An official agency of the same State of Louisiana which had banished French from the schools a few decades before, CODOFIL represented official recognition for what was becoming known as the Louisiana French renaissance movement (Gold et al. 1979–80; Henry 1982; Baird 1977). Under the direction of its chairman, former U.S. Congressman James Domengeaux, CODOFIL became the driving force behind the preservation of French in Louisiana. Attacking the problem on political, educational and psychological fronts at once, CODOFIL spearheaded the establishment of policies restoring the French language in the educational system, even at the elementary level. Teachers were imported from France, Belgium and Québec to put these new policies into effect and to help train native Louisianans who would eventually replace them (Ancelet 1988). Today, there is a renewal of interest and favor among the Cajuns for the French language and the culture it helps to define. Among the black Creoles, long preoccupied with racial issues, the linguistic renaissance has been much slower, though an interest in this part of their heritage has begun to emerge as the problems of segregation are increasingly resolved.

Most of the stories presented in this collection are not antiquities. They represent the continuity of the core of Cajun folklife in the midst of the Americanization process. The tellers are almost invariably from a rural background. Even those who now live in urban areas, such as Lafayette, still have strong attachments to family farmlands nearby. The language of the tales, the details, the character and the conflicts are all richly reflective of this common background. The lifestyles of the tellers are reflected most obviously in the more active genres, especially the joke, tall tale and historical tale, which feature the quirks and preoccupations of farmers, ranchers, hunters and fishermen. This factor is not absent even in other genres, such as animal tales and magic tales, in which it may be less immediately apparent. The Creole version of the lazy cricket (type 280A; no. 15), for example, plays the accordion, conforming to local tradition, while his neighbor the ant works, and he is eventually left to freeze outside on stalks of sugar cane. The ant, incidentally, speaks English in the tale, reflecting the stereotypical industriousness of that segment of the population. The

Cajun version of Jean l'Ours (type 513B; no. 20) wins his preliminary competitions with the king in areas that resemble a local 4-H fair: best bulls, best hogs, and best dogs. After Jean wins the hand of the king's beautiful daughter, the king, described as a multi-millionaire, gives his riches and his castle to the hero. Not to be outdone, the Cajunized Jean l'Ours gives the king a river to fish in during what is in effect his retirement, the perfect gift in a society where fishing is an important avocation.

The Study

The first scholars to study the oral tradition of French Louisiana in the early part of this century were primarily interested in tracing the French and African origins of traditional tales. Undoubtedly this approach was due in part to the linguistic and cultural particularities of the region, but it also conformed to the prevailing folklore methodology of the times which placed a premium on European folktales, like those collected by the Grimms in Germany (1944), or on animal tales, like those that inspired Joel Chandler Harris to write his Uncle Remus stories (1955). When Alcée Fortier collected stories among the black Creoles in New Orleans, he focused almost exclusively on animal tales, underscoring the historical and cultural connections between Louisiana and Africa (1895). In the 1920s and '30s, Calvin Claudel (1948) and Corinne Saucier (1949) searched for fairy tales and numbskull stories which would demonstrate the connections between Louisiana and France. Although the incidental presence of more popular genres like jokes and tall tales in her 1940's collection paralleled the discipline's broadening view of oral tradition, like that of her predecessors, the focus of Elizabeth Brandon's study was on the vestiges of French tradition (1955).

Preoccupation with European and African antecedents blurred the image of Louisiana French oral tradition unnecessarily. Basically, scholars found only what they were looking for. Despite the almost touristic approach of many scholars, Louisiana is not simply a French or African cultural outpost. In his study of America's regional cultures, folklorist Richard Dorson notes an important American influence in the culture of South Louisiana, finding that "distinctively French elements are not as conspicuous as might be expected in the Cajun folklore" (1964:231). The fact is that the Cajuns and black Creoles have less connection to France and Africa and more connection to North America (where they have spent the last three centuries) than "purists" like to admit. While it is true that interesting parallels can be drawn between the Old World and Louisiana, it would be a mistake to neglect the other quite active aspects of the Cajun and Creole cultural blend.

Alcée Fortier was the first to systematically collect Louisiana French oral tradition. A professor at Tulane University at the end of the nineteenth century, Fortier was particularly interested in the black Creole culture of New Orleans. His *Louisiana Folk-Tales*, a collection of African Caribbean-style animal tales, remains a standard reference work for the study of Louisiana folklore. The method of transcription he devised to render the Louisiana Creole dialect falls somewhere between linguistics and literature and resembles Joel Chandler Harris's renditions of black English dialect. Fortier was an active folklorist. He founded the New Orleans Folklore Society, which later became the Louisiana Folklore Society, and

also served as president of the American Folklore Society in 1894.

After Fortier, the study of Louisiana French oral tradition lagged until Corinne Saucier began her work in the 1920s. The Americanization of the Louisiana educational system made studies of the state's French heritage difficult, so she went to the George Peabody College for Teachers in Nashville, Tennessee, where she produced a Master's thesis entitled, "Contes et chansons louisianais en dialecte français avec notes linguistiques" (1923). Later she went to Québec to pursue her studies under the direction of Luc Lacourcière at the Université Laval where there was considerable interest in the Louisiana French situation because of Québec's stake in the survival of the French language and culture in North America. Saucier's dissertation, "Histoire et traditions de la paroisse des Avoyelles en Louisiane," completed in 1949, included a collection of folktales which were later published in 1972 in English translation as *Folk Tales from French Louisiana* (1972). Calvin Claudel completed his dissertation, "A Study of Louisiana French Folktales in Avoyelles Parish," at the University of North Carolina in 1948. More active as a folklorist than Saucier, he drew upon his initial research to produce numerous articles for the *Journal of American Folklore* and other scholarly journals. Claudel published several articles on the French folklore of America in collaboration with Joseph Medard Carrière, author of *Tales from the French Folklore of Missouri* (1937). In the 1940s, Elizabeth Brandon came to Louisiana from Russia by way of Québec where she was studying under Luc Lacourcière at the Université Laval. Her dissertation, "La Paroisse Vermillon: Moeurs, dictons, contes et légendes," was completed in 1955 and published in series in *Bayou* from 1955 to 1957 (nos. 64-69). Claudel, Saucier and Brandon were all forced to leave Louisiana to study its French culture.

At the same time, a few studies were being carried out in Louisiana, though not strictly speaking in folklore. At Louisiana State University in the 1940s, professors James Broussard, Hoguet Major, and John Guilbeau directed research projects among graduate students who collected folk songs and tales for their studies of Louisiana's French dialects (e.g., Voorhies 1949). Strictly speaking, however, these studies were concerned with linguistics and not the literary and cultural aspects of the oral repertoire. During the 1950s, students in Marie Del Norte Theriot's French classes at the University of Southwestern Louisiana added a cultural context to their studies of the language by gathering stories, songs, games, and proverbs. This early research in Louisiana's colleges and universities, originally intended to lay the groundwork for a linguistic description of Cajun and Creole French, unfortunately has since remained undisturbed in file drawers and on library shelves.

Among the most active defenders of Louisiana French culture were folklorists like Alan Lomax, Harry Oster, and Ralph Rinzler who were primarily interested in Cajun and Creole music. Advocates of cultural self-preservation, they helped launch a program designed to recycle music in the schools and to make cultural heroes of musicians at festivals. They were less concerned with ancient survivals in the tradition than with the survival of the tradition itself (Ancelet 1984 and 1989). In contrast, the few researchers interested in the oral tradition of the area made no attempt to preserve the traditions they studied. After the establishment of CODOFIL in 1968, those involved in the Louisiana French renaissance realized that the language does not exist in a vacuum and undertook to preserve the culture

that it helps to define. With the presentation of the first Tribute to Cajun Music festival in 1974, Cajun and Creole musicians became officially involved in CODOFIL's struggle. The same year, CODOFIL discretely became involved in the collection of the area's oral tradition. Stories were recorded to be used in the production of French radio programs. In 1977, this modest collection of a few dozen reels served as the basis for the establishment of a folklore archive at the University of Southwestern Louisiana. The collection has continued to grow, including by 1993 about eight hundred hours and thousands of stories.

The large number of tales collected since 1974 clearly indicates that oral tradition is alive and well in French Louisiana despite the frequent predictions of the tradition's impending demise. These predictions are invariably based on a static definition of culture. If, on the other hand, change is viewed as a sign of life, a natural factor of social and cultural development, and if oral tradition is considered within this active context, then quite different conclusions can be drawn. The first folklorists, who collected before the discipline understood the importance of a story's context and function, had a necessarily limited view of oral tradition. They found little more than the animal tales and fairy tales they asked of their informants. The interpretation of these limited resources created a false impression which led to glum predictions for the future of the tradition. The rumored death of Cajun and Creole oral traditions proved to be greatly exaggerated. This contemporary study shows taletelling to be quite vigorous and constantly changing.

The Louisiana French repertoire can be divided into three basic categories, one based on vestiges, another on popular tradition, and the third on historical experience. The first category includes animal tales and fairy tales, often the only genres included in past collections. These tales are part of the passive repertoire usually only revived by certain storytellers at the request of a persistent folklorist. They are nevertheless an important part of the oral heritage and storytellers who perform them are revered as important bearers of tradition. The second category includes jokes and tall tales. Those who tell these are not always revered. More often they are taken for granted, or tolerated at best. Their stories are called nonsense at least as often as tales, but the role these jokers play in their communities is an important one which in some ways parallels that of the medieval jesters. Through their humor, they reflect contemporary developments in their society's collective sense of identity. Their stories well up naturally and spontaneously, without solicitation and even despite protests. The third category, embracing legends and historical tales, has been ignored by past scholars of Louisiana oral tradition. Yet the tellers of these stories are appreciated locally as guardians of a shared past.

When Corinne Saucier asserted in her introduction to *Folk Tales from French Louisiana* that her collection was small but "representative . . . of our Southern Louisiana form of oral tradition known as folklore, a heritage that is disappearing in our mechanized age" (Saucier 1972), she was thinking in narrow terms. To her and other early Louisiana folklorists, the study of French and African survivals was an integral part of the attempt to describe a simplified cultural history of Cajun and Creole tradition. Today, these survivals are still considered important, but only as two ingredients in the complex cultural *mélange* in South Louisiana, a part of the American frontier which was also affected by the Native Americans,

Spaniards, Germans, Swiss, Italians, Scots, Irish, English, and more recently Lebanese, Syrians, and Vietnamese, who have contributed to the regional melting pot. The oral repertoire has adapted its genres with shorter forms like jokes and tall tales, reflecting the pace of modern times. Stories are told in French, English and a combination of the two, reflecting the bilingual makeup of the population. Further, the admission of historical narratives into the canon of oral tradition has greatly increased the tale stock. In the past, researchers have consistently set up their studies of Cajun and Creole oral tradition as would-be autopsies, yet its vital signs seem to be quite healthy. It is, in fact, difficult to avoid hearing, in groups of two or more in South Louisiana bars, barbershops and barbeques, *"T'as entendu le conte pour . . ."* ["Have you heard the one about . . . ?"]

The Repertoire

The tales included in this collection have been placed in fairly standard categories: animal tales, magic tales, jokes, tall tales, legends and historical tales. While most fit comfortably within these generic tags, there are some that walk the boundary between two categories. For example, Edward Deshotels' story about the giant alligator bridge has elements that could make it a tall tale, but since Mr. Deshotels gave specific references such as highway signs referring to the event, I have included it in the legendary tales. Stanislaus Faul's story about the mare's eggs is usually classified as a joke, but since he cast Bouki and Lapin as the characters in his telling, I have included it in the animal tales. On the other hand, tall tales include a certain amount of details from real life in order to help disorient the listener, which does not automatically place them among the historical tales. These cases admittedly required a judgment call on my part and I regularly deferred to the apparent feeling of the storyteller for the kind of story he or she was relating.

Contes d'animaux / Animal Tales

Animal tales require tellers and their audiences to share certain conventional understandings. In these tales, animals speak, cry, laugh and reason like humans. This characterization also allows for a simplification of roles. Animal characters can become the incarnation of a human trait: cleverness (the rabbit, the fox, the turtle), ignorance (the wolf, the bear, the hyena), malice (the spider, the monkey), brute strength (the elephant, the lion). The symbolic nature of animal characters allows tellers, especially members of oppressed communities such as medieval peasants and ante bellum slaves, to indirectly criticize the social order.

The characterization of Louisiana animal tales is based on a confluence of French and African traditions. The two categories of animal tales point to these origins. In some, the characters are the same as those featured in La Fontaine's *Fables* and the *Roman de Renart* from French tradition, such as the fox, the wolf, the bear, and the crane. In others, the two main characters are the wily, amoral trickster, Compère Lapin (Rabbit) and his clumsy, unwitting victim, Compère Bouki (Wolof for "hyena"), obviously from West African oral tradition where the traditional trickster is the hare and the dupe is the hyena. Other characters can appear in these stories, such as Elephant, Snake, Cat, Dog, Turtle, but it is interesting to note the absence—in South Louisiana as elsewhere in the United States—of the

malicious spider, an important character in African and Caribbean oral tradition. (cf. Dorson, 1964 and Abrahams, 1970). These African-influenced tales are generally associated with the black Creole community, but they are also popular among white Cajuns, who probably learned them because of the close cultural contact between the two groups. This is best represented in this collection by Martin Latiolais who spoke Creole as well as Cajun French and used both in his tales. In fact, the principal characters of black Creole tales appear as far up the Mississippi Valley as Missouri (Carrière 1937), the results of a French frontier connection as well as the river's use in the slave trade. Black Creoles also borrowed and adapted European tales, such as Ben Guiné's remarkably creolized version of "The Ant and the Lazy Cricket." The cultural crossover evident in animal tales parallels the shared character of the cuisine, music and architecture of the two groups.

In both groups, tellers talk about Bouki and Lapin in conversation almost as if these imaginary animals were human neighbors. Tales are frequently framed by comments and judgments concerning the personalities of the characters and the implications of their actions. Storytellers thus lift these characters out of the purely fictional time of the tales to bring them into the quasi-real time often associated with legends. Comments of this sort often focus on Lapin. All tellers exhibit at least some ambivalence toward his unrelenting exploitation of Bouki. He is sometimes admired, sometimes comdemned, but always considered amusing.

Just as Lapin and Bouki can appear almost human, people can come to acquire reputations and references associated with the characters. Clever rascals are said to be as smart as Lapin, while gullible, foolish or accident-prone people are sometimes nicknamed Bouqui.

Louisiana animal tales, so heavily collected in the past, are now fading from the active repertoire, though some can still be found, primarily in the parishes east of Lafayette (especially St. Landry, St. Martin and Iberia) where black Creole culture is strongest, as opposed to the predominately Cajun prairies to the west. Even in the areas of strongest Creole influence, however, one must search diligently for tellers of animal tales and ask specifically for them once one is found. Some grandparents use these stories, with their animal characters and uncomplicated plots, as oral cartoons to entertain their television-generation grandchildren. Formula tales, which often cast animals and even objects as characters with human traits, are also increasingly rare, but the verbal artistry they require makes them popular in elementary school French classes. Thus, these stories, which once served as popular entertainment for audiences of all ages during evening visits called veillées, are now reserved for pre-adolescents and persistent folklorists.

Contes merveilleux / Magic Tales

The rapid pace and electronic distractions of modern times makes finding time for the performance of long oral narratives difficult. Magic tales, with their often complex plots filled with amazing demonstrations of skill, adventurous quests for fabulous treasures and populated by princes and princesses, heroes and heroines who almost always succeed in the end, tend to be long. They flourished in the days before radio and television when stories and songs were needed to fill long otherwise empty evenings. Today, it is rare that one has or takes the time to listen to one of these oral masterpieces. Magic tales have given way to shorter forms like the joke which can be told in a moment, without interrupting the flow of everyday life. These days, magic tales are heard almost exclusively by conscientious folklorists, but they remain majestic expressions of oral tradition.

The language of these tales tends to be more formal and possesses a vocabulary and a syntax that are older than contemporary speech. For example, the use of the formal pronoun *vous* is virtually unknown in everyday Cajun French conversation. Consequently it almost never occurs in most genres of this collection. Yet it appears frequently in the magic tales, indicating a feeling about the level and antiquity of language associated with this venerable genre. In addition to the formality of the relationships implied by the use of *vous* in these tales, there is also a vocabulary which reflects another time. Words such as *carnassière* [hunting bag] and *romaines* [counter-balanced scales], which have faded from contemporary French, regularly send transcribers to historical dictionaries.

On the other hand, the details of these stories are sometimes adapted in interesting ways to reflect the constantly changing values of Cajun life. In Louisiana, for example, where the concept of royalty is no longer familiar, a king is described as a multi-millionaire, and the princess becomes simply *"la fille du roi"* [the king's daughter]. The king also acts suspiciously like a Cajun farmer, taking great pride in his pigs, bulls and hunting dogs. He also retires from the throne to fish in the pond that Jean l'Ours gives him.

To some extent, the magic tale became less frequently told, in part, because of the time needed to develop its complex structure. In some cases, only fragments remain of what were undoubtedly longer tales, and even these resurface only with much probing, as storytellers dutifully search through their memories on request to find even a trace of this fading part of the oral tradition.

The attrition of magic tales can be attributed only in part to their length. Some storytellers who feel that they do have the time will develop even a simple joke plot to extraordinary lengths by dwelling on details. The more likely reason is the almost exclusive channel of transmission of the stories from adults to their children and grandchildren. As schools began punishing children for speaking French, parents avoided inflicting on them what came to be considered a social liability. The tales were a part of the cultural heritage closely associated with the language and suffered along with it.

Farces / Jokes

The joke is easily the most popular oral genre in the Louisiana French repertoire, as it is in much of the Western world. Joketelling has suffered little from the effects of mass media entertainment and continues to enliven social gatherings of all sorts. Past researchers, pre-occupied with French and African antecedants, long neglected jokes, yet many are variants of international tale types and motifs.

On the surface, jokes are funny, but they are also dead serious. People define them-selves in part by what makes them laugh. Jokes which may seem otherwise ordinary at first consideration may conceal deeper psychological or cultural currents. Moreover, they offer excellent evidence of the vitality of Louisiana's French heritage. Tellers often prefer to tell their stories in French, even when they learned them from Anglo-American sources.

Traditional jokes can define a culture from the inside. Within their own cultural context, Cajuns and Creoles have never hesitated to laugh at themselves. There are, for example, many stories based on the clever little hero who always manages to avoid direct confrontation with obviously superior forces and eventually succeeds at least in escaping danger by his wits. (See, for example, Félix Richard's "La jument verte," in this collection). Other jokes indirectly reflect specific aspects of the Cajun world view. Exiled from their native Acadia by the British in 1755, the Cajuns finally arrived in Louisiana where they voluntarily and selectively withdrew from the mainstream. Visitors today can still find it difficult to penetrate the remnants of the protective barriers that were developed in the eighteenth century.

Une fois, il y avait un étranger qui s'a arrêté devant une vieille maison pour demander comment arriver chez tel untel. Il y avait un vieux bougre assis sur sa galerie et il lui a demandé ayoù la maison à Joe Babineaux était.

Le vieux bougre dit, "Well, tu vas dans le chemin-là jusqu'à t'arrives à la terre à Marius Thibodeaux, et là, tu tournes à la gauche. Là," il dit, "tu vas aller jusqu'à ayoù il y avait un grand chêne qu'a été arraché dans l'ouragon de '42." Il dit, "Et là, tu tournes à droit," il dit, "et ça va être sur ce chemin-là, juste l'autre bord du chemin d'ayoù Rhéul Cormier a été tué dans ce rendez-vous des années passées."

"Mais," il dit, "espère une minute." Il dit, "Si je connaissais ayoù tout ces places sont, j'aurais pas besoin des directions."

Once there was a stranger who stopped in front of an old house to ask how to get to so-and-so's house. There was an old fellow sitting on the porch and he asked him where Joe Babineaux's house was.

The old fellow said, "Well, you go down this road until you get to Marius Thibodeaux's land, and then you turn left. Then," he said, "you're going to go until where that big oak tree was uprooted by the hurricane of '42." He said, "And then, you turn right," he said, "and it'll be on that road, just across the road from where Rhéul Cormier was killed in that duel years ago."

"Well," he said, "wait a minute." He said, "If I knew where all those places where, I wouldn't need directions."

Le vieux bougre dit, "Si t'as besoin des directions, peut-être que t'as pas d'affaire d'aller là-bas du tout." (Stanislaus Faul, Cankton, 1982)

The old fellow said, "If you need directions, maybe you've got no business going there at all."

Jokes from within a culture are one thing; jokes at the expense of a culture are quite another. Inside of Cajun culture, there are many jokes based on foolishness.

Un jour, Touchet a été à la pêche avec Boudreaux dans son nouveau bateau. Ça faisait juste quelques minutes qu'ils étaient sur l'eau quand la machine a tombé dedans l'eau. Boudreaux a sauté dans l'eau après. Touchet, lui, il s'a penché pour voir quoi c'est qu'il faisait en bas-là, et il a vu son partner après hâler la corde pour tout ça il y avait moyen, après essayer de partir la machine en bas de l'eau. Il l'a regardé pour un bon bout de temps, après escouer sa tête, puis là, il crie, "Espèce de couillon! Hâle ton choke!" (Elmo Ancelet, Lafayette, 1979)

One day, Touchet went fishing with Boudreaux in his new boat. They had been out on the water only a few minutes when the motor fell into the water. Boudreaux jumped into the water after it. Touchet leaned over to see what he was doing down there, and he saw his partner pulling on the cord for all he was worth, trying to start the motor under water. He looked at him for a while, shaking his head, then he yelled, "You fool! Pull your choke!"

However, in an intercultural context, foolishness can become a weapon in a sometimes bitter ethnic duel, such as the doubly racist slur: "The only thing more dangerous than a nigger with a knife is a Cajun with a pencil" (overheard in a bar, 1978).

The earliest surviving Cajun tales reflecting intercultural influences and tensions were the commercial recordings of Walter Coquille, the "Mayor of Bayou Pom Pom," made in the 1930s. These were at least as much in Cajun English dialect as in Cajun French, and showed already the results of change in Cajun society. Coquille's stories made gentle but penetrating fun of Cajuns who found themselves confronted for the first time with the complexities of the modern world.

This collection focuses on the French-language oral tradition of south Louisiana. Thus, there are no stories in English included here. Although animal tales and magic tales are seldom told in English, jokes often are; and to understand the influence of English-language American culture on the Cajun and Creole societies, one must take this more active genre into consideration. Since the 1930s, a cycle of stories based on the social and linguistic evolution of the Cajuns and Creoles has emerged. These stories, which often play on the difficulties that French-speakers encountered when they tried to use the newly-imposed English language, are often told in English. Some of these are at the expense of Cajuns or Creoles, taking for granted their place toward the bottom of the social ladder. Often the setting for this oral sub-genre was the school. It was assumed that the Cajuns had no place in the classroom. Relatively few had had the opportunity to attend school regularly

before 1916, when free mandatory public education was established in the state. Finally in school, but equipped only with poorly learned English at best, young Cajuns seemed stupid and recalcitrant. In the following joke told by Justin Wilson, a well-known comedian from Mississippi, now living in Denham Springs, Louisiana, the influence of school is subverted at home.

> You know, lady an' gentlemans, I got a frien' an' he got a li'l boy chirren an' one day las' year he brought hisse'f home from school an' he say, "Pa-pa, I got a problem."
>
> Pa-pa say, "Well, we all got problem, son."
>
> "But you jus' don't unnerstan', Pa-pa. I got 12 problem."
>
> Pap say, "W'at you meant by dat?"
>
> He say, "Rit-ma-tick. I got 12 problem r'at chere. De teacher done tole me dat she want to fine the common denominator for averyone dem twelve problem."
>
> His pa-pa say, "Whoo! You all still lookin' fo' dat damn t'ing? We was lookin' fo' dat w'en I was a boy." (Justin Wilson, with Howard Jacobs, *Justin Wilson's Cajun Humor*).

This story, of course, underscores the difficulty of educating the Cajuns, while also making fun of their accent when speaking English. Wilson tells his stories, some original, some recycled international ethnic jokes, in a heavy, imitation-"Cajun" dialect which reflects the difficulty Cajuns had learning English years ago, but Wilson's Cajuns do not only have trouble with English. When confronted by "real French," they are just as perplexed:

> Dis young lady from New Or-lee-anh study dat good French at dem Too-lane University, an' one mornin' she was squat in a dock blin' in Sout'wes' Lewisana an' she say to her Cajun guide like dis: "Quelle heure est-il?"
>
> De guide scratch his head an' he say, "Lady, dem wasn't teal, dem was mallard." (Wilson and Jacobs 1974)

This story reflects an all-too-pervasive attitude among many Cajuns, that their simple patois could never be used to communicate to "real French-speakers."

Many people in south Louisiana find such stories funny and retell them, disregarding the underlying message. On the other hand, there are many other stories that reflect the positive social changes which have occurred in French Louisiana since World War II. One of the new heroes to emerge in both French- and English-language oral tradition is Boudreaux who travels through the wide world seeing everything in his own terms:

> Boudreaux went to Chicago, you know, to visit his daughter who lived out there. And she had mailed him directions to get to her house. And he was doing pretty good for a while, but then he missed a turn. There were so many cars on the road, it made him nervous. So he pulled over on the side of the road and was

about to make a U turn when a policeman came running up yelling, "Hey, man, you can't do that!"

Boudreaux looked at the road and said, "Yeah, I believe I've got enough room," and took off. (Don Montoucet, Scott, 1990)

Sometimes the humor of new-found pride can sound a bit aggressive:

This guy shot a duck, and he wounded it, but it trailed off before it died, and it fell on the other side of a fence. And he was just about to cross the fence. He was between the barbed wire, like that, and he heard somebody, "Ain, ain. Ain, ain." He turned around and he saw a man coming. "Ain, ain." He was an old Cajun, you know. He said, "Tu peux pas faire ça, nègre." You know, "You can't do that, man. That's my land. Ça, c'est ma terre." The hunter said, "Excuse me." He didn't talk French, you know. He said, "I shot a duck and it fell over there on the other side of the fence." The man said, "Ouais, mais, that's my land. That's sacred." The hunter said, "Yeah, but that's my duck. That's my limit." "My land . . ." "My duck . . ." So the hunter said, "Well, that's something. How we gonna fix this?" The man said, "Ha! I don't know. We can do what they used to do in the old days." He said, "What's that?" "Well," he said, "we can kick each other until one gives up." "Goddam," he said, "that sounds rough," he said, "but if that's the only way. . . ." So the man said, "My land." And he kicked him as hard as he could in the nuts. That hunter fell sitting down. He fell on his back. He didn't move for a few minutes. He was in a cold sweat. After a while, he pushed himself up. He got up slow. He shook his head. He said, "Goddam, that hurt! My turn." The old man said, "Hey, it's no use to argue for a duck. Go ahead and take it." (Willert Menard, Ossun, 1988)

Most times, however, humor simply calls attention to or exaggerates the natural quirkiness of real life, as in the stories told by an emerging group of contemporary Cajun comedians, Justin Wilson's real Cajun counterparts, including Dave Petitjean, Ralph Begnaud and A.J. Smith. Smith, for example, a native of Lafayette, now living in Lake Charles, gives the following twist to a familiar modern scene:

Two dogs are sitting under a tree talking. And they see a kid walking by, listening to music on one of those Walkmans with the earphones, you know. And that kid was dancing and turning and shaking every which way like that. And nobody else could hear anything. And one of those dogs says to the other one, "Look at that, man. If we did that, they'd worm us." (A.J. Smith, Lake Charles, 1988)

The characters and storylines can be found in the oral tradition of many other cultures around the world. Stories that can be translated are often told in English for audiences that cannot understand French. Yet there are certain characteristics that seem consistent in both languages, such as an undeniable appreciation for the clever rascal. Another Cajun come-

dian, Ralph Begnaud, incorporates the familiar tradition of the humbling retort as part of a more complex cultural "sting" operation.

> On a transatlantic flight, a Cajun found himself sitting next to a man in a three-piece suit. When the Cajun tried to make conversation, he was cut off abruptly by the other man who told him that he was a Harvard scientist on his way to do research at Oxford and that he did not wish to speak to anyone so far below his level. "Come on," the Cajun insisted, "I'm on my way to the North Sea to work offshore for a while. I've never left South Louisiana before this and I'm so excited!"
>
> "Please," the Harvard man protested, "we obviously have nothing in common, so I would prefer that you not speak to me for the rest of the flight."
>
> "What makes you think you're so smart?" the Cajun asked.
>
> "Look," the Harvard man said, "I don't think I even have to answer that. You are hardly near my level of intelligence."
>
> "Why don't we make a little bet?" the Cajun said. "One hundred dollars on one question each. I'll ask you a question and you ask me a question. Since you're so much smarter than me, will you give me 5 to 1 odds?"
>
> "Sure. This might teach you a lesson and shut you up for the rest of the trip."
>
> "Okay, then, if you can't answer my question, you give me five hundred dollars. If I can't answer your question, I'll give you one hundred dollars. I'll go first. What has yellow hair, blue eyes, green skin, red scales, and lives in the sea, but comes on land to eat?"
>
> The Harvard man thought about it and admitted, "I'm afraid I must say that I don't know." He handed over five one hundred dollar bills to the Cajun.
>
> "Thanks," the Cajun said.
>
> "Now wait a minute," the Harvard man said, "just what does have yellow hair, blue eyes, green skin, red scales, and lives in the sea, but comes on land to eat?"
>
> "Hell, I don't know either," said the Cajun, and he gave him back one of the hundreds. (retold from Ralph Begnaud, Lafayette, 1991)

Once jokes are admitted into the oral repertoire to be studied, the tradition appears in no danger of disappearing. Even in a world of computers and television, people need to tell stories. They adapt style, repertoire, and even language to the dizzying pace and changes of modern times and tell stories which reflect their history and culture just as their ancestors did.

Menteries et contes forts / Lies and Tall Tales

In Louisiana there is a difference between *menterie,* a lie told to amuse, and *mensonge,* a lie told to deceive. As one storyteller, Revon Reed, put it, "You know, your typical Cajun is a

great liar, and naturally loves to brag." Cajun storytellers are often artistic liars, which is not to say that they are devious, but simply that they love telling tall tales. This genre is among the easiest to collect because, unlike animal and magic tales, tall tales are highly public and often told to strangers. As these tales are often told as tests of gullibility, the presence of a collector—so disruptive in the collection of some genres—may even serve as a spur for fresh artistic creations. Consider, for example, the title and contents of Vance Randolph's collection of Ozark tall tales, *We Always Lie to Strangers*.

While animal tales are concentrated in the bayou regions east of Lafayette, tall tales are more common in the prairies to the west where the Cajuns grew up as cowboys in the tradition of the western plains. This lying tradition has roots in Europe, but was likely reinforced by the perception of the first settlers that anything seemed possible on this huge, rich, wide-open continent. When asked by a documentary film producer how he managed to have such a lush, productive garden, Cajun musician Marc Savoy answered, "I throw a few seeds down and run like hell to get out of the way of the growing plants." As is evident in this example, tall tales can also emerge without warning in the course of a conversation. They are often based on familiar activities, such as farming, fishing and hunting, and can develop out of just about any description of everyday reality. In South Louisiana, as in most of the United States, men are generally recognized as the primary tellers of tall tales, though women are often present when the stories are told and active as listeners and responders.

Tall tales require a complicity between the teller and the members of his audience who tacitly agree to suspend the rules of reality for awhile. Other times, the teller deftly manipulates fact and fiction to surprise his audience in the end. These stories are typically told with straight-face and mock earnestness. They often elicit as many groans as they do laughs. Those most familiar to the tradition can serve as accomplices, pretending there is nothing remarkable about the narrative being developed. Paradoxically, those who appreciate the story most may show the least reaction. Many of the best tales are based on two liars trying to outdo each other and seeing how much they can get away with, while others play on the humorous retorts of indignant liars forced to reduce their stories.

Contes de Pascal / Pascal Stories

There has been for years in the town of Mamou, Louisiana, a specialized lying tradition called Pascal stories. These stories are spontaneous oral creations which form an ongoing system of exaggerations, lies, and nonsense that is quite popular among those who participate in sessions of Pascal stories. True Pascal stories are not performances of "fixed" texts, but instant improvisations, often conversational in nature. They seem to be limited to Mamou, a town where the toughness and originality of frontier tradition still exist (though I have encountered similar ongoing systems in other small towns). More specifically, the Pascal tradition was centered at one time in the bars along the one-block long stretch of Sixth Street, between Main and Chestnut. In these bars, including Fred's Lounge, Manuel's Bar

and especially the Casanova Bar, certain groups of men meet nearly every morning (except Sundays) in order to eventually play a popular local game of cards called *bourré*. These men are almost all retired and spend their abundant free time in these bars drinking, playing cards, and talking. All of these activities play important functions in their lives, providing an escape from boredom and an opportunity to participate in a folk group whose members share a similar situation. The entertainment involved in drinking, playing cards, and talking is escalated to the level of social obligation and even of faithfully executed ritual. Consequently, some of these men become alcoholics, gamblers, and superb storytellers. The solidarity of the group gives meaning to their lives. If someone does not show up one day, his absence is sorely felt by all. With such a strong sense of community, it is not surprising that, at one point, this group developed its own "language," the system of Pascal stories.

In order for the system to be effective, and indeed for it to make any sense at all, the participants must understand the ground rules for original production. This sort of competence in talking Pascal is comparable to the linguistic competence involved in the original production of any language. When a speaker formulates a sentence, he assumes that his listeners will understand the code system he is using. He produces an utterance which he assumes will have meaning and relevance for those who share that system. In the same way, on a different level, the participants in Pascal tradition exploit a shared competence in this system of oral tradition to tell and understand appropriate stories.

A normal day in the bars spans three phases: the first, drinking; the second, talking; the third, playing cards. The context for the stories usually develops before noon in the bars, somewhere between early morning hangovers and cards. The first members of the community begin to arrive around 8:30 A.M. This early in the morning, conversations tend to be rather quiet. For these hardcore participants, the first task is that of drinking in order to work up to the "normal" level of daytime intoxication. As the morning wears on, a certain circle of close friends finds itself coming together in each bar. There are definite groups peculiar to each bar, although there are some unattached drifters. As a group assumes its final constituency, the conversation becomes more animated and stylized, and in some groups the first mention of Pascal and his friends can be heard. By 10:00 A.M., the day is usually well under way in terms of drinking and members have built up enough steam to begin "serious" storytelling. While waiting to begin the final phase, playing cards, the members bide their time by launching into stories about Pascal before moving into the game room around 12:30 or 1:00 P.M. Storytelling may continue, though generally to a lesser degree, around the card tables during the afternoon.

Although the barroom provides the usual context for telling Pascal stories, it is not exclusive. A similar situation occurs during informal dinner parties, called *soupers,* given by one or more members of the barroom groups. Basically, the same pattern is followed. First, there is an initial gathering highlighted by drinking. As a rule, these parties are so informal that invitations are not involved. The word is simply passed around. Second, while waiting for the supper to be prepared, the participants entertain themselves with Pascal stories. The meal replaces the card game as the third phase in this case. It is important to note that, like the card game, the supper is only an excuse for getting together. There are in fact many

accounts of the prepared supper being altogether forgotten in the heat of the talking.

What is actually produced during the speech event called talking Pascal is artistic nonsense. The stories told are not traditional texts in the way the magic tale, for example, is traditional. In the magic tale, there is a basic plot or structure which is performed as a story. In talking Pascal, the stories are created in conversation. It is essentially a group effort, with individual parts offered by members of the group as they alternately take control of the floor; each talker helps shape the story by contributing narrative material which applies to the current theme. Occasionally one especially imaginative person might attain firm enough control of the floor to perform alone for several minutes. Someone eventually challenges him, though, contributing further to his idea or even taking over the floor with a change of subject if the performance begins to falter. The ideal, in any case, is not the retelling of traditional stories, nor even the recombination of past themes or plots. Instead, it is the obligation of the talkers to produce and develop a new idea, a new theme. The responsibility of each teller is to improvise his part of the story, to hatch an appropriate idea and then to develop it according to the rules defined by the expectations of the other members of the group with at least a passive competence in the tradition.

The protagonist of most of the stories is Pascal himself. The origin of this character is not clear, but all versions agree that it was based on a real person. According to one variant, the fictional Pascal was inspired by Pascal Guillory, a local policeman well-known for his sometimes over-zealous enforcement of the local speed limit laws. Out of this notion grew several stories about Pascal catching speeders despite the fact that the town was too poor to buy him anything but a bicycle. He is said to have learned to ride on the electrical wires. From this vantage point, he would see speeders coming from far away, and descend upon them as they approached:

Irving Reed: Oh, défunt Pascal, ils l'avaient mis *state trooper*. Et les chars étaient à course, dans le temps de la guerre. Et ils lui ont donné un *bicycle*. Il courait après les chars, il pouvait pas les attraper. Ça fait, il a ôté les *tires*, et il courait dessus les fils de téléphone avec son rim, juste dessus les *rims*. Et quand il arrivait-là, il sautait en avant-là, il sautait en avant du char. Son *bicycle*, il était dressé, ouais! Il pouvait parler, "Monsieur Pascal." Il parlait, ouais, le *bicycle*!
BA: Oh?
IR: Ouais! Il l'appelait "Mister Pascal." Il parlait en anglais.

Irving Reed: Oh, old Pascal, they made him a state-trooper. And cars were speeding everywhere during the war. And they gave him a bicycle. He went after the cars. He couldn't catch them. So he took off the tires and he rode on the telephone lines on the rims. And when the car arrived, he would jump off in front of the car. His bicycle was well-trained! It could talk, "Mr. Pascal." The bicycle could talk.

BA: Oh?
IR: Yeah! It called him Mr. Pascal. It spoke English.

This bicycle has been an important feature in the Pascalian fantasy. Often stories mention the extraordinary speeds that he was able to attain with it, up to 700 mph, which made

possible an array of other marvelous feats such as cutting tornadoes in half with a razor blade mounted on the handlebars.

Another variant maintains that Pascal was one of the regulars at the card table, and that the tradition developed out of a comment made when he arrived late for the game one day. He explained that the delay was due to the uncomfortable ride he had had on his mule:

BA: Ça a commencé comme ça avec les contes de Pascal?

Alexandre Manuel: Ouais, depuis ces années-ça-là. Il venait, il jouait à la petite *game*-là, à un et trois sous. Et mon frère lui a demandé, il dit, "Comment t'as arrivé ici, Pascal?"

"Well," il dit, "je veux te dire . . . sûr pas dessus une lame de rasoir, mais ça sent comme ça!"

BA: That's how the Pascal stories started?

Alexandre Manuel: Yeah, since that time. He'd come, he used to play the low-stakes game, for one to three cents. And my brother asked him, he said, "How'd you get here, Pascal?"

"Well," he said, "I'll tell you, surely not on a razor blade, but it feels that way!"

His fellow card players took off from that simple statement and spun what were the beginnings of the full-blown Pascal tradition with a story about razorback mules. Whatever the origins of this character, his renown has far surpassed his modest beginnings.

Pascal the hero is variantly described as tall and thin:

IR: Pascal, il avait six pieds quatre pouces et il pesait quatre-vingt-neuf livres. Il était fin comme une aiguille.

IR: Pascal was six foot four inches and he weighed ninety-nine pounds. He was as thin as a needle.

or

Hube Reed: Pascal, il avait douze pieds de haut et il pesait soixante livres.

Hube Reed: Pascal was twelve feet tall and he weighed sixty pounds.

Cut of the same trickster cloth as Compère Lapin of the animal tales, Pascal is a champion of the practical joke and a successful rascal.

Pascal is neither omnipresent, nor even dominant in the cycle of stories that bears his name. His importance comes from his vintage and his longevity in what has become a rather fluid tradition. The second most important character is Jim Israel, Pascal's friend and right-hand man. Jim is the hero of many stories based not on his physical appearance, but on his many exploits. He is always involved in grandiose schemes: going to the moon (in any number of outlandish ways) or reflooding the Pacific Ocean after a terrible drought.

Pascal's neighbor, Olide, appears to have been more important in the early development of the tradition than later on. He is the brother of Tante Auroc and the boyfriend of the infamous witch, Tante Coque. Despite having his heart transplanted to his back to avoid *mal au cœur* [lit. "heart ailment" = nausea], he died unexpectedly on his birthday, February 32, at the tender age of 123.

Mayo Israel is sometimes the butt of the practical jokes performed by his brother Jim and his friend Pascal. He is also an important member of the supporting cast. In one tale, Mayo stays behind in Mamou to furnish supplies by giant slingshot to Pascal who is swimming to Japan to visit Jim. In another, he is fooled when Pascal and the gang divide the moon: they give him the dark side. This eventually proves to be a blessing as the soil is especially rich there.

Some minor characters have appeared with more or less consistency. The devil rules in hell, but is hen-pecked there by his wife, Tante Coque, the witch. In fact, according to rumors, she is rather highly placed in the hierarchy of hell. She hates Pascal and tries frequently to kill him by various means. Some are animals, such as Pascal's three-ounce dog which is as fast as its master and a great hunter despite its small size, and Boulé Sévenne, Alexandre Manuel's legendary bull whose photograph alone weighs fifteen pounds. A veritable army of supporting characters come and go as needed in the ongoing production of the stories. Sometimes real people, living and recently deceased, are also added to the cast. They are usually active storytellers such as Alexandre Manuel:

HR: Alex s'est fait un *brass knuckle* l'autre jour. Il a dit à la fin il y avait un bougre qui le chinquaillait. Il a pris deux de ces grosses enclumes qu'ont des cornes-là. Il les a brasées ensemble comme ça. Là, il a fait des trous pour mettre son *brass knuckle*. Quand quelqu'un le chinquaille, il a un gros bœuf dessus une charette à bœuf. Il met son *brass knuckle* dessus cette charette. Là, il vient *park* en avant-là et cil-là qui l'a chinquaillé, quand il voit son *brass knuckle, he hit the back door.* Le gros taureau, il avait des cornes, cher Bon Dieu. Ça aurait pris un yinquis quinze minutes pour voler de chaque bout des cornes. C'était un *longhorn,* ça appelait ça.

HR: Alex had some brass knuckles made for himself the other day. He finally said that there was a fellow who was bothering him. He took two of those big anvils with horns on the ends. He welded them together like this. Then he made some holes for his fingers. When somebody bothers him, he has a big bull hitched to an ox cart. He has his brass knuckles on that cart. Then he parks out front and anyone who bothers him, when he sees those brass knuckles, he hits the back door. The big bull had horns, good Lord. It would have taken a sparrow fifteen minutes to fly from one tip of the horns to the other. They called those longhorns.

As certain characters have attained well-defined roles within the system, certain settings have also become well-established. Perhaps the most popular setting for Pascal tales is the moon, or the way there. One of the earliest accounts told of Pascal and Olide's attempt to get to the moon, long before the American astronauts made it there, of course.

Revon Reed: L'autre on contait pour le même Pascal et Olide, quand ils allaient à la lune, longtemps avant qu'on parlait des astronauts puis tout ça. Ça voulait aller à la lune; à tout moment ça parlait de ça. La vieille tante avait quelque sous. Ils ont emprunté, je crois, cinq, vingt piastres. Puis ils on fait une des

Revon Reed: Another one that was told about Pascal and Olide, when they went to the moon, long before anyone was talking about astronauts and all that. They wanted to go to the moon; every once in a while, they talked about that. The old aunt had a few pennies. They borrowed five or fifteen dollars. And

ces *capsules*-là pour aller à la lune. Et tout a été bien. Je crois il avaient deux ou trois machines à coudre et ils ont mis ça . . .

BA: Des machines à coudre?
RR: Ouais, des machines à coudre. Et là, Pascal avait attrapé des éclairs, tu vois? Il a passé tout l'hiver; il guettait les ouragons et puis quand les éclairs frappaient, il les mettait dans un sac. Ça, c'était leur énergie, leur *power take-off,* les éclairs. Et ils ont tout mis ça ensemble d'une manière assez pour les deux monter, puis ils ont parti. Et tout allait bien. Et les chances sont, ils auraient été les premiers pour arriver à lune, *except* ils estiont près à arriver quand, tout d'un coup, la lune s'est couchée. Ça pouvait pas la trouver. Ils avaient oublié amener un *flashlight.*

they made one of those capsules to go to the moon. And everything went well. I think they had two or three old sewing machines and they put them on.
BA: Sewing machines?
RR: Yeah, sewing machines. And then, Pascal had caught some lightning bolts, you see? He spent all winter watching the storms and when lightning struck, he'd put it in a sack. That was their energy, their power take-off, the lightning bolts. And they put all this together such that the two could get up, and they took off. And everything was going well. And chances are they would have been the first to arrive on the moon, except that they were about to arrive when, all of a sudden, the moon set. They couldn't find it in the dark. They had forgotten to take along a flashlight.

The moon has come to symbolize, in Pascal talk, the land of fantasy par excellence, "up there" where anything can happen. It provides the loosely defined setting, removed from familiar reality, safe from scrutiny, and appropriate for even the wildest adventures. Originally populated by little green men with one eye in the middle of their foreheads, the moon soon became the domicile of the departed heroes of the legendary past: Olide, Bouki, Pascal, and Mayo (who provides the place with water by spitting on rocks—reminiscent of Moses in the desert). The moon is thus similar to the Greek concept of Hades or the Norse concept of Valhalla where departed heroes are maintained in a semiphysical sense. Though Pascal and friends may come back to Earth for occasional adventures, they have escaped the mundane existence of this world. Their absence is expressly regretted by the tellers who frequently allude to their own aspirations to go "up there" one day to join all of their heroes.

Elvin Fontenot: Alex, t'es sûr longtemps dû d'aller là-bas.
AM: On peut aller asteur!
HR: On peut aller asteur! Ça prends 300 années. Quand je vas mettre mon cœur de caouaine, écoute! Quand je vas me faire opérer, on va laisser notres femmes.

Elvin Fontenot: Alex, you've been meaning to go there for a long time.
AM: We can go now!
HR: We can go now! It takes three hundred years. When I have my sea turtle heart, listen! When I have my operation, we'll leave our wives.

The home of the fictional Pascal, while he was still with us, was as elusive as the hero himself. Its location differs according to various reports, but it is usually referred to in the past to place it and Pascal beyond scrutiny.

BA: Mais ayoù c'est qu'il reste quand il est ici?

AM: *Well*, il a resté à Mamou ici. Mais quand son cheval est mort, il a *gone* et il a jamais revenu. Et moi, je l'ai pas vu pour plusieurs années.

BA: C'était pas lui qui restait à l'Anse à Guiguiche?

AM: Ouais, il a resté là, mais ils ont tué son cheval. Il a *give up*.

BA: Ayoù c'est ça, l'Anse à Guiguiche?

AM: C'est l'autre bord de Chataigner, ça. Je peux pas bien nommer.

BA: L'autre bord de bord ici?

AM: Ouais, mais c'est une drôle de place, là. Le soleil paraît jamais là.

BA: But where does he live when he is here?

AM: Well, he used to live here in Mamou. But when his horse died, he left and never came back. And I haven't seen him for years.

BA: Isn't he the one who lived in L'Anse à Guiguiche?

AM: Yeah, he lived there, but they killed his horse. He gave up.

BA: Where is L'Anse à Guiguiche?

AM: It's on the other side of Chataigner. I can't really say.

BA: The other side of this side?

AM: Yeah. But it's a funny place. The sun never rises there.

Other fantasy lands employed in the Pascal tradition are Hell (a perpetual barbecue of people) and Africa (popular for its obvious exotic potential). Both of these settings fulfill the same thematic need as does the moon. The essential requirement of the setting of a Pascal tale is that it be "somewhere else," away from too-close examination. Finally, the Mamou area itself is obviously a useful setting for some aspects of the tales, usually as a point of departure or return. The tradition makes use of familiar surroundings for the purposes of pseudorealism, intensifying the lies by toying with the deliberate misuse of facts and by disarming the listener with vague familiarities and references to the real world.

In its most usual form, the method of producing the Pascal story is in conversational exchange between at least two active performers who, ideally, challenge one another to adopt new directions as the session develops. Ideal production involves performing with another talker, vying with him for the floor, but taking care to avoid shutting him off completely.

HR: Il a un *winch*-là que . . . il peut hâler Mamou ici, s'il trouverait bien, parce qu'il a un bon *dead man*. Rien que le cable est deux pieds. Non, à peu près gros comme ça, hein Alex? À peu près un pied et demi, son cable en acier?

AM: Il est terrible. Tout je veux te dire, il y avait un village qu'il aimait pas et il a pris sa *balloon* et son . . .

HR: Il l'a accroché et puis il l'a hâlé à peu près vingt miles à côté là-bas.

AM: Il était . . . Non, il était là-bas dans la Chine. Il était à collé le petit village dans la Chine.

HR: He has a winch that . . . He could haul Mamou here, if he wanted to, because he has a good dead man. The cable alone is two feet [thick]. No, about this big, eh Alex? About a foot and a half, his steel cable.

AM: It's really something. All I can say is that there was a town he didn't like and he took his balloon and his . . .

HR: He hooked it and he hauled it about twenty miles away.

AM: He was . . . No, he was over in China. He was next to a little town in China.

BA: Avec tout le monde?
AM: Mais il a fendu l'affaire.
HR: Le soir, il l'a mis dessus un *rack*.
AM: C'est ça qu'a fait une partie du *Pacific*, tu comprends?
HR: Ouais.
AM: Le *Pacific*.
HR: Je crois c'est à Guam ou dans les *Philippine Islands,* Manila. Pas Manila?
AM: Ouais, Manila. J'étais là. J'ai vu ayoù c'est qu'il l'a fait.
HR: Alexandre était là. Il était docteur.
AM: Et la boucane brûle toujours.
HR: Ils se sont jamais aperçu. Il a mis son cable tout le tour de son petit village, et puis il a accroché son . . .
AM: Ça l'aimait pas. Ça voulait pas il se pose là. Quand il se posait, ça faisait une explosion.
HR: Mais!
BA: Comment il a fait pour le couper en deux?
AM: Mais avec le passe-partout à Bouki!
HR: Bouki avait un passe-partout, les dents étaient à peu près deux pieds, hein? Le passe-partout était à peu près cinquante pieds de long, des deux manches.
AM: Il l'a scié par petits bouts. Il l'a pas fini tout d'un coup. Il l'a scié . . .
HR: Ouais. Je me rappelle bien de ça. J'avais trois mois.

BA: With all the people in it?
AM: But he split the thing.
HR: One night, he put it on a rack.
AM: That's what formed part of the Pacific, you understand.
HR: Yeah.
AM: The Pacific.
HR: I think it was in Guam or in the Philippine Islands. Manila. Not Manila?
AM: Yeah, Manila. I was there. I saw where he did it.
HR: Alexandre was there. He was a doctor.
AM: And it's still smoking.
HR: They never noticed. He put his cable all around the little town, and he tied it to his . . .
AM: They didn't like him. They didn't want him to land there. Every time he landed, there was an explosion.
HR: Well!
BA: How did he cut it in two?

AM: Well, with Bouki's crosscut saw!
HR: Bouki had a crosscut saw, the teeth were about two feet long, eh? The crosscut saw was about fifty feet long, between the handles.
AM: He cut it into little pieces. He didn't finish right away. He sawed . . .
HR: Yeah, I remember it well. I was three months old.

Additionally, an essential aspect of Pascal performance involves the participation of the members of the "audience" who play the role of "straight men." Questions asked by members whose competence is more passive inspire new directions for the talking and, consequently, assure the continuance of the performance. There is a definite talent involved in asking appropriate and effective questions intended to directly inspire more talking, as illustrated in the following excerpt which arose out a discussion about beards and shaving.

EF: Mais Jésus Christ s'a jamais rasé, Lui.
HR: Jésus Christ, c'était le premier *hippy* jamais on a eu. Des grands cheveux et une grande barbe, c'est Lui qu'a commencé l'affaire des *hippies*.

EF: Well, Jesus Christ never shaved.
HR: Jesus Christ was the first hippy ever. Long hair and a long beard, He's the one who started the hippy thing.

EF: T'es sûr il y avait des ciseaux. Je sais pas comment il l'a *trim*.
HR: Il y avait pas des ciseaux ces temps-là. Il y avait des haches à deux talons. Des petites haches, ça pesait à peu près trois tonnes. Le monde était gaillard dans le vieux temps.

EF: Are you sure there were scissors? I don't know how He trimmed it.
HR: There were no scissors in those days. There were two-edged axes. Little axes, they weighed about three tons. People were strong in those days.

Pascal tales are essentially spontaneous creations within a traditional framework formulated by a certain community of storytellers for a specific cultural purpose. The ideal is not to reproduce "fixed" texts, but to produce a new idea, appropriate to the tradition, and to entertain the audience by developing a story according to the rules of the tradition. As the tradition came of age, some excellent past performances have occasionally been retold. In this respect, the tradition seems to be tending toward the development of traditional texts, but spontaneous performance within the traditional framework has remained the ideal for the most active storytellers.

Contes légendaires / Legendary Tales

Legendary tales appear often enough in Louisiana French oral tradition. Based on belief and often told as true, they serve as means for tellers to explore the boundaries between the everyday and the supernatural. Certain stories—such as *le juif errant* [The Wandering Jew], *la chasse galerie* [The Wild Hunt], and *les feux follets* [Will o' the Wisp]—are versions of international legend types, adopted by storytellers and adapted to the social, cultural and geographic context of the region. Others come directly from the local context and try to explain its special phenomena, such as place names. Some of these serve as testimonials of the powers of the *traiteur* (faith healer). Occasionally a complete tale is told to illustrate the legend in question, but more usually only a passing reference is made which is understood by most. When someone is lost or late, for example, one might hear, "He must have followed a *feu follet*," and most people understand the reference. If not, a full story might be told for the benefit of the uninitiated. Thus, for a visitor from outside the culture, or a curious folklorist, one might patiently relate the legend, but ordinarily it functions without narrative development or explanation.

Some of the most popular Louisiana French legends are about buried treasure and mysterious events experienced by those who seek it. It is true that a substantial amount of money was buried in south Louisiana. During the Civil War and shortly afterward, some Southerners buried their money to protect it from Yankee pillagers as well as vigilante gangs. The almost hereditary mistrust of banks among descendants of the French also drove many Cajuns to hide their wealth. Sometimes these suspicious folks died without telling anyone, including unsuspecting family members, about their hidden treasure.

The activities of Jean Lafitte along the Louisiana coast also contributed to the stock of buried treasure tales in Louisiana French oral tradition. A corsair to the French, a pirate to his victims, and a hero to the Americans during the War of 1812, Jean Lafitte became an important character in the cycle of Louisiana legends, as much for his style as for his exploits. It is said that when the new American governor C.C. Claiborne offered one thousand dollars for his head, Jean Lafitte made a counter-offer of ten thousand dollars for the governor's head.

Buried treasure stories, known throughout the world, often involve the intervention of malevolent spirits and other strange occurrences. According to some, the spirits in the stories are the souls of those who buried the treasure in the first place who are trying to preserve it for those destined to find it. Others suggest that the pirates always buried a person or an animal with their loot so that the restless spirit would guard it.

Histoires vraies / Historical Tales

A functional definition of story enlarges the scope of oral tradition beyond fiction to include tales—about duels, fights and practical jokes; about heroes, villains, and clever rascals; about personal courage during hard times; about incredibly fortunate accidents—and even tall tales based on fact, all paralleling the most popular elements in oral fiction.

If story is defined functionally as a relatively constant oral text told (and retold) for the entertainment of listeners (whether for its humor, horror, or adventure value), then many oral history accounts qualify as tales. Such accounts, requested again and again by listeners, eventually enter into the active repertoire of oral tradition and begin to take on forms to fit the telling experience. They may or may not stick closely to the facts; historical truth is often secondary to psychological truth and stylistic concerns. After dozens and even hundreds of tellings, the teller's feelings about the event, as well as his or her sense of how it should be related, matter at least as much as the actual facts.

Unlike historians and folklorists, storytellers are primarily occupied with entertaining their audiences. The storification of oral history involves such oral performance devices as the casting of personal characters to convey a story, the development of plot structures and dénouements, and the enhancement of roles and events, especially endings. There is, however, an ongoing tension between fact and fiction in the style of the narrator, who must conform enough to history to make his or her story function as oral history. Tellers often find it necessary to insist that their stories are not oral fiction. Truth is indeed sometimes stranger than fiction, and embellished truth can be so strange and interesting that the storyteller's *genre* comes into question, tacitly or otherwise. At this point, there are a few classic expressions or assurances: "This may seem like a joke (tale), but it's the truth;" "Now, this was told to me for the truth (for cash);" the slightly less committed, "If I'm lying, I'm lying after——;" or the ultimate parry, "And this is no damn lie!"

Stories concerning local heroes often contain claims establishing a personal connection between the teller and the hero as a form of self-corroboration. For example, expressing disbelief becomes impossible or at least impolite when the teller attributes the story to a family member.

A good indication that a story is emerging out of a conversation about the past is a change in oral style, a shift to a language associated with oral fiction. A narrator may go from a general description of how things used to be to a story illustrating his point. A common transition indicator is a reference to a specific time: "Times were tough then. I remember, one day we. . . ." Other indicators include specific details, scene descriptions, and attributed dialogue.

In their transformation to story characters, individuals typically become formalized. Their attributes are often exaggerated and they tend to become larger than life. Stories about Martin Weber, a well-known constable on the south Louisiana prairie frontier, invariably describe him as a heroic peacekeeper, capable of handling any situation with brute justice, despite overwhelming odds. Although, in fact, he carried a pistol he is usually described as armed only with sticks. His already impressive law enforcement record is regularly enhanced to have him succeed over hordes of invading *Marais-bouleurs* [Marsh-bullies], the local band of ruffians, to show him capable of picking men up by the seat of their pants and collar and throwing them out of doors and windows, without ever losing a single battle. Exaggeration is a common, even necessary element in the development of heroes. It is not done with an intent to deceive. Instead, it occurs quite unconsciously in an attempt to reflect accurately the way the teller feels about the person, and to make the specific reference conform to the generally held notions of the hero's stature.

Further indications of the storification process include other echoes of folktale style. The occurrence of events in groups of three, for example, is more than incidental. Story form is sometimes so dominant that it slightly (or not so slightly) bends the facts, without altering them essentially, to make them fit the oral mold. The entertainment of listeners is as important to the teller as the transmission of facts. The result is a marriage of the two influences. Oral history informants often bring an otherwise undocumented past to life, but in their own terms. They know instinctively that the most interesting stories about the old days are artful blends of fact and style.

General Observations

This collection would appear to demonstrate three things. First, instead of being extinct, as previous scholars have repeatedly predicted it would be, Louisiana French oral tradition is still alive, though greatly transformed. Second, this tradition is generically much more complex and varied than has been shown until now. Third, past studies which focused almost exclusively on the French and African influences on Louisiana French tradition failed to

take into consideration important influences from other elements in South Louisiana's mini-melting pot of cultures, as well as America's larger melting pot. The Cajuns and Creoles have, after all, been in North America for nearly four centuries.

I have attempted in the annotation to these tales to situate Louisiana French oral tradition in several pertinent contexts: French, Creole, and American, as well as international. The stories presented here were chosen from the thousands I have collected since 1974 to represent the broad range I have observed since I was a child growing up in this culture, as I waited for a ride home in my father's barber shop or waited for supper during the many *veillées* [evening visits] my family hosted and attended. While my primary focus was on stories with contemporary currency, I also made an effort to find and include vestiges of past tradition, those told only when a folklorist asks about them. Since I was interested in the historic, geographic and linguistic backgrounds of this oral tradition, I searched for variants in France and French Canada (especially in Québec, New Brunswick and Nova Scotia), in Africa and the black Creole islands of the Caribbean and the Indian Ocean, in Mexico and Central and South America, in the United States (especially in the South), and in England. Other international variants were sometimes helpful to demonstrate the broad distribution of certain stories even when they appear to be firmly rooted in regional tradition, especially in the case of legendary material.

These stories collected since 1974 show that Louisiana French oral tradition is not disappearing; they also show that it is changing rapidly in response to current realities. While animal tales and magic tales can still be found (though with great difficulty), jokes, tall tales and historical tales are hard to avoid. These more common forms have adapted to the rhythm of contemporary life. New forms such as the Pascal stories give evidence to the vitality of the tradition.

Some researchers who claim that oral tradition is dying make this claim because they would like to have the last word on the subject they are studying. Others think of tradition only as a fixed stock of material that is preserved more or less well by an ethnic or regional group under constant threat from modernization. But if tradition is thought of as an ongoing process, it becomes obvious that, as a culture changes, its traditions are adapted to reflect its new needs and interests. Stories survive, outliving those who predict their demise. We still tell tales that are thousands of years old. Though oral tradition is often described as a fragile thread, it also has the characteristics of a resilient fabric.

There is in fact a warp and weave in the transmission of tradition. There are two forces involved, one synchronic and the other diachronic, and the survival of tradition comes from the intersection of the two. One comes out of the past and the other comes across the present. The repertoire of the first is a carefully and consciously preserved oral legacy of tales handed down from generation to generation. That of the other is more spontaneous, made up of jokes, lies and silly stories that are current for a few days or weeks. The first is linear and depends on the fragile thread that links generations. The other is cyclical and emerges instantaneously in response to current events, then disappears again, sometimes for years, only to reemerge when circumstances conjure it.

At the intersection of these diachronic and synchronic influences, a new story based on a real event can become a tale which is handed down to posterity if it becomes part of a storyteller's active repertoire. Conversely, an old tale which is only a vague memory in the inactive repertoire can reemerge because of current events. Old stories can be lost within a limited tradition if young people don't learn them from older tellers. But the older tellers don't only hand stories down to the younger people in their own circles. They also tell them across to other members of their own generation who then can also transmit them down in other circles. When this occurs, a story can acquire contemporary details which make it appear new to young people hearing it for the first time and even to older people who simply don't recognize it in its new incarnation. In this way, the warp and woof of diachronic and synchronic threads support each other in a rich and resilient fabric in which oral tradition constantly renews itself.

On the other hand, there is a significant threat to Louisiana French oral tradition in the diminishing number of young French speakers. Since the creation of the Council for the Development of French in Louisiana (in 1968) and the subsequent reestablishment of French education in the state, many young people are able to learn the language of their ancestors in schools. However, the transmission of the language in the home has been slow to reappear, and the future of the language itself is far from sure. Yet, now that the stigma of being Cajun and Creole has been removed, a surprising number of young adults from the middle generations have begun speaking the language they learned in secret during the decades when it was still considered a liability. Louisiana French society has consistently shown itself to be remarkably adaptive and activists have chosen to bet that it will somehow adapt once again.

Not surprisingly, stories told in French tend to represent an insider's point of view, while many of those told in English tend to represent an outsider's perspective. At the same time, the difficulty in preserving the French language in Louisiana places constant pressure on the repertoire. Stories that do not depend on language can be translated into English. Storytellers are more interested in the reaction of their audiences than in the complex issues of cultural and linguistic preservation. They instinctively tell their stories in whatever language will most likely get a laugh from their friends. Nevertheless, there is a large part of the repertoire that is still told in French by choice. There are many reasons for this. First, many of the best older tellers are more at ease in French. Their vocabulary and sense of rhythm are stronger in their affective language. Moreover, French can sometimes serve as a secret code with which one can limit one's audience, excluding children from risqué jokes or outsiders from inside jokes, for example. Furthermore, the French language remains an important cultural marker that can serve to underscore the origins and allegiances of a storyteller. Many storytellers choose to tell their stories in French to demonstrate their Cajun or Creole ethnicity.

The range of this collection shows that the Louisiana French repertoire has been affected by its several contexts. The historical ties to France and Africa are still evident, especially in the vestiges (animal tales and magic tales), but one must not neglect to consider the other social, geographic and cultural ties that link South Louisiana to its other

influences, including other western Europeans and native Americans. The animal tales and magic tales underscore Louisiana's place in the French-speaking and Creole-speaking worlds. But the more contemporary repertoire shows that it is also a part of the American South, with tales about the horrors of slavery, and part of the American frontier, with tales about fantastic hunting and fishing trips and unbelievable crops. Certain legends indicate a French-American connection, while an overlap of some stories with Missouri French tradition underscore the legacy of the French presence in the Mississippi Valley. The popularity of jokes points to a connection with the rest of the United States and the modern western world in general. Some of these are based on preoccupations common to places where two cultures and/or two languages are trying to coexist.

Thus, the joke which tickles us in our most sensitive spots in a given situation is at least as important to an understanding of a culture as a venerable fable. Stories which pit Vieux Nèg and Vieux Boss against each other reflect the ongoing battle between wits and strength among blacks and whites, and this is at least as important as the stories about Bouki and Lapin which reflect similar issues back to an even earlier time. A Pascal story, rooted in the spontaneous creation of Mamou's bar life, can be as impressive a reflection of cultural fantasy as a magic tale rooted in a European past. Legendary tales and historical tales are necessarily regional, inextricably linked to their place; yet, they are also international, as their themes are based on the preoccupations of men everywhere who try to understand and interpret their surroundings and experiences.

The Language

Though this is not a linguistic study, a discussion of the linguistic issues necessarily involved in the transcription and translation of the tales may be useful. Ironically, the most common means of communicating oral tradition research is print. Folklorists have long needed to render in written form the particular ways people speak. Until recently, many storytellers recorded by folklorists could not write at all. Even now, most are not familiar enough with the craft of writing to transcribe their own stories as effectively as they tell them. They know instinctively too that talking and writing are different things. So folklorists do it for them, and for their own purposes.

The most obvious problem involved in transcribing other people's stories include the impossibility of reducing the oral performance to print (Burrison 1989, 11–16). There are also linguistic issues involved, whether tacitly or otherwise. When this question was debated by Dennis Preston and Elizabeth Fine in the *Journal of American Folklore* some years ago (Preston 1982; Fine 1983; Preston 1983), I found myself siding firmly with Preston. Meticulous sound-by-sound transcription, including all hesitations and false starts, can be dull and difficult to read, while interpretive transcription requiring judgment calls on the part of the transcriber makes some purists uncomfortable, and adaptations designed to represent accent and/or dialect can turn transcriptions into an impossible word game for readers. An unfortunate number of published transcriptions wander aimlessly somewhere between literature and linguistics.

Transcribed language must function in the absence of the speaker. Some writers choose to impose a dialectal pronunciation on their readers, either because their texts are to serve as scripts for radio or theatrical presentation, or because they want to impress their readers, for whatever reasons, that the "speaker" speaks differently. Ideally, transcriptions with no linguistic intentions or pretentions primarily communicate ideas and information, not sounds, capturing as much as possible the ease and eloquence of the speaker. Transcriptions which try to do both linguistics and communication often stumble between the two. After all, spelling is only a set of mutually agreed upon symbols used to represent language. Literary or eye dialect tricks like ellipses and altered spellings often make written statements unnecessarily confusing to readers, while the utterances they represent were clear to the listeners who understood immediately the message of the speaker. Transcribers should answer a few basic questions before approaching a text. Are they dealing with sounds or ideas? Is rendering pronunciation worth confusing the message?

All transcription is fatally flawed. It is impossible to capture oral tradition in its entirety on the page. Some folklorists have valiantly experimented with innovative new methods to include as much contextual information as possible, such as tone, volume, pauses, laughter, gestures, spatial considerations, and audience reaction (e.g. Fine 1984). Yet no transcription, no matter how elaborate, can ever reproduce the storytelling event (Burrison 1989, 14). And after a point, this style of transcription becomes hopelessly cluttered and reads like a complicated screenplay or a map. From a reader's point of view, the most successful transcribers may be the ones who limit their roles to that of intermediaries, focusing on the message and the most readable aspects of performance. When Kenneth Goldstein recommended that fieldworkers collect as much information as possible (Goldstein 1964), he did not, I suspect, mean that every bit of this information should be published, nor that this should serve as a substitute for original fieldwork. The serious researcher interested in issues not represented in a particular style of transcription should consult the original recordings or, better yet, arrange to attend a real performance in its own context.

The translations of these stories are fairly literal. I had no interest in creating what Dennis Tedlock has called "performable translations" (Tedlock 1983). The English translations here are faithful and straightforward. They are, I hope, readable, but they are not intended to replace or displace the transcriptions, only to help the reader not fluent in French to understand the stories represented.

In the French-speaking, the issue of transcription is further complicated by the imposing presence of centralized standard-setting institutions. Throughout this century and the last, there was a deliberate effort in France to homogenize regional dialects and accents to conform to the language as it had become institutionalized in the era of French kings and later in the French republic and commerce. Differences came to be considered errors. Expressions to indicate that something is different from the "standard" include *"Cela ne se dit pas"* (That is not said), and *"Ce n'est pas du français"* (That is not French), as though deviations from the "standard" are excluded from the language.

Recently, however, this perception has been mitigated by the growing influence of Québecois and Acadian literature and music, as well as a new interest in linguistic decentralization in France. On a more academic level, some French researchers have become interested in *le patrimoine* (national heritage), leading to a renewed interest in folklore and ethnic studies. In the early 1970s, a team of linguists and anthropologists at Université de Provence (Aix-Marseille I), led by Jean-Claude Bouvier, formed the *Centre de Recherches Méditerranéennes sur les Ethnotextes, l'Histoire orale et les Parlers régionaux* (CRÉHOP). Based on the study of what they called *ethnotextes* (ethnotexts), this team of French scholars effectively rediscovered the study of folklore through anthropological linguistics. Their study was not exclusively academic; it included an activist side as well. They specifically intended to influence contemporary culture with these studies by making available genuine elements of *le patrimoine* to artists, writers, filmmakers, and especially to teachers and schools (Bouvier et al 1980:97), recycling traditional culture through contemporary channels. Yet, despite the fact that the CRÉHOP was heavily populated with linguists, the *"Conventions pour la transcription des ethnotextes"* (Conventions for the transcription of ethnotexts) described

in its manifesto, *Tradition orale et identité culturelle,* insisted on transcriptions *"en graphie normalisée"* (in normal, accepted spelling), though it did insist on the preservation of morphology and lexicology (Bouvier et al 1980:133). That is, texts should be transcribed word for word, but using the French language for spelling. CRÉHOP directors invited linguists to study the linguistics of the texts, but cautioned that such concerns, while parallel and possibly illuminating, should not tread on the study of ethnotexts. In essence, the rule is: if studying the language itself, use linguistics; otherwise, do not confuse textual information with transcription methods which obscure meaning.

While the French rediscovered the value of oral tradition as recently as the 1970s; the French Canadians, led by luminaries such as Marius Barbeau, Germain Lemieux and Luc Lacourcière, and more recently Jean-Claude Dupont, Conrad Laforte and Jean-Pierre Pichette, have actively collected, studied and published their folklore for the better part of this century. In Québec, preserving *le patrimoine* was a matter of social, cultural and political identity and survival. Folklorists helped to define Québec by providing it with information about its own past and traditions. Early researchers in Québec tended to transcribe dialects with an insistence on indicating pronunciation. Threatened by Anglophone dominance, the French language was rightly considered a critical identity marker. Many Québecois also felt a need to resist what they considered cultural colonialism from France. Many of the studies in the series *Les Archives de Folklore,* published by Université Laval, featured transcriptions designed to reflect dialectal pronunciation and preserve the particularities of Québecois speech with ellipses and non-standard spellings. Unfortunately, these techniques also made reading difficult (e.g., Schmitz 1972). The same is true of Father Lemieux's work in Ontario, published in the series *Les vieux m'ont conté.*

In New Brunswick and Nova Scotia, there was a similar move to include sociocultural baggage in the transcription of Acadian French dialects. Early works sought to justify the linguistic peculiarities of Acadian speech by tracking words and expressions to earlier versions of the French language (Poirier 1964 and 1977; Maillet 1971). Many transcribers of Acadian oral tradition also felt compelled to reflect sounds in visual form, as in Catherine Jolicœur's *Le Vaisseau fantôme* (1970). By the time she published *Les plus belles légendes acadiennes* (1981), however, Jolicœur had joined the growing number of French Canadian folklorists publishing texts in rewritten form. The publishing industry there is apparently unable to place collections of transcribed oral tradition in the lucrative educational market because educators cannot or will not use the non-standard dialect transcriptions in the classroom. The education system is, after all, intended to cure the very ills highlighted by such transcriptions. Despite the valiant efforts of Jean-Pierre Pichette and Éditions Quinze whose *Mémoires d'homme* series has attempted to regularize spelling while keeping transcriptions verbatim (Pichette, in Laforte 1978: 11–18) most presses, including the Presses de l'Université Laval, which formerly had insisted on exact word-for-word, if not sound-by-sound transcriptions, now publish collections of folklore in which the transcriptions are reworked in a form that would be acceptable in schools. This goes beyond spelling to alter vocabulary, sentence structure, and style.

One of the most important collections of French-American oral tradition was Joseph Médard Carrière's *Tales from the French Folk-Lore of Missouri* (1937). Carrière's painstaking transcriptions capture the accent and dialect of the Old Mines French-speakers. But when Rosemary Hyde Thomas began trying to make use of this material to revive French in the region, she too was forced to rewrite and translate the tales (Thomas 1981). Though her intent was not to import the "standard" French language from the outside through text books, the altered spellings in the original transcriptions made them unusable in a classroom setting.

In South Louisiana, transcribing oral tradition implies a certain *parti pris,* whether the transcriber admits it or not. The Creole spoken by blacks in some areas resembles the Creole dialects used in parts of the Antilles. There, linguists, educators, and literary figures have been struggling for decades to produce a written form which distinguishes their language from French. Setting aside the debate on that question for a moment, Cajun French is a different matter. Most of what the Cajuns say can easily be rendered in written form by simply using the French language, though Cajuns have generally not done this themselves. An already complex socio-linguistic situation was compounded during the first half of this century by a hostile climate which actively sought to eliminate the French language in Louisiana as part of the Americanization of the Cajuns. Both Cajun French and Creole were long stigmatized, denounced as dialects unfit for preservation. They certainly had no place in the classroom. Even once French began to be taught again as a foreign language in Louisiana schools, teachers regularly told students that knowing some Cajun or Creole French was worse than none at all. Thus, there is virtually no history of literacy in French among most active Louisiana French speakers as their language has remained at the level of oral tradition. Consequently, the contemporary transcriptions of folklorists and linguists represent a major part of the written form of the language as it is spoken in the region.

Over the years, Louisiana French oral tradition has served as grist for the linguist's mill (cf. Read 1931; Ditchy 1932; Phillips 1936). Dozens of M.A. and Ph.D. candidates have produced theses and dissertations on various aspects of Louisiana French linguistics (cf. Parr 1940; Voorhies 1949; Guilbeau 1950). Tales and songs isolate speakers for long uninterrupted passages which are easier to handle than conversation, which can be impressionistic, rapid, and elliptical. Instead of building systematically on past research, though, generally these scholars and students had a tendency to reinvent the wheel as an exercise in producing and justifying yet another clever system to render one or more of Louisiana's regional French dialects in written form.

Folklorists have also contributed to the pool of available transcriptions. Alcée Fortier provided transcriptions of New Orleans black Creole animal tales in his *Louisiana Folk-Tales in French Dialect and English Translation* (1895). His rendering of accent and pronunciation in visual form is such that most readers must now listen to themselves reading the stories aloud to understand them. Fortier's transcriptions have not been reprinted since the turn of this century; some were, however, rewritten in "standard" French in a collection destined to serve as a reader (St. Martin and Voorhies 1980).

Corinne Saucier used altered spellings to reflect pronunciation and apostrophes to indicate elision in her transcriptions of Louisiana French tales from Avoyelles Parish (1956). She published excerpts from her dissertation in the original French in the *Memoirs of the American Folklore Society* series, in Louisiana, however Saucier was only able to publish the English translations of the tales in her collection *Folk Tales from French Louisiana* (1972). The same is true of Calvin Claudel, who published some of his original transcriptions in scholarly articles (cf. Claudel 1944: 287–299), but his *Fools and Rascals* (1978) contained only English translations. Elizabeth Brandon published some material from her dissertation on the folklore of Vermilion Parish in the journal *Bayou* (1955), but again transcriptions of the original texts failed to reach the Louisiana French public. To be sure, these folklorists were only following the fashion of their times. Yet the effect of these non-standard transcriptions was to give the impression that the Cajuns and Creoles spoke the way they did because they did not know better, and to reinforce the notion that the language they spoke was indeed so different from French that it was not worth preserving and certainly unfit for the classroom.

Cajun French is a close enough variant of the French language to justify the use of standard orthography in most cases. The Cajuns do not always speak according to French rules, yet Cajun French does not differ from "standard" French any more than other regional variations of the French language among speakers of comparable social and cultural background. Whether or not a particular Cajun can write, his or her language can be transcribed with a few adjustments for lexical and syntactical changes. Though divided at first, today most serious Louisiana French specialists seem to agree that Cajun French is a variant of the French language and is best rendered using the French system with minor adjustments. I based my transcription method on a line of reasoning similar to the one described by linguist Becky Brown in her word level analysis of the syntax of Cajun French: "insofar as it *is* a French variety, genetically related to and mutually intelligible with metropolitan French, that orthography as a point of departure is logical. The purpose is to *recover* a tradition, not invent one" (Brown 1988). My method also resembles that used by the series *Mémoires d'homme*, directed by Jean-Pierre Pichette for Éditions Quinze (in Laforte 1980). Essentially I wrote everything word for word, as it was narrated, using the French language for spelling, leaving out only obvious false starts which contributed nothing to the discourse. My guiding principle was that spelling could be altered only for the sake of syntax, not only to render pronunciation. Even then, I avoided inventing spellings unless I could not find a preexisting source, which was rare. An example includes words which consistently retain the liaison sound from the plural in all forms; these are preceded with *z-*, as in *un z-oiseau*. For terms not in contemporary dictionaries (*asteure, cil [celui]*), I checked etymological and historical dictionaries. I traced most Acadian sources in the works of Poirier (1964 and 1977) and Maillet (1971). For regionalisms and borrowings from other languages, especially Spanish and certain Native American languages (*grègue, chaoui*), I found references in the studies of Ditchy (1932), Phillips (1936), and Read (1931). I also tried to be faithful to the grammar and syntax of spoken Cajun French. When this posed an orthography problem, as in the variant conjugation of certain verbs, I used historical spellings when possible

CAJUN AND CREOLE FOLKTALES

(*ils estiont, ils vouliont*). Otherwise, I tried to follow a parallel from the French language (*je vas, tu vas, il va*) and checked my case with contemporary linguists working in Louisiana French (Richard Guidry, Becky Brown, etc.). Some ambiguities were impossible to eliminate while preserving the integrity of this system. The best example is *"plus,"* a homograph of the word for "more" (pronounced [plys]) and the negative indicator for "no more" (almost always pronounced [py]) which functions in Cajun French without *"ne"*. Despite the possibility for confusion in isolated cases (*Il y en a plus dans la maison*, which could mean "There are more in the house" or "There are no more in the house"), I opted to preserve the orthography of the existing form, leaving its meaning to be supported by context.

Creole is another case altogether, complicated by its greater distance from the French language (Broussard 1942; Morgan 1959 and 1960; Valdman 1981). Many Creole specialists have opted for the creation of new writing systems that seek, as Robert Chaudenson put it, *"d'éviter les incohérences du code graphique français"* [to avoid the inconsistencies of the French writing system] (1984, personal communication; see also Chaudenson 1974:I, xxxv–xxxvi). The Creole storytellers I recorded were more interested in getting me to understand their stories, than in making a statement concerning linguistic purity. Though I had studied their language enough to understand it, they knew that my native language was Cajun French. Being all more or less bidialectal (Cajun French and Creole), they all made an unconscious effort to Frenchify their Creole in order to communicate more directly. Moreover, Louisiana Creole is already relatively less creolized than the dialects from the West Indies. The result in the Creole stories of this collection is an essentially French dialect laced with Creole elements. I chose to render them as such, generally using French orthography. For the obvious Creole elements, I tried to follow the rules developed by Chaudenson (1974) for the Indian Ocean and Valdman (1981) for the West Indies. I also referred to the works of Broussard (1942) and Morgan (1959 and 1960). Briefly, there is a reduction to a single form in the present, with other tenses indicated by markers: *pé,* or *apé* + participle = progressive; *té* + participle = past preterite; *té pé,* or *té apé* + participle = past imperfect; *sé* + participle = conditional; *va* + participle = future; and so on. The personal pronouns are *mo* (I), *to* (you), *li* (he or she), *nous* or *on* (we), *vous* (you, formal) / *vous autres* (you, plural), *yé* (they).

The Storytellers

Unless specifically described as black Creoles, the narrators are Cajuns.

Clence Ancelet is my father's older brother. Born in Ossun on the northwestern corner of Lafayette Parish, he was one of the first generation from his area to settle in town in search of a better life. He moved to Lafayette in 1943 and has lived there since then, though he maintains a close contact with his native rural neighborhood. His family and friends consider him a "good talker." He has a phenomenal memory and a deep knowledge of the area's oral history and genealogy. He worked for a while in a farm supply store, but was forced to retire early for medical reasons. Since then, he has done a little fishing and hunting, tended a small but highly productive urban garden, faithfully visited his friends and family, told a few jokes, and talked about the old days with anyone who will listen.

Elmo Ancelet is my father. Like his brother and many of his neighbors, he also left the family farm as a young man. He worked in the CCC camps during the 1930s and then joined the Navy during World War II. After the war, he became a barber and moved in with his brother Clence for a while before moving with his new wife to Cankton, a small town near the rural community of Ossun where he was born. Elmo moved his family back to Lafayette a few years later and has lived there since then. As a barber, he has acquired the requisite avocations of philosopher, political analyst, ethnologist, psychologist, historian, and storyteller. Most of his stories are told to him by his clients and "don't stay with [him] for long." His rapidly changing repertoire is thus a fair barometer of the current oral tradition.

Maude Mayer Ancelet is my mother. She has storytelling on both sides of her family tree. Her father, Valery Mayer, was a locally renowned storyteller and practical joker. Her mother, Ida Chautin Mayer, and many of her aunts and uncles are fine storytellers in their own right. Most of their repertoire of family stories focuses on the adventures and unexpected turns of real life. During Prohibition, for example, both sides of the family were active in bootlegging operations. They all grew up on the farm and experienced the floods of 1927 and 1940, as well as several hurricanes. My grandfather was also a traveling salesman, and operated a liquor store for a while. These experiences furnished hundreds of stories which are now being enjoyed and enhanced by subsequent generations.

Ralph Begnaud, from Lafayette, is one of the new breed of Cajun stand-up comics. His repertoire is part localized international joke types and part original observations of the quirks of daily life in South Louisiana. He honed his craft, first as a class clown in school,

Elmo Ancelet in his barbershop in Lafayette, Louisiana, cutting the hair of his grandson Jean.

and then as a automobile salesman. He now devotes himself full-time to performing his huge repertoire of stories.

Évélia Boudreaux was born and still lives on a farm near Carencro, in northern Lafayette Parish. She comes from a long line of female storytellers, including her mother, Clotile Richard, and a great-aunt from nearby Grand Coteau. Since my first visit with Mrs. Boudreaux in January, 1974, I have noticed a remarkable progression in her style, her delivery, and her repertoire. During our first meeting, I was struck by the careful way in which she told her tales. She took the recording session to be a very serious affair. Her sense of mission was so strong, in fact, that she was brief and little stiff, and spoke in a language laden with formality, but she told some exceptional tales and I was sure she had known more. I returned to visit her a year later, because I suspected that she might remember more stories with a little encouragement, but our first visit had been encouragement enough and she had already begun to mine her own memories. She announced immediately that she had several new stories to tell me, and when I returned home afterwards, she had already left a message that I should come back the next day because there were a few stories she had forgotten to tell me. During these second and third visits, she told her stories with no less sense of mission, but she felt more comfortable with the recording process, and was thus more at ease than the first time. She felt freer to improvise and embellish her stories, and she

demonstrated a mastery of oral style, as only the best storytellers can. Since then, Mrs. Boudreaux has come to understand the importance of her traditional artistry; she has continued to explore her past for stories from her childhood and has rebuilt a remarkable repertoire of traditional stories. She often is invited to participate in storytelling presentations and workshops at festivals and in school programs designed to teach younger generations about the importance of preserving the French language and culture in Louisiana.

Inez Catalon, a Creole from Kaplan in Vermilion Parish, is an excellent singer of Louisiana French ballads and *complaintes*. She and her mother were recorded as early as the 1940s by folklorist Elizabeth Brandon. In 1974, I rediscovered her while doing fieldwork in preparation for the first Tribute to Cajun Music festival in Lafayette. Since then, she has sung at several festivals, including the New Orleans Jazz and Heritage Festival, the Smithsonian Festival of American Folklife in Washington, and *À la mode de chez nous,* a concert tour presented by the National Council for the Traditional Arts. Her charm derives in large part from her quick wit and unflappable character, which also make her a fine storyteller. She is not at all afraid to shock her audiences, keeping them off-balance with racy and irreverent humor. She also tells—without the least self-consciousness—stories about the atrocities suffered by the black Creoles during the vigilante era when some took the law into their own hands and others were forced to respond in kind. She also delights in telling legends and stories about superstitions and then laughing about people who would believe such things.

Andrew (André) Chautin is my mother's uncle. He was born in the Pacanière region near Leonville in St. Landry Parish. He moved around in search of work and now lives in Gillis, just north of Lake Charles, near the edge of the French part of Louisiana, in Calcasieu Parish. He is one of many natural comedians in his family. Most of his stories are based in reality. He is one of those people who are simply good at noticing the humor in everyday life. Many of his stories come from his escapades with brother-in-law and longtime partner, and my grandfather, Valery Mayer, as well as from his own brothers and sisters. He continues to speak French, though he lives in an English-speaking community.

After recording Mrs. Mary Fentroy, who told me several Bouki and Lapin tales, I asked her if she knew anyone else around Cade, in Iberia Parish, who might tell me some stories. She sent me to see Mrs. **Carrie Charles,** an elegant Creole woman who lived nearby in a little farmhouse completely hidden from the road by trees. She lived alone by her own choice and was self-sufficient despite her advanced age. She had no formal education, but had carefully provided an education to each of her children, who now live and work in Lafayette. Mrs. Charles told me two long animal tales in a highly creolized French. Her storytelling style was simple and unassuming, but reflected a deep, almost stoic strength.

I met **Frank Couppel** during a fieldwork trip east of the Atchafalaya Basin. I arrived in Bayou Pigeon, a little town clinging to the levee which runs along the swamp, hoping to find a situation similar to Pierre Part, where I had found a great number of singers and storytellers a few years before. The percentage of French-speakers seemed to be as high, but I had a hard time making initial contacts. All of the usual resource people (parish priest, grocer, barber, etc.) suggested, as usual, that I try talking to the elders of the community.

Evélia Boudreaux, on the *galerie* of her home near Carencro, Louisiana, 1970.

A storytelling performance with Barry Jean Ancelet and Stanislaus "Tanisse" Faul at his home in Cankton, Louisiana, 1985.

One of them, Mr. Couppel, had moved to nearby Bayou Sorrel. His was one of only two French-speaking families in that surprisingly English-speaking town. After several misses, I finally found his house which had been built facing the bayou, formerly the town's main means of transportation, instead of the new road which now connected it with the outside world. Like most of his neighbors, he had gathered moss and fished for a living when he wasn't working on road and canal crews for the oil industry. He didn't know his exact age, but knew that he had been born sometime in the 1890s. He had hardly begun rummaging his memories when he came upon the story of Ste. Geneviève which he had learned from his mother. His Cajun French was reminiscent of the language of the Acadian Maritimes in Canada. He and his two sons were among the few who still spoke French in Bayou Sorrel, and they maintained close contacts with their French-speaking neighbors down the levee in Bayou Pigeon, Pierre Part, and Belle Rivière.

Odette Coussan lives in Carencro, in Lafayette Parish, where she has taught French for many years. She is an eloquent and well-respected member of her community. She uses the oral tradition she learned in her own family to help teach Louisiana French culture along with the language.

Edward Deshotels lives in Mamou and his brother **Elby** lived in Reddell, both in Evangeline Parish. The northern edge of what is called Cajun country was actually settled largely by French Creoles. These twin brothers were renowned in the region both as singers and as storytellers. Though a hard-working farmer and rancher, Elby was known to leave his tractor in the middle of his fields to run to the grocery store in town to have a quick cup of coffee and tell a story or two when the notion struck him. Their father, Marcellus Deshotels, taught them most of their stories and songs. The Deshotels family has played an important role in the preservation of Cajun culture. In the 1950s, Marcellus was one of the principal sources of information on the Mardi Gras when community leaders in nearby Mamou reestablished the traditional run there. The Deshotels twins have preserved their family traditions in their musical recordings and storytelling sessions.

Lazard Daigle was an active storyteller before the mass media invasion. I heard from friends and neighbors that he was a good talker, but when I met him at his home in Pointe Noire, in Acadia Parish, he claimed to be no longer able to tell stories. His repertoire was in fact only a fragment of what it once had been, but his mastery of oral style revealed that his natural storytelling talent had not dimmed. With a little encouragement, he may have been able to reconstruct some of his former repertoire, as Mrs. Boudreaux has done. Unfortunately, though, Mr. Daigle died before a second visit could be arranged.

Westley "Kit" Dennis was born in 1897 at Loudun, the old Montgomery family plantation which is now part of the city of Lafayette. He worked on a farm all his life and excelled in the training of horses. Even in his 80s he was frequently asked to help train an especially difficult pony. He has never owned an automobile, more comfortable with his own horse-drawn methods of transportation. Many of his stories describe the time when vigilante posses roamed the countryside intimidating members of the Creole community. His tales are horrifying, but also remarkably non-judgmental; he insists that he has always preferred to look to the opportunities of the future. His French is slightly creolized, but

resembles closely the French spoken by his Cajun neighbors in the countryside where he lives near Scott, in Lafayette Parish. I first met Mr. Dennis while directing a fieldwork project for students from the University of Southwestern Louisiana in 1981. Since then, he has worked with folklorist Patricia Rickels, participating in storytelling presentations at events such as the Lafayette Native Crafts Festival.

Witness Dugas was born in rural St. Landry Parish, but he was raised between Scott and Ossun in Lafayette Parish. When married, he left the farm for a salaried job making doughnuts at the Café du Monde in New Orleans. Later, he came back with his wife to raise his family in Lafayette where he got a job as a butcher in a commercial meat-packing house. Now retired, he works long hours in his garden which has gotten almost as big as his repertoire of jokes and tall tales.

I've known Witness's son, **Rick Dugas,** since high school. He also is an avid story-teller, specializing in contemporary forms such as jokes and tall tales. He has a knack for hearing and remembering the most current material floating around and is consequently an invaluable resource for up-to-the-minute information from the field. Once when I was do-ing research for a paper on the relationship between oral tradition and Cajun identity, I asked him if he knew any jokes about Cajuns. His first answer was, "Yeah, but I don't think I should tell them to you. I mean, I know who you are." I insisted that this was for scholarly purposes and that I really did need to hear those stories. So he agreed and asked matter-of-factly, "OK, what do you want, upgrade or downgrade?"

Stanislaus "Tanisse" Faul was born in Cankton, in St. Landry Parish, when the town was still called Coulée Croche (Crooked Creek). He lived there most of his life as a tenant farmer. He came from a family of musicians and storytellers. His oral style made his huge repertoire come alive as only a true storyteller's can. His stock of tales, among the largest I encountered in my years of collecting, included the full range of Louisiana French oral tradition: animal tales, magic tales, jokes, tall tales, legends and historical narratives. Within his community, he had a reputation as a joker which he enthusiastically cultivated. He insisted that he so enjoyed making people laugh that they could laugh at his expense, if no other subject came to mind. For someone who grew up in the Marais-bouleur, a region once renowned for its toughness, Mr. Faul was a remarkably gentle man. Despite his lack of formal education, his Cajun French language was rich with generations of traditional learn-ing. His tales often sent transcribers to historical and etymological dictionaries where they invariably found the words he used so effortlessly and unselfconsciously. Carl Brasseaux, an historian and my colleague at the Center for Louisiana Studies at the University of South-western Louisiana, first introduced me to his longtime friend and former neighbor in 1980. "Mr. Tanisse" was delighted, but also genuinely astonished that anyone might be interested in his stories. Almost immediately, his wide repertoire and deft style earned him invitations to participate in various storytelling events at festivals and on radio and television, to his even greater amazement. Yet he took to this more public forum with the same quiet grace and ease that he displayed telling stories to visitors while sitting in his favorite rocking chair at home or leaning against a hoe in his large garden.

Mary Fentroy lived in the town of Cade, near the Bayou Teche, in Iberia Parish. Her son, the principal of an elementary school in nearby Parks, told me a few tales in English when I was looking for storytellers there. He suggested his mother when I said I was interested in French tales. Education and the English language were very important to Mrs. Fentroy, yet she spoke with great respect also of her own French-influenced black Creole heritage. Her repertoire consisted almost exclusively of animal tales which she told in a moderately creolized French.

Adley Gaudet is retired, but stays active and in touch with the daily life of his native Bayou Pigeon by working part-time at Valia's, a combination bar/grocery store to which most of the people in town go at least once a week. This is where I found him during an improvised fieldwork trip east of the Atchafalaya Basin. A hunter, fisherman, former oilfield worker, like most of his friends and neighbors, Mr. Gaudet is also an excellent teller of tall tales based on life in the basin. His speech is typical of the Cajun French dialect spoken in the more isolated regions where the modernizing influences of contemporary French are less evident. He was incredulous at first that someone might be interested in his tales, but within minutes he became intrigued by my project and called a few other storytellers from the area to tell them to come in that afternoon to record their stories.

Léonard and Samuel Gautreaux live in the countryside near Cecilia, in St. Martin Parish. These two brothers are very serious about searching for buried treasure with everything from metal detectors to spirit controllers. "Anything that works," declared Léonard. Their stories about their own exploits and those of others are practically inexhaustible, especially when they are playing off of each other.

Richard Guidry, originally from Gueydan, in southern Vermilion Parish, has a degree in French from the University of Southwestern Louisiana. He has taught French in the bilingual education program in St. Martin Parish, and now supervises the French education program for the Louisiana State Department of Education. While helping me to find contacts among Creole storytellers along the Bayou Teche, he told me several stories that he had learned from his own family tradition. He has since developed methods and materials to use Louisiana French culture in the classroom.

Elizabeth Landreneau, of Mamou, in Evangeline Parish, is a well-known storyteller who delights in shocking her audiences with risquée stories, despite the fact that she looks like the very prototype of the "nice little old lady." She is from the same family of musicians that produced Adam and Cyprien Landreneau and plays a mean harmonica herself.

Claude Landry lives in Bayou Pigeon where he is known as a great teller of jokes. His oral style is highly developed and his timing is flawless. He never fails to produce a few chuckles at informal social gatherings and improvised storytelling sessions in his neighborhood. He has worked on boats and in the oilfield. When I recorded him in the mid-1980s, he was in his forties and spoke a French typical of his generation with lots of English influences.

Martin Latiolais lived in Catahoula, in St. Martin Parish, near the levee which runs along the western edge of the Atchafalaya Basin. He worked on boats and in the oilfield, but

Photo by Ginette Vachon

Martin Latiolais in his home, telling "Bouki et Lapin et le bonhomme en *coal tar.*"

always preferred commercial fishing. Like so many "retirees," he never really stopped work-ing. When I first met him, he was out in his yard repairing window screens. He was quick to abandon this project, though, when I asked him if he told any old stories. He spoke with equal fluency in Cajun French, Creole, and English, despite his lack of formal education. He told me his stories in Cajun French because he instinctively felt that I would understand them better that way. He was quick to point out that he had learned most of his stories from an old and dear friend named Willie Johnson who despite his name spoke no English and who had a huge repertoire which could provide stories throughout a day-long hunting or fishing expedition without repetition. Mr. Latiolais regretted not learning more of his friend's stories.

Azalée Malveaux, a Creole, is the grandmother of one of my wife's students. Her granddaughter recorded the story of Petit Pouce as part of a school French class project. When I heard the recording, I immediately called to see if I might come for a visit. When I arrived, I recognized Mrs. Malveaux's husband, Gradney, who had been the custodian at Cathedral-Carmel High School when I was in school there in the 1960s. Mrs. Malveaux learned her stories from her family as a child and was proud, but a little surprised, that one

Ida Mayer and her daughter Maude Ancelet, Easter 1978, participating in a traditional Cajun pâquer contest as Maude's daughter Jody looks on. At the Mayer home, Easter has also been a time for relatives to exchange family stories.

of them had been useful to her granddaughter in school and had even attracted the attention of a university professor. She is shy and subsequently declined to participate in public storytelling sessions, but has genuinely enjoyed the newfound value of her stock of French tales.

Ida Chautin Mayer is my maternal grandmother. She developed a reputation as a child for her wit and her love of practical jokes. Many of her brothers supplemented their incomes during the Depression by making moonshine in the woods of their native Pacanière region along the Bayou Teche between Leonville and Arnaudville in St. Landry Parish. She eventually married the perfect partner. Her husband, Valery Mayer, was renowned for his exploits as a traveling salesman and an elusive bootlegger. He also regularly entertained gatherings of family and friends with his seemingly inexhaustible store of stories. My grandmother jokingly complained that she could never stay mad at her husband, no matter how bad the situation, no matter how outrageous his behavior, because he could always make her laugh. Most of her stories are based on the adventures and misadventures of her own life.

Willert Menard is married to my sister. He grew up on a farm near Cankton with his mother and father and ten brothers (no sisters). His father, Evril Menard, was a locally popular musician. Willert now lives in Ossun, near Lafayette where he works as a butcher. He is also an avid hunter and fisherman. He is a great audience with an easy laugh for the performers in our family. Otherwise he is usually quiet and reserved. Occasionally, however, he regales us with a joke he's just heard. His disarmingly spare performance style adds to the effect of his stories which are usually outrageous.

Norris Mitchell was visiting Mr. Westley Dennis one day when I arrived to record a few tales. When he heard that his friend could no longer remember any animal tales, he happily contributed one story, included here, explaining why the dog chases the rabbit. His French consistently resembled the prairie Cajun and Creole dialects in ordinary conversation but he clearly shifted into a Creole-influenced dialect when he began his story, indicating his family's Bayou Teche background.

Wilson "Ben Guiné" Mitchell lived in the Promised Land, a section of the town of Parks in the heart of the Bayou Teche country in St. Martin Parish. I first met this exceptional storyteller by sheer luck. His grandson won a footrace to my truck when I asked a group of children playing along the side of the road for directions to the home of another lead. During the interview, the child listened to the questions I was asking and suggested on the way back that his grandfather told the kind of stories we were seeking. When we arrived at Ben Guiné's house, he was just sitting down to supper. He pushed away a steaming plate full of crawfish étouffée when his wife explained that the people at the door were interested in hearing some old stories. His repertoire consisted of animal tales, jokes, and historical tales, all told in a heavy Creole dialect and regularly punctuated with gestures and movements. Though his role as an active storyteller had been diminished by the invasion of mass media, he still possessed a remarkable mastery of oral style. For him, a story was not only a memory, but a living tradition which involved visual and tactile support to enhance the oral performance. His storytelling was like oral music. Even those who understood little of what

Wilson "Ben Guiné" Mitchell in his garden, Parks, Louisiana, 1975.

Photo by Barry Jean Ancelet

Photo by Ginette Vachon

Félix Richard at home with his wife Rena in Cankton, Louisiana, 1978.

he said sat spellbound by his voice. He eventually was featured on Louisiana Public Broadcasting in a series of storytelling segments, which revived interest in this master storyteller within his own community. Thus the media that once robbed him of his status as a culture hero finally helped to restore some of that same status while he was still alive.

Don Montoucet, a native of Scott, is a well-known musician and was instrumental in efforts during the 1970s to revitalize the Cajun music scene by working with young people. He is also a master mechanic, a carpenter, an electrician, a concrete-finisher, a welder, a schoolbus driver, and a gifted teller of jokes. He enjoys a good story no matter who's telling it, often laughing at least as much as his audience at his own performances.

Edward Morin was a blacksmith in Pointe Bleue, in Evangeline Parish. He was known especially for his tall tales, most of which he learned from his father-in-law. His stories were generally rooted in his family tradition, using family members as characters. I met him briefly through the efforts of Revon Reed, a master storyteller in his own right.

Clotile Richard spent the last years of her life near Carencro, in Lafayette Parish with her daughter Évélia Boudreaux, also featured in this collection. She told me several stories while I was recording her daughter who had learned many of the stories from her mother. Still quick-witted at 90, she was generally content to let her daughter have the floor, but contributed a more developed ending to one of the magic tales that Mrs. Boudreaux told. A deeply religious woman, she also contributed a few interesting traditional prayers.

Félix Richard was a master carpenter, musician, and storyteller. Originally from the Marais-bouleur, he lived most of his life near Cankton (formerly Coulée Croche), in St.

lxix

Landry Parish. A well-known musician, he first played guitar and sang in house dances and dance halls with the now-legendary band leader and accordionist Aldus Roger. Later he learned the accordion, but he quit playing altogether when he married and started raising a family. He eventually picked up the instrument again to participate in the renewal of Cajun music which developed since the early 1970s. In addition to his musical talents, Mr. Richard was also an excellent storyteller with a remarkable oral style. In disarmingly relaxed fashion, he weaved oral fiction in and out of ordinary conversation. A true man of words, he possessed a rich vocabulary and he developed his stories carefully, slowly, and in great detail, turning what might otherwise have been a short joke into a full-blown folktale.

A. J. Smith was born and raised in Lafayette, but now lives near Lake Charles where he works in the oil industry. He is another of the new breed of Cajun stand-up comics who are drawing on Louisiana French oral tradition for their working repertoire. Though A.J. tells some localized versions of internationally known jokes, his forte is finding humor in everyday life, especially in the confrontation between traditional and modern lifestyles.

Fred Tate was a native of Mamou and owner of the legendary Fred's Lounge, for many years the site of Revon Reed's well-known live Saturday morning radio show, featured often in national and international news reports, and a mecca for visitors to south Louisiana's Cajun country. As the owner and bartender of his lounge, he heard stories every day and remembered the best ones for retelling himself. His brief and direct style produced stories typical of his occupation, short enough to slip in between the draft beer and mixed drinks, and strong enough to shock even his inebriated clientele.

Bernice Wiltz lives along Bayou Teche between Parks and Pont Breaux, in St. Martin Parish. When I first met her, she was still very active despite her eighty years, still attending the horse races regularly. She told me in Creole a few stories that she had learned from her father, a deeply religious man who had also taught his whole family traditional French canticles and prayers.

Pascal Storytellers and Participants in Mamou, Evangeline Parish:

Elvin Fontenot (EF) was a member of the group of Pascal storytellers. Although his participation was usually limited to provoking the more active talkers with well-conceived and well-timed questions, he occasionally took the floor to develop at least part of a story.

Burke Guillory (BG) was superintendent of schools for Evangeline Parish. He was part of a circle of friends who gathered regularly for suppers which doubled as storytelling sessions, usually featuring tall tales. His tales and his "lies" are still a part of the oral tradition of this group, though he died some years ago. His participation in the Pascal tradition was limited, however, to retelling memorable tales he heard from the most active talkers who regularly refused to retell their stories.

Alexandre Manuel (AM) was a native of Mamou. Some insist that it was he who

Photo by Ginette Vachon, 1977

Revon Reed as master of ceremonies for a Saturday morning live broadcast of Cajun music, Fred's Lounge, Mamou. Revon told many of his tales in Fred's Lounge, both on and off the air. Fred's Lounge has also served as a popular site for exchanging Pascal stories.

started telling stories about Pascal. According to local tradition, Pascal Guillory was complaining one day about an uneasy ride he had had on his underweight mule. Alexandre is said to have retorted, "Must be a razor-backed mule!" He was one of the most popular storytellers in the bars of Mamou where he spent almost every morning with his drinking and storytelling buddies.

Irving Reed (IR) lived just outside of Mamou, his hometown. He was the brother of Revon and Hube Reed, and one of the best storytellers of the Pascal tradition. I met him at his home, since he was bedridden by then, but he still had the spark of spontaneous oral creation, refusing to retell any stories and choosing instead to launch a new one for the recording session his brother Revon had helped to set up.

Hubert Reed (HR), another of the Reed brothers from Mamou, excels in the Pascal genre on the strength of his wildly vivid imagination. He was a frequent visitor in the bars along Sixth Street during the heyday of the tradition. In another life, he might have been a great novelist or a celebrated filmmaker. Instead he is a gifted storyteller who is underappreciated at best in his own environment. A waitress once told me when I asked if she knew where he was: "I can't understand why you're interested in all that foolishness. We try to get away when we see him coming." Hube is a driven man; he tells his stories to all around him, whether anyone is listening or not.

Revon Reed (RR) is a retired schoolteacher. He completed the Master's degree in English at Boston University. When ethnomusicologists Harry Oster and Ralph Rinzler came

to do fieldwork in south Louisiana in the 1960s, they quickly found in Revon Reed a key contact person and a presenter to explain the musical tradition in national and international festivals where Cajun and Creole musicians were beginning to perform. He accompanied several groups to the Newport Folk Festival in the late 1960s. Already the host of the live radio show broadcast over KEUN from Fred's Lounge every Saturday morning, he also became involved in the promotion and preservation of his own Cajun culture in other ways. He even published a book, *Lache pas la patate* (Montréal: Parti Pris, 1976), which focused on the culture and traditions of French Louisiana. In addition to all this, Revon is a gifted storyteller. Swallow Records released several commercially produced recordings of his stories told in French under the pseudonym Nonc Hilaire.

The Tales

Except when otherwise indicated in this study, tale types refer to Antti Aarne's standard classification, *The Types of the Folktale: A Classification and Bibliography*, revised by Stith Thompson, and motifs refer to Stith Thompson's *Motif-Index of Folk-Literature*. References to Baughman are from Ernest Baughman's *Type and Motif Index of the Folktales of England and North America*. Types and motifs preceded by (AF) refer to the manuscript of an annotated index of French language oral tradition prepared at Université Laval's Archives de Folklore under the direction of Luc Lacourcière and Margaret Low. References to frequently cited titles are shortened to the part underlined in the bibliography (pp.205–212). *Journal of American Folklore* references are shortened to *JAF*.

Contes d'Animaux / Animal Tales

1. Le gros baril de beurre / The Big Barrel of Butter (Martin Latiolais, Catahoula)

This tale is a Creole variant of type 15 *The Theft of Butter (Honey) by Playing Godfather.* It is one of the most widely known animal tales in French-speaking Louisiana, in the American South and in the West Indies. Flowers lists twenty references in her study of West Indies folktales, including a version from Bermuda in which the quarrel which develops in this story is said to be at the heart of the inimical relationship between dogs and cats. In *Folktales of the Antilles, French and English,* Parsons has a variant from Grenada with a similar explanation (I, pp. 77–78). In that variant, the cat steals the butter from the dog using names such as "Just-Start," "Quarter," "Half-Gone," and "All-Done." He then relieves himself in the empty pot and throws the contents at the dog's head. Klipple reports an African variant in which the rabbit fools the antelope and then proposes a truth test (motif K981). An English-language Louisiana version was told by Clifford Blake *(Louisiana Folklife* 1980). In *American Negro Folktales,* Richard Dorson presents a variant by his star storyteller, J. D. Suggs (no. 1, pp. 68–71) with a similar test. In the same collection (no. 2, pp. 71–75), John Blackmore includes interesting contemporary details: the rabbit steals food from an ice box and the duped bear is chased by a fox with a shotgun. Burrison reports two Southern versions, "Brother Rabbit Steals the Lard" *(Storytellers,* p. 94) in which the clever rabbit exchanges places with the possum to avoid detection and punishment; and "Brother Rabbit Steals the Butter" (pp. 155–156), in which the butter-filled rabbit is killed and cooked in the end. There are two versions in Carrière's collection of Missouri French tradition: "Bouki p'is Lapin" (no. 6) and "Entamé, À Moiquié Mangé, Tout Mangé" (no. 7). In both stories, type 15 is followed by type 175 *The Tarbaby and the Rabbit,* after the discovery of the theft by Bouki. The use of Bouki and Lapin in Missouri French tradition indicates a Mississippi River Valley connection through Louisiana to West Africa. Bouki is Wolof for "hyena," the traditional dupe of the hare in the oral tradition of the Sene-Gambia region.

This type is also common in the French tradition of animal tales featuring the clever fox and the stupid wolf (Renart and Isengrin, in the medieval *Roman de Renart).* Geneviève Massignon reported a French variant in *Folktales of France* (no. 54, pp. 189–192, "The Fox and the Wolf") in which type 15 is followed by types 1 *The Theft of Fish,* 2 *The Tail-Fisher,* and 34 *The Wolf Dives into the Water for Reflected Cheese.* The unfortunate wolf finally dies in the last episode.

3

The Archives de Folklore at Laval University in Québec has at least 42 versions of type 15 from North American French tradition. French Canadian variants almost always cast the clever fox and the bumbling wolf. This tale is often linked with other animal tale types, especially types 1 and 2, as in France, and 41 *The Wolf Overeats in the Cellar.* The names of the children to be baptized always indicate the theft in progress. See, for example, "Le Renard parrain" in Conrad Laforte's collection *Menteries drôles et merveilleuses* (no. 4, pp. 63). Elisabeth Brandon has a Louisiana version of this tale in her doctoral dissertation on the folklore of Vermilion Parish, "Bouqui et Lapin et la récolte" (II, no. 58, pp. 365–367), which is based on the false godfather plot, but without the telling names.

It is interesting to note that this version concludes without what might be considered a just resolution: Lapin has eaten all the butter, but is not punished for it.

Là, quand ils travaillaient comme ça-là, Lapin s'avait mis comme un prêtre, tu vois? Il baptisait les enfants. Mais, ils s'avaient acheté un baril de beurre, un gros baril de beurre.

Ça fait, ils étaient après piocher dans le clos. Voilà, à tout moment, Lapin dit ça à Bouki, il dit, "Heup! Quelqu'un m'appelle."

Ça fait, Bouki dit, "Ah! Va!" (Il croyait il collectait, tu vois?)

Il allait. Il revenait. "Comment ils l'appellent, Lapin?"

"Commencé," il disait. (Mais il avait commencé manger le baril de beurre, tu vois?)

Ça fait, tout à l'heure—ils piochaient un petit peu—tout à l'heure, "Heup! Bouki, il y a quelqu'un qui m'appelle encore."

"Mais va, Lapin."

Lapin allait, il mangeait un peu de beurre. Puis là, il revenait.

"Comment il l'appellent, Lapin?"

"Un quart," il dit.

"Mais ça, c'est des drôles de noms quand même! Hé bien!" Piochent un petit peu encore.

Tout à l'heure, "Un autre qui m'appelle-là, Bouki!"

Ça fait, Bouki dit, "Va, Lapin." Ça fait, ça part.

Il revient. "Comment ils l'appellent, Lapin?"

"La moitié." Il avait mangé la moitié du

Now, when they worked together like that, Lapin posed as a priest, you see? He baptized children. But they had bought a barrel of butter, a big barrel of butter.

So, they were hoeing in the field. Every now and then, Lapin says to Bouki, he says, "Hup! Somebody's calling me."

So, Bouki says, "Ah! Go!" (He thought he was getting paid, you see?)

He would go. He'd come back. "What did they call it, Lapin?"

"Started," he'd say. (But he had started eating in the butter barrel, you see?")

So, a little later, they were hoeing a little, a little later, "Hup! Bouki, somebody's calling me again."

"Well, go, Lapin."

Lapin would go, he'd eat a little butter. And then he'd come back.

"What did they call it, Lapin?"

"Quarter," he says.

"Well, those sure are funny names! Oh, well." Hoe a little more.

A little later, "Another one's calling me, Bouki!"

So, Bouki says, "Go, Lapin." So, he leaves.

He comes back. "What did they call it, Lapin?"

"Half." He had eaten half the barrel of

baril de beurre.

Ça fait, ils piochent un petit peu encore. "Heup! Bouki, il y a un autre qui m'appelle."

"Va, Lapin." Ça a parti.

Il revient encore. "Comment ils l'appellent, hein?"

"Trois quarts," il dit.

Ça fait, ils ont pioché un peu encore. Ça l'appelle encore.

Bouki dit, "Va, Lapin." Il part. Il va.

Il revient *back*. Il dit, "Comment ils l'appellent, Lapin?"

Il dit, "Fini. Et c'est la dernière fois," il dit, "il y n-a plus de beurre." Il avait tout mangé le beurre.

BA: Il était malin, Lapin?

ML: O, il était malin, Lapin. T'as raison pour ça.

butter.

So, they hoed a little more. "Hup! Bouki, there's another one calling me."

"Go, Lapin." He left.

He comes back. "What did they call it, eh?"

"Three quarters," he says.

So, they hoed a little more. They called him again.

Bouki says, "Go, Lapin." He leaves. He goes.

He comes back. He says, "What did they call it, Lapin?"

He says, "Finished. And that's the last time," he says, "there's no more butter." He had eaten all the butter.

BA: He was clever, Lapin?

ML: Oh he was clever, Lapin. You sure are right.

2. *Bouki et Lapin et le bonhomme en* coal tar / *Bouki and Lapin and the Little Tar Man (Martin Latiolais, Catahoula)*

This tale belongs to type 175 *The Tarbaby and the Rabbit*, with motif K581.2 "Briarpatch punishment for rabbit," easily one of the most widely known animal tales of all. It is found in the oral tradition of many cultures: Spanish, Indian, Japanese and Philippine, among others. It seems to be especially popular among Hispanic Americans who had 29 published versions listed in the Aarne-Thompson index, West Indians who had 35, and Africans who had 39. In certain African versions, the tarbaby is replaced by another trap, often a wax statue or even a tortoise shell covered with glue, as in the Creole tales from the Indian Ocean. The trickster, in Africa as well as in the West Indies, is often represented by the hare or the spider. The dupe is normally the hyena or the wolf, but can also be the dog or the cat. Among the Creoles of the Indian Ocean, it is the hare who tricks the monkey and other animals, including the panther and the rhinoceros (cf. *Lièvre Grand Diable*). Another version, from Nevis (Parsons, *Antilles* II, p. 326), casts a dog and a man. It is interesting to note that Nancy, or Anansi, the spider common to Africa and the West Indies, is hardly found in African American tradition. There are at least 21 French American versions in Québec's Archives de Folklore, of which only one is Canadian and it is from a Native American source. In an Ojibwa tale (Coffin, *Indian Tales of North America*, no. 34, pp. 136–138), the turtle gets itself thrown into a river to be drowned. Ordinarily, in the Native American tales, Coyote plays the role of the trickster, although the skunk also occurs (*Indian Tales of North America*, no. 38 [Comanche]), the duck (no. 36 [Ute]), as well as other animals. In a

Southern version reported by Burrison, "The Tar Baby" (*Storytellers*, pp. 152–154), the scene is a cabbage patch, but the tar baby episode is followed by the briar patch ending as here.

This tale is certainly the best known animal tale in Louisiana. Dolores Henderson contributed an African-American version and Max Grieg a Cajun English language version to *Folktales of Louisiana*. (Note the English term "coal tar" is used to refer to the tarbaby.) In "Brer Turtle" (Saucier, *French Louisiana*, no. 31, p. 87) Lapin is replaced by the turtle who dupes the goat and finally pushes it into the river. In the same collection, "Brer Rabbit" (no. 33, p. 88), all the elements of the story of the tarbaby are present except the tarbaby itself, which becomes simply a trap. Alcée Fortier presents another Louisiana variant, "Piti Bonhomme Godron," in "Bits of Folklore," *Transactions and Proceedings of the Modern Language Association*, vol. 3 (1887), pp. 101–168. In that long and complex version, Compère Lapin refuses to help the other animals to dig a well. He is eventually arrested but escapes punishment by a judgment rendered in his favor. He then steals water and is caught by means of the tarbaby only to escape into the briars.

Une fois, il a fait une grosse sécheresse, et Bouki dit à Lapin, il dit, "*Well*, faudra on se fouille un puits."

Lapin dit, "moi, j'ai pas besoin de puits. Je bois la rosée le matin."

Ça fait, Bouki a fouillé un puits. Ça fait, le matin, il voyait des traces autour de son puits, des traces à Lapin autour de son puits. Ça fait, il dit, "Coco de Lapin, je vas t'installer!"

Il s'a fait un bonhomme en *coal tar*, un bonhomme qui ressemblait à Bouki, tu vois?

Là, Lapin a venu le soir pour voler de l'eau. Il a vu le bonhomme, et a cru que c'était Bouki. "Mais," il dit, "je vas t'installer, Bouki!" Il fout un coup de poing, le poing reste collé. Il fout un autre coup de poing, l'autre poing reste collé. Il fout un coup de pied, le pied reste collé. Il fout un autre coup de pied, l'autre pied reste collé. Ça fait, il a foutu un coup de tête, la tête reste collée. Un coup de ventre, le ventre reste collé.

Ça fait, le lendemain matin, Bouki lève. Lapin était collé après son bonhomme en *coal tar*. Et il dit, "Ah! Coco Lapin, là je te tiens. Mais," il dit, "je vas t'installer!"

Ça fait, il s'a attrapé un gros tas de branches. Il s'a fait un gros feu. Il y avait une grosse talle d'éronces au ras-là, tu vois?

Once, there was a great drought, and Bouki says to Lapin, he says, "Well, we'll have to dig a well for ourselves."

Lapin said, "I don't need a well. I drink the morning dew."

So, Bouki dug a well. So, the next morning, He saw tracks around his well, rabbit tracks around his well. So, he says, "Rascal Lapin, I'll fix you!"

He made himself a little man out of coal tar, a little man that looked like Bouki, you see?

Then Lapin came during the night to steal water. He saw the little man, and thought it was Bouki. "Well," he says, "I'll fix you, Bouki!" He hit him with his fist. The fist stayed stuck. He hit him again. The other fist stayed stuck. He kicked him, his foot stayed stuck. He kicked him again, the other foot stayed stuck. So, he butted him with his head, his head stayed stuck. Hit him with his belly, his belly stayed stuck.

So, the next morning, Bouki gets up. Lapin was stuck on his little tar man. And he says, "Ah rascal Lapin, now I've got you. And," he says, "I'll fix you!"

So, he grabbed a big pile of branches. He made a big fire. There was a big briar patch nearby, you see?

Ça fait, il dit, "Lapin, je voulais te brûler, mais je veux te jeter dans les éronces-là!" Il dit, "Lapin je veux te jeter dans les éronces pour bien te graffigner."

"O non!" il dit, "Bouki," il dit, "fait pas ça!"

"Ouais," il dit, "c'est ça, je veux faire avec toi, te jeter dans les éronces."

Ça fait, il le garroche dans les éronces.

Mais Lapin dit, "Yahou! C'est là mon papa et ma maman m'ont élevé, dans les éronces!"

So, he says, "Lapin, I wanted to burn you, but I'd rather throw you into those briars!" He says, "Lapin, I want to throw you into the briars to really scratch you."

"Oh, no!" he says, "Bouki," he says, "don't do that!"

"Yeah," he says, "that's what I want to do with you, throw you into the briars."

So, he threw him into the briars.

But Lapin says, "Yahoo! This is where my dad and mom raised me, in the briars!"

3. *Le petit bonhomme en* coal tar / *The Little Tar Man (Wilson "Ben Guiné" Mitchell, Parks)*

In this variant of the preceding tale, Lapin, usually the trickster who always wins and is never caught, is trapped by the little tar man. Of all the African variants listed by Klipple, only one [Malinke] has the thief escaping the trap by means of his wits: the rabbit is thrown into the dew. Carrière, in his study of Missouri tradition (no. 6), has a version in which the rabbit fools Bouki into throwing him into the morning dew. In the Indian Ocean (*Lièvre Grand diable*, pp. 43–57), the hare also has himself thrown into the morning dew supposedly to simmer. In his Uncle Remus stories (*Uncle Remus*, no. 2), Joel Chandler Harris leaves Brer Rabbit stuck to the tarbaby trap, only to dedicate a whole tale later (no. 4) to his escape. The defeat of the rabbit is not common in Louisiana and when this storyteller left Lapin stuck to the little tar man, one of the listeners, Richard Goldry, expressed surprise and asked why he had ended the tale in this way. He answered with brutal simplicity, "It was time to catch Lapin, you see?"

Ouais, mais, Bouki té gain un jardin. Li acheté un homme, et fait un petit n-homme en *coal tar* dans le milieu du jardin.

Ah, *well,* Bouki vient, li gardé comme ça-là. Lapin vient, li gardé comme ça-là. Li hélé li, li dit, "Qui c'est ça, cil-là?"

À rien répond pas.

"O!" li dit, "c'est bligé d'être quelque chose de malicieux que Bouki rangé moi," li dit, "M'alé couri apé li, n-homme.

Quand il a arrivé là-là, il sacré gaillard-là un coup de poing. "Cabô!" Ça, c'était les jambes en bas, vous comprends?

Yeah, well, Bouki had a garden. He bought a man and made a little tar man in the middle of the garden.

Ah, well, Bouki came and looked at him like this. Lapin came and looked at him like this. He yelled to him, he said, "Who is this?"

Nothing answered nothing.

"Oh!" he said, "this must be malicious thing that Bouki has prepared for me." He said, "I'll go and grab the man."

When he arrived, he stung the guy with his fist. "Kabo!" he hit him on his legs, you understand?

Li dit, "Moi dis toi lâcher moi, moi té toi!"

C'est comme ça!

"Moi dis toi lâcher moi, moi gain l'autre oui! Moi dis toi lâcher moi, moi gain l'autre, oui! Li piqué un autre coup encore! Li lâché pas, li resté collé! Li resté collé! Li—Là, li voyé la tête, tout quelque chose resté collé comme ça-là.

Ah ouais, mais Bouki toujours resté en arrière. Lapin sorti devant.

RG: Mais cette fois-là-là, Bouki sorti en avant!

BG: Ouais, mais, li sorti en avant, mais li tient bon li, vous comprends ça? Bien là, c'était temps pour traper Lapin, vous comprends? C'était passé. C'était temps pour traper li! C'est pas une affaire, non. Pas jouer avec Lapin, non!

He said, "Let me tell you, I'd let me go if I were you!"

That's the way it was!

"I'd let me go if I were you. I have another! I'd let me go if I were you. I have another!" He stung him with another blow. He didn't let go. He stayed stuck! He stayed stuck! He—Then, he hit him with his head, everything stayed stuck.

Oh yeah, but Bouki always came out behind. Lapin came out ahead.

RG: But this time, Bouki came out ahead!

BG: Yeah, but he came out ahead, he had him, you understand? Well then it was time to catch Lapin, you understand? It was past time. It was time to catch him! That's really something. You can't play around with Lapin!

4. *Dans la grosserie / In the Grocery (Elby Deshotels, Rydell)*

This tale belongs to type 41 *The Wolf Overeats in the Cellar.* The characters are usually in a forbidden place. One of them escapes and the other, who is greedy, is caught. In La Fontaine's literary version (*Fables*, XVII, "La belette entrée dans un grenier"), the victim is not brought by ruse, but a rat explains why it can no longer escape. Klipple describes several different African variants, including one from the Hottentot tribe in which the jackal and the hyena are in the white man's house; and another from the Hausa in which a dog and a jackal are in the home of a newlywed couple and drink their oil. Parsons has a parallel version in *Antilles* (no. 16, p. 36, "Too Swollen to Escape.")

In this version, Lapin knows where to find food during a famine. Lapin agrees to take Bouki along, with the understanding that they must leave when the time comes. But by then, Bouki is having such a good time eating that he refuses. There is not the password often associated with this type. The characters simply pass though a hole in the floor under a loose plank. Later, Bouki tries to escape but can no longer fit through the hole, having eaten too much ice cream. The storekeeper assumes that Bouki is the one who has been stealing the whole time and makes him work off the theft. When Bouki finds him later, Lapin, in true trickster fashion, shows no remorse and assumes no part of the guilt. Calvin Claudel has a Louisiana variant in *Fools and Rascals* ("Bouqui and Lapin in the Smoke House," pp. 26–27).

Il y avait deux malfaicteurs, une fois. Il y en a un, son nom, c'était Bouki, et l'autre, c'était Lapin. Et Lapin était tout le temps gras. Il était en bonne condition, et Bouki était tout le temps, tout le temps maigre.

Et un jour, Bouki dit, "Lapin, pourquoi t'es si gras?" Il dit, "Comment se fait que t'es tout le temps, tout le temps gras et en bonne condition?"

Ça se fait, Lapin lui a dit, "Si tu veux venir me joindre, à soir, je vas te montrer."

Ça se fait, Bouki a été le joindre. Lui et Lapin a parti. Il y avait un beau clair de lune. Ils ont arrivé à une grosserie. Et Lapin s'est traîné dessous la grosserie. Il a arrivé droit dessous le milieu du plancher. Il y avait une planche qu'était déclouée. Ça se fait, il a poussé la planche et il s'est traîné dedans la grosserie.

Il dit à Bouki, "Asteur, Bouki, tu vas te conduire." Et il dit, "Je veux pas tu fais un cochon avec toi-même!"

Ils ont arrivé à une grosse caisse, et ils l'ont ouvert. Et quand ils l'ont ouvert, dedans le milieu de la caisse, il y avait une jarre, elle était pleine de crème. Et Lapin a commencé à manger, mais Bouki était beaucoup gourmand. Il attrapait ça avec ses deux mains. Et il mangeait à pleine gueule. Ça lui tombait à chaque bord de la bouche.

Il dit à Bouki, il dit, "Bouki, je t'ai dit de pas faire un cochon avec toi-même." Et il dit, "C'est l'heure on *gone.*"

Mais Bouki dit, "J'en ai pas assez."

Il dit, "On ferait mieux de s'en aller, le jour est après se faire." Il dit, "Le marchand va ouvert la boutique. On va se faire prendre." Il dit, "C'est l'heure on *gone.*"

Mais bouki voulait pas *gone.* Ça se fait, Lapin a été, puis il a passé dedans la planche, et lui, il s'en a été, et Bouki a resté.

Il a mangé jusqu'à son ventre était au moment de casser. Et quand il a cru qu'il en avait assez, il est venu pour passer. Il pouvait plus passer. Le trou était pas assez gros pour lui passer. Il était pris.

There were these two rascals, once. One's name was Bouki and the other was Lapin. And Lapin was always fat. He was in good shape, and Bouki was always, always skinny.

And one day, Bouki says, "Lapin, why are you so fat?" He says, "How is it that you are always fat and in such good shape?"

So Lapin told him, "If you want to join me tonight, I'll show you."

So Bouki went to meet him. He and Lapin left. The moon was bright. They arrived at a grocery store. And Lapin crawled under the grocery. He arrived just under the middle of the floor. There was a plank that had come unattached. So he pushed the plank and he crawled into the grocery.

He says to Bouki, "Now, Bouki, you must behave yourself." And he says, "I don't want you to make a pig of yourself."

They arrived in front of a big box, and they opened it. And when they opened it, in the middle of the box, there was a jar which was full of cream. And Lapin started eating, but Bouki was very greedy. He was grabbing it with both hands. And he was stuffing his face. It was dripping from both sides of his mouth.

He says to Bouki, he says, "Bouki, I told you not to make a pig of yourself." And he says, "It's time to leave."

But Bouki says, "I haven't had enough."

He says, "We'd better go, the day is breaking." He says, "The storekeeper will open soon. We'll get caught." He said, "It's time to go."

But Bouki didn't want to leave. So Lapin went and passed under the plank, and he left, and Bouki stayed.

He ate until his belly was about to burst. And when he thought he'd had enough, he came to pass. He couldn't. The hole wasn't big enough for him to pass through. He was stuck.

Ça se fait, il a été. Il s'est caché dans le coin de la boutique. En même temps, le marchand est venu. Il a rentré. Il a vu les pistes de crème par terre, et tout quelque chose. Et il a été, et il a trouvé Bouki. Il était assis dans le coin de la boutique.

"Ah," il dit, "C'est toi, mon malfaicteur!" Il dit, "C'est toi qu'après voler ma crème aussi longtemps. Mais," il dit, "tu vas payer pour!" Il dit, "Faudra tu frobis le plancher. Faudra tu nettoyes toute ma boutique." Et il dit, "Faudra tu peintures."

Il l'a fait travailler toute la journée, toute la journée! L'après-midi tard, il lui a dit qu'il pouvait *gone*.

Ça se fait, Bouki connaissait ayoù il pouvait trouver Lapin. Droite dessous un gros chêne de mer. Il a été, Lapin était couché. Il était après dormir. Il l'a réveillé.

Ça se fait, Lapin a dit, "Qui c'est qu'il y a eu avec toi? Comment ça se fait tu ressembles si effarouché?" Il dit, "Tu ressembles abîmé!"

"Mais," il dit, "j'ai travaillé toute la journée, toute la journée." Il dit, "J'ai mangé assez, je pouvais pas passer en travers du trou et," il dit, "Le marchand m'a attrapé."

"Ah," il dit, "c'est ça je t'ai conté." Il dit, "Je t'ai dit, il fallait tu te conduis, puis pas faire un cochon avec toi-même." Il dit, "Tu vois, quand tu m'écoutes pas, comment c'est."

So he went. He hid in a corner of the store. About the same time, the storekeeper arrived. He came in. He saw the tracks of cream on the floor, and everything. And he went and he found Bouki. He was sitting in a corner of the store.

"Ah," he says, "so you're the one, you rascal." He says, "You're the one who's been stealing my cream for so long. Well," he says, "you're going to pay for it!" He says, "You're going to have to scrub the floor. You're going to have to clean up my whole store." And he says, "You're going to have to paint."

He made him work all day long, all day long! Late that afternoon, he told him he could go.

So Bouki knew where he could find Lapin. Right under a big live oak. He went, Lapin was lying down. He was sleeping. He woke him up.

So Lapin said, "What happened to you? Why do you look so frazzled?" He says, "You look beat."

"Well," he says, "I worked all day long, all day long." He says, "I ate so much, I couldn't pass through the hole and," he says, "the storekeeper caught me."

"Ah," he says, "that's what I told you." He says, "I told you you had to behave yourself, and not make a pig of yourself." He says, "You see, when you don't listen to me, how it is."

5. *En haut la terre ou en bas la terre / Above or Below Ground (Martin Latiolais, Catahoula)*

This variant of type 9B *The Crop Division* is related to type 1030 which is also a crop division tale between the ogre (giant, devil) and the hero. There seem to be two basic ways in which this story can be set up. The versions casting humans and/or anthropomorphic spirits (such as St. Michael and the Devil) tend to focus on the cleverness of the hero. The dupe usually chooses above or below the ground first, then the hero chooses a crop to his

exclusive advantage. Tales casting animals, as in this Louisiana version, tend to focus simply on the stupidity of the dupe. The pair plants a crop first, then the dupe chooses unwisely, motivated by greed or a misunderstanding of the true value of the shared commodity.

There are many English and British American versions. (See Baughman.) There are seven versions in the Archives de Folklore at Laval, including one recorded by Brandon (II, no. 59, pp. 368–372), "Bouki et Lapin et la récol'e d'pistaches." Another Louisiana variant is presented by Joseph Médard Carrière and Calvin Claudel (*JAF* 56, pp. 41–42) and Carrière has two versions in *French Missouri*, no. 22 (9B) and no. 62 (1030: between St. Michael and the Devil). In African tradition, stories concerning *The Unjust Partner* (type 9) are grouped together by Klipple though the crop division is never present, usually one hunter tricks another as they divide their common prey. Burrison has a Southern variant of type 1030, "Bobtail Outwits the Devil" (p. 162), in which the partners first plant beans and corn, then sweet potatoes and Irish potatoes. In another Southern variant, Leonard Roberts' *South from Hell-fer-Sartin* (no. 39, pp. 114–115), the main characters are also Bobtail and the Devil, but the Devil is finally outwitted over hogs, not a common crop.

Là, une autre fois (ils étaient associés, tu vois), ils ont fait une récolte. Ça fait, la première année, ils ont planté des patates, juste des patates. O! C'était beau, ces lianes de patates-là.

Ça fait, Lapin dit à Bouki, "Choisis ça tu veux, ça qu'est en haut la terre ou ça qu'est dans la terre."

Ça fait, Bouki dit, "Je vas prendre ça qu'est en haut la terre. C'est beau."

"Mais," il dit, "ôte tes lianes que je fouille mes patates."

Ça fait, il fallait Bouki coupe les lianes. Il a pas pu faire à rien avec ça, tu vois.

Ça fait, Lapin a fouillé ses patates. Bouki a pas eu à rien.

Ça fait, l'année d'après, ils ont planté du maïs. Le maïs était beau. C'était magnifique.

Ça fait, Lapin dit à Bouki, "*Well*, rechoisis ça tu veux encore cette année. Je te donne à choisir."

"Mais," il dit, "tu me blufferas pas cette année. Je vas prendre ça qu'est dans la terre!"

"Mais," il dit, "prends ça qu'est dans la terre!"

Ça fait, Lapin a cassé son maïs. Bouki a fouillé. Il y avait rien dans la terre.

Then, another time (they were associates, you see), they made a crop. So the first year, they planted potatoes. Oh, it was beautiful to see those potato vines.

So Lapin says to Bouki, "Choose what you want, what's above the ground or below the ground."

So Bouki says, "I'll take what's above the ground. It's beautiful."

"Well," he says, "take out your vines so that I can dig for my potatoes."

So Bouki had to cut his vines. He couldn't do anything with them, you see?

So Lapin dug his potatoes. Bouki had nothing.

So the next year, they planted corn. The corn was beautiful. It was magnificent.

So Lapin says to Bouki, "Well, choose again what you'd like this year. I'll leave the choice to you."

"Well," Bouki says, "you won't fool me this year. I'll take what's below the ground."

"Well," he says, "take what's below the ground."

So Lapin broke his corn. Bouki dug. There was nothing in the ground.

6. Tiens bon, Bouki! / Hold Him, Bouki! (Martin Latiolais, Catahoula)

This tale is a variant of type 47A *The Fox Hangs by his Teeth to the Horse's Tail, Hare's Lip*. Often the trickster is a hare who laughs so hard at his victim's misfortune that he splits his lip, thus explaining the origin of the hare lip. Klipple found two African versions and Flowers gives several versions from the West Indies, most of which have the hare lip ending. In this Louisiana version, the humor is based on the rabbit's insistence that Bouki hold the bear and on Bouki's hopeless answer. Similar endings are reported by Fausset (*JAF* 40, p. 222, "Rabbit Ties Fox's Tail to Dead Horse," and p. 241, "Try Him, Try Him"), as well as by Dorson in *American Negro Folktales*, pp. 83–86, no. 8, "Take My Place" (with the ending, "How in the hell can I hold him with ne'er foot touching the ground?") The only version found in the Archives de Folklore (coll. Lacourcière, no. 2778) casts a chicken, a rooster and a bull. Burrison has a similar story from Georgia, "Brother Buzzard and the Lazy Mule" (p. 96), which he associates with motif K1047 "The bear bites the seemingly dead horse's tail," and which includes a similar challenge from Brother Crow to "Try 'im!"

Tu vois, il y a un *joke* pour Bouki et Lapin aussi. Ils étaient à la chasse dans le bois. Et, ça fait ils ont vu un ours après dormir, couché après dormir. Ça fait, Lapin (il bluffait tout le temps Bouki, tu vois), il dit à Bouki, "Attrape sa queue!"

Ça fait, Bouki a parti. En peu de temps, il approchait l'ours. Il a fait un tour après la queue. Ça a réveillé l'ours, il y a pas de doute. L'ours a parti avec.

Lapin était à côté, il disait, "Tiens bon, Bouki! Tiens bon, Bouki!"

Il dit, "Comment tu veux moi, je tiens bon, mes quatre pattes, elles touchent pas par terre!"

D'après moi, l'ours était après courir manière vite. Bouki, il touchait pas par terre!

You see, there's a joke about Bouki and Lapin, too. They were hunting in the woods. And so they saw a bear sleeping, lying down sleeping. So Lapin (he was always tricking Bouki, you see), he says to Bouki, "Catch his tail!"

So Bouki left. In no time, he approached the bear. He took a wrap on his tail. This woke the bear, of course. The bear took off with him.

Lapin was off to the side, he said, "Hold him, Bouki! Hold him, Bouki!"

He says, "How do you want me to hold him, none of my four feet is touching the ground!"

I guess the bear was running pretty fast. Bouki wasn't even touching the ground!

7. Lapin joue banjo / Lapin Plays the Banjo (Carrie Charles, Cade)

This tale, in strong Louisiana Creole dialect, is a variant of type 183* *The Hare Promises to Dance*. Laval's Archives de Folklore has another Louisiana version, "Tortie" (Turtle), included by Fortier in *Louisiana Folktales* (p. 28), also from Louisiana Black Creole tradition. Compare also "The Deer Escapes from the Fox," in Dorson's *American Negro Folktales* (no. 15). Motif K606.2 "The trickster escapes by making his captors dance," which figures prominently in this tale, is well-known in African tradition. In the version presented here,

unusually long for a Black Creole animal tale, Lapin is the amoral trickster, stealing and lying without the least remorse. When he finally escapes, he doesn't even let on to his own family that he's been in trouble. It is also interesting that Lapin escapes by playing the banjo, an American instrument with African origins.

Il y a une fois que Compère Bouki té gain une maison, et li té gain six petits. Et tous les jours, yé té parti, té couri pêcher. Et Compère Lapin té guetté quand yé té parti, et li té rentré en dedans la maison-là, et li té mangé tout ça li té gain cuit. Et quand li té fini mangé tout ça li té gain cuit, li té parti. Li té chappe'. Li té gain nique pas loin-là.

Li té resté là tout la journée, là li té vini. Là li té vini, li té gardé. Li té jamais capab connaît qui c'est qui té mangé yé manger.

Et Compère Lapin continué fait ça-là . . . deux mois. Il t'apé comme créver la faim, il té pas gain à rien pour manger plus que poisson li té trapé quand li té couri à la coulée.

Et il y a un jour, Compère Lapin couri, pi li mangé tout ça il y avait là. Mais là, li assis, une fois li fini mangé, tellement son l'estomac plein, li assis. Et pi, li plus parti. Et là, quand li *do* décidé pour parti, yé trapé là, li t'apé dormi. Dormi volé li, li t'apé dormi. Ça fait, Compère Bouki rentré là. Li mandé li, "Ça t'apé fait là?"

Li dit, *"Well,"* li dit, "la pluie t'apé vini," li dit, "mo arrêté ici chez toi. Mo té connais toi bien."

Mais li dit, "Mais, c'est pas tout," li dit. "Ça qui mangé tout manger qui té là?"

Li dit, "Mo pas connais."

Li dit, "Mais, c'est bligé toi qu'apé manger tout no manger. Il y a deux mois, nous apé couri pêcher. Chaque fois nous reviens, il y a pas manger."

Ça fait, li dit yé, *"Well,"* li dit, "c'est pas moi qui mangé manger-là."

"Well," Compère Bouki dit, "si c'est toi qui mangé," li dit, "m'alé trapé toi et m'alé

There was a time when Compère Bouki had a house, and he had six children. And every day, they left to go fishing. And Compère Lapin would watch when he would leave, and he would go into the house, and he would eat everything that he had cooked. And when he finished eating everything he had cooked, he would leave. He would escape. He had a nest not far away.

He stayed there all day, then he'd come. He'd come, he'd look. He was never able to figure out who had eaten all his food.

And Compère Lapin contined doing that, for two months. He was almost dying of hunger, he had nothing to eat but the fish he caught when he went to the creek.

And one day, Compère Lapin went, and he ate everything that was there. But then, he sat down, once he'd finished eating, so full was his stomach, he sat. And then, he didn't leave. And then, when he did decide to leave, he was sleeping, they caught him there, he was sleeping. Sleep stole him away, he was sleeping. So Compère Bouki came home. He asked him, "What are you doing there?"

He says, ""Well," he says, "It was starting to rain," he says, "I stopped here at your house. I know you well."

But he says, "But that's not all," he says. "Who ate all the food that was there?"

He says, "I don't know."

He says, "Well, it must be you who are eating all our food. For two months now, we're going fishing. Every time we come home, there is no food."

So he says to him, "Well," he says, "I'm not the one who ate the food."

"Well," Compère Bouki says, "if you are the one who ate it," he says, "I'll catch you,

marrer toi, et m'alé tailler toi." Et li trapé li, li marré li, li taillé li, mais li jamais dit quand même.

Ça fait, li resté marré là trois jours. Et li té gain un—Compère Bouki té gain un banjo dans la maison-là. Li dit, "Compère Bouki," li dit, "trape banjo toi gain là," li dit. "Mo connais," li dit, "mo capab jouer banjo bien, ouais!"

Commence jouer banjo-là. Ça fait, quand Compère Bouki voit que Compère Lapin t'apé jouer banjo-là, et pi c'était des si vaillantes danses, li dit, li commencé à inviter so z-amis, et li dit, "To connais," li dit, "samedi nous gain un gros bal ici." Li dit, "Compère Lapin icitte avec banjo-là. Mo té pas connais li té capab jouer avec ça."

Ça fait, quand samedi soir vini, o, yé tous vini, un gros bande. Et Compère Lapin commencé jouer, mais yé tous commencé danser au ras où il t'apé jouer.

Il dit, "Vous autres, danse pas au ras moi comme ça." Li dit, "Vance là-bas! Pi danse un peu plus loin." Ça fait, yé commencé danser. O, yé dansé, yé trouvé comment c'était si joli.

Et là, tout d'une escousse, Compère Lapin dit Compère Bouki, li dit, "To gain moi amarré-là, m'apé jouer bien, mais si to sé démarré moi," li dit, "là, to sé tendé quelque chose." Li dit, "M'a jouer quelque chose to jamais tendé."

Ça fait, li démarré li. Quand li démarré li, et c'est vrai, li joué une danse enfin-là, yé té peut pas arrêter danser, mais li toujours fait yé signe vancer là-bas. Après li fait yé signe pas danser au ras li, vancer là-bas, mais li continué jouer et là, après ça, so maman vini.

So maman dit, "Mais, mo jamais té connait," li dit, "to té connait jouer banjo comme ça." Li dit, "C'est mo qui élevé toi," et li dit, "mo jamais té connait toi té connait jouer banjo comme ça."

and I'll tie you up and I'll whip you." And he caught him, he tied him up and he whipped him, but he never admitted it.

So he stayed tied for three days. And there was a—Compère Bouki had a banjo in the house. He says, "Compère Bouki," he says, "get that banjo you have there," he says. "I know," he says, "I'm able to play the banjo well, you know."

Started playing the banjo. So when Compère Bouki saw that Compère Lapin was playing the banjo, and they were such nice songs, he says, he started inviting his friends and he says, "You know," he says, "Saturday we'll have a big dance here." He says, "Compère Lapin here with this banjo. I didn't even know he could play it."

So when Saturday night arrived, oh they all came, a big bunch of people. And Compère Lapin started to play, but they all started dancing next to where he was playing.

He said, "You all, don't dance next to me like that." He says, "Go on over there! Dance a little farther away." So they started dancing. Oh, they danced, they found that it was so beautiful.

And then, all of a sudden, Compère Lapin says to Compère Bouki, he says, "You have me tied up, I'm playing pretty good, but if you would untie me," he says, "then you would really hear something." He says, "I'll play something that you never heard before."

So he untied him. When he untied him, and it was true, he played such a fine tune that they couldn't stop dancing, but he still signaled for them to go on. After he signaled them to not dance next to him, to go farther away, but he continued to play and then his mother came.

His mother says, "Well, I never knew," she says, "that you knew how to play the banjo like this." She says, "I'm the one who raised you," she says, "and I never knew you could play the banjo like this."

Li dit, "Mam, il y a longtemps mo té connait. Mo apprends jouer banjo, mais mo té jamais oulé personne connait ça mo té connait."

Ça fait, li joue une autre danse. Ça té so troisième danse. Quand li joue l'autre danse, li—yé continué après danser, pi après *brag on* li, li dit yé *"Go ahead,* avance là-bas toujours! Li dit, "Avance!" li dit. Tout d'une escousse, li jette banjo-là par terre, li dit yé, *"Good-bye!"* li dit, *"I'm gone!"*

Ça fait, quand li parti, c'était juste une la-poussière. Compère Bouki té derrière li, mais li jamais pu trapé li, c'était juste une la-poussière qui t'apé voler. Yé té pas la peine-là du tout. C'était juste une la-poussière qui t'apé voler en l'air.

Ça fait, quand li rendu chez li, so femme et so petit, yé dit, "Mais comment ça se fait to t'apé galoper comme ça, to tout trempe comme ça?"

"O," li dit, "c'était semblé comme si la pluie t'apé vini," li dit, "ça fait, mo parti, mo galopé," li dit, "mais là, mo à la maison." Li dit, "Mo fini avec ça."

He says, "Mom, I've known how to do this for a long time. I learned to play the banjo, but I never wanted anyone to know what I knew."

So he played another tune. That was his third tune. When he played another tune, he—they continued to dance and to brag about him. He says to them, "Go ahead, go on over there still farther!" He says, "Go on!" he says. All of a sudden, he threw the banjo down and said to them, "Good-bye!" he says, "I'm gone!"

So when he left, there was only a cloud of dust. Compère Bouki was after him, but could never catch him, there was only a cloud of dust. It was no use to try. There was just a cloud of dust blowing in the wind.

So when he got back home, his wife and his children said, "Well why are you running like this, you're all wet?"

"Oh," he says, "it seemed like it might rain," he says, "so I left, I ran," he says, "but now, I'm home." He says, "I'm done with all that."

8. *Les oeufs de jument / The Mare's Eggs (Stanislaus "Tanisse" Faul, Cankton)*

This tale is a variant of type 1319 *Pumpkin Sold as an Ass's Egg* (see Bolte and Polívka, I, pp. 317 and following). This story is widely known throughout the world; Thompson reported 29 variants from Germany, 34 from Ireland, and 39 from France. Baughman also described several Anglo-American versions and Laval's Archive de Folklore listed 18 French American variants.

The animal which appears to emerge when the pumpkin is thrown into the briarpatch (usually a rabbit) can be misunderstood to be several sorts. In "The Irishman and the Pumpkin," an African American variant reported by Dorson in *American Negro Folktales* (no. 242), the egg is supposedly that of a mule. The same is true of an Appalachian version, "The Mule Egg" (pp. 136–138), in Jones and Wheeler. Conrad Laforte included a version from Québec in *Menteries drôles et merveilleuses* (pp. 229–232), in which it is a "mare's egg," as in the present text, which is eventually sold to a man who "hatches" it with the help of his wife before seeing the young "colt" run off.

It is interesting to note that this white Cajun storyteller switches to a black Creole dialect toward the end, a reflection of the probable origins of this tale which features Bouki and Lapin.

Là, Bouki était après casser des giraumons. Lapin dit, "Bouki, ça, c'est pas des—Quoi c'est que tu fais avec ça?"

"Mais," il dit, "je mange ça. C'est des giraumons."

"Ah!" il dit, "c'est pas des giraumons. C'est des œufs des jument." Il dit, "Si tu veux connaître quoi c'est, passe et puis garroche donc un dans la talle d'éronces. Tu vas voir, c'est des petites juments qui vont sortir."

Il a garroché un giraumon. Il y a un lapin qui a sorti. Il dit, "'Garde, moi té dit ça."

Et Bouki a jamais voulu manger un giraumon après ça.

Now, Bouki was harvesting pumpkins. Lapin said, "Bouki, those are not—What are you doing with those?"

"Well," he said, "I eat them. They are pumpkins."

"Ah!" he said, "They aren't pumpkins. They are mare's eggs." He said, "If you want to know what they are, go and throw one in the briarpatch. You'll see, little horses will come out."

He threw a pumpkin. A rabbit came out. He said, "Look, I told you."

And Bouki never wanted to eat a pumpkin after that.

9. Lapin, Chat et les chestnuts / Lapin, Chat and the Chestnuts (Mary Fentroy, Cade)

In order to place this tale in their *Catalogue raisonné,* Luc Lacourcière and Margaret Low created a new type number, (AF) 9D *The Division of the Chestnuts.* Thompson had already described a similar plot in motif K231.1.2 "Mutual agreement to divide the food. Trickster eats other's food and then refuses to divide his own." A literary version can be found in La Fontaine's *Fables* (IX, 17, "Le Singe et le chat"), with a monkey as trickster. The chestnut story is followed by a moral comment in which La Fontaine clearly implicates the greedy provincial princes of his day. In her study of Antilles oral tradition, Parsons described a variant (no. 90, "Greedy Cat") in which the cat steals all the fish and is then chased by the dog. Burrison includes a version from west Georgia, "The Cat, the Monkey, and the Chestnuts" (p. 34), which he associates with motif K171.9 "Monkey cheats fox of his share of bananas."

In this Louisiana version, the clever rabbit fools the cat and makes him do all the work while he eats the roasted chestnuts. The deftness which is ordinarily associated with the cat is opposed here to the cleverness of the rabbit.

Il y avait un lapin et pi un chat qui té apé *roast* des *chestnuts* dans le feu, parce qu'ils té verts. C'est tel comme des pistaches.

Ça fait, li dit, "Mais, quoi fé to va pas—viens, Chat, toi, to capab, to galopes des rats,

Once there was a rabbit and a cat who were roasting chestnuts in the fire because they were green. This is just like peanuts.

So, he says, "Well, why don't you go. Come here, Chat, you're able, you chase rats,

to fais tout quelque chose, to sé capab gain un ou deux, et pas brûler toi-même, et juste prends to patte et hale yé." Li dit, "Moi, mo va rester ici." Li dit, "Juste mets to patte et hale yé." Li dit, "Moi, mo peux pas, moi. Moi, mo pas l'homme grand comme toi. Toi, to gain longues jambes. *Go ahead* et trapé yé et quand to va mettre cil-là sur la terre, moi, mo va haler li *back*. Tu vas essayer traper l'autre."

"All right."

Ça fait, quand pauvre Chat-là t'apé manière brûler li-même. *"Go ahead.* Trapé un l'autre. Nous autres va gain assez t' à l'heure." Et Lapin juste t'apé manger tout quelque chose pauvre Chat-là té halé.

Quand pauvre Chat-là fini, li dit, "Hé! Mo souhaite pas que mo va pas souffert mais mo brûlé moi-même. Là, ça se fait, combien nous autres gain?"

Li dit, "Combien nous autres gain? Mo té croit il y avait plus que ça. To té halé ti brin-là. Ça to halé, mo mangé yé tout."

Ça fait, li té pas gain à rien pour l'autre du tout.

you do all sorts of things, you would be able to catch one or two without burning your-self, just take your paw and pull them." He says, "I'll stay here." He says, "Just put your paw in and pull them." He says, "I can't. I'm not the big man you are. You have long legs. Go ahead and catch them and when you'll put them down, I'll pull them back. You'll try to catch another one."

"All right."

So, when poor Chat was kind of burning himself, "Go ahead. Catch another one. We'll have enough in a while." And Lapin was just eating everything that poor Chat was pulling.

When poor Chat finished, he says, "Hey! I hope I won't suffer but I've burned myself. Now, so, how many do we have?"

He says, "How many do we have? I thought there were more than that. You pulled this little bit. I ate all you pulled."

So, there was nothing at all for the other one.

10. *Le chien et le lapin / The Dog and the Rabbit (Norris Mitchell, Scott)*

This tale, related to type 200 *The Dog's Certificate* which explains why dogs smell each other now, is more precisely a variant of type 200C* *Hare and Hunting Dog Conduct a Store* which explains why dogs now chase hares (rabbits). (Consider also motif A2494.4.4 "Enmity between dogs and rabbits.") Thompson mentions only four Romanian variants in the type index, but there is at least one other published variant in Joel Chandler Harris's *Nights* (no. 61, "Why Mr. Dog Runs Brother Rabbit"), in which the rabbit is chased because he has stolen the dog's new shoes. In this Louisiana French variant, the dog loses his money by putting his check under his tail to cross the river. He mistakes the rabbit's white tail for his lost check, which explains why the dog still chases the rabbit today.

It is interesting to note that this black Creole storyteller uses Cajun French throughout most of the story, but reverts to his native Creole dialect in the speech of the animal charac-ters.

Ça, c'est pour le chien et le lapin. Ils étaient des grands amis dans le temps. Ça

This is about the dog and the rabbit. They were good friends in those days. So

fait, ils ont été ensemble. Il y a un homme qui les a engagés, les deux. Ils ont travaillé. Ça fait, l'homme les a payé chacun leur chèque. Et ils ont parti.

Ils ont arrivé ayoù il y avait une rivière pour passer. Le chien lui dit, "Lapin, comment on va passer sur de l'eau-là?"

Lapin dit, "Mets ton chèque en bas ta queue et puis nage jusqu'à l'autre bord."

Ça fait, le chien le regarde, il dit, "Comment tu dis ça?"

Ça fait, Lapin a fait comme ça. Lapin a mis son chèque et lui, il a mis le sien et ils ont parti à nager. Mais là, il y avait une lame d'eau qui vini. Une lame d'eau qui les a foutus dedans. Ça fait, il a été voir s'il pouvait trouver son chèque mais il était *gone*. L'eau avait pris son chèque.
Lapin était là-bas. Il dit, "Dépêche-toi!"

Ça fait, il a parti derrière Lapin, mais Lapin était sur la butte. Le chien dit, "Tu connais mon affaire? Mo perdu mo chèque!"

"O," Lapin dit, "gros sacré imbécile! Mo dit toi mettre-le en bas to la-queue. Là, de l'eau sé pas prendre ton chèque. Mais," il dit, "ça, c'est une affaire quand même!" Lapin, lui, il a *gone* et Lapin a la queue blanche. Ça fait, Lapin a levé sa queue et puis il a *gone*.

Il a regardé Lapin, il dit, "Tu connais une affaire? C'est lui qui a volé mon chèque!" Et il a parti après.

Et c'est pour ça il course Lapin jusqu'à asteur.

they went together. There's a man who hired them both. They worked. So the man paid each one with a check. And they left.

They arrived at a place where there was a river to cross. The dog says, "Lapin, how are we going to cross this water?"

Lapin says, "Put your check under your tail and swim to the other side."

So the dog looks at him, he says, "What do you mean?"

So Lapin did this. Lapin put his check and then he did the same and they took off swimming. But then a wave came along, a wave that swamped them. So he went to see if he could find his check but it was gone. The water had taken his check.

Lapin was over there. He says, "Hurry up!"

So he took off behind Lapin, but Lapin was on the hill. The dog says, "You know what my problem is? I've lost my check!"

"Oh," Lapin says, "you big damn imbecile! I told you to put it under your tail. Then the water would not have taken your check. Well," he says, "that's really something!" Lapin took off and Lapin has a white tail. So Lapin lifted his tail and took off.

He looked at Lapin, he says, "You know something? He's the one who stole my check!" And he took off after him.

And that's why he chases Lapin to this day.

11. *Éléphant et Serpent / Elephant and Serpent (Mary Fentroy, Cade)*

This tale, type 155 *The Ungrateful Serpent Returned to Captivity,* is very popular in black oral tradition. Klipple found 28 African versions. In most of those variants, the animal saved from death wants to bite or eat its rescuer once it is safe. But it is then killed or replaced in the trap by a helpful third party playing the role of impartial judge. Occasionally, however, justice is not rendered, as in the variant collected among the Kwéli in which a leopard saves a serpent which then wants to bite it; the antelope which intervenes as judge

is killed by the leopard and eaten by the serpent! Flowers reports only four variants from the West Indies. In his *Index of Mexican Folktales*, Robe presents 33 versions of this type and classes the animals according to the level of their ingratitude. They are, in descending order, serpents, lions, alligators, tigers, jaguars, wolves, and a giant. The clever decision of the "impartial" judge is, of course, the second deception of the foolish ingrate. The first occurs when the "victim" insists on seeking arbitration in the first place. The Uncle Remus version (Harris, *Nights*, no. 46, pp. 281–287, "Brother Wolf Still in Trouble") has Brer Rabbit helping Brer Wolf out from under a rock. Brer Wolf decides upon emerging that this would be a good time to take revenge on Brer Rabbit for all his previous troublemaking including a recent scalding of Brer Wolf. Brer Tarrypin is consulted to determine the legality of all this and he has everyone get back into their original positions to judge the situation. Once Brer Wolf is under the rock again, Brer Tarrypin announces his decision that Brer Rabbit was "wrong" to interfere with Brer Wolf's problems, and that everyone should go on about their original business, leaving Brer Wolf back under the same rock. In his *American Negro Folktales* (no. 22, pp. 106–109, "The Farmer and the Snake"), Dorson records a much more cynical version of this tale by master storyteller J. D. Suggs in which a farmer warms the snake he has just rescued in his shirt. The revived serpent bites the farmer who then dies. On the other hand, in La Fontaine's literary version (*Fables*, "Le Villageois et le serpent" [VI, 23]), it is the man who kills the snake. In an African-American English language version by Clifford Blake (*Folktales of Louisiana,*) Brer Rabbit returns the snake to captivity before he is bitten. In this Louisiana Creole variant, the rabbit saves the elephant by replacing the serpent in his original position under the log under the guise of seeking a fair judgement.

Li té fait frette, frette, frette! Ça se fait, Eléphant dit, au bout de la nuit, "Nous autres va geler. Faut essayer couri où nous autres capab d'être *safe* parce que si nous autres reste ici, la neige, tout quelque chose apé tomber. Mo pas connais ça qui rivé nous autres." Ça fait, li dit, "Moi, mo va prendre une chance. Mo va essayer couri. Mo va commencer en bas et mo va essayer monter en haut," li dit, "en haut le *mountain*."

Ça fait, li commencé marcher, l'Eléphant commencé marcher. Là, li manière entendre un bruit. Li dit, "Mais ça, mo apé entendre quelque chose. Mo *wonder* qui c'est ça."

Arrive. "O, Monsieur Eléphant!"

Mais li dit, "Qui diable c'est ça? Quelqu'un té dans tout ce frette-là, yé peut pas aider yé-même. Laisse-moi couri voir."

Ah bien, la serpent té en bas une bûche. Li té essayé sauver li-même, parce qu'il fait si frette.

It was cold, cold, cold! So Éléphant says, "We're going to freeze. We have to try to go to a safe place because, if we stay here, the snow and everything is falling. I don't know what will happen to us." So he says, "I'm going to take a chance. I'm going to try to go. I'm going to start down here and I'm going to try to make it to the top," he says, "to the top of the mountain."

So he started walking, Éléphant started walking. Then he kind of heard a noise. He says, "Well, I hear something. I wonder what it is."

Arrives. "Oh Mister Éléphant!"

Well, he says, "What in the devil is that? Someone is in all this cold and can't help himself. Let me go and see."

Oh well, the serpent was under a log. He was trying to save himself because he was so cold.

Li dit, "Ça il y a avec toi?"

"O!" li dit, "Mo près-là pour geler icitte. Mo essayé en bas un *log*, mais comment? Mo pas chaud encore. Mo va geler. To peux pas aider moi un peu?"

Li dit, "Ah bien, *all right.*" Li dit, "Mo va aider toi. Si mo aide toi, to crois to capab aider toi-même? Si mo laisse toi sors en bas *log*-là?"

Li dit, "Peut-être bien."

Li dit, *"Let's roll it over."*

Là, li dit, "Mais mo *still* frette. Mo peux pas fait à rien. O! Mo frette!"

Li dit, *"All right,* ah bien, moi, mo apé couri en haut *mountain."* Li dit, "Rentre ici, mets-toi, mets-toi sur le côté mo vieille jambe. To va chauffer toi là, parce que moi, mo pas frette."

So, li fait ça. *Now,* li commencé réchauffer. Là, li manière grouiller. Eléphant a gardé li, li dit, "Ça il y a avec toi?"

Li dit, "Mo veux descendre, mais mo gain l'envie pour mordre toi."

"Mais quoi fait to va mordre moi?" Li dit, "Moi, mo t'apé essayer aider toi parce que— J'ai réchauffé—Là, toi, to veux mordre moi?"

Li dit, "Mais to té pas connait mo té une serpent? C'est ça mo fais, moi."

"Ah," li dit, "o non, mais là, ça fait pas bien. To pas apé traiter moi bien. Ah bien, si to veux mordre moi, allons un petit bout-là." Li dit, "Nous autres va joindre là avec Compé Lapin. Nous autres va demander li. Si li dit faut to mordre moi, m'a quitter toi mordre moi."

Li dit, "Compé Lapin! Mo vini demander vous une question."

Li dit, "Mais ça il y a? Mais ça il y a?"

Li dit, "Mo joindre une serpent-là. Mo entends li t'apé crier comme s'il t'apé pélé moi. Ça fait, mo couri voir. Bûche-là té en haut li. Là li té peut pas sorti. Et là, li té tout frette, tout frette. Moi, mo juste ôté *on* li. Et

He says, "What's wrong with you?"

"Oh!" he says, "I'm about to freeze here. I tried to get under this log, but how? I'm not warm yet. I'm going to freeze. Couldn't you help me a little?"

He says, "Oh well, all right." He says, "I'll help you. If I help you, do you think you'll be able to help yourself? If I let you out from under this log?"

He says, "Maybe."

He says, "Let's roll it over."

Then, he says, "But I'm still cold. I can't do anything. Oh! I'm cold."

Then he says, "All right, oh well, I'm going to the top of the mountain." He says, "Come in here, put yourself next to my old leg. You'll heat yourself up there, because I'm not cold."

So he did this. Now, he started getting warmer. Then he started to move. Éléphant looked at him, he says, "What's the matter with you?"

He says, "I want to go down, but I feel like biting you."

"Well why are you going to bite me?" He says, "I was helping you because—I warmed—Now you want to bite me?"

He says, "Well didn't you know that I'm a snake? That's what I do."

"Ah," he says, "oh no, but now, that's not right. You're not treating me right. Ah well, if you want to bite me, let's go a little farther." He says, "We'll meet Compé Lapin there. We'll ask him. If he says you should bite me, then I'll let you bite me."

He says, "Compé Lapin! I've come to ask you a question."

He says, "Well, what's wrong? What's wrong?"

He says, "I met a serpent. I heard him crying as though he were calling me. So I went to see. There was a log on him. And he couldn't get out. And then, he was very cold, very cold. I just took it off of him. And then,

là, tellement li té frette, mo dis, 'Mettez-toi en bas mon bras, mo va chauffer toi. Quand to chauffé, to capab *go ahead.*'"

Là, li dit, "Et li tourné mordre toi?"

Li dit, "O oui!"

"Ayoù c'était? Ayoù to . . . ?"

Li dit, "Allons marcher, m'a montrer toi où bûche-là y est."

Yé marché, yé marché. Quand Eléphant voit bûche-là, li dit, "To vois bûche-là, là-bas?"

Li dit, "Oui. Ça, c'est bûche qu'était *on* li."

Li dit, "Ah bien, mettez li où li té. Laissez-moi voir li. Mo va juge bien. Mo oulé juge li bien. Mettez-li côté bûche-là."

Li metté li, Serpent, côté bûche-là. Là, li dit, "C'est là li té? To sûr?"

"O oui! C'est là li té! C'est là mo prends li, mo méné li jusqu'à li té oulé mordre moi."

Li dit, "Ah bien, juste tournez bûche-là." Là, li dit, "Là, quittez li là."

he was so cold, I said, 'Put yourself under my arm, I'll heat you up. When you're warm, you can go ahead.'"

Then, he says, "And he turned to bite you?"

He says, "Oh, yes!"

"Where was this? Where did you . . . ?"

He says, "Let's walk, I'll show you where the log is."

They walked, they walked. When Eléphant sees the log, he says, "Do you see that log over there?"

He says, "Yes." That's the log that was on him."

He says, "Ah well, put him where he was. Let me see it. I'll judge well. I want to judge well. Put him next to the log."

He put Serpent next to the log. Then he says, "Is that where he was? Are you sure?"

"Oh yes! That's where he was! That's where I found him. I carried him until he wanted to bite me."

He says, "Ah well, just turn the log." Then he says, "Now, just leave him there."

12. *Hibou et z-oiseau / Hibou and the Bird (Bernice Wiltz, Parks)*

This tale belongs to the new type [AF] 236A *Contest between Birds: To Fast or to Sing Longer* created by Lacourcière and Low for their *Catalogue raisonné* (four variants listed). The basic plot involves the ruse of the small bird to nourish itself despite having to share its find with the larger owl by proposing a game: each bird will take a worm only after singing its own song; the small bird's song is short, while the owl's is long. In all the variants listed, the storytellers imitated the songs of the birds in question. Brandon presented a version from Vermilion Parish in Louisiana, "Le Conte du Moqueur et Hibou"[The Tale of the Mockingbird and the Owl] (II, p. 354) which has the birds singing as follows:

Moqueur:	Si bi yo ta la la.
Hibou:	Kou ta la la
	Bin à fenallé ta la la.

Alcée Fortier has a variant, "Mamzelle Moquère" (no. 14, pp. 34–36), as well as Joel Chandler Harris, "The Wise Bird and the Foolish Bird" (*Nights*, no. 66). The songs tran-

scribed by Harris are as follows:

Sma't bud:	"Tay-tay tenando wanzando waneanso"
Fool bud:	"Tay-tay tenando wanzando olando"

Harris goes on to comment on the African origins of this tale. In this Louisiana version, the slow song of the owl is what prevents him from eating as fast as the small bird whose song is short and rapid.

Il n-avait Hibou et pi un z-oiseau en haut un arbre. Et là, c'était—N-arbre-là té gain un creux. Et creux-là té gain des petits des-vers en dedans. Ça fait Hibou et pi z-oiseau dit, "Mo pari mo ca chanter mieux que toi."

Hibou dit, "O non! O non!"

Ça fait, Hibou commencé. Li fait comme ça "Cou cou tralala! Cou cou tralala!"

Ça fait, il té resté là. Le z-oiseau dit comme ça, "C'est mo kèn tour. Cri-cri! Cri-cri! Cri-cri! Cri-cri! Cri-cri! Cri-cri!"

Ça fait, chaque fois li té chanté, le z-oiseau té chanté, li té rentré dans le n-arbre. Li té attrapé un des-vers. Ça fait, Hibou continue, "Cou cou tralala!" jusqu'à so la voix-là vini faible. Li chantait un et faisait son cinq ou six fois. En dernier li vini, li té près peut plus chanter. Li dit, "Cou cou tralala. Cou cou tra . . . la . . . la."

Z-oiseau dit, "Mais on dirait toi peux plus chanter."

Li dit, "Non, non, mo peux plus chanter."

Mais z-oiseau t'apé nourri li-même, mais Hibou té pas apé nourri li-même.

Quand ça a tourné garder, z-oiseau recommencé chanter encore, "Cri-cri! Cri-cri! Cri-cri! Cri-cri! Cri-cri! Cri-cri! Cri-cri!"

Quand li fini chanter, Hibou té commencé, "Cou cou tra . . . la . . . la!" et li tombé "Boum!" par terre. Li té plus chanté du tout.

Ça fait, z-oiseau gagné li. Ouais, z-oiseau gagné li.

There was Hibou and a bird up in a tree. And there was—The tree was hollow. And there were some little worms in the hole. So Hibou—And the bird says, "I'll bet I can sing better than you."

Hibou says, "Oh no! Oh no!"

So Hibou started. He did like this, "Coo coo tralala! Coo coo tralala!"

So he stayed there. The little bird says this, "It's my turn. Cri-cri! Cri-cri! Cri-cri! Cri-cri! Cri-cri!"

So each time he sang, the bird sang, he went into the tree. He caught a worm. So Hibou went on, "Coo coo tralala!" until his voice became weak. He would sing and make his sound five or six times. When he came near the end, he could almost sing no longer. He says, "Coo co tralala. Coo coo tra . . . la . . . la."

The bird says, "Well one would say that you can no longer sing."

He says, "No, no, I can no longer sing."

The bird was feeding itself, but Hibou was not.

When they turned around to look, the bird started singing again, "Cri-cri! Cri-cri! Cri-cri! Cri-cri! Cri-cri! Cri-cri! Cri-cri!"

When he finished singing, Hibou started, "Coo coo tra . . . la . . . la!" and he fell "boom!" on the ground. He didn't sing anymore.

So the bird beat him. Yes, the bird beat him.

13. Le renard et le raisin / The Fox and the Grapes (Évélia Boudreaux, Carencro)

Paradoxically, the tale type 59 *Fox and the Sour Grapes* is so well known in literary tradition (e.g., Aesop, no. 33; la Fontaine, II, 21) that it is actually rather poorly represented in collections of oral tradition. The Archives de Folklore in Québec have only two collected versions. The narrative has also become proverbial in that the simple mention of the sour grapes is enough to conjure up the story. Mrs. Boudreaux learned this version from her mother through oral tradition. It is interesting that in oral tradition as well as literary tradition, the fox is trying to eat grapes, which these carnivores don't normally eat at all.

Le renard était dans le bois où ils habitent et, toujours, il avait beaucoup faim. Et il était après chercher pour trouver du manger. Et il a vu des belles grappes de raisins haut d'un arbre. Et il s'est dit à lui-même, "Ça serait beaucoup bon, ce raisin. J'aimerais beaucoup d'en manger. Il est un peu haut. Je vais essayer de sauter et essayer de l'attraper."

Et il sautait et il sautait, mais il venait pas près du raisin, et il s'est découragé.

Il dit, "Je peux pas l'attraper. Ou," il dit, "je le veux pas quand même." Il dit, "Il est trop aigre, quand même." Il dit, "Je le veux pas."

Et il est parti. Il s'en a été.

The fox was in the woods where they live and, in any case, he was very hungry. And he was looking around to find something to eat. And he saw some beautiful bunches of grapes up high in a tree. And he said to himself, "That would be very good, those grapes. I would like very much to eat some of them. They are a bit high. I'll try to jump and try to catch them."

And he jumped and he jumped, but he didn't come close to the grapes, and he became discouraged.

He said, "I can't catch them. And," he said, "I don't want them anyway." He said, "They are too sour anyway." He said, "I don't want them."

And he left. He went away.

14. Les petits ouaouarons / The Little Frogs (Évélia Boudreaux, Carencro)

This tale is related to type 277A (motif J955.1) *The Frog Tries in Vain to be as Big as the Ox*. Klipple reported five African variants including one from the Wolof in which a butterfly tries to fly to the sun. In a Mexican variant (Wheeler, p. 221), a young toad tries to be as big as a house. In *American Negro Folktales*, "Bullfrog and Terrapin (no. 21, p. 106), Dorson notes his belief that the tale has a reference to motif J955.1, apparently referring to a confrontation between a frog and a truck. La Fontaine's *Fables* has a literary parallel, "La Grenouille qui veut se faire aussi grosse que le bœuf" (I, 3). There is in Louisiana French fakelore a similar "tale" which proclaims the crawfish to be the bravest animal in the world. Braver than the American eagle or the Russian bear which run off the railroad tracks when the train comes, the crawfish raises its pinchers in defiance instead.

Une fois, il y avait une grosse bande de petits ouaouarons. Les petits ouaouarons

Once there was a big gang of little frogs. The little frogs were getting to be pretty

23

commençaient d'être joliment gros. Ils commençaient d'être assez gros pour sauter et aller trouver du manger et jouer.

Ça fait, un jour, la maman dit à les petits ouaouarons, "Je suis partie à la chasse et faut vous autres se comportes bien. Faut vous soies pas canaille, faut pas vous autres vas trop loin. Tu sais, il y a un tas de bêtailles qui peut vous manger."

Mais, après la maman était partie, les enfants, comme toute autre petite chose, monde ou bêtaille, ils vont jouer et le jeu les emporte. Ils ont joué et ils se sont éloignés de leur nid. Il y en a un des petits ouaouarons qu'a vu un gros bœuf, et le bœuf lui a fait peur, tellement il était gros. Il s'est sauvé, et quand il a arrivé chez lui, sa maman était déjà arrivée. Et elle dit, "Où tu sors, mon petit?"

Il dit, "Maman," il dit, "j'étais rendu loin! Et j'ai vu une bêtaille qu'était beaucoup grosse!"

"Mais," elle dit, "comment gros?"

Il dit, "Attends, maman," il dit, "je vas te montrer."

Il s'est gonflé et il s'est gonflé, et elle a dit, "Gros comme ça?"

Il dit, "Beaucoup plus gros," et il s'est gonflé et il s'est gonflé jusque tout à l'heure, il a gonflé de trop et il a cassé ouvert et il est mort et il a pas pu montrer à sa maman comment gros la bêtaille il avait vu était.

grown up. They were getting to be big enough to jump and go off to find food and to play.

So, one day, the mother says to the little frogs, "I'm going hunting and you all must behave yourselves. You mustn't be naughty, you mustn't go off too far. You know, there are many animals who can eat you."

Well, after the mother had gone away, the children, like any other little ones, human or animal, went to play and they got carried away with the game. They played and went far from their nest. One of the little frogs saw a big bull and the bull scared him, so big was it. He ran and when he arrived home, his mother was already back. And she said, "Where are you coming from, my little one?"

He said, "Mother," he said, "I was far away! And I saw an animal that was very big!"

"Well," she said, "how big?"

He said, "Wait, Mother," he said, "I'll show you."

And he puffed himself up and he puffed himself up, and she said, "That big?"

He said, "Much bigger," and he puffed himself up and he puffed himself up until, after a while, he puffed up too much and he burst open and he died and he was not able to show his mother how big the animal was that he had seen.

15. Froumi et Grasshopper / Ant and Grasshopper (Wilson "Ben Guiné" Mitchell, Parks)

This tale is a version of type 280A *The Ant and the Lazy Cricket*. For a literary version, see La Fontaine's "La Cigale et la fourmi" (*Fables*, I, 1). In her study of African folktales, Klipple reported a Dahomean variant and a Kwéli variant in which the cricket is in need during the rainy season. In Robe's *Index of Mexican Folktales* (p. 506), there is a variant in which an ant gives grain to the starving cricket, but the ant refuses to continue this charity when it learns that the cricket spends the summer months sucking the grain. In Uncle Remus, "Why Mr. Cricket Has Elbows on His Legs" begins with a cricket playing music all summer and seeking shelter when winter comes, but then the tale changes direction, with

the cricket hiding in the chimney of a house where it continues to play a fife. Soon the man tired of the noise and poured hot water down the chimney which caused it to fall on the cricket. The cricket kicked so hard that it unjointed its legs.

In this Louisiana variant, Ben Guiné introduces a bit of local color by describing the Grasshopper as an accordion player whose musical interests prevent him from working with the ant. In South Louisiana tradition, musicians are often looked upon as marginal members of society. Also the accordion is a particularly loud instrument, suggesting the volume of cricket chirping one can hear on Louisiana summer evenings. When Ben Guiné announced the title of this story, Richard Guidry, a Louisiana French language specialist present during the session, gently suggested that "grasshopper" in French was "sauterelle". Ben Guiné countered, "Oui, sauterelle. C'est comme ça mo, mo pelle li Grasshopper" [Yes, sauterelle. What I call him is Grasshopper], deftly asserting his role as storyteller. In conclusion, Ben Guiné gave his notion of the moral of this story: "There is nothing more intelligent than an ant, but what could be more stupid than a grasshopper?'

Ah, *well*, et ça semble vrai, tout ça, vous comprends? Une froumi travaille tout l'été. Il t'apé ramasser des quoi et pi il emplit une maison. Il mandé Grasshopper, comme ça, li dit, "Comment ça se fait to viens pas aider moi? Mo pourras donne toi quelque chose."

"O!" Grasshopper dit, "O non!" Li dit, "Moi, mo pas gain le temps pour embêter avec toi!" Li dit, "Mo joue l'accordéon pour mon *living*."

Froumi dit, *"All right, go ahead,* mais," li dit, "mo va, quand li parti, sauterelle, commencer mettre du manger à côté." Li met.

Et là, *well,* quand ça rivé dans l'hiver, il y avait la glace. Tout quelque chose té glacé! Vous comprends ça? Tout quelque chose té glacé! Froumi, li, té dans sa maison.

Li cogné, "Tac, tac, tac."

Li dit, "Hé, hé, hé, *who's there?"*

Li dit, "C'est moi, Grasshopper, *let me in!"*

Li dit, "To pas connais comment mo dis toi dans l'été-là? Mo travaille avec vous autres." Et li dit, "T'étais apé jouer la musique." Li dit, "O, *poor Grasshopper, go and play for your living!"* Li frémé sa petite porte, "Cabô!" Li té couché dans sa maison et Grasshopper té gelé. Yé trouvé li en haut les

Ah, well, and all this seems true, you understand? An ant works all summer. He was gathering things and filling a house. He asked Grasshopper, like this, he said, "Why don't you come and help me? I will then give you something."

"Oh!" Grasshopper said, "Oh no!" He said, "I don't have time to fool around with you." He said, "I play the accordion for a living."

Froumi said, "All right, go ahead, but," he said, "when that cricket is gone, I'm going to start putting food away." He did.

And then, well, when winter arrived, there was ice. Everything was frozen! Do you understand this? Everything was frozen! Froumi was in his little house.

He knocked, "Tack, tack, tack."

He said, "Hey, hey, hey, who's there?"

He said, "It's me, Grasshopper, let me in!"

He said, "Don't you know what you told me during the summertime? I would have worked with you." And he said, "You were playing music." He said, "Oh, poor Grasshopper, go and play for your living!" He closed his little door, "Kabo!" He was asleep in his house and Grasshopper was frozen.

cannes maïs. C'est pas vrai, ça? Hein?

Li travaille tout le temps l'été, mais quand ça fait froid, vous p'alé oir li. Vous peux passer en haut où li gain nique-là. Li dans sa maison, li. Mais Grasshopper, li dans l'été, c'est là li n-homme. C'est là li n-homme. Ça apé jouer, mais quand ça fait frette-là, li gelé, li voulait rentrer, mais Froumi dit li, "O non! Peux pas vini. O non!" Et ça semble vrai, hein? Il n'y a rien qu'est plus malin qu'une froumi, mais ça qu'est plus bête qu'un *grasshopper?*"

They found him high on the cornstalks. Is this not true?"

He works all summer long, but when it's cold, you won't see him. You can pass right over his nest. He's in his house. But Grasshopper, in the summertime, that's when he's a man. That's when he's a man. He was playing, but when it turned cold, he froze. He wanted to come in, but Froumi said to him, "Oh no! You can't come in. Oh no!" And it seems true, doesn't it? There is nothing more intelligent than an ant, but what could be more stupid than a grasshopper?

16. *Neige casse la patte de la froumi / The Snow Breaks the Ant's Foot* (Inez Catalon, Kaplan)

This cumulative formula tale is a variant of type 2031 *Stronger and Strongest.* Robe's *Index of Mexican Folktales* includes 15 versions of this type, all parallel to this version. For example, a California version unfolds as follows: an ant breaks its foot in the snow and is sent in turn to blame the sun, the clouds, the wind, the wall, the rat, the cat, the dog, the stick, the fire, the water, the bull, the knife, the blacksmith, death, and finally God, who admits that He is the strongest of all.

Brandon collected two Louisiana variants in Vermillon Parish: "La Religieuse" [The Nun] (II, no. 45, pp. 338–339) which is based on the following chain: God, man, bull, water, fire, stick, dog, rat, wall, wind, cloud, sun, snow, and "La Froumi" [The Ant] (II, no. 46, pp. 340–342), from the same storyteller presented here, but recorded more than twenty years earlier, in which the earth ends the chain by accepting the title of strongest.

Neige casse la patte de la froumi. Elle dit, "Neige, neige, c'est toi qu'es si fort que ça, tu casses ma patte?"

Neige dit, "Non, c'est pas moi qu'es si fort que ça. Le soleil me fend."

Elle dit, "Soleil, soleil, c'est toi qu'es si fort que ça, tu fends neige, neige casse ma patte?

Soleil dit, "Non, c'est pas moi qu'es si fort que ça. Le nuage me couvre."

Elle dit, "Nuage, nuage, c'est toi qu'es si fort que ça, tu couvres soleil, soleil fend neige, neige casse ma patte?"

Snow breaks the ant's foot. She says, "Snow, Snow, is it you that is strong enough to break my foot?"

Snow says, "No, I'm not so strong. The sun melts me."

She says, "Sun, Sun, are you strong enough to melt Snow, and Snow breaks my foot?"

Sun says, "No, I'm not so strong. The cloud hides me."

She says, "Cloud, Cloud, are you strong enough to hide Sun, Sun melts Snow, and Snow breaks my foot?"

"Non, c'est pas moi qu'es si fort que ça. Le vent me pousse."

"Vent, vent, c'est toi qu'es si fort que ça, tu pousses nuage, nuage couvre soleil, soleil fend neige, neige casse ma patte?"

"Non, c'est pas moi qu'es si fort que ça. Le mur me guette."

"Mur, mur, c'est toi qu'es si fort que ça, tu guettes vent, vent pousse nuage, nuage couvre soleil, soleil fend neige, neige casse ma patte?"

"Non, c'est pas moi qu'es si fort que ça. Le rat me perce."

"Rat, rat, c'est toi qu'es si fort que ça, tu perces muraille, muraille guette vent, vent pousse nuage, nuage couvre soleil, soleil fend neige, neige casse ma patte?"

"Non, c'est pas moi qu'es si fort que ça. Le chat me tue."

"Chat, chat, c'est toi qu'es si fort que ça, tu tues rat, rat perce muraille, muraille guette vent, vent pousse nuage, nuage, couvre soleil, soleil fend neige, neige casse ma patte?"

"Non, c'est pas moi qu'es si fort que ça. Le chien me tue."

"Chien, chien, c'est toi qu'es si fort que ça, tu tues chat, chat tue rat, rat perce muraille, muraille guette vent, vent pousse nuage, nuage couvre soleil, soleil fend neige, neige casse ma patte?"

"Non, c'est pas moi qu'es si fort que ça. Le bâton me tue."

"Bâton, bâton, c'est toi qu'es si fort que ça, tu tues chien, chien tue chat, chat tue rat, rat perce muraille, muraille guette vent, vent pousse nuage, nuage couvre soleil, soleil fend neige, neige casse ma patte?"

"Non, c'est pas moi qu'es si fort que ça. Le feu me brûle."

"Feu, feu, c'est toi qu'es si fort que ça, tu brûles bâton, bâton tue chien, chien tue chat, chat tue rat, rat perce muraille, muraille guette vent, vent pousse nuage, nuage couvre soleil, soleil fend neige, neige casse ma patte?"

Cloud says, "No, I'm not so strong. The wind pushes me."

"Wind, Wind, are you strong enough to push Cloud, Cloud hides Sun, Sun melts Snow, and Snow breaks my foot?"

"No, I'm not so strong. The wall stops me."

"Wall, Wall, are you strong enough to stop Wind, Wind pushes Cloud, Cloud hides Sun, Sun melts Snow, and Snow breaks my foot?"

"No, I'm not so strong. The rat pierces me."

"Rat, Rat, are you strong enough to pierce Wall, Wall stops Wind, Wind pushes Cloud, Cloud hides Sun, Sun melts Snow, and Snow breaks my foot?"

"No, I'm not so strong. The cat kills me."

"Cat, Cat, are you strong enough to kill Rat, Rat pierces Wall, Wall stops Wind, Wind pushes Cloud, Cloud hides Sun, Sun melts Snow, and Snow breaks my foot?"

"No, I'm not so strong. The dog kills me."

"Dog, Dog, are you strong enough to kill Cat, Cat kills Rat, Rat pierces Wall, Wall stops Wind, Wind pushes Cloud, Cloud hides Sun, Sun melts Snow, and Snow breaks my foot?"

"No, I'm not so strong. The stick kills me."

"Stick, Stick, are you strong enough to kill Dog, Dog kills Cat, Cat kills Rat, Rat pierces Wall, Wall stops Wind, Wind pushes Cloud, Cloud hides Sun, Sun melts Snow, and Snow breaks my foot?"

"No, I'm not so strong. The fire burns me."

"Fire, Fire, are you strong enough to burn Stick, Stick kills Dog, Dog kills Cat, Cat kills Rat, Rat pierces Wall, Wall stops Wind, Wind pushes Cloud, Cloud hides Sun, Sun melts Snow, and Snow breaks my foot?"

"Non, c'est pas moi qu'es si fort que ça.
L'eau m'éteint."

"Eau, eau, c'est toi qu'es si fort que ça, tu
éteins feu, feu brûle bâton, bâton tue chien,
chien tue chat, chat tue rat, rat perce
muraille, muraille guette vent, vent pousse
nuage, nuage couvre soleil, soleil fend neige,
neige casse ma patte?"

"Non, c'est pas moi qu'es si fort que ça.
Le boeuf me boit."

"Boeuf, boeuf, c'est toi qu'es si fort que
ça, tu bois eau, eau éteint feu, feu brûle
bâton, bâton tue chien, chien tue chat, chat
tue rat, rat perce muraille, muraille guette
vent, vent pousse nuage, nuage couvre soleil,
soleil fend neige, neige casse ma patte?"

"Non, c'est pas moi qu'es si fort que ça.
Le cable me tient."

"Cable, cable, c'est toi qu'es si fort que
ça, tu tiens boeuf, boeuf boit eau, eau éteint
feu, feu brûle bâton, bâton tue chien, chien
tue chat, chat tue rat, rat perce muraille,
muraille guette vent, vent pousse nuage,
nuage couvre soleil, soleil fend neige, neige
casse ma patte?"

"Non, c'est pas moi qu'es si fort que ça.
L'arbre me tient."

"Arbre, arbre, c'est toi qu'es si fort que
ça, tu tiens cable, cable tient boeuf, boeuf
boit eau, eau éteint feu, feu brûle bâton,
bâton tue chien, chien tue chat, chat tue rat,
rat perce muraille, muraille guette vent, vent
pousse nuage, nuage couvre soleil, soleil fend
neige, neige casse ma patte?"

"Non, c'est pas moi qu'es si fort que ça.
La racine me tient."

"Racine, racine, c'est toi qu'es si fort que
ça, tu tiens arbre, arbre tient cable, cable tient
boeuf, boeuf boit eau, eau éteint feu, feu
brûle bâton, bâton tue chien, chien tue chat,
chat tue rat, rat perce muraille, muraille
guette vent, vent pousse nuage, nuage couvre
soleil, soleil fend neige, neige casse ma
patte?"

"Non, c'est pas moi qu'es si fort que ça.

"No, I'm not so strong. The water puts
me out."

"Water, Water, are you strong enough to
put out Fire, Fire burns Stick, Stick kills Dog,
Dog kills Cat, Cat kills Rat, Rat pierces Wall,
Wall stops Wind, Wind pushes Cloud, Cloud
hides Sun, Sun melts Snow, and Snow breaks
my foot?"

"No, I'm not so strong. The bull drinks
me."

"Bull, Bull, are you strong enough to
drink Water, Water puts out Fire, Fire burns
Stick, Stick kills Dog, Dog kills Cat, Cat kills
Rat, Rat pierces Wall, Wall stops Wind, Wind
pushes Cloud, Cloud hides Sun, Sun melts
Snow, and Snow breaks my foot?"

"No, I'm not so strong. The rope holds
me."

"Rope, Rope, are you strong enough to
hold Bull, Bull drinks Water, Water puts out
Fire, Fire burns Stick, Stick kills Dog, Dog
kills Cat, Cat kills Rat, Rat pierces Wall, Wall
stops Wind, Wind pushes Cloud, Cloud
hides Sun, Sun melts Snow, and Snow breaks
my foot?"

"No, I'm not so strong. The tree holds
me."

"Tree, Tree, are you strong enough to
hold Rope, Rope holds Bull, Bull drinks
Water, Water puts out Fire, Fire burns Stick,
Stick kills Dog, Dog kills Cat, Cat kills Rat,
Rat pierces Wall, Wall stops Wind, Wind
pushes Cloud, Cloud hides Sun, Sun melts
Snow, and Snow breaks my foot?"

"No, I'm not so strong. The root holds
me."

"Root, Root, are you strong enough to
hold Tree, Tree holds Rope, Rope holds Bull,
Bull drinks Water, Water puts out Fire, Fire
burns Stick, Stick kills Dog, Dog kills Cat,
Cat kills Rat, Rat pierces Wall, Wall stops
Wind, Wind pushes Cloud, Cloud hides Sun,
Sun melts Snow, and Snow breaks my foot?"

"No, I'm not so strong. The earth holds

La terre me tient."

"Terre, terre, c'est toi qu'es si fort que ça . . . ?"

"Oui! C'est moi qu'es si fort que ça!"

me."

"Earth, Earth, are you so strong. . ."

"Yes! I am so strong."

17. Bicoin et les choux / Bicoin and the Cabbage (Odette Coussan, Carencro)

This cumulative tale is a variant of type 2015 *The Goat who Would not Go Home*. There is a close parallel in Geneviève Massignon's *Folktales of France*, "Coué or Couette" (no. 39, p. 136), in which the chain is as follows: goat, dog, stick, fire, water and finally the bull, which accomplishes the required task and begins the process which will eventually send the goat back into its pen. In this Louisiana version, the chain continues past the bull to the axe which breaks the whetstone which sharpens the knife which bleeds the bulls, and so on. The resolution strains logic in that the bulls drink the water which then must put out the fire which then must burn the stick. Somehow, it all works out in the end and the cabbage patch is successful. In his study, *The Survival of French in the Old District of Ste. Genevieve*, Ward Dorrance includes a version from Missouri, "La Vieille Femme pi son cochon" [The Old Woman and her Pig] (p. 128). In Laval's Archives de Folklore, there is a sung version collected by Luc Lacourcière from Benoît Benoît of Tracadie, New Brunswick, "Briquet." This Louisiana variant is chanted up to the last line which is said with an appropriate I-told-you-so tone. This tale likely came to the storyteller from black Creole origins as indicated by the dialect of the first and last lines.

Eh! O! Toi soigneras mes choux!

J'ai été chercher Bicoin pour soigner mes choux. Mes choux veut pas profiter. Eh! O! Bicoin, toi soigneras mes choux!

J'ai été chercher les chiens pour mordre Bicoin. Les chiens veut pas mordre Bicoin. Bicoin veut pas soigner mes choux. Mes choux veut pas profiter. Eh! O! Bicoin, toi soigneras mes choux!

J'ai été chercher bâton pour battre les chiens. Bâton veut pas battre les chiens. Les chiens veut pas mordre Bicoin. Bicoin veut pas soigner mes choux. Mes choux veut pas profiter. Eh! O! Bicoin, toi soigneras mes choux!

J'ai été chercher le feu pour brûler bâton. Le feu veut pas brûler bâton. Bâton veut pas battre les chiens. Les chiens veut pas mordre Bicoin. Bicoin veut pas soigner mes choux.

Hey! Oh! You'll take care of my cabbage!

I went to get Bicoin to care for my cabbage. My cabbage won't grow. Hey! Oh! Bicoin, you'll take care of my cabbage!

I went to get the dogs to bite Bicoin. The dogs won't bite Bicoin. Bicoin won't care for my cabbage. My cabbage won't grow. Hey! Oh! Bicoin, you'll take care of my cabbage!

I went to get a stick to beat the dogs. The stick won't beat the dogs. The dogs won't bite Bicoin. Bicoin won't care for my cabbage. My cabbage won't grow. Hey! Oh! Bicoin, you'll take care of my cabbage!

I went to get the fire to burn the stick. The fire won't burn the stick. The stick won't beat the dogs. The dogs won't bite Bicoin. Bicoin won't care for my cabbage. My

Mes choux veut pas profiter. Eh! O! Bicoin, toi soigneras mes choux!

J'ai été chercher de l'eau pour éteigner le feu. De l'eau veut pas éteigner le feu. Le feu veut pas brûler bâton. Bâton veut pas battre les chiens. Les chiens veut pas mordre Bicoin. Bicoin veut pas soigner mes choux. Mes choux veut pas profiter. Eh! O! Bicoin, toi soigneras mes choux!

J'ai été chercher les boeufs pour boire de l'eau. Les boeufs veut pas boire de l'eau. De l'eau veut pas éteigner le feu. Le feu veut pas brûler bâton. Bâton veut pas battre les chiens. Les chiens veut pas mordre Bicoin. Bicoin veut pas soigner mes choux. Mes choux veut pas profiter. Eh! O! Bicoin, toi soigneras mes choux!

J'ai été chercher couteau pour saigner les boeufs. Couteau veut pas saigner les boeufs. Les boeufs veut pas boire de l'eau. De l'eau veut pas éteigner le feu. Le feu veut pas brûler bâton. Bâton veut pas battre les chiens. Les chiens veut pas mordre Bicoin. Bicoin veut pas soigner mes choux. Mes choux veut pas profiter. Eh! O! Bicoin, toi soigneras mes choux!

J'ai été chercher la meule pour aiguiser couteau. La meule veut pas aiguiser couteau. Couteau veut pas saigner les boeufs. Les boeufs veut pas boire de l'eau. De l'eau veut pas éteigner le feu. Le feu veut pas brûler bâton. Bâton veut pas battre les chiens. Les chiens veut pas mordre Bicoin. Bicoin veut pas soigner mes choux. Mes choux veut pas profiter. Eh! O! Bicoin, toi soigneras mes choux!

J'ai été chercher la hache pour briser la meule. La hache a brisé la meule. La meule a aiguisé couteau. Couteau a saigné les boeufs. Les boeufs a bu de l'eau. De l'eau a éteigné le feu. Le feu a brûlé le bâton. Bâton a battu les chiens. Les chiens a mordu Bicoin. Bicoin a soigné mes choux. Mes choux ont bien profité. Eh! O! Bicoin, m'a pas dit toi, toi soigneras mes choux!

cabbage won't grow. Hey! Oh! Bicoin, you'll take care of my cabbage!

I went to get the water to put out the fire. The water won't put out the fire. The fire won't burn the stick. The stick won't beat the dogs. The dogs won't bite Bicoin. Bicoin won't care for my cabbage. My cabbage won't grow. Hey! Oh! Bicoin, you'll take care of my cabbage!

I went to get the bulls to drink the water. The bulls won't drink the water. The water won't put out the fire. The fire won't burn the stick. The stick won't beat the dogs. The dogs won't bite Bicoin. Bicoin won't care for my cabbage. My cabbage won't grow. Hey! Oh! Bicoin, you'll take care of my cabbage!

I went to get the knife to bleed the bulls. The knife won't bleed the bulls. The bulls won't drink the water. The water won't put out the fire. The fire won't burn the stick. The stick won't beat the dogs. The dogs won't bite Bicoin. Bicoin won't care for my cabbage. My cabbage won't grow. Hey! Oh! Bicoin, you'll take care of my cabbage!

I went to get the whetstone to sharpen the knife. The whetstone won't sharpen the knife. The knife won't bleed the bulls. The bulls won't drink the water. The water won't put out the fire. The fire won't burn the stick. The stick won't beat the dogs. The dogs won't bite Bicoin. Bicoin won't care for my cabbage. My cabbage won't grow. Hey! Oh! Bicoin, you'll take care of my cabbage!

I went to get the axe to break the whetstone. The axe broke the whetstone. The whetstone sharpened the knife. The knife bled the bulls. The bulls drank the water. The water put out the fire. The fire burned the stick. The stick beat the dogs. The dogs bit Bicoin. Bicoin cared for my cabbage. My cabbage grew well. Hey! Oh! Bicoin, I told you that you would take care of my cabbage!

Contes Merveilleux / Magic Tales

18. Petit Poucet / Little Poucet (Évélia Boudreaux, Carencro)

This tale is a variant of type 327B *The Dwarf and the Giant,* known around the world. See Bolte and Polívka, *Anmerkungen* (I, no. 15, p. 124, and no. 56, p. 499) for an extensive analysis. This type is particularly well-known in the oral tradition of the French-speaking world. The second revision of the Aarne-Thompson index (1961) lists three French versions, eight West Indian versions and 57 French American versions (type 327 in general, from Laval's Archives de Folklore). Baughman's Anglo-American index lists six variants including one in English from a Louisiana Creole source (Fausset, *JAF* 40, pp. 255–56). In *Le conte populaire français* (p. 306), Paul Delarue gives a complete analysis of the story and classifies all variants under the single type 327, which he refuses to subdivide insisting that all variations fall comfortably within it. According to Delarue, the complete text of this type was not found in oral tradition before the appearance of Charles Perrault's literary version in *Contes de ma mère l'oye,* in 1697. Delarue maintains that it is this literary version which eventually entered into oral tradition where it became immensely popular.

A French variant, "Jean et Jeannette," collected by Delarue's student, Geneviève Massignon, for Dorson's Folktales of the World series (*Folktales of France,* no. 50, pp. 170–175), has the two heroes, a young boy and his sister, in a version of type 327 (Massignon did not subdivide the type either) in which the ogre is a demon. The editor attributes this transformation to the influence of Christianity in the Languedoc region. A French American variant collected by Carrière in the Old Mines region of Missouri (*Missouri,* no. 20), casts three sisters, the youngest of whom is called Finette. She escapes from the ogre's house and has her sisters rescued. The sisters then become jealous of her and the tale shifts to the Cinderella story (type 510A) at that point.

This story is very popular in Louisiana French tradition. In "Poucette," a Louisiana variant collected by Saucier (*French Louisiana,* no. 13, pp. 49–50), the hero, who bears the same name as the one presented below, has eight brothers and sisters who all go to the giant's house when they are abandoned. There they are saved by Poucette who exchanges the blue nightcaps for the white ones worn by the giant's own children (cf. type 1119, motif K1611; recorded in the repertoires of southern English-speaking blacks and whites). The giant kills his own children while the hero flees with his brothers and sisters to find the road which will take them home. John Guilbeau collected five variants for his linguistic study of Lafourche Parish French (pp. 371–378; 382–389; 390–395; 396–401; 402–407). In four

of them, Petit Poucet is abandoned in the woods three times with his brothers and sisters. Twice he leads them back home by following trails he has left (nails and buttons, gravel and buttons, or rocks and gravel). The third time he leaves a trail of bread crumbs which are eaten by the birds. Wandering in the woods, they finally go to the home of the giant and his wife, always marked by a red light. As in the version presented here, the giant's wife tries to warn the children, but it is Petit Poucet's exchange of nightcaps (white for red) that ultimately saves them, and they escape with the giant's boots and money (N538.2 "Treasure stolen from giant [devil]"). One of the versions is similar, but Petit Poucet has only brothers. They find their way out of the woods only once by following his trail of gravel. The next time his trail of bread crumbs is eaten. In two of the versions, instead of exchanging nightcaps, he takes the crowns from the heads of the giant's children. Only two of the storytellers specified that the giant's boots were fast (a variant of D1521.1 "Seven league boots"). In one of these, the giant's treasure is a bootful of money. In the versions collected by Fortier ("Piti garçons et Géant," *Louisiana Folktales* I, pp. 82–85) and by Brandon ("'Tit Poucet," thèse, II, no. 11, pp. 247–250), there are several brothers at the giant's (or ogre's) house, and there is an exchange of bonnets. In Brandon's variant, the devil takes his seven league boots to catch the children who have stolen his treasure, but Petit Poucet also succeeds in stealing his boots.

The initial episode of "Petit Jean Micuicuic," in *Les Aventures de Petit Jean: Contes créoles de l'Océan Indien* (pp. 95–96), describes a child who avoids being eaten by the wolf when he cuts his father's hair and changes places with him, though there is no mention of magic boots, nor of stolen treasure, both suggested by Mme Boudreaux in the following Louisiana variant. It is interesting to note that Mme Boudreaux skims over the more brutal parts of the story, especially the evils done to the children. She relates only vaguely the abandoning of Petit Poucet by his brothers and sisters in the woods, and the death of the child without a bonnet who is inadvertently eaten by his own father, the old devil.

Il y avait une famille, ils avaient plusieurs enfants et le dernier, ils appelaient Petit Poucet. Et Petit Poucet était plus *smart* que les autres et il était aimé plus par le papa et la maman. Comme il était le dernier, ils avaient plus de temps pour jouer et pour l'aimer que les autres et ses frères et ses sœurs étaient jaloux. Les autres enfants étaient jaloux de lui.

Ça fait, un bon jour, les enfants se sont mis ensemble et ils ont dit, "On va faire quelque chose avec lui. Quoi bien on pourra faire? On peut pas l'endurer, lui, avoir toutes les bonnes choses et d'être aimé plus qu'on est aimé. On aime pas ça et on va faire quelque chose avec lui."

There was a family that had several children and the last of these they called Petit Poucet. And Petit Poucet was smarter than the others and he was loved more by the father and mother. Since he was the last child, they had more time to play with him and to love him than the other children and his brothers and sisters were jealous. The other children were jealous of him.

So, one fine day, the children got together and they said, "We're going to do something with him. What can we do? We can't stand it that he has all the good things and that he is more loved than we are. We don't like that and we're going to do something with him."

Ça fait, ils se sont compris qu'ils auriont pris le wagon et attelé les chevaux dessus et ils auriont été *ride* dans le bois. Et Petit Poucet, lui, il était beaucoup *smart,* comme j'ai déjà dit, et il était intelligent. Il guettait quoi c'est les autres faisaient. Et quand il les a vus tous se mettre ensemble, il s'est caché et il écoutait quoi ils ont dit. Alors, il connaissait qu'ils voulaient aller *ride* dans le wagon et ils auriont fait quelque chose avec lui. Il s'est ramassé une poche de pierres et il s'est assis en arrière dans le wagon. Et toutes les distances, il lâchait une pierre. Toutes les distances, il lâchait une pierre.

Ils ont voyagé dans le bois. Ils ont arrêté. Et ils ont fait semblant d'aller marcher dans le bois. Et quand ils ont été un peu loin, ils ont tous parti et ils sont rentournés au wagon. Les chances sont, ils ont couru pour pas que Petit Poucet peuve les rattraper. Et toujours, ils ont quitté Petit Poucet dans le bois tout seul. Et il a cherché pour trouver son chemin. Il cherchait pour les pierres, mais il trouvait plus les pierres.

Ça fait, il a vu une maison, et il dit, "La nuit est après prendre." Il dit, "Je vas risquer d'aller à la maison. Ici dans le bois, les bêtailles vont me manger, et j'aurai peur, moi tout seul."

Il a été à la maison et il a appelé. La maîtresse de la maison a sorti. Il lui a dit quoi c'est qu'était son tracas. "Mais," elle dit, "ça ici, c'est la maison du vieux diable, et le vieux diable va te manger à soir."

"Mais," il dit, "je vas prendre une chance, si vous voulez, que le vieux diable me mange." Il dit, "J'aimerais mieux que le vieux diable me mange que les bêtailles dans le bois, et d'être tout seul dans le noir." Ça fait, il dit, "Je vas prendre une chance."

"Mais," elle dit, "*Okay!* Rentre." Il a rentré.

Elle a préparé à souper de bonne heure. Elle connaissait que le vieux diable aurait arrivé plus tard et elle voulait que les enfants

So they agreed that they would take the wagon and hitch the horses to it and they would take a ride in the woods. And Petit Poucet was very smart, as I already said, he was intelligent. He watched what the others were doing. And when he saw them all get together, he hid and he listened to what they said. So he knew that they wanted to go for a ride in the wagon and that they were going to do something to him. He picked up a pocketful of pebbles and he sat in back of the wagon. And every once in a while, he would drop a pebble. Every once in a while, he would drop a pebble.

They traveled into the woods. They stopped. And they pretended to take a walk in the woods. And when they were pretty far away, they all left and returned to the wagon. Chances are that they ran so that Petit Poucet could not catch up with them. Anyway, they left Petit Poucet all alone in the woods. And he searched to find his way. He looked for the pebbles, but he couldn't find them.

So he saw a house, and he said, "Night is falling." He said, "I'll take a chance on going to the house. Here in the woods, the animals will eat me, and I will be afraid all alone."

He went to the house and he called out. The mistress of the house came out. He told her about his troubles. "Well," she said, "this is the home of the old devil, and the old devil will eat you tonight."

"Well," he said, "I'll take my chances, if you don't mind, that the old devil might eat me." He said, "I would prefer that the old devil eat me than the animals in the woods where I would be all alone in the dark." So, he said, "I'll take that chance."

"Well," she said, "Okay! Come in." He went in.

She prepared supper early. She knew that the old devil would arrive later and she wanted the children to be in bed by the time

soient tous couchés pour quand il serait arrivé pour pas qu'il s'aperçoive qu'il y en avait un d'étrange.

Et quand le souper était fini, elle a mis ses enfants couchés et tous ses enfants à elle avaient un petit bonnet sur la tête. Mais Petit Poucet en avait pas un. Quand les enfants se sont endormis, il a ôté le bonnet à un et il l'a mis sur sa tête à lui.

Quand le vieux diable a arrivé, il dit, "Snff, snff! Ouuu! Je sens de la viande fraîche."

"O!" elle dit. "Tu t'imagines ça."

"Snff, snff! O!" il dit, "non! Je sens de la viande fraîche."

Elle dit, "Viens souper." Elle dit, "Le souper est paré. J'ai cuit de la viande. C'est ça tu sens."

Il a été. Il a soupé. Après il était couché, il était pas satisfait. Il sentait toujours de la viande fraîche, il disait. Ça fait, il a été. Il a passé à côté des lits de ses enfants et il a touché. Et il y en avait un qu'avait pas un petit bonnet. Ça fait, il a ramassé cil-là qu'avait pas de petit bonnet et il a fait quelque chose avec. Il avait dit c'était de la viande fraîche, ça fait, les chances sont, il l'a tué pour le manger.

Et là, Petit Poucet avait peur. Et il avait vu ayoù le vieux diable avait ôté ses bottes et mis son argent. Ça fait, quand le vieux diable s'a recouché, il a volé les bottes du vieux diable et l'argent et il a parti. Il a mis les bottes à vieux diable. Elles estiont grandes et il aurait marché plus vite avec ces bottes.

Ça fait, il a marché, marché. Et le jour s'a fait et il a retrouvé un ou deux des pierres. "O!" il dit, "je suis sur mon chemin." Ça fait, il a continué, il a retrouvé sa maison. Il a retourné.

Et quand il a arrivé avec l'argent et les bottes du vieux diable, sa famille était contente de le voir parce qu'il était riche et

he arrived so that he wouldn't notice that there was a stranger among them.

And when supper was finished, she put her children to bed and each one of her children had a little nightcap on his head. But Petit Poucet didn't have one. When the children fell asleep, he took the nightcap from one of them and he put it on his own head.

When the old devil arrived, he said, "Snff, snff! Ooo! I smell fresh meat."

"Oh!" she said, "You're imagining things."

"Snff, snff! Oh!" he said, "No! I smell fresh meat."

She said, "Come and eat your supper." She said, "Supper is ready. I cooked some meat. That's what you smell."

He went. He ate supper. After he was in bed, he wasn't satisfied. He claimed he still smelled fresh meat. So he went. He passed alongside the beds where his children were sleeping and he touched them. And there was one of them that didn't have a little nightcap. So he picked that one up, the one without the nightcap, and he did something to it. He had said that it was fresh meat, so chances are that he killed it to eat it.

Then, Petit Poucet was afraid. He had seen where the old devil had put his boots and his money. So when the old devil went back to bed, he stole the old devil's boots and his money and he left. He put on the old devil's boots. They were very big and he could walk faster with them on.

So he walked and walked. And day broke and he was able to find one or two of his pebbles. "Oh!" he said, "I'm on my way." So he continued and he found his home again. He returned home.

When he arrived with the money and boots of the old devil, his family was happy to see him because he was rich now and they

eux, ils étaient beaucoup pauvres. Ça fait, ça leur faisait leur vie beaucoup plus facile. Et ils l'ont accepté. Ils estiont contents avec lui après ça.	were very poor. So this made their lives much easier. And they accepted him. They were happy with him after all that.

19. Petit Pouce / Little Pouce (Azalée Malveaux, Judice; recorded by her granddaughter, Jennifer Ardoin)

This tale is a simplified variant of type 303 *The Twins or Blood-Brothers*. For detailed studies, see Kurt Ranke's *Die Zwei Brüder* and Bolte and Polívka (I, 528ff). This tale can be one of the most complex, and richly developed in European tradition (cf. Grimm, no. 60). Leonard Roberts has one long and relatively complex version, "Magic White Deer" (no. 157) in *Sang Branch Settlers*, which the storyteller Jim Couch attributes to the French side of his family. Most other versions collected in America tend to be shorter and simpler. Roberts has two other variants in *South from Hell-fer-Sartin*, "Alice and Ben" and "Jack and his Dogs" (pp. 19–22), both of which basically focus on the same episode featured in this Louisiana version, motif B524.1.2 "Dogs rescue fleeing master from tree refuge." The latter of the two tales in Roberts is very close to this one, casting a single hero, with his mother and his dogs as helpers. There is, however, no life taken here, and the hero jumps from one tree to another to avoid being chopped down, instead of restoring the tree he is in with magic eggs. It is interesting to note that the name of the young hero of this Louisiana version, told by a black Creole, resembles that of Petit Poucet, the thumbling hero of French oral tradition (see tale 18 in this collection), while the names of the dogs, Miblé, Toumadaïe and N'Daye, seem African in origin. Roberts, in his note to this tale, speculates that the variants collected in Kentucky "appear to have come from the South, perhaps with the general movement of slaves to and from collecting stations in the Bluegrass" (p. 213).

William Bascom (1992: 155–200) argues convincingly that this tale has strong African affinities. He types it as Part IV of 315A *The Cannibal Sister*, although none of the African tales he found has apparent connections to the larger type. In all, he lists 117 variants, with 58 from Africa, 25 from North America, 33 from the Caribbean and South America and one from Spain. The dogs' names range from descriptive translations, such as "Cut to Pieces," Swallow Up" and Clear the Remains" in a Yoruba tale from Nigeria, to transcriptions of sounds with no explored meaning, such as Akangs, Anhosay and Andilo in a Creole tale from Haiti. As in this Louisiana variant, the calling of the dogs' names is a significant part of most of the stories cited by Bascom.

Mrs. Malveaux performed this tale as cante fable, singing the lines of the man as he is chopping the trees, and the lines of Petit Pouce as he is calling his dogs. In my step-grandfather's version, the hero also sang for his three dogs named Gaillum, Singo, and Moliseau. In *Folktales of Louisiana*, Alfred Anderson, a black English-speaking narrator from

Donaldsonville, also has the hero chant the names of his four dogs: Rover, Counselor, Daddy-o, and Jim.

Une fois, c'était un petit garçon. Son nom, c'était Petit Pouce. Il avait trois chiens. Un chien s'appelait Miblé. L'autre s'appelait Toumadaïe. Et l'autre, N'Daye.

Un jour, le petit garçon dit à sa mère, il était parti faire la chasse dans le bois. Mais il aurait quitté ses trois chiens amarrés. Ça fait, il dit à sa mère, il dit, "Mam, si je retourne pas *back*," il dit, "lache mes chiens. Eux va connaître ayoù me trouver."

Ça fait, la mère, elle a dormi. Elle a oublié le petit garçon. Quand elle s'a réveillée, il y avait un moqueur qu'était après amener du train côté de sa fenêtre. Ça l'a réveillée. Ça fait, elle a pensé de lacher ses chiens.

Et le petit garçon, il était après marcher dans le bois. Il a vu un vieux n-homme qu'avait une scie dans ses mains. Il sciait les arbres. Il avait une serpent et une tortue qui l'aidaient. Et puis il disait à petit garçon qu'était dans l'arbre, il dit, "Faut tu viens par terre. Je veux t'attraper."

Mais le petit garçon avait un *rubber shoot* dans ses mains qu'il tirait avec des pierres. Chaque fois le vieux homme sciait l'arbre par terre, le petit garçon se trouvait dans un autre arbre. Et puis il était après appeler ses chiens. Il disait, "Miblé, Miblé, Toumadaïe, N'Daye."

Et le vieux homme disait, "Serpent, Tortue, vini m'aider." Il sciait l'arbre. Il allait [chanté], "A zouinga zouinga, tou la la. A zouinga zouinga, tou la la. A zouinga zouinga, tou la la. Serpent, Tortue, vini m'aider."

Le petit garçon était là [chanté], "Miblé, Miblé, Toumadaïe, N'Daye."

[chanté] "Serpent, Tortue, vini m'aider. A zouinga zouinga, tou la la. A zouinga zouinga, tou la la."

Quand petit garçon avait dernier arbre pour grimper en dans, le vieux homme avait

Once there was a little boy. His name was Petit Pouce. He had three dogs. One was named Miblé. Another was named Toumadaïe. And the other, N'Daye.

One day, the little boy said to his mother, he was going to hunt in the woods. But he would leave his three dogs tied up. So he said to his mother, he said, "Mom, if I don't come back," he said, "let my dogs go. They'll know where to find me."

So the mother fell asleep. She forgot about the little boy. When she awoke, there was a mocking bird making noise next to her window. This woke her up. So she thought about letting the dogs go.

And the little boy, he was walking in the woods. He saw an old man who had a saw in his hands. He was sawing trees. And he had a snake and a turtle helping him. And he said to the little boy who was in the tree, he said, "You must come down. I want to catch you."

But the little boy had a slingshot in his hands that he used to shoot rocks. Every time the old man would saw a tree down, the little boy would be in another tree. And he was calling his dogs. He would said, "Miblé, Miblé, Toumadaïe, N'Daye."

And the old man would said, "Snake, Turtle, come and help me." He would saw the tree. He went [chanted], "A zouinga zouinga, tou la la. A zouinga zouinga, tou la la. A zouinga zouinga, tou la la. Snake, Turtle, come and help me."

The little boy was there [chanted], "Miblé, Miblé, Toumadaïe, N'Daye."

[chanted] "Snake, Turtle, come and help me. A zouinga zouinga, tou la la. A zouinga zouinga, tou la la.

When the little boy had one last tree to climb, the old man had almost sawed the tree

presque scié l'arbre par terre. Quand les trois chiens ont arrivé, eux a attrapé vieux homme. Eux a tout déchiré ses culottes. Et puis eux a tué la serpent. Eux a tué la tortue. Et le petit garçon s'en a retourné *back* chez lui.

Et c'est comme ça que ça a arrivé, et c'est tout.

down. When the three dogs arrived, they caught the old man. They tore up his pants. And then they killed the snake. They killed the turtle. And the little boy went back home.

And that's how it happened, and that's all.

20. Jean l'Ours et la fille du roi / Jean l'Ours and the King's Daughter (Elby Deshotels, Reddel)

This tale is related to type 513B *The Land and Water Ship*, without the initial episode about the ship that could travel on land and sea. In *Le conte populaire français*, Delarue lists 37 variants of type 513. Louise Bernard studied the French American versions of this story (Archives de Folklore manuscript). For an international study, see Bolte and Polívka, *Anmerkungen* (II, pp. 79–96). See also the Grimms' nos. 71 and 134 for other parallels.

In sub-type B, the hero has a specific goal to obtain the hand of the princess. He is assisted in this quest by his fabulous friends, either before or for the occasion. Often the friends help the hero in numerous tasks imposed by the king. See, for example, Parsons, *Antilles* (I, p. 62) in which the hero must accomplish four tasks in order to obtain the princess's hand. Versions of 513B have been collected from Spanish speakers in Louisiana, as well as English-speaking blacks and whites in the South (cf. Baughman).

In "Le P'tsit bateau qui allait sus mer et pis sur terre," a French American variant collected by Carrière in *Missouri* (no. 30), as well as in the Louisiana variant presented here, the hero has five friends. In the Missouri version, the hero must prove himself in numerous tests before the final race for which the princess is the prize. The Louisiana story simply alludes to the early competition as Jean l'Ours shows the king his superior pigs and hunting dogs. In both variants, Jean l'Ours finally earns the princess. In other versions, he doesn't always accept her in the end. In one French variant (Massignon, *Contes de l'ouest*), he refuses to take her after having won her.

Klipple describes a variant from the Congo in which the spider (in this case the hero) obtains the princess with the assistance of the turtle, the woodpecker, the rat and mosquito. But he gives her back to the king in exchange for her value in cash, according to tribal custom, when his companions are unhappy with her.

In another Louisiana variant collected by Saucier in the 1930s (*French Louisiana*, pp. 41–43, "The Millionaire, His Daughter and Her Suitors"), after the quest for the land and water ship, the hero's great runner wins the race and his great eater wins the pork eating contest, making it possible for the hero to marry the millionaire's daughter. The hero then shows the same sort of gallantry as in the present text by giving the millionaire his boat. The

notion of the hero who is richer than the king can also be found in such traditional Cajun songs as "Cadet Rousselle" and "Trois jolis tambours."

The runner who is asleep on a pine knot toward the end of this story is reminiscent of the traditional race between the tortoise and the hare (type 275A; motif K11.3) in which the rabbit is so far ahead in the race that he stops to rest. He falls asleep and loses the race. Here, the Great Runner manages to win the race after all with the help of the other marvelous companions.

Jean l'Ours (John the Bear) is a name commonly given to the hero in French oral and storybook tradition. Like Juan Oso (also John the Bear) in Spanish tradition, and Jack (of beanstalk and giant-killing fame) in English tradition, Jean l'Ours is an Old-World hero transplanted in the New. Unlike Juan Oso and Jack, however, Jean l'Ours appears only rarely in folktales recently collected in the United States.

It is interesting to note how elements of this story are affected by the transplantation of French oral tradition to the Louisiana context. Now the king's millions make him important, not his crown. His daughter is not the stereotypical Cajun brown-eyed brunette, but a blue-eyed blonde. She is a rare beauty, a "Jolie Blonde" of the sort that has long fascinated Cajun musicians and singers. Jean l'Ours eventually wins her over with his bravado and talent, and he addresses her father with no inkling of subordination. Though he can't match the king's riches, he wisely competes on his own turf, where he excels in ways admired by country people, farmers and hunters, by having superior pigs, bulls and hunting dogs. After he and his companions have won the final race, the king gives Jean l'Ours his money and his castle, effectively retiring from his position. Not to be outdone, Jean l'Ours gives the king his superior animals and a fine river to fish in during his retirement.

Je suis surement pas un conteur de contes, mais j'ai appris des contes, quand j'étais petit avec mon père et ma mère. Et mon papa, c'était un chanteur et c'était un raconteur de contes. Son nom, c'était Marcellus Deshotels. Et dans ce temps-là ils aviont pas beaucoup des affaires à faire d'autre chose que d'assir et se conter des contes. Et moi, j'ai appris une partie des contes. Et il y a un conte il contait, c'était pour Jean l'Ours et la fille du Roi.

Le Roi était beaucoup, beaucoup riche. Il était millionaire un tas de fois. Et il était beaucoup jaloux, beaucoup jaloux. Il avait une belle fille. Elle avait des grands cheveux jaunes, et les yeux bleus. Et il quittait pas personne parler avec sa fille. Et il avait tout le temps dit qu'il aurait fallu que quelqu'un la gagne pour la marier.

I'm certainly no storyteller, but I learned some stories when I was young from my father and my mother. My father was a singer and a storyteller. His name was Marcellus Deshotels. In those days, there wasn't much to do other than sit around and swap stories. And I learned some of those stories. And there was one story he told about Jean l'Ours and the king's daughter.

The king was very, very rich. He was a millionaire several times over. And he was very jealous, very jealous. He had a beautiful daughter. She had long blonde hair and blue eyes. And he didn't allow anyone to talk to his daughter. He had always said that it would be necessary to win her in order to marry her.

Et il y avait un jeune homme, son nom, c'était Jean l'Ours. Et il a déménagé au ras de chez le Roi un jour. Et Jean l'Ours avait beaucoup de la capacité. Et il était beaucoup glorieux de ça il avait. Il avait les plus beaux cochons il y avait. Tout ça Jean l'Ours avait, c'était le meilleur. Et il croyait qu'il avait le meilleur coureur il y avait. Et dans son organisation, il avait le Grand Coureur, le Grand Tireur, le Grand Souffleur, et le Grand Crieur, et le Bon Entendeur; il entendait beaucoup bien.

Ça se fait, un jour la fille du Roi a été, elle s'est baignée. Il y avait un beau lac, et elle allait les après-midi; elle s'est baignée. Et Jean l'Ours a approché, et il a tiré des pierres après.

Elle lui dit, "Jean l'Ours, je connais c'est toi qu'es là. Mais," elle dit, "si mon père t'attrape, il va couper ton cou!"

Il dit, "Je suis venu ici, la fille du Roi, pour te demander pour me marier." Il dit, "Je t'ai pas jamais vue, mais je connais que t'es réellement une belle fille." Il dit, "Je veux te marier."

"Bien, mais," elle dit, "tu peux pas me marier autrement que mon père, me dit que tu m'as gagnée," Et elle dit, "Si tu veux prendre tes chances, peut-être que tu pourrais me marier."

Ça se fait, un jour, il y a eu un encan de cochons, et le Roi a arrivé avec une belle bande de cochons. Et il a commencé à dire comment ses cochons étaient beaux, et comment ils estiont gros, ils estiont ci, ils estiont ça. Et Jean l'Ours lui a dit, "Mon Roi, c'est pas des beaux cochons que vous avez." Il dit, "Vous devriez voir les miens."

Ça se fait, il l'a invité, et le Roi a été, et surement ceux à Jean l'Ours étaient un tas plus beaux que les siens.

Et un jour, il a rejoint le Roi dans le bois, il était à la chasse. Et Jean l'Ours avait tué deux gros chevreuils. Et le Roi avait pas de

And there was a young man whose name was Jean l'Ours. And he moved next to the king one day. And Jean l'Ours was very capable. And he was proud of all he had. He had the most beautiful pigs in the land. All that Jean l'Ours had was the best. And he thought that he had the best runner in the land. In his organization, there was the Great Runner, the Great Shooter, the Great Blower, and the Great Yeller, and the Great Listener; he listened terribly well.

So one day, the king's daughter went to take a bath. There was a beautiful lake and she went there in the afternoons to bathe. And Jean l'Ours approached and threw stones near her.

She said to him, "Jean l'Ours, I know it's you who are there. But," she said, "if my father catches you, he will cut your throat!"

He said, "I've come here, daughter of the king, to ask you to marry me." He said, "I've never seen you, but I know that you are a very beautiful girl." He said, "I want to marry you."

"Fine, well, you can't marry me. I can't marry you unless my father tells me that you've won me." And she said, "If you want to take a chance, maybe you could marry me."

So one day, there was a hog auction, and the king arrived with a beautiful band of pigs. And he started saying how his pigs were beautiful, and how they were fat, they were this and they were that. And Jean l'Ours told him, "My king, those pigs that you have are not beautiful." He said, "You should see mine."

So he invited him over and the king went and, sure enough, the pigs of Jean l'Ours were much more beautiful than the king's own.

And one day, he met the king in the woods where he was hunting. And Jean l'Ours had killed two big deer. And the king

rien. Il avait pas tué rien. Il dit à le Roi, "Si t'aurais des chiens de chasse, des taïaux comme ça moi, j'ai, tu pourrais tuer un chevreuil."

Le Roi dit, "J'ai les meilleurs taïaux il y a qui chassent."

Ça se fait, Jean l'Ours a lâché ses taïaux, et dans peu de temps, ils ont ramené un chevreuil, et ils l'ont tué. Et il dit à le Roi, "J'aimerais marier ta fille."

Le Roi dit, "Jean l'Ours, tu peux pas marier ma fille. Ça prendrait des mille et des millions de piastres, et des bijouteries, et tout ça qu'il y aurait dans le monde, pour ma fille.

Jean l'Ours, il dit à le Roi, "Je vas te parier que mon coureur peut courir plus vite que le tien." Et le Roi avait le plus beau coureur, le plus vite il y avait. Il pouvait courir vite comme le vent. C'était un grand sauvage.

Ça se fait, un jour, ils ont eu un rendez-vous. Ils ont fait un rendez-vous et Jean l'Ours avait amené tous ses hommes avec lui. Il fallait ça court cinq cents milles. Ça se fait, Jean l'Ours avait son Grand Coureur, et le Roi avait son Grand Sauvage.

Ça se fait, quand le pistolet a craqué, le Grand Sauvage a parti loin devant le coureur à Jean l'Ours. Et dans l'après-midi tard, ils ont vu le sauvage qu'était après revenir et ça voyait pas l'homme à Jean l'Ours. Ça se fait, Jean l'Ours a appelé son Bon Entendeur. Il lui dit, "Mets ta tête sur la terre, peut-être tu vas l'entendre. Il est peut-être après dormir."

Ça se fait, le Bon Entendeur a mis sa tête par terre. Il dit, "Je peux pas l'entendre. Il y a trop de train." Il dit, "L'herbe est après élever." Ça se fait, il a été dans le brûlé, ayoù il y avait pas d'herbe. Il a mis sa tête, il dit, "Je l'entends, il est après ronfler."

Ça se fait, il dit à Bon Tireur, "Grimpe dans la tête du grand pin, et vois si tu peux le voir." Ça se fait, il a grimpé dans le grand

had nothing. He had killed nothing. He said to the king, "If you had hunting dogs like mine, you could kill a deer."

The king said, "I have the best hounds in the land."

So Jean l'Ours turned his hounds loose and in no time at all they returned with a deer and the hunters killed it. And he said to the king, "I would like to marry your daughter."

The king said, "Jean l'Ours, you can't marry my daughter. It would take thousands and millions of dollars, and jewels, and all the riches in the world to marry my daughter."

Jean l'Ours said to the king, "I'll bet you that my runner can run faster than yours." And the king had the finest runner, the fastest in the land. He could run like the wind. It was a Great Indian.

So one day, they had a rendezvous. They arranged a rendezvous and Jean l'Ours brought all of his men along with him. The race was to be 500 miles long. So Jean l'Ours had his Great Runner and the king, his Great Indian.

So, when the pistol shot rang out, the Great Indian took off way ahead of Jean l'Ours' runner. And late in the afternoon, they saw the Indian coming back, but they couldn't see Jean l'Ours' man. So Jean l'Ours called his Great Listener. He said to him, "Put your head on the ground, maybe you'll hear him. Maybe he's sleeping."

So the Great Listener put his head down on the ground. He said, "I can't hear him. There's too much noise." He said, "The grass is growing." So he went to a burnt spot, where there was no grass. He put his head down, he said, "I hear him. He's snoring."

So he said to Great Shooter, "Climb up to the top of that tall pine tree and look to see if you can see him." So he climbed in the

pin; il l'a vu. Il avait sa tête dessus un nœud de bois gras. Et il a pris sa mire, il était au dessus de deux cents miles. Il a pris sa bonne mire avec sa grande carabine; il a tiré et il a ôté le nœud de bois gras dessous la tête du Grand Coureur.

Et le Grand Crieur, il a crié, "Le sauvage est après venir si vitement. C'est l'heure. Faut tu viens."

Et l'homme à Jean l'Ours a parti pour courir, mais il avait son Bon Souffleur avec lui. Avant le sauvage a arrivé, il dit à Bon Souffleur, "Écoute, tu pourrais pas nous souffler une mer," il dit, "quelque chose pour l'arrêter?"

Il dit, "Il est assez au ras," il dit, "faudra je souffle juste dedans une narine parce qu'il y aura un tremblement de terre et," il dit, "je vas tout tuer tout le monde il y aura alentour d'icitte." Ça se fait, il a mis son doigt sur un bord de son nez et il a soufflé dans une narine, et ça a fait une crevasse qu'avait des mille de pieds de creux. Et les pierres et tout ça, ça tombait.

Il dit à son Grand Souffleur, "Resouffle," il dit, "une petite orage, un ouragan, pour l'empêcher d'arriver." En même temps, le Grand Coureur à Jean l'Ours a cassé la ligne, ils estiont moins qu'un demi-pouce de différence, mais il avait gagné.

Ça se fait, Jean l'Ours était planté. La fille du roi, elle est venue, elle s'est envoyée dedans ses bras. Elle dit, "Jean l'Ours, tu m'as gagnée. Je suis pour toi. T'as tout mon amour."

Ça se fait, le Roi, il a dit, "Jean L'Ours, faudra tu viens avec moi à la maison." Il dit, "J'ai des choses je veux te donner." Ça se fait, il l'a amené dans sa maison. Et il l'a amené dans une grande chambre qu'il y avait beaucoup, beaucoup des valises tout le tour de la chambre. Et il a ouvert ces valises, et ils estiont pleins des bijouteries, des rubis, et tout ça qu'tu peux t'imaginer qui valait des millions et des millions de piastres. Il dit,

tall pine; he saw him. He had his head on a pine knot. And he took sight; he was more than two hundred miles away. And he took his good sight with his long rifle; he shot and he knocked the pine knot from under the Great Runner's head.

And the Great Yeller yelled, "The Indian is coming so very fast. It's time. You've got to come."

And Jean l'Ours' man started to run, but he had his Great Blower with him. Before the Indian arrived, he said to Great Blower, "Listen, couldn't you blow us a sea," he said, "something to stop him?"

He said, "Well, he's so close," he said, "I'll have to blow through only one nostril because otherwise there will be an earth-quake and," he said, "I'll kill all the people around here." So he put a finger on one side of his nose and he blew through one nostril, and this made a split in the earth that was thousands of feet deep. And rocks—And everything was falling.

He said to his Great Blower, "Blow again," he said, "a little storm, a hurricane, to prevent him from arriving." At the same time, Jean l'Ours' Great Runner crossed the line, and they were less than half an inch apart, but he had won.

So Jean l'Ours was there. The king's daughter came and she threw herself into his arms. She said, "Jean l'Ours, you've won me. I'm all yours. You have all my love."

So the king said, "Jean l'Ours, you must come with me to my home." He said, "I have some things I want to give to you." So he took him home. And he took him into a big room where there were many, many suitcases all around the room. And he opened the suitcases and they were full of jewels, of rubies, and everything you can imagine that was worth millions and millions of dollars. He said, "Jean l'Ours, I give you this." And he said, "I give you my castle." And he said, "I

"Jean l'Ours, je te donne ça." Et il dit, "Je te donne mon *castle*." Et il dit, "Je te donne tout ce que j'ai; c'est pour toi."

Et Jean l'Ours, il a dit, "Je vous remercie pour ça que vous m'as donné, mais," il dit, "j'ai quelque chose que je veux vous donner, moi aussitte." Ça se fait, il lui a donné ses chiens. Il lui a donné ses bœufs. Il lui a donné ses cochons. Et il lui a donné une grosse rivière pour lui pêcher dedans. Et Jean l'Ours avait la fille du Roi.

Ça, c'est la finition du conte à Jean l'Ours et la fille du Roi.

said, "I give you my castle." And he said, "I give you all that I have; it's all yours."

And Jean l'Ours said, "I thank you for what you have given me, but, " he said, "I have some things I want to give you as well." So he gave him his dogs. He gave him his bulls. He gave him his pigs. And he gave him a big river to fish in. And Jean l'Ours had the king's daughter.

That's the end of the tale of Jean l'Ours and the king's daughter.

21. L'histoire de Sainte Geneviève / The Story of Saint Genevieve (Frank Couppel, Bayou Sorrel)

This tale is a variant of type 883A *The Innocent Slandered Maiden* and is related also to types 706 *The Maiden Without Hands* and 712 *Crescentia*, without developing the role of the girl's healer and without the element of amputation. Delarue noted four French versions and there are several versions in the Creole oral tradition of the islands of the Indian Ocean. Laval's Archives de Folklore had five French American variants of type 883A, which is also well-known in Spanish, German, Italian, Danish, Polynesian and Jewish oral traditions, among others. For an analysis, see Bolte and Polívka (I, p. 305, no. 1). For a study of the abandoned woman, see Stith Thompson, *The Folktale* (pp. 109–110 and 120–125). Compare also type 713* *The Warrior and his Wife* which develops a similar plot.

In her headnote to "Geneviève de Brabant" (*French Louisiana*, no. 1, pp. 19–21), Saucier refers to the medieval legend based on the story of Marie de Brabant, accused by her husband Louis IV and executed in 1256 (cf. René de Cérisier, *L'Innocence reconnue, ou Vie de Ste Geneviève de Brabant*, 1638). The short version presented by Saucier contains the same elements: the husband who goes away to war leaves his wife in the care of a king who tries to seduce her (type 713*); when she refuses, the king sends a letter to the husband accusing her of infidelity (motif K2117); the husband demands her execution, but she is abandoned in the forest instead (Q438, K512.2) where she lives for a number of years, nourished by the milk of a doe (cf. B535., T611.7); she and her child are at last found by the husband; the doe follows them and dies later on the tomb of her mistress (F981.6, B301.1).

This tale, generally long, is among the longest collected recently in Louisiana French tradition. Among the five versions in Laval's Archives de Folklore, there is a version by François Saint-Laurent of Gaspé, "Le Prince de Marinca" (coll. Charles-Marius Barbeau, ms. no. 117), which is 65 pages long in transcription. The name Geneviève is often associated

with the long-suffering heroine in French tradition (cf. "Conte de Geneviève," coll. Madeleine Doyon, ms. no. 10, Archives de Folklore).

Type 883A also exists in African tradition. Klipple reported two versions from the Hausa region including one from the Samali tribe, "The Girl Without Legs" in which a sultan leaves his daughter with a priest who then tries to kiss her. She is slandered and abandoned with her legs cut off. (Compare to Œdipus who is abandoned in the woods with his feet tied so tightly that they swell, rendering him unable to walk.) Her legs grow back and she marries the son of another sultan and finally finds her father, who has the priest's throat cut upon discovering the truth. In another African version, from the Soho tribe, there is a double slander: the same woman finds herself first banished by her father when her school teacher falsely accuses her of having slept with him, then again by her husband when a servant accuses her of the same transgression.

Il y a l'histoire de Ste. Geneviève. Ça, c'est une belle histoire, mais je peux pas la raconter, moi. C'était une toute petite fille. Depuis l'âge, elle allait voir ses amis, elle les traitait tous bien. Et quand elle a venu grande, elle s'a mariée.

Justement quand elle était mariée, la guerre s'a déclarée pour son mari. Et ils ont venu le prendre. Et là, il a dit qu'il fallait pas qu'elle se tracasse, qu'il allait parler au roi pour la soigner, pour prendre cas d'elle. Mais c'est que le roi, lui, il aurait voulu la prendre pour sa femme. Et elle voulait pas, jusqu'à ce que, quand le roi a vu ça, lui il a fait tuer son gardien qu'elle avait, et puis il l'a blâmée, elle. Ils l'ont mise en prison.

Là, quand elle a été en prison, la petite fille qu'elle avait guérie—elle avait guéri une petite fille qui était décomptée. Elle avait travaillé pour, et elle l'avait guérie. Ça fait que là, quand elle était vieille, elle l'a gardait tout le temps. C'était Geneviève, qu'ils l'appelaient. Et elle gardait Geneviève pareil comme sa mère.

Ça fait que là, elle était tournée tout à l'envers qu'elle était, qu'elle était criminelle, qu'elle fréquentait tous les hommes. Et là, son mari, quand il a lu cette lettre, il a cru que c'était vrai, lui. Il a fait une autre lettre pour envoyer au roi, lui dire que—et elle avait un petit—il a dit dessus la lettre qu'il

There's the story of Saint Geneviève. That's a beautiful story, but I can't tell it. There was a little girl. From the time she was old enough, she visited her friends. She treated them all well. When she grew old enough she married.

Just when she was married, war was declared and her husband was called to serve. They came to get him. And then, he said that she shouldn't worry, that he would speak to the king to have her protected, to take care of her. But it happened that the king wanted to take her for himself. And she did not want this, to the point where, when the king saw this, he had her guardian killed and he blamed her. They put her in prison.

Then when she was in prison, the little girl whom she had healed—she had healed a little girl who was considered hopeless. She had worked for her and had healed her. So then, when she was older, she kept her always with her. Geneviève was her name. And she looked upon Geneviève as a mother.

So then, she was treated as the opposite of what she really was, as though she were a criminal, as though she went out with men. And then, her husband, when he read the letter, he thought it was true. He wrote a letter to send to the king telling him to—and she had a child—he said in the letter that he

fallait qu'il détruit Geneviève et son petit parce qu'il voulait pas de souvenance si elle était tournée comme ça.

Là, il a rencontré un de ses *partners*. Il avait été *mail* la lettre. Il a rencontré un de ses *partners*. Il dit, "D'ayoù tu viens?" Il dit, "Tu sembles peineux."

"*Well*," il dit, et il lui conte l'affaire.

"Je peux pas croire que tu crois ça," il dit. "Tu crois pas que c'est vrai, ça? Moi, je sais que Geneviève était trop bonne pour faire des tours comme ça. Moi, à ta place, j'irai retirer cette lettre."

Ça fait qu'il a viré de bord. Il a été pour retirer la lettre, mais elle était partie. Ça fait, elle a été au roi. Ça fait que le roi—Geneviève était en prison—il a fait le cas paraître. Et il a lu la lettre au monde, ça que son mari disait, il fallait qu'il la détruit et tout. Et il a dit qu'il fallait que deux hommes, qu'il fallait qu'ils vont la prendre à onze heures le soir et puis aller la tuer, la détruire.

Mais la petite fille, elle était rendue grande et elle avait été au cas, celle-là qu'elle avait guérie. Et quand le cas a fini, elle a été à la prison. Elle a cogné à la fenêtre de la prison et Geneviève s'a levée. "Qui ce qui est là?" elle dit. Et là, elle lui a dit que c'était elle, elle se nommait, et qu'elle avait venu lui porter une triste nouvelle. Elle dit que, "Tu vas être tuée ce soir, et je voulais voir si tu voulais me donner des commandements, quelque chose pour que je dis à ton mari. Tu sais que je sais que tout ce qui se fait là, que c'est toute des menteries, mais c'est le roi qui veut ça."

Ça fait que, "Bien," elle dit, "va me chercher un cahier, des plumes et de l'encre. Je vas lui écrire une lettre." Ça fait qu'elle a écrit une lettre. Tu devrais voir tout ce qu'elle a dit sur cette lettre-là. Et quand elle a fini la lettre, elle dit, "Je te pardonne parce que je sais que c'est des mensonges que t'as eu de contés, parce que moi, j'ai pas rien sur ma

must kill Geneviève and her child because he wanted no memory of her if she had gone wrong.

Then he met one of his friends. He had gone to mail the letter. He met one of his friends. He said, "Where do you come from?" He said, "You look so full of pain."

"Well," he said, and he told him the story.

"I can't believe that you believe this," he said. "You don't believe this could be true? I know that Geneviève was too good to do such things. If I were in your place, I would get that letter back."

So he turned around. He went back to retrieve the letter, but it had left. So it went to the king. So the king—Geneviève was in prison—he brought the case to trial. And he read the letter to everyone, what the husband had written, that she should be killed and everything. And he said that two men should take her at eleven o'clock at night and kill her, put her to death.

But the little girl, whom she had cured, was grown up now and attended the trial. And when the trial ended, she went to the prison. She tapped at the prison window and Geneviève got up. "Who's there?" she said. And then she said that it was she, she named herself and said that she had come bearing sad news. She said, "You will be killed tonight, and I wanted to see if you wanted to give me a message, something that I should tell your husband. You know that I know that all this is a lie, but it's the king who wills it."

So, "Good," she said, "go and get me a tablet, pens and some ink. I'll write him a letter." So she wrote a letter. You should have seen all that she included in that letter. And when she finished the letter, she wrote, "I forgive you because I know that you were told lies, because my conscience is clear. With all that has happened, my conscience is

conscience. Tout ce qu'a été fait, j'ai pas rien sur ma conscience." Elle dit, "Ça a tout été fait par le roi, mais je te pardonne. Tout ce que te demande, c'est de secourir le monde, surtout les vieilles veuves." Elle a écrit toute espèces de choses.

Là, le soir, ils sont venus la prendre, et ils l'ont amenée dans le bois pour la tuer. Ça fait qu'elle, elle savait qu'ils allaient la tuer, mais ces bougres qui ont été la prendre, eux, ils savaient pas qu'elle savait. Et là, quand ils ont arrivé dans le bois, il y en a un qui dit, "*Well*, je veux que tu me donnes ton petit."

"Mais," elle dit, "quoi vous autres veux faire avec?"

Ça fait, il dit, "On a été envoyé par le roi pour te tuer, toi et ton petit, et on est obligé de le faire parce que si nous autres, on le fait pas, on va être tué."

"Mais," elle dit, "je veux vous autres me laisses parler un élan."

Alors ils ont dit, "Tu peux dire tout ce que tu veux."

"Bien," elle dit, "vous autres sais que ça, c'est tout des mensonges qu'il y a eu de contés. Moi, j'ai rien sur ma conscience. Ça a tout été fait par le roi." Elle dit, "Vous autres vois la lune?" C'était pleine lune. Elle dit, "Vous autres vois la lune, comment ce qu'elle est brillante? Mais à chaque fois que la lune sera pleine lune, que vous autres vas regarder, elle sera rouge de sang si vous autres me détruis."

Ho! C'est que ça les a travaillés joliment. Et elle dit, "Vous autres vois les feuilles de bois blanc qui tremblont? Vos visages vont trembler toute votre vie comme ça."

Ho! Ils ont dit, "*Well*, on est obligé de te tuer quand même, parce qu'il a dit qu'il fallait qu'on emporte tes yeux."

Mais elle dit, "Tuez ce chien qui vous suit, et puis ôtez-lui les yeux pour porter au roi."

"O, mais," ils disent, "il va reconnaître que c'est pas tes yeux."

clear." She said, "It was all the king's doing, but I forgive you. All that I ask is that you help people, especially old widows." She wrote all sorts of things.

Then, that night, they came to take her away, and they took her to the woods to kill her. So she knew that she would be killed, but the fellows who went to get her didn't know that she knew. And when they arrived in the woods, one said, "Well, I want you to give me your child."

"Well," she said, "what do you want to do with him?"

So he said, "We've been sent by the king to kill you and your child, and we are obliged to do it because if we don't, we will be killed."

"Well," she said, "I want you to let me speak for a while."

So they said, "You can say what you like."

"Fine," she said, "You know that those were all lies that were told. My own conscience is clear. It was all the king's doing." She said, "Do you see the moon?" The moon was full. She said, "Do you see how bright the moon is? Well, every time you look at the moon when it will be full, it will be blood red if you kill me."

Ho! This worried them considerably. And she said, "Do you see the trembling leaves on the white oak? Your faces will tremble that way the rest of your lives."

Ho! They said, "Well, we're obliged to kill you anyway, because he said that we were to bring back your eyes."

Well she said, "Kill that dog that is following you and then take out its eyes to take to the king."

"Oh, but," they said, "he will realize that they are not your eyes."

Elle dit, "Tracassez-vous pas. Le roi est bien tracassé asteur. Il voudra pas les voir, ces yeux-là." Elle dit, "Moi, je voudrais que vous autres me laisses ici dans le bois, ayoù je pourrais mourir par ma bonne mort. Vous autres aurais pas besoin de me tuer."

"Mais," ils disent, "si tu veux nous promettre—"

Elle dit, "Je vous promets de jamais ressortir."

Ils ont dit, "Si tu veux promettre de pas ressortir, on va te laisser." Et ils l'ont laissée.

Et quand ils ont arrivé au roi, ils ont présenté les yeux, mais il a dit qu'il voulait pas les voir, et qu'il voulait pas les revoir, eux, qu'il fallait qu'ils laissent la ville ce soir-là. Ils voulait pas les revoir dans la ville. Ça fait, les bougres ont été obligés de laisser la ville.

Là, la guerre a été et a été. Quand la guerre a fini, c'était le lendemain, la neige tombait. Elle s'a mis à marcher dans le bois; c'était un grand bois. Elle a trouvé une route d'une bêtaille. Ça fait qu'elle a dit en elle-même, "Je vas suivre cette route. Peut-être qu'elle a un abri en quelque part."

Elle a parti; elle a suit cette route-là. Elle a arrivé dans une place, ça dit que c'était une caverne, comme un rocher qu'il y avait, et il y avait un appartement là-dedans. Elle s'a fourrée là-dedans. Elle dit, "Well, on serait bien ici, mais on a pas rien à manger." Elle se disait à elle-même, "Well, il faudra—" Elle a laissé son petit là et elle a pris à roder à l'entour. Là, elle a trouvé de l'eau, une source d'eau qui coulait. Ça fait que là, ils avient de l'eau. "Mais," elle dit, "oui, mais, c'est pas tout. Juste avec de l'eau, on pourra pas vivre." Ça fait qu'elle s'a retourné dans sa caverne. Là, elle était là-dedans et le soir-là, c'était une brebis, une chevreuil qui a arrivé pour se fourrer dans la caverne, mais c'est que quand elle l'a vue, elle voulait pas rentrer. Elle a commencé à la caresser jusqu'à

She said, "Don't worry. The king is very troubled now. He will not want to see those eyes." She said, "I would like for you to leave me here in the woods where I will be able to die a natural death. You wouldn't need to kill me."

"Well," they said, "if you will promise us—"

She said, "I promise you that I will never go back."

They said, "If you will promise never to go back, we will leave you." And they left her.

And when they arrived before the king, they presented the eyes, but he said that he did not want to see them, and that he did not want to see the two men ever again, that they should leave the city that very night. He did not want to see them again in the city. So the fellows had to leave the city.

Meanwhile, the war went on and on. Then the war ended; the next day, snow was falling. She started walking in the forest; it was a big forest. She found the trail of an animal. So she said to herself, "I'll follow this trail. Maybe there's a shelter somewhere."

She left; she followed the trail. She arrived at a place where there was a cavern, like a rock and there was a room inside. She went inside. She said, "Well, it would be nice in here, but there is nothing to eat." She was talking to herself, "Well, I'll have to—" She left her child there and she began to wander nearby. There she found water, a spring which was flowing. Then they had water. "Well," she said, "this is fine, but we need more. We can't live just on water." So she returned to the cavern. Then she was in there, and that night, a doe came to the cavern, but when it saw her, it didn't want to come in. She started caressing it until finally it came in. And it had a swollen udder. It had lost its young. She caressed it until she was able to start milking it to have some milk. So

qu'elle a rentré. Et elle avait un gros pis; elle avait perdu ses petits. Ça fait qu'elle l'a tant caressée jusqu'à qu'elle a commencé à la traire pour avoir du lait. Ça fait que ça donnait du lait à elle et son petit.

Et là, elle a resté là-dedans. Il y a pas beaucoup d'apparences que ça peut se faire, mais ça dit qu'elle a resté là sept ans de temps. Et son petit était moyen. Ils parlaient tout le temps.

Ça fait qu'un jour, elle a tombé bien malade. Ça fait qu'elle dit, "Moi, je vas mourir."

Il dit, "Mourir, mais quoi c'est ça, mourir?"

"Mais," elle dit, "mourir, quand tu vas voir que je vas plus souffler, et je vas plus parler, et je vas plus battre mes yeux, mes lèvres vont venir noires, je serai morte. Tu pourras partir à t'en aller droit sur le soleil. Tu marcheras toute la journée. Ça va te prendre deux jours. Quand tu vas arriver que la nuit va te prendre, tu couches là et tu repartiras le lendemain matin."

"Ho!" il dit. "Non, moi, je vas pas faire ça. J'aime mieux rester avec les bêtes farouches."

"O," elle dit, "non. Tu peux pas faire ça. Faut que tu me promets de t'en aller."

"Mais," il dit, "quand moi, je vas arriver là-bas, ils vont faire avec moi pareil comme ils ont fait avec toi. Ils vouliont te tuer."

Elle dit, "O, non! Ils vont pas te tuer. Tu vas demander pour ton père. Il va te ramasser et tu vas être bien soigné."

"Bien, mais," il dit, "je te promets, alors. Je vas faire ça."

Mais là, elle est pas morte. Elle a revenu mieux. Ça fait que quand elle a été mieux, elle commençait à rodailler encore. Ça fait qu'un jour, elle dit, "Demain matin, moi, je vas partir de bon matin. Je vas marcher toute la journée. Quand je crois qu'il va être midi, je vas virer de bord, essayer de trouver des fruits." Il y avait des fruits marrons, mais ils

this provided milk for her and her child.

So she stayed there. It doesn't seem possible, but they say that she stayed there seven years. And her child was growing. They talked all the time.

So one day, she became very ill. So she said, "I'm going to die."

He said, "Die, what is it to die?"

"Well," she said, "dying, when you see that I'm no longer breathing, and I'm no longer talking, and I'm no longer blinking, my lips will turn black, I'll be dead. You will leave and follow the sun. You will walk all day long. This will take you two days. When you see that night is falling, you will sleep there and leave again the next day."

"Ho!" he said. "No, I won't do that. I would prefer to stay here with the wild animals."

"Oh," she said, "no. You can't do that. You must promise me that you will go away."

"But," he said, "when I arrive there, they will do to me what they did to you. They will want to kill me."

She said, "Oh, no! They won't kill you. You will ask for your father. He will take you in and take good care of you."

"Fine, then," he said, "I promise you. I will do this."

But then she didn't die. She got better. So when she was better, she started wandering again. And one day, she said, "Tomorrow morning, I am going to leave very early. I'll walk all day long. When I think it is noon, I'll turn around to come back, trying to find fruit." There was wild fruit, but they had eaten everything nearby. She said, "There is

les avaient tous dépensés alentour. Elle dit, "Il y a plus de fruits ici. Je veux essayer d'en trouver d'autre. Mais tu resteras dans la caverne. Sors pas avant que je reviens."

"O!" il dit, "je vas rester."

Ça fait qu'elle a parti le matin et quand elle a arrivé le midi, qu'il était proche midi, il y avait une petite montagne. Elle a monté sur la montagne et là elle a vu un loup qui s'en venait avec un mouton. Il l'apportait. Mais il a arrivé là au ras d'elle. Elle avait toujours une branche, elle portait un bâton. Elle lui a flanqué un coup de branche. Il a roulé en bas en hurlant. Là, il a parti à s'en aller. Là, elle a pris le mouton pour essayer de lui faire boire du lait—elle s'avait emporté du lait—mais le mouton a crevé. Ça fait qu'elle dit, "*Well*, je vas essayer d'enlever la peau si je peux trouver quelque chose pour"—Ça fait qu'elle a descendu en bas de la montagne et elle a trouvé de quoi qui coupait. Elle a remonté, elle lui a ôté la peau et puis là, elle se l'a mise sur le dos, et elle a parti à s'en aller.

Et quelques jours avant ça, elle était assise, elle était bien jongleuse. Elle a sorti. Il dit, "Quoi ce qu'il y a, maman? On dirait que t'es jongleuse."

"Oui," elle dit, " "toi, tu t'aperçois pas. Moi, j'ai plus de linges pour me couvrir et ayoù ce que je vas en prendre?"

"Ho! Mais si le Bon Dieu est aussi bon que tu dis," il dit, "Il va te donner du linge." Elle a été obligée de sourire.

Là, quand elle a eu enlevé la peau de mouton, elle s'en a retourné. Et elle a arrivé tard le soir. La nuit était pour prendre. Quand elle a arrivé un peu près, elle a crié. Le petit, qui était dans la montagne, il a sorti. Il a parti à l'autre bord quand il l'a vue. Il a viré de bord en criant. Il l'avait pas reconnue. Là, elle a crié dessus, elle s'a fait connaître.

"Oui, mais," il dit, "pardieu, quoi ce que t'as sur le dos, cette affaire que tu portes? C'est pour ça que je t'ai pas reconnue."

no more fruit here. I want to try to find some more. But you stay near the cavern. Don't come out until I return."

"Oh!" he said. "I'll stay."

So she left in the morning and when it was almost noon, there was a little mountain. She climbed up onto the mountain and she saw a wolf coming with a sheep. It was carrying it. And it came right next to her. She always had a branch, she carried a stick. She hit it with the branch. It rolled down howling. Then it ran away. Then she took the sheep and tried to make it drink some milk—she had brought along some milk—but the sheep died. So she said, "Well, I'll try to skin it, if I can find something to"—So she went down the mountain and found something to cut with. She went back up and skinned it and then she put the skin on and left.

Several days before this, she had been sitting, and thinking deeply. She went out. He said, "What's the matter, mother? You seem pensive."

"Yes," she said, "you don't notice, but I no longer have any clothes to wear and where will I find something?"

"Ho! Well if God is as good as you say," he said, "He will provide you with clothes." She had to smile.

When she had skinned the sheep, she returned. She arrived late in the evening. Night was falling. When she arrived fairly close, she called out. The child, who was in the cave, came out. He ran away when he saw her. He turned around crying. He didn't recognize her. Then, she called out to him; she made herself known.

"Yes, but," he said, "by God, what is that on your back, what are you wearing? That's why I didn't recognize you."

Mais elle lui a conté l'affaire pour le mouton.

"O! mais," il dit, "je t'ai dit que le Bon Dieu aurait pas te laissée comme ça." Elle voulait se faire une robe avec ça.

Là, le cavalier, lui quand il s'en a revenu, la petite fille a été de ville en ville pour lui donner la lettre. Geneviève lui avait cacheté la lettre, et elle lui avait donné. Et elle lui avait dit de pas la donner avant que son mari arrive et de lui donner dans ses mains. Ça fait, quand il s'en a revenu, elle a marché loin de chez eux pour lui donner la lettre. Et il a lu la lettre. Il a lu tout ce que Geneviève lui avait dit dessus. Là, il a vu que c'était vrai, ça que. . . .

Ça fait, quand ils ont arrivé où ce qu'il avait pour débarquer, le roi était là. Et il fallait qu'il ôte le pied de dedans l'estrier pour qu'il descend de sur le cheval. Ils étiont tous sur des chevaux. Et quand il a été pour lui ôter son pied, il dit, "Touche pas mon pied, criminel que t'es." Au roi, il a dit ça. Il dit, "Avoir tout conté les mensonges que tu m'as contés, me faire condamner ma Geneviève. Quand on va rentrer dans le château, toi, tu vas pas monter sur le *stage*. C'est moi qui vas monter. C'est moi qui vas parler. Toi, tu vas aller dans la prison où ce que Geneviève était." Il a dit tout ça au roi.

Ça fait que là, quand ils ont rentré, le bougre, lui, il a monté sur le *stage* et il a lu la lettre que Geneviève avait écrit au monde. Tout ce qui est dessus. Eux devaient entendre tout ce qu'elle avait dit. Jusqu'à la, ça a passé comme ça. Là, lui, après de ça, ils faisiont des belles parties, ils l'invitaient, mais il voulait jamais aller. Ça fait qu'un jour, il dit, "Si vous autres veux aller à tel et tel bois," il dit (c'était là que Geneviève aurait été tuée, il croyait), "là j'irai."

"Bien, mais," ils ont dit, "on va aller là." Ça fait qu'ils ont parti avec des mulets et des charrettes et des bagages et ils ont été dans ce

So she told him about the sheep.

"Oh! well," he said, "I told you that God wouldn't leave you like that." She wanted to make herself a dress with it.

Meanwhile, the knight, when he returned, the little girl searched for him from town to town to give him the letter. Geneviève had sealed the letter and given it to her. And she had said not to give it to anyone until her husband returned and to give it to him in his very hands. So when he returned, she walked far away from her home to give him the letter. And he read the letter. He read all that Geneviève had written there. And he saw that it was true, that. . . .

So when they arrived where they were to dismount, the king was there. And he had to take his foot out of the stirrup to get down from his horse. They were all on horseback. And when he went to help him dismount, he said, "Don't touch my foot, criminal that you are." He said this to the king. He said, "After all the lies you told me, causing me to condemn my Geneviève. When we get back to the castle, you will not take the podium. I will take it. I will talk. You will go to the same prison as Geneviève." He said all this to the king.

So when they went inside, the fellow mounted the podium and read the letter that Geneviève had written before all the people. Everything that was in it. They had to listen to all that she had written. Until then, everything had been allowed to slip by. Then afterwards, they gave fine parties and invited him, but he never wanted to go. So one day, he said, "If you would like to go out to a certain forest," he said (this is where Geneviève supposedly had been killed, he thought), "then I would go."

"Fine, well," they said, "we'll go there." So they left with mules and carts and baggage and they went into that forest and they made

bois-là, et ils ont bâti un camp et ils ont commencé à chasser, faire la chasse.

Ça fait qu'un jour, il chassait à cheval, lui, mais il allait toujours dans le bois à l'entour où il croyait Geneviève avait été tuée. Ça fait qu'un jour qu'il voit un chevreuil, une brebis, enfin. Il essayait de l'approcher pour la tirer, mais elle s'échappait toujours. Ça fait qu'il a amarré son cheval et il a parti par derrière et il l'a suit jusqu'à la caverne ayoù ce qu'elle se tenait. Là, elle s'a fourrée dans la caverne, et il a été tout doucement à la porte. Il voulait tuer la brebis. Là, Geneviève était là dedans. Elle a sorti. Elle dit, "Monsieur, tuez pas ma brebis. C'est la vie de moi et mon petit, ça."

Là, il l'a reconnue lui. Il dit, "O, Geneviève! Retire-toi de moi. Je sais que c'est pas toi. C'est ton esprit qui me parle. Ça peut pas être toi."

Là, elle l'a reconnu. Elle dit, "O, *Lord!*" Il s'appelait Lebouche. Elle dit, "O, Lebouche! C'est moi-même. Touche voir ma main."

Il touche sa main, et il dit, "Mais oui, ta main est bien glacée. Il y a plus de vie dans toi du tout. C'est juste ton esprit qui parle."

Elle a dit, "O, non! Je te garantis que c'est moi. Regarde mon alliance que tu m'as donnée à l'autel de l'église quand on s'a marié." Et il voulait pas la reconnaître quand même. Elle s'a levé les yeux aux ciel et elle a demandé au Bon Dieu qu'il peuve la reconnaître. Là, ça fait qu'il a venu qu'il l'a reconnue.

"Bien mais," il dit, "on va prendre le cheval et on va s'en aller." Ça fait qu'ils ont parti.

Quand ils ont arrivé où ce qu'était leur *gang*, ils se sont tous rassemblés et ils ont parti, mais la brebis les suivait. Ça fait qu'ils ont été chez eux et il a préparé une bâtisse à cette brebis pour la mettre dedans, et il la soignait bien. Pauvre Geneviève, ça faisait

camp and started hunting.

So one day, he was hunting on horseback, but he always went to the part of the forest where he thought Geneviève might have been killed. So one day, he saw a deer, a doe, in fact. He tried to approach it to shoot it, but it kept getting away. So he tied his horse and he took off the back way and followed it to the cavern where it lived. Then it went inside the cavern, and he went very quietly up to the opening. He wanted to kill the doe. And Geneviève was inside. She came out. She said, "Sir, don't kill my doe. It's the livelihood of my son and me."

Then he recognized her. He said, "Oh, Geneviève! Go away from me. I know it can't be you. It's your spirit talking to me. It can't be you."

Then she recognized him. She said, "Oh, Lord!" His name was Lebouche. She said, "Oh, Lebouche! It is I. Here, touch my hand."

He touched her hand and said, "Well, yes, your hand is icy. There is no life in you at all. It's only your spirit talking."

She said, "Oh, no! I assure you that it is I. Look at my wedding ring, the one you gave me at the altar of the church when we were married." And he still didn't want to admit it was she. She raised her eyes to heaven and asked God that he should recognize her. Then he finally recognized her.

"Well, then," he said, "we'll take the horse and we'll leave." And they left.

When they arrived at the camp, they gathered together and they left, but the doe followed them. So when they arrived home, he prepared a home for the doe to live in, and he took good care of it. Poor Geneviève had been milking it for seven years. It was a

sept ans de temps qu'elle l'avait trait. C'était une bonne laitière. Ça fait, il l'a soignée pareil comme si elle aurait été une de leurs enfants.

Là, un jour, Geneviève est morte. Et ils ont parti l'enterrer. Et la brebis les a suit. Elle s'a couchée sur la tombe. Et là, il allait la chercher. Il l'emmenait chez lui. Il lui offrait toute espèce de bon manger. Elle voulait pas manger. Elle se virait de bord. Elle retournait. Elle se couchait sur la tombe. Mais là, elle a crevé sur la tombe de Geneviève.

Là, ça finit l'histoire, mais j'en conte pas la moitié.

good provider of milk. So he took care of it as though it were one of their own children.

Then one day, Geneviève died. And they went to bury her. And the doe followed them. It lay down on the tomb. And then he went to get it. He brought it back home. He offered it all sorts of good things to eat. It didn't want to eat. It would turn around and return to lay down on the tomb. And then, it died on Geneviève's tomb.

There, that's the end of the story, but I only tell half of it.

22. Fin Voleur / The Master Thief (Stanislaus "Tanisse" Faul, Cankton)

This variant of type 1525A *The Master Thief* is the longest of this collection, linking several episodes of clever theft. For an analysis, see Bolte and Polívka (III, p. 33 and following, p. 379, p. 390 [no. 2] and p. 393). Compare also Grimm no. 192, "The Master Thief." Tales of the master thief abound throughout the world. Type 1525 is one of the most popular English-language tales in the South. See, for example, Carl Lindahl's two studies, "Who is Jack?" in *Fabula* 29 (1988): 380–382; and "Jack, My Father, and Uncle Ray (1994).'" It is also popular in French and Creole oral traditions. Laval's Archives de Folklore reported 56 variants. Flowers mentioned 21 West Indian versions, though most of them fall better under type 1 *The Theft of Fish*. Several of the versions (from Andros, Sainta Lucia, and Nevis) present the episode involving the disguised man who steals from the king. In the Jamaican and Guadeloupan versions (Parsons II, no. 102, "Maît'e volé'"), the last episode involving the exchange of places in the sack (cf. type 1737 *The Parson in the Sack to Heaven;* motif K842). Petit Jean is cast in stories of the same sort from the Indian Ocean islands. Burrison has a Georgia variant, "Jack the Rogue" (p. 137–140), which ends after the wedding test. Another tale in Burrison's collection, "Whistlin' Jimmy" (p. 143–145), a variant of type 1535 *The Rich and the Poor Peasant*, ends with the sack exchange episode.

In "Fin voleur ou les pantoufles d'or," a French American version from Missouri (Carrière, no. 65), the storyteller described thievery as a profession, which seems to be an important part of this type. The hero, who has the same nickname as the one in this Louisiana variant, leaves home to learn a trade in order to qualify for the hand of the emperor's daughter. He learns to steal and passes several tests required by the emperor (stealing a pair of oxen, a horse, and the sheet from the queen's bed) to win the hand of the princess. Stealing as a trade is also found in "Jack and the Doctor's Girl" (Chase, *Jack Tales*, no. 13), in "Le Méquier à p'tsit Jean (Dorrance, *The Survival of French in the Old Mines District of Ste*

Geneviève, pp. 115–116), and in "Jack qui prend le trade de voleur" (Archives de Folklore, coll. Bouthillier / Labrie, no. 2334, du Nouveau-Brunswick).

Another name often associated with the master thief in French American oral tradition is Roclore (Raquelore). It is common in versions of the tale from Québec and the Acadian Maritimes. Saucier included two variants of this type in *Folk Tales from French Louisiana* (nos. 14 and 15), both with Roclore as the thief. Calvin Claudel had two more variants in *Fools and Rascals*; one starred Franck Rascal and the other, Roclos.

In the following variant, Fin Voleur learns his trade and then rejoins his family to help save it from dire straits. He attracts the attention of the king by audaciously sending for the king's scales to weigh his wagon full of gold. He then succeeds in stealing the king's horse (putting the guards to sleep with an intoxicating liquor), his cattle herd, and the queen's wedding band and the sheet from her bed (by disguising a pig as himself). The king finally arrests him and has him put in a sack to be drowned in the river, but he escapes by tricking another into taking his place. In the end, he succeeds in having the king and his guards thrown into the river instead. They are duped into thinking that that is where he got his beautiful horse. Brandon had four versions of the exchange of places in the sack (K840) in her collection from Vermilion Parish in Louisiana (II, nos. 29 to 32, pp. 306–313), and another, told by Creole narrator Enola Matthews, appears in *Folktales of Louisiana*.

Il y a l'histoire de Fin Voleur, mais c'est proche un embarras, tellement c'est long.

C'était un homme et une femme. Ils étaient beaucoup pauvres et ils avaient trois petits garçons, trois garçons. Il y en a un qui était petit encore. Ça se fait, les deux grands ont dit, "On peut pas le faire comme ça. Pap peut pas nous donner une vie à les trois." Il dit à son frère, "Moi et toi, on va partir, chacun un cheval, et les premiers deux chemins on va rencontrer, on va prendre chacun un."

"O!" le petit dit, "moi, je veux aller aussi et on va trouver trois chemins."

"O!" ça dit, "tu peux pas venir. Toi, t'es trop petit."

"O!" il dit, "ouais, je veux aller."

Ça fait, ils l'ont mis en arrière d'un de leurs chevaux et ils ont partis. Ça fait, ça venait manière sur l'après-midi, ils ont rencontré un trois-chemins. Ils l'ont prêché, mais il voulait son chemin lui aussi. Ça part, ils ont pris chacun leur chemin. Ils ont cherché des *jobs*. Lui, la nuit l'a pris, le petit,

There's the story about Fin Voleur, but it's almost a bother, it's so long.

There was a man and a woman. They were very poor and they had three little boys, three sons. One of them was still little. So the two older ones said, "We can't make like this. Pop can't support the three of us." One said to the other, "You and I will leave, each on horseback, and the first fork in the road we come to, we'll split up."

"Oh!" said the youngest, "I want to go too and we'll look for a three-way fork."

"Oh!" they said, "you can't come. You're too young."

"Oh!" he said, "yes, I want to go."

So they put him up on horseback behind one of them and they left. So by the afternoon, they finally found a three-way fork in the road. They pleaded with him, but he insisted on going his way as well. They left, each taking a fork in the road. They looked for jobs. Night fell on the youngest who was

à pied. Il s'a assis sur le bord du chemin. Il pleurait. Il y a deux voleurs qui passaient, à cheval les deux. Ils entendaient cet enfant-là pleurer. Ça fait, ils ont été. Ils ont arrêté voir, et il a dit son histoire. Là, ça a dit, "Si tu veux te mettre fin voleur, on va te prendre et on va t'emmener avec nous autres."

"*Well,*" il dit, "*all right.*" Ils l'ont emmené avec eux autres. Ils ont fait leurs vols. Ils ont rentourné. Ils l'ont soigné. Ils l'ont élevé. Quand il est devenu assez fort, ils l'ont envoyé voler comme eux autres. Et il portait le nom de Fin Voleur.

Mais ils s'avaient jamais rencontré, eux autres les trois, avant lui, il était homme. Il était vieux. Il a venu assez *smart* dans les voleurs, eux autres, ils l'ont mis lui le *boss,* puis il les envoyait ayoù il voulait voler. Il a eu assez d'argent. Il s'a pris une grosse paire de beaux chevaux et un wagon. Il les a dit, il les envoyait assez loin que ça lui donnait plein de temps de faire des rassemblements. Eux autres, ils étaient après revenir, il fallait qu'il fait à souper. Et ils auriont fait un souper pour eux autres le soir.

Quand il était petit, il avait attrapé un coup de pied de cheval. Un cheval l'avait cogné sur le front. Ça lui faisait une marque. Ça fait, il avait gardé son chapeau par dessus la marque. Il a chargé son wagon de piastres. Il en a mis plein, mais il l'a couvert. Il a attelé ses chevaux, puis il a parti, lui. Il a été chez sa maman. Il a arrivé là-bas, ses frères étaient là. Mais il avait son chapeau. Il dit au monde, il dit, "Je pourrais rester ici à soir?"

"Mais," ils ont dit, "sûr, tu peux rester." Il a mis ses chevaux dans l'hangar. Il a dételé son wagon. Il a rentré.

La vieille femme était tracassée. Elle avait le souper de paré. Elle dit, "Je sais pas quand mon garçon va arriver; j'espère l'autre." Et lui le disait pas. Ça fait, tout d'un escousse, ça dit, "Mais nous, on va souper. Quand lui, il va arriver, il va manger." Ils se sont mis à table. Il dit, "Regardez la marque ici."

on foot. He sat by the side of the road. He was crying. Two thieves happened by, both on horseback. They could hear a child crying. So they went. They stopped to see, and he told them his story. Then they said, "If you would like to become a master thief, we'll take you with us."

"Well," he said, "all right." They took him with them. They stole. They returned. They took care of him. They raised him. When he was old enough, they sent him to steal just like them. And he bore the name Fin Voleur [Master Thief].

But they never met again, the three brothers, until he was a grown man. He was older. He had become rather smart among the thieves, and they had made him the boss, and he sent them where he wanted them to steal. When he had enough money, he took a big pair of beautiful horses and a wagon. He told them, he sent them so far away that he would have plenty of time to get his things together. They would come back and he had to cook supper for them. They would have supper together that night.

When he was little, he had been kicked by a horse. A horse had kicked him on the forehead. This had left a mark. So he had kept his hat on to hide the mark. He loaded his wagon with money. He put a lot on it, but he covered it. He hitched his horses and he left. He went to his mother's house. He arrived and his brothers were there. But he had his hat on. He said to everyone, he said, "Could I stay here tonight?"

"Well," they said, "sure, you can stay." He put his horses up in the barn. He unhitched his wagon. He went in.

The old woman was worried. Her supper was ready. She said, "I don't know when my son will arrive; I'm waiting for the other one." And he said nothing to her. So suddenly they said, "Well, we'll just eat. When he arrives, he'll eat." They sat at the table. He said, "Look at this mark."

O! Ça les a fait une excitation, voir que c'était lui qui était revenu. Ça fait, ils ont fait leur veillée, magnifique. Le lendemain matin, —eux autres restaient au près de leur roi. Le Roi était pas loin. Le lendemain matin, il dit à sa mère, il dit, "Maman, tu vas aller chez le Roi demander pour ses balances pour peser mon argent."

Elle dit, "Mon garçon," elle dit, "non, ça va pas faire."

Il dit, "Ouais, va." Elle a été.

Le Roi dit, "Ah, c'est ça, et il est un fin voleur."

Elle dit, "Ouais, je connais pas." Elle dit, "C'est un tas d'argent, un tas d'argent, un wagon plein."

"Mais," il dit, "regarde. Amène les romaines et pèse son argent. Qu'il le pèse. Mais il a pour venir à soir voler mon cheval dans l'écurie avec la garde tout le tour."

Hmmm.

Elle est arrivée en pleurant.

Il dit, "Qui il y a, maman? Quoi il y a?"

"O!" elle dit, "je vas pas te dire, parce que tu peux pas le faire."

Il dit, "Maman, j'ai fait des tours *smart*." Il dit, "Je peux le faire, ouais. Dis-moi."

Elle dit, "Le Roi dit qu'il faut tu vas à soir voler son cheval dans l'écurie avec la garde tout le tour."

"O! Ça, c'est pas rien, Maman."

Elle dit, "Tu peux pas."

Il dit, "Tu vas voir."

Il s'a préparé un *hack* et il a attelé un de ses chevaux dessus. Il a mis toute qualité de boissons, mais tout en espoir pour les endormir. Les boissons dans des bouteilles, il a mis tout ça dans son *hack*. Il a arrivé là l'après-midi tard.

"Hé!" il dit, "On dirait comme si vous avez quelque chose de guetté. Vous avez la garde tout autour du magasin."

Il dit, "Ouais, on est après espérer Fin Voleur venir voler le cheval."

Oh! They were excited to see that it was he who had come home. So they had their evening visit, it was magnificent. The next day—They lived next to their king's house. The king was not far away. The next day, he said to his mother, he said, "Mama, you'll go to the king and ask him for his scales to weigh my money."

She said, "My son," she said, "no, that won't do."

He said, "Yes, go." She went.

The king said, "Ah, so that's it and he's a master thief."

She said, "Yes, well, I don't know." She said, "There's a lot of money, a lot of money, a wagon full."

"Well," he said, "look. Take the scales and weigh his money. But he must come tonight to steal my horse from the stall with the guard posted all around."

Hmmm. . . .

She arrived in tears.

He said, "What's the matter, Mama? What's the matter?"

"Oh!" she said, "I'm not going to tell you because you can't do it."

He said, "Mama, I've done clever tricks." He said, "I can do it. Tell me."

She said, "The king says that tonight you must steal his horse from the stable with the guard posted all around."

"Oh! That's nothing, Mama."

She said, "You can't."

He said, "You'll see."

He made himself a hack and he hitched one of his horses to it. He loaded all sorts of drinks, all with a mind to putting them to sleep. Drinks in bottles, he put all of this in his hack. He arrived late in the afternoon.

"Hey!" he said, "it would seem that you have something under guard. You have a guard posted all around the barn."

One said, "Yes, we're waiting for Fin Voleur to come and steal the horse."

"O!" il dit. "Là, il peut pas le faire."

"O!" il dit. "Non, non, il le fera pas."

Et le vieux Roi, il restait à la maison. Il laissait les autres faire.

Il dit, "Mais regardez, venez boire un bon *drink*." Il dit, "Ça va vous réveiller. Ça va vous donner meilleur à guetter."

Le vieux bougre a goûté, et c'était bon. Il a bu un gros *drink*.

Il dit, "Ça vous gênerait que je vas donner un *drink* à les hommes là-bas qui sont après guetter?"

"O! Non, ça gêne pas."

Il a été. Il a dit ça, qu'il avait apporté de la boisson pour eux boire. Quand ils en ont bu, ça, ils ont tous dormi. Puis il a volé le cheval et il s'en a retourné.

Ça se fait, le lendemain matin, il dit à sa maman, "Maman," il dit, "allez dire à le roi de venir chercher son cheval." Il dit, "Moi, je veux pas le cheval."

Ça fait, elle a été, contente que peut-être ça aurait tout arrangé.

"Non," il dit, "je veux pas le cheval. Qu'il le garde, mais," il dit, "à soir, il faut il vient voler mon troupeau de bêtes avec la garde tout autour."

Là, elle voyait pas de chance. Elle a retourné en pleurant encore. Elle lui dit ça.

"Mais," il dit, "C'est pas rien. Je vas le faire."

Mais s'il allait pas, s'il volait pas ça, ils l'aurient pendu à neuf heures le lendemain matin. Il disait rien.

Elle dit, "T'as pas de chance."

Ça fait, il a guetté. Quand ils ont parti, deux hommes à cheval ont parti chercher les bêtes là-bas en arrière du bois, dans une grande savane. Il les a guettés. Quand ils ont parti, lui, il a été en arrière d'eux là-bas au commencement du bois. Quand ils ont sorti avec la bande de bêtes pour les ramener, ils ont vu un homme pendu. Il s'a pendu après un arbre. Il s'a pendu.

Ça dit, "Ah, ça doit être un autre fin

"Oh!" he said. "Now he can't do it."

"Oh!" he said. "No, no, he won't do it."

And the old king stayed in the house. He let the others take care of it.

He said, "Well, listen, come and have a good drink." He said, "It will wake you up. It'll help you to keep better watch."

The old fellow tasted and it was good. He took a big drink.

He said, "Would it bother you if I go and give a drink to the men over there keeping watch?"

"Oh! No, it won't bother."

He went. He said that he had brought drinks for them to drink. When they had drunk, it put them all to sleep. Then he stole the horse and he went home.

So the next day, he said to his mother, "Mama," he said, "go and tell the king to come and get his horse." He said, "I don't want the horse."

So she went, happy that maybe everything was resolved.

"No," he said, "I don't want the horse. Let him keep it, but," he said, "tonight, he must steal my herd of cattle with the guard posted all around."

Then she saw no hope. She returned weeping again. She told him this.

"Well," he said, "That's nothing. I'll do it."

But if he didn't succeed, if he didn't steal this, they would hang him at nine the next morning. He said nothing.

She said, "You don't have a chance."

So he watched. When they left, two men left on horseback to round up the cattle on the other side of the woods, on an open prairie. He watched them. When they left, he went behind them at the front of the woods. When they came out with the herd of cattle to lead them home, they saw a man hanging. He had hung himself in a tree. He had hung himself.

They said, "That must be another master

voleur. Pendu." Ça fait, ils ont *go ahead* avec leurs bêtes. Ça allait pas vite, tu sais. Quand ils ont dépassé assez loin, il a parti, il a été là-bas en avant là-bas. Il s'a rependu encore.

Ça a arrivé là. "Un autre! Ça, ça doit être deux fins voleurs qui étaient ensemble. Ils les ont attrapés et ils les ont pendus."

Quand ils ont quitté, il a retourné encore. Il a été loin en avant là-bas encore. Mais quand ils ont arrivé là-bas, ils ont dit, "Mais regarde un autre, ça, c'est le troisième." Ça dit, "Allons voir ayoù l'autre là-bas, combien loin ça donne."

Quand ils ont parti au galop, lui, il a justement poussé les bêtes chez lui là-bas.

Le lendemain matin, il dit à sa mère, il dit, "Va, dis à le roi je veux pas les bêtes. J'ai pas de place pour. Qu'il vient les chercher."

Ça a arrivé. "Ah," il dit, "non, mais," il dit, "je vas le prendre." Il dit, "À soir, il faut qu'il vient voler le drap sur le lit de ma femme, elle couchée dessus, et son alliance dans son doigt."

Ouf! Elle voyait pas de chance. Ça fait, elle lui dit ça.

Il dit, "C'est pas rien, ça non plus."

"O," elle dit, "quoi tu peux faire?"

Il s'en a été. Il s'a tué un cochon. Il a fait un bonhomme. Il a mis tous le débris du cochon-là, puis le sang. Il s'a fait un positif bonhomme! Il a mis un ressort après et une corde. Tous les autres étaient tous après guetter sur un bord. Il a venu par en arrière et il l'a mis acadiaque sur la barrière. Puis il a halé sur la corde comme s'il voulait traverser, mettre une jambe en long. Là, il la rehalait. Quand ils l'ont vu, ils l'ont défoncé.

"Mais," il dit, "là, on l'a, le coco, Fin Voleur. On l'a." Il dit, "Vous autres vas aller l'enterrer quinze pieds de creux."

Ils ont parti avec les pelles. Lui a été aussi en arrière. Ça fait, Fin Voleur, lui, dans

thief. Hanged." So they went ahead with their cattle. They weren't going fast, you know. When they had gotten far enough past him, he left and went on ahead. He hung himself again.

They arrived there. "Another one! They must be two master thieves who were together. They were caught and hanged."

When they left, he went again. He went far ahead again. And when they arrived there, they said, "Well, look, another one. That's the third." They said, "Let's go see the others. How far back were they?"

When they left at a gallop, he simply pushed the cattle to his house.

The next day, he said to his mother, he said, "Go and tell the king that I don't want his cattle. I don't have room for them. He may come and get them."

They arrived. "Ah," he said, "no, but," he said, I'll catch him." He said, "Tonight, he must come to steal the sheet from my wife's bed, with her lying on it, and the wedding ring from her finger."

Ouf! She didn't see a chance. So she told him this.

He said, "That's nothing either."

"Oh," she said, "what can you do?"

He left. He killed a pig. He made a mannekin. He put all the insides of the pig and the blood in it. He made an honest-to-God mannekin! He put an elastic band on it and a rope. All the others were watching on one side. He came from behind and placed it astraddle on the fence. Then he pulled on the rope as though it was trying to cross, putting one leg over. Then he pulled again. When they saw it, they burst it.

"Well," he said, "now we've got him, that rascal, Fin Voleur. We've got him." He said, "You all are going to go and bury him fifteen feet deep."

They left with the shovels. He [the king] went too, behind them." So Fin Voleur,

ce temps-là, il est rentré. La lampe était pas allumée. Il a fait semblant d'allumer la lampe. Il dit, "Là, on l'a." Il dit, " On l'a enterré quinze pieds de creux." Il a soufflé la lampe. Il a été se coucher. Là, il a poussé avec ses pieds. Quand il a eu le drap de poussé au pied là-bas, il dit, "Vieille, t'as ton alliance?"

"Mais," elle dit, "ouais."

Il dit, "Allons voir." Il dit, "Tu connais, il est assez malin." Elle lui a donné. Il dit, "Je vas aller à la lampe voir." Il a été à la lampe, fait comme s'il avait été la voir. Il l'a mis dans sa poche. Il l'a repassée au ras de la main de cette-là. Il dit, "O, laisse-moi aller voir. Pas sûr qu'il vont l'enterrer creux comme ça, non, si je vas pas."

Psht! Il a échappé avec le drap et l'alliance de la femme.

Ça fait, le lendemain matin, il fallait la vieille femme va pour lui ramener ça. Il l'a pas voulu. Il dit, "Non, on va l'attraper." Et il dit, "Pour à soir, on veut le noyer."

Là, elle voyait pas de chance là, sûr. Si eux le coursaient, il fallait eux l'attrapent. Ça fait, lui, il a été assez malin. Il s'a préparé une chandelle. En cachette. Il a été, puis il a mis la chandelle allumée au bas de la saule de la maison. Ça fait, pour l'heure il s'aura laissé attrapé, la maison aurait été après brûler. Ça fait, ils ont venu. Ils l'ont attrapé. Ils l'ont mis dans un sac et ils ont parti avec à pieds, tu connais, l'apporter. Il fallait le noyer dans la rivière. Ça fait, il y en a un qui dit, "Cô! La grosse boucane là-bas!"

Ça dit, "Ouais!"

"Mais," il dit, "mais, ça, c'est ma maison, d'après moi, qui est en feu." Ça fait, ils ont tout foutu le sac là et ils ont parti au feu. Ça fait, tout à l'heure, le bougre a entendu des chaînes et des colliers, tu connais. Il savait quelqu'un était après passer avec des chevaux attelés avec des agrès.

Il disait, "Je vas pas marier la fille du roi! Vous autres peux me noyer mais je marieras

during this time, came back. The lamp was not lit. He pretended to be lighting the lamp. He said, "Now we've got him." He said, "We buried him fifteen feet deep." He blew out the lamp. He went to bed. Then he pushed with his feet. When he had pushed the sheet to the foot of the bed, he said, "Wife, do you have your wedding ring?"

"Well," she said, "yeah."

He said, "Let's see." He said, "You know, he's so clever." She gave it to him. He said, "I'll go to the lamp to see." He went to the lamp, pretended that he was looking at it. He put it in his pocket. He passed it next to her hand. He said, "Oh, let me go and see. I'm not sure that they'll bury him deep enough if I'm not there."

Psht! He slipped away with the sheet and the woman's wedding ring.

So the next morning the old woman had to go to take these back to the king. He didn't want them. He said, "No, we'll catch him." And he said,"Tonight we want to drown him."

Then she surely didn't see a chance. If they chased him, they were sure to catch him. So he was clever enough. He prepared a candle. In secret. He went and he placed the lighted candle under the beam of the house. So by the time that he would let himself be caught, the house would be burning. So they came. They caught him. They put him in a sack and they left with him on foot, you know, carrying him. They had to drown him in the river. So one of them said, "Ko! Look at all that smoke over there!"

They said, "Yeah!"

"Well," he said, "but, that's my house, seems to me, that is on fire." So they threw the sack there and they left to go to the fire. So after a while, the fellow heard chains and collars, you know. He knew that someone was passing with horses in harness.

He said, "I won't marry the king's daughter! You all can drown me, but I won't

pas la fille du roi!"

Le jeune homme—c'est que lui, il aurait voulu la fille du roi. Il dit, "Quoi il y a?"

Il dit, "Les autres veut je marie la fille du roi, mais," il dit, "ils pourront me noyer, mais je vas pas la marier."

Il dit, "Si je te sors et je te démarre, et tu vas emmarrer moi." Il dit, "Moi, je pourras la marier."

"O," il dit, "Tu peux la marier si tu veux, mais moi, je la veux pas." Le bougre l'a démarré du sac, puis il s'a fourré en dedans. Lui, il l'a bien amarré et puis il a monté sur les chevaux, deux beaux chevaux, puis il a parti et il s'a caché.

Tout à l'heure, ils ont revenu. Quand il les a entendus après venir, le jeune homme, il a commencé à crier, "Ouais, je vas la marier, la fille du roi! Ouais, je vas la marier!"

"Ah," le vieux Roi dit, "non, tu la marieras pas." Il dit, "On va te noyer, mon enfant-de-garce de voleur, de coquin." Ça fait, ils l'ont apporté. Ils ont été. Ils l'ont jeté, mais le bougre était caché. Là, ils s'en ont retourné. Tout à l'heure, eux étaient après charrer l'après-midi tard. L'autre bougre s'en revenait avec la paire de beaux chevaux et des belles agrès.

Ça fait qu'il dit, "Ça là, c'est Fin Voleur."

"O," le roi dit, "non, on l'a noyé, amarré dans un sac."

"Ah! O!" eux dit. "C'est lui!"

Il dit, "Allez voir, allez l'arrêter," il dit. "Il est libre asteur." Ils ont été. Ils l'ont arrêté. C'était *sure enough* lui. Ça fait, ils l'ont fait aller, mais il dit, "Comment t'as fait pour sortir?"

"Ah!" il dit, "je suis pas content. Vous autres m'as pas garroché tout à fait assez loin." Il dit, "J'ai pas pu choisir les chevaux que j'aurais voulu. Je pouvais pas, mais," il dit, "un peu plus loin, là, il y a des beaux chevaux."

Eux autres dit, "Plus beaux que ça?"

marry the king's daughter!"

The young man—the thing is that he would have liked to marry the king's daughter. He said, "What's the matter?"

He said, "They want me to marry the king's daughter, but," he said, "they can drown me, but I won't marry her."

He said, "If I let you out and untie you, and you tie me up," he said, "I could marry her."

"Oh," he said, "you can marry her if you like, but I don't want her." The fellow untied the sack, and then he got inside. He tied him up well, then he mounted the horses, two beautiful horses, and he left and hid.

After a while, they came back. When he heard them coming, the young man, he started yelling, "Yeah, I'll marry her, the king's daughter! Yeah, I'll marry her!"

"Ah," said the king, "no, you won't marry her." He said, "We're going to drown you, you son-of-a-gun of a thief, of a bum." So they carried him. They went. They threw him, but the real fellow was hiding. Then they came back. After a while, they were talking late in the afternoon. The other fellow was coming back with the pair of beautiful horses with the beautiful harnesses.

So he said, "There, that's Fin Voleur."

"Oh," the king said, "no, we drowned him tied up in a sack."

"Ah! Oh!" they said, "That's him!"

He said, "Go and see, go and stop him," he said. "He's free now." They went. They stopped him. It was sure enough him. So they made him go, and he said, "How did you manage to get out?"

"Ah!" he said, "I'm not happy. You all didn't throw me quite far enough." He said, "I wasn't able to choose the horses that I would have liked. I couldn't, but," he said, "a bit farther, there are some really beautiful horses."

They said, "More beautiful than that?"

Il dit, "Ouais."

Ça dit, "Tu pourrais nous mettre là?"

"O," il dit, "ouais."

Ça fait, il les a amarrés. Il y en avait trois. Il a amarré les trois, et puis il les a garrochés dans l'eau.

C'est un *smart*. Ça, c'est tout.

He said, "Yeah."

They said, "Could you get us there?"

"Oh," he said, "yeah."

So he tied them up. There were three of them. He tied all three up and then he threw them in the water.

There's a smart guy. That's all.

23. *Le voyageur / The Traveller (Évélia Boudreaux, Carencro)*

This tale is about a traveller who is looking for a cemetery in each land that he visits. This is a variant of type 726 *The Oldest on the Farm*. Baughman lists two versions, one from Missouri and the other from Michigan. In *American Negro Folktales* (no. 224, "The Old Man"), there is a variant in which the old man explains that he is weeping because his father has beaten him for having dared to answer his grandfather, who is himself so old that there is nothing left of him but a wrinkle. In this Louisiana variant, motif F571.2, "Sending to the older," is present, though not until the seventh generation. The longevity of the men that the traveller meets explains the absence of a cemetery in the town. This is a popular story in the South. Burrison has a Georgia variant, "Remarkable Longevity" (p. 194); Jones and Wheeler have an Appalachian version in *Laughter in Appalachia* (p. 95); and Randolph has an Ozark version in *Sticks in the Knapsack* (pp. 8–10).

There is a similar joke in Louisiana tradition which has the old man decline to take the traveller to meet his father because he is going to his own father's wedding. This version takes a different turn: the old man explains that his grandfather is marrying not because he wants to, but because he has to.

Une fois, il y avait une autre qu'était beaucoup riche, et il savait pas qu'est-ce faire avec sa vie. Un jour, il a décidé de voir le pays. Il a voyagé de place en place, de ville en ville, et toujours, il avait intérêt de visiter les cimetières. C'étaient les choses qui l'intéressaient le plus. Il aimait voir tout d'autres choses aussi, mais toujours, à chaque place, c'était le cimetière qui l'attirait.

Un jour, il a arrivé à une ville. Elle était beaucoup grande. Il cherchaient pour trouver le cimetière. Il allait auprès les églises. Il ne voyait pas de cimetière, et il était tracassé.

Once, there was another man who was very rich, and he didn't know what to do with his life. One day, he decided to see the country. He travelled from place to place, from city to city, and always, he was interested in seeing the cemeteries. The cemeteries are what interested him most. He liked to see everything else, but in each place, the cemetery was what really attracted his attention.

One day, he arrived in a city. It was very big. He looked to find the cemetery. He went to the churches. He saw no cemeteries, and he was troubled.

Il passe à une maison, et voit un beaucoup vieux homme qu'était après pleurer. Il dit, "Voilà ma réponse. Je vas connaître là ayoù le cimetière est." Il a arrêté. Il dit, "Bonjour, le vieux."

Il dit, "Bonjour."

Il dit, "Je vois vous êtes en peine. Vous avez perdu quelqu'un de votre famille?"

Il dit, "Non, j'ai pas perdu personne de ma famille." Il dit, "C'est papa qui m'a fouetté!"

"O! Votre papa vous a fouetté," il dit. "Ouais, mais quel âge vous avez?"

"Mais," il dit, "moi, j'ai quatre-vingt-dix ans."

"Et," il dit, "euh, vous veux dire votre papa vit toujours?"

Il dit, "Ouais, mon papa est en arrière la maison après parler avec mon grand-père." Il dit, "Il a été le rejoindre à la cour et," il dit, "ils sont après parler en travers de la barrière, à la mode des vieux."

"Mais," il dit, "j'aimerais beaucoup de voir votre papa et votre grand-père!"

Ce fait, il a amené le voyageur pour rencontrer son papa et son grand-père. Et il dit, "Je suis intéressé de connaître où le cimetière." Il dit, "Où je vas, c'est toujours les cimetières j'aime visiter, mais," il dit, "je vois à présent la raison que je trouve pas le cimetière." Il dit, "Le monde vit tellement vieux, il y en a pas pour enterrer!"

He passed a house, and saw a very old man who was crying. He said, "There's my answer. I'll find out where the cemetery is." He stopped. He said, "Hello, old man."

He said, "Hello."

He said, "I see that you are in pain. Have you lost someone in your family?"

He said, "No, I haven't lost anyone on my family." He said, "My father spanked me!"

"Oh! Your father spanked you," he said. "Yes, but how old are you?"

"Well," he said, "I'm ninety years old."

"And," he said, "uh—you mean to tell me that your father is still living?"

He said, "Yeah, my father is behind the house talking with my grandfather." He said, "He went to meet him at the fence and," he said, "they are talking across the fence just like old folks."

"Well," he said, "I would very much like to meet your father and your grandfather!"

So he took the traveller to meet his father and his grandfather. And he said, "I'm interested in finding the cemetery." He said, "Wherever I go, I always like to visit the cemeteries, but," he said, "I understand now why I haven't found the cemetery here." He said, "People live to be so very old that there is no one to bury!"

24. Cendrillonne / Cinderella (Martin Latiolais, Catahoula)

This tale is, despite its title, a variant not of 510A Cinderella, but of type 565 The Magic Mill (see Grimm, no. 103; Bolte and Polívka II, p. 438), a tale often told to explain how the sea became salty: a stolen mill produces salt uncontrollably, burying the thief and sinking his boat in the previously fresh-water ocean. Compare "Why the Sea is Salt," collected by Parsons (Antilles II, no. 50, p. 351) and "Comment la mer est devenue salée," collected by Marius Bareau (in the Archives de Folklore which had eight versions of this tale). In this Louisiana version, Cendrillonne is the name of the good witch who gives the

magic pudding pot to two poor orphans. Flowers lists another version collected by Parsons on Andros Island ("Feeding the Family," no. 91, p. 140) in which a barrel of flour is given to a poor woman to feed her family. In this Louisiana variant, the magic pot also nourishes a hungry family until it is misused. See also Baughman's motif X1812(a) "Cook bakes enormous pudding; it falls, crushes people;" with both variants listed from New England.

Une fois, il y avait une vieille femme avec deux enfants, un petit garçon et une petite fille. Ils étaient orphelins. Ça fait, ils étaient misérables. Ça allait couper des petites branches dans le bois pour faire leur feu, tu vois? Ils avaient proche pas rien pour manger.

Ça fait, ils ont rencontré une—il y avait une vieille petite Cendrillonne, ils appelaient dans le temps. Ils ont rencontré Cendrillonne dans le bois.

Ça fait, Cendrillonne dit, "Qui vous autres fais là, z-enfants?"

Ils dit, "*Well,* on est après se casser des petites branches pour se chauffer." Ils dit, "On est pauvres. On a proche juste du gru pour manger, de la farine maïs."

"Mais," elle dit, "je vas vous donner une chaudière, avec deux petits bâtons." Elle dit, "Ça, ça va vous aider. Et vous autres vas juste mettre la chaudière-là sur le feu, qu'a rien en dedans, et vous autres vas cogner avec les petits bâtons au bord de la chaudière. Ça va faire de la bouillie. Là, quand la chaudière sera pleine, vous autres vas recogner, 'Arrête, chaudière.'" Ça fait, elle dit, "ça va arrêter faire la bouillie."

Ça fait, ils ont parti avec la chaudière, trop contents. Ils ont arrivé là-bas, ils l'ont glissé sur le feu, ils ont cogné la chaudière, "Bouille, chaudière." Chaudière a commencé faire la bouillie. Ça fait, elle était pleine. "Tac! Arrête, chaudière." Chaudière a arrêté. Ils ont mangé leur bouillie.

Ça fait les petits a parti *back,* aller jouer, tu vois? Ça fait, la faim a pris la vieille femme. Ça fait, elle dit, "Je vas me faire de la bouillie." Met la chaudière sur le feu. Cogne.

Once there was an old woman who had two children, a little boy and a little girl. They were orphans. So they were miserable. They would go out and cut little branches in the woods to make their fire, you see? They had almost nothing to eat.

So, they met a—there was a little old Cendrillonne, as they called her in those days. They met Cendrillonne in the woods.

So Cendrillonne said, "What are you doing there, children?"

They said, "Well, we're breaking little branches so we will be able to warm ourselves." They said, "We are poor. We have only grits to eat, corn meal."

"Well," she said, "I'm going to give you a pot, with two little sticks." She said, "That will help you. And you will simply place the pot on the fire, with nothing in it, and you will strike the little sticks on the side of the pot. This will cause it to make pudding. Then, when the pot will be full, you will hit it again, 'Stop, pot.' So," she said, "it will stop making pudding."

So they left with the pot, very happy. They arrived, they slid it onto the fire, they hit the pot, "Boil, pot." The pot started making pudding. So then it was full. "Tack! Stop, pot." The pot stopped. They ate their pudding.

So the little ones went back out to play, you know? So the old lady was suddenly hungry. So she said, "I'll make myself some pudding." Put the pot on the fire. Hits. "Boil,

"Bouille, chaudière." Chaudière a commencé à bouillir. Mais là, elle a oublié la manière pour arrêter la chaudière.

Ça fait, la chaudière a commencé à faire de la bouillie, ça a commencé à déborder, tomber par terre. Ça a rempli la maison. Ça a commencé à sortir dans les portes. Ça a pris les rues. Ça fait, pour que le monde s'en aillent dans les rues, fallait ils mangent leur *way*. Ça a tout rempli les rues avec de la bouillie!

pot." The pot started boiling. But then, she forgot the way to stop the pot.

So the pot started making pudding, it started overflowing, falling on the floor. It filled the house. It started going out the doors. It flowed into the streets. Soon, in order for people to go about in the streets, they had to eat their way. All the streets were filled with pudding!

25. Petit Jean et le diable / Petit Jean and the Devil (Lazard Daigle, Pointe Noire)

The types involved here, 1049 *The Heavy Axe* and 1115 *Attempted Murder with Hatchet*, are often found among the episodes associated with type 1640 *The Brave Tailor* (cf. Grimm, no. 183; Bolte and Polívka III, p. 333). Laval's Archives de Folklore had only one version. Compare "Jean Vaillant" in Carrière's *Missouri* (no. 69). *Folktales of France* has a version from the collection of Geneviève Massignon (no. 4, "Le Tailleur") which includes a similar deception in the woods, and Brandon had a Louisiana version, "Tit Jean et les géants" (II, no. 26), in which the hero escapes an attempted murder. Such tales—especially type 1115—have been popular in English-language versions in the Appalachians and the Ozarks, and are often associated with Jack the Giant Killer. See, for example, Leonard Roberts' *Old Greasybeard* (nos. 25 and 132), and *Sang Branch Settlers* (no. 140). Compare also "Jack in the Giant's New Ground" in Richard Chase's *Jack Tales* for more episodes associated with the brave tailor cycle. Petit Jean is also a popular hero in the oral tradition of Indian Ocean Creoles. See, for example, *Les aventures de Petit Jean: Contes créoles de l'Océan Indien*. In "Soudin," a variant from Rodrigue Island (*Lièvre Grand diable*, pp. 105–117), three hoodlums write "Soudin, d'un coup de révolver, tue cinq cent mille hommes" [Soudin, with one pistol shot, kills five hundred thousand men] on the coat of a drunk who must then pass several tests before the king.

Petit Jean s'avait engagé avec un géant. Le vieux diable, on l'appelait. Et le diable arrachait des arbres, c'était pour desserrer le bois. Il attrapait les arbres et il les arrachait. Il les mettait sur son épaule et il allait les mettre dans un tas. Et le Petit Jean a venu, il a regardé ça un bout de temps et il pouvait pas faire ça. Il était pas proche assez fort.

Petit Jean had hired on with a giant. The old devil we called him. And the devil uprooted trees, this was to clear the woods. He would grab the trees and uproot them. He would put them on his shoulder and go and pile them up together. And Petit Jean came, he watched this for a while and he couldn't do this. He was not nearly strong enough.

Ça fait, il a été se chercher un grand cable et il a pris à cerner plusieurs arbres à la fois, et le diable lui a demandé quoi il voulait faire. Il dit, "Ça va trop doucement, un à la fois. On va arracher un tas à la fois."

"O, non," il dit, "tu vas ruiner ma terre!"

Ça fait, il l'a arrêté. Quand ça a venu le soir pour se coucher, il lui a donné une chambre pour Petit Jean se coucher. Et Petit Jean a entendu le géant a dit à sa femme, "Cet homme-là est plus fort que moi. Je vas le tuer ce soir. Je veux pas personne plus fort que moi."

Ça fait, Petit Jean a entendu ça. Il a sorti. Il s'a attrapé un *log* et il l'a mis dans son lit, et puis il s'a fourré quelque part. Il s'a caché.

Ça fait, dans la nuit, le diable a pris un gros bâton et il a venu sacré un coup qu'il croyait que c'était Petit Jean, mais c'était un *log*. Et là, il s'a vitement ôté de là. Il a été se coucher.

Ça fait, Petit Jean a pris le *log*. Il a retourné le mettre à la même place. Et il s'a couché dans le lit. Le matin quand il s'a réveillé, le géant guettait voir si—Il croyait qu'il l'avait tué. Mais Petit Jean s'a levé. Ils se sont mis à table après déjeuner. Il a pris à déjeuner et le géant lui a demandé comment il avait dormi.

"Mais," il dit, "j'ai bien dormi. Il y a des maringouins ou quelque chose qui s'a posé sur moi dans la nuit. Ça m'a réveillé, mais autrement, j'ai bien dormi!"

So he went to get a big rope and he put it around several trees at once, and the devil asked him what he intended to do. He said, "This is going too slowly, just one at a time. We'll pull up many at one time."

"Oh no," he said, "you'll ruin my land!"

So he stopped him. When the time came that night to go to sleep, he gave Petit Jean a room to sleep in. And Petit Jean heard the giant say to his wife, "This man is stronger than me. I'll kill him tonight. I don't want anyone stronger than me."

So Petit Jean heard this. He went out. He got a log and he put it in his bed and then he hid somewhere. He hid.

So during the night, the devil took a big stick and he came to strike what he thought was Petit Jean, but it was a log. And then, he got out of there fast. He went to bed.

So Petit Jean took away the log. The next morning when he awoke, the giant was watching to see if—He thought he had killed him. But Petit Jean got up. They sat at table to eat breakfast. He ate some breakfast and the giant asked him how he had slept.

"Well," he said, "I slept well. There were some mosquitoes or something that lit on me during the night. This awoke me, but otherwise, I slept well."

26. Barbe-bleue et Barbe-rouge / [Bluebeard] and [Redbeard] (Lazard Daigle, Pointe Noire)

This tale is a fragmentary variant of type 301A *Quest for a Vanished Princess*, without the fabulous companions of 301B *The Strong Man and his Companions*, nor even the rescue of the princess, the basis for most of the tales in the cycle of type 301 *The Three Stolen Princesses*, one of the most widespread types in the world. This type is well-known in French

and Creole oral traditions. Laval's Archives de Folklore had 111 French American versions and Delarue listed 96 French versions (sub-types A and B combined). Klipple mentioned only two African variants (from the Congo and Madagascar), which may point to this type's European origins.

In a version from Missouri, "Jean l'Ours," collected by Carrière (no. 10), there is a bearded dwarf, as in the present text, who defeats Tord-chêne [Oak Twister] and Joueur d'Palets [Stone Player] before being beaten in turn by Jean l'Ours [John the Bear]. The fight exposes the hole by which to descend to the underworld (motif F92). Once down the hole, Jean l'Ours rescues the three princesses, but is abandoned by his friends. He finally succeeds in coming back up to the top of the hole on the back of an eagle, but without losing part of his anatomy (motif B322.1 "The hero gives his own flesh to feed the animal which carries him," often associated with the escape from the underworld). In a French version, "Little Fourteen" (no. 46 in *Folktales of France*), there are the gifted companions of type 301B, the descent to save the princesses, and the loss of a leg to feed the animal which carries the hero back.

Flowers described 11 variants from the West Indies. In one of these, "La Oreja del Diablo" (no. 11, from Puerto Rico), the young prince descends into a well to save the princesses. He fights the devil at the bottom of the well and cuts off one of his ears, but he cannot get back out on his own. The devil then proposes to take him back up in exchange for the restitution of his ear.

The bearded nature of the little man seems to be an important element of this tale. In another Louisiana version presented by Brandon (II, no. 13), there is a similar bearded dwarf, 'Tit Barbe-bleue [Little Bluebeard] who is defeated by 'Tit Palais [Little Castle] after having defeated his two companions. 'Tit Palais chases him down the hole and kills him and his mother. He is lifted back up by a flock of blackbirds to whom he must feed a part of his leg. He manages to replace the missing part later. There is a similar bearded villain in Appalachian versions of type 301. In Leonard Roberts' *Old Greasybeard* (no, 11), the hero traps an evil dwarf's beard in a split log; the dwarf rips his beard off while fleeing; and the hero follows the trail of blood to a hole in the ground. Compare also to "Old Fire Dragaman" in Chase's *Jack Tales* (no. 12).

There are also obvious comparisons with the first part of the English epic poem in which Beowulf defeats Grendel, first ripping the monster's arm off in the great hall and then following it down into the hole where he kills its mother as well. There is no princess to rescue, only the mighty struggle between the hero and the monster, as in an English-language Missouri version of type 301 in which the hero rips off the leg of a bear (Randolph, *Sticks in the Knapsack*, pp. 17–18).

In this Louisiana version, the struggle is only briefly evoked. The storyteller insisted that he had forgotten most of the tale, remembering most clearly the escape from the hole.

Il y avait deux hommes, Barbe-rouge et Barbe-bleue, des hommes avec des grandes barbes. Ils s'aviont battu. Il y avait un qui	There were two men, Barbe-rouge and Barbe-bleue, men with long beards. They had fought. One had defeated the other. Barbe-

avait battu l'autre. Barbe-bleue s'avait fait battre. Et il avait de la grande barbe.

Ça fait, Barbe-rouge l'a pris et il lui a séparé la barbe et l'a passée par dessus d'une branche dans un arbre et l'a amarrée. Et il avait les mains d'amarrées et les pieds d'amarrés, et la barbe amarrée après l'arbre. Il était pendu en haut-là.

Il s'a débattu, débattu jusqu'à qu'il a tombé. Il s'a dépris. Et il avait peur de l'autre. Il s'a fourré dans un trou dans la terre et quand il a été dans le trou, il s'a aperçu qu'il était dans un autre pays-là. Et il a resté un bout de temps, puis là, l'ennui l'a pris. Il était seul. Il voulait s'en revenir, mais il pouvait pas, parce qu'il avait pas moyen de sortir. Il lui aurait fallu des ailes d'oiseau pour sortir.

Ça fait, il y avait un gros, gros, gros z-oiseau qui restait là. Et il a été joindre le z-oiseau. Le z-oiseau lui a dit, "Ouais je peux te sortir, mais ça va prendre de quoi. Il faudra tu me donnes à manger. Ça va prendre cent moutons."

Ça fait, il y avait des moutons alentour, dans ce gros trou, dans ce pays-là. Ça fait, il a tué cent moutons et il les a amarrés de quelque manière et puis ça a parti.

En allant en haut, à tout moment, le z-oiseau disait, "Donne-moi du mouton!" Et il lui passait un morceau de mouton, et "Donne-moi du mouton!" Quand il a arrivé en haut, il y avait plus de moutons. Juste pas assez de moutons pour le sortir. Il a fallu qu'il se coupe un morceau après sa jambe à lui pour le dernier morceau. Autrement il l'aurait réchappé.

bleue had been beaten. And he had a long beard.

So Barbe-rouge took him and parted his beard and passed it over a branch and tied it. And he tied his hands and his feet together and his beard to the tree. He was hanging there.

And he struggled and struggled until he fell. He freed himself. And he was afraid of the other one. He hid in a hole in the ground and when he went into the hole, he noticed that he was in another land. And he stayed for a while, but then he was overwhelmed with loneliness. He was all alone. He wanted to return, but he couldn't because he didn't have the means to come out. He would have had to have wings like a bird to come out.

So there was a great big bird which lived there. And he went to meet the bird. The bird told him, "Yeah, I can take you out, but I'll need something. You'll have to feed me. It will take one hundred sheep."

So there were sheep nearby, in this big hole, in this land. So he killed one hundred sheep and he tied them in a certain way and they left.

Going up, from time to time, the bird would say, "Feed me some sheep!" And he would give it a piece of sheep, and "Feed me some sheep!" When he arrived near the top, there were no more sheep. Not quite enough sheep to make it out. He had to cut a piece of his own leg to give it one last piece. Otherwise it would have dropped him.

27. La famille qu'avait perdu la petite fille / The Family That Had Lost the Little Girl (Évélia Boudreaux, Carencro)

This tale is a variant of type 769 *Dead Child's Friendly Return to Parents* with motif E324 ". . . frequently to stop weeping." For a discussion of this element in English ballad tradition, see Child 78 (II, p. 328 and following; III, p. 244 ff.; V p. 241). Laval's Archives de Folklore had one version from the Gaspé peninsula in which the child appears in a dream carrying buckets full of tears. In an Acadian version from the Canadian Maritimes, "Enfants espiègles," collected by Jolicœur in *Les plus belles légendes acadiennes*, there are two children. Compare also a Hungarian version, "The Restless Dead Man" (no. 10, in Dégh's *Folktales and Society)*, in which the dead man cannot rest because the tears shed for him have wet his pillow. In this Louisiana version, the child appears to her mother in a vision to tell her that she cannot keep her candle lit because of her parents' tears. For a discussion of this type, see also Bolte and Polívka (II, p. 485).

Il y avait une famille qu'a perdu une petite fille. Et la famille pouvait pas se refaire de la perte de l'enfant. Et ils pleuraient. Presque tout le temps, eux étaient après pleurer.

Un jour, la maman a eu une vision. Elle a vu plein de petits enfants après faire une marche, et ils étiont tous habillés en blanc, et ils avaient tous des chandelles. Et elle a vu la petite fille à elle avec sa chandelle, mais sa chandelle était éteinte. Et tous les autres, leurs chandelles étaient allumées.

Alors, elle a demandé à sa petite fille, et elle dit, "Chère, comment se fait toi, ta chandelle est pas allumée?"

Elle dit, "Maman," elle dit, "vous autres pleures pour moi." Elle dit, "Le Bon Dieu aime pas que vous autres pleures pour moi." Elle dit, "Faut vous autres acceptes que le Bon Dieu m'a pris." Et elle dit, "Quand vous autres pleures, vous autres éteins ma chandelle." Et elle dit, "Les autres, les parents ont accepté leur mort." Et elle dit, "Ils pleuront pas. Leurs chandelles restent allumées. Alors," elle dit, "il faut pas vous autres continues à pleurer pour moi comme ça." Et elle dit, "Faut vous autres acceptes que le Bon Dieu m'a pris." Et elle dit, "Il me voulait."

There was a family that lost a little girl. And the family couldn't get over the loss of the child. And they wept. Almost every day, they wept.

One day, the mother had a vision. She saw lots of little children marching, and they were all dressed in white, and they all had candles. And she saw her own daughter with a candle, but her candle was not lit. And all the others' candles were lit.

So she asked her daughter, she said, "Dear, why is your candle not lit?"

She said, "Mother," she said, "you all weep for me." She said, "The Good Lord does not like for you to weep for me." She said, "You must accept that the Good Lord has taken me." And she said, "When you weep, you put out my candle." And she said, "The others' parents have accepted their death." And she said, "They don't weep. Their candles stay lit. So," she said, "you must not continue to weep for me like this." And she said, "You must accept that the Good Lord has taken me." And she said, "He wanted me." She said, "I belong to the Good Lord."

Elle dit, "J'appartiens au Bon Dieu." Et elle dit, "Il m'a pris quand Il a été paré. Ça fait," elle dit, " Faut vous autres acceptes votre croix," elle dit.

And she said, "He took me when He was ready. So," she said, "you must accept your cross," she said.

Farces / Jokes

28. *La prière d'Osée / Osée's Prayer (Inez Catalon, Kaplan)*

This tale is a variant of the well-known motif J217.0.1.1, "Trickster overhears man praying for death to take him. . . ." Baughman found variants from New Jersey, Virginia, North and South Carolina, Florida, Mississippi, Illinois, and Michigan, the majority being from African American sources. Dorson had two of the most frequent episodes associated with this type in "Efan Prays" (*American Negro Folktales*, no. 47, pp. 143–145). In the first, Efan escapes running and his wife remarks, "Lord, you just wants to quit. You can't catch Efan cause he's barefooted." Then, when the master overhears Efan praying for the death of the white people, he is angry and strikes with an ax handle, to which Efan responds, "Oh, Lord, don't you know a white man from a nigger?" See also Parsons (no. 340, p. 321) for versions from the West Indies, Brewer (*Dog Ghosts*, pp. 117–18) for an African American version from Texas, and Fauset (no. 141, p. 93) for versions from the black English-speaking community in Nova Scotia.

In the Uncle Remus version ("Death and the Negro Man," no. 4, in Joel Chandler Harris' *Uncle Remus and His Friends*), the master gives such a shock to the slave he has overheard praying for death that the slave escapes through an open window and hides in the woods for a week before returning to work harder than ever.

Brandon had a version in her thesis, "Le vieux nègue qu'était paré à mourir" (II, no. 44) which ends this way:

> Boss: "Oh Michel. . . ."
> Michel: "Dis-moi pas là." [Say that I'm not here.]
> Sa femme: "Ça fait pas rien au Bon Dieu, mais va!" [It makes no difference to the
>   Lord, but go on!]

It is interesting to note that, in the version presented here, Madame Catalon switches to the black Creole dialect of the Bayou Teche region when reporting the speech of Osée. Though herself a black Creole, this storyteller's natural speech is not Creole but the Cajun French of her native Vermilion Parish. The fact that she insisted on having Osée speak this way may indicate the way she feels about the character, or the historical nature of the story.

Osée, tous les soirs, il se mettait à genoux puis il faisait sa prière. Et puis, il disait, "Mon Dieu, quand Vous sé d'être paré	Osée, every night, would get down on his knees to pray. And he would say, "My God, when You are ready for Osée, Osée will

69

pour Osée, Osée paré pour aller." Et tous les soirs, c'était la même chanson. Il se mettait d'à genoux, et puis il finissait sa prière, "O Dieu! Quand Vous sé d'être paré pour Osée, Osée paré pour aller."

Ça fait, ils se sont mis dessous les soliveaux, en haut-là. Puis-là, ça commençait à appeler, "Oséééé!" de loin, tu connais, "Oséééé!"

"Osée pas paré, mo dis Vous! Osée pas paré, mo dis Vous!"

be ready to go." And every night, it was the same song. He would get down on his knees, and he would finish his prayers, "Oh God! When You are ready for Osée, Osée will be ready to go."

So, they hid behind the beams upstairs. And then, they started yelling, "Osééée," from far off, you know, "Osééée."

"Osée isn't ready now, I'm telling You! Osée isn't ready now, I'm telling You!"

29. La vieille fille qui voulait se marier / The Old Maid Who Wanted To Marry (Clotile Richard, Carencro)

This tale is a variant of type 1476 *The Prayer for a Husband*. A clever rascal usually overhears the old maid's prayer and promises her a husband if she will complete some ridiculous task. Baughman found numerous variants of this type in England as well as in North America (New York, North Carolina and Missouri). See Bolte and Polívka (III, p. 120) for a discussion of this type. In the Grimm brothers' version, "The Maid of Brakel" (no. 139), the old maid prays to St. Anne for her husband. When the hidden rascal tells her that she will not get her husband, she retorts, "Hold your tongue and let your mother speak," thinking that the young Virgin Mary is interfering. There are 12 French versions mentioned in Thompson.

Most of the Québecois versions in Laval's Archives de Folklore have the old maid praying at the foot of St. Joseph's statue. See, for example, the collections of Laforte (no. 22, "L'habit, la vie, l'mari") and Lacourcière (no. 565, "St. Joseph et la vieille fille"). In the latter tale, a rascal hides behind the statue and refuses the old maid's prayer for a husband. She is so surprised to hear the statue "talk" that she jumps on it and grabs its neck causing it to fall over on her. She exclaims, "Débarque donc, St. Joseph. T'es pire qu'un jeune!" [Get off, St. Joseph, you're worse than one of the boys]. This response comes directly from Québecois tradition in which religion fell along with religious authority during the rebellion in the middle of this century and in which good cussing typically involves a subversion of religious terms (hostie [host], tabernacle, calice [chalice]). There is a parallel version from New Brunswick in the collection of Catherine Jolicœur, "La vieille fille dans le poulailler" [The Old Maid in the Chicken Coop; no. 851]. In this version, the old maid is ashamed to pray aloud outside. So she hides in the chicken coop and lifts her head in prayer. At that moment, chicken droppings fall into her open mouth. Her reaction, "Bonne Ste Viarge, j'ai reçu vos grâces, b'en c'est amer!" [Good Holy Virgin, I've received your grace, but how bitter it is], is a remarkable reflection of the downtrodden culture of the Maritime Acadians.

The variant presented here depends on the confusion between the English word "who" and the owl's hoot. Mme Richard had obviously heard the story first in English, but was in the habit of telling her stories in French. She did not, however, feel it necessary to change the bird's cry to create confusion with the French "qui" [who], as for example in the "kee kee" cry of the sparrow or the kildeer. What could, on first consideration, be thought of as a defective telling may be instead an unconscious reflection of the region's cultural reality on the part of the storyteller. For Mme Richard, it is not surprising that God speaks English, just like any other person in power. But the old maid's final answer in French demonstrates that she knows that He understands her language, even if He doesn't choose to speak it, just like many in south Louisiana, including her own great-grandchildren.

C'était une vieille fille qui voulait se marier. Et puis, elle avait pas d'avantage. Ça fait, elle avait été consulter sa grand-mère. Ça fait, sa grand-mère l'a dit, "Mais, si tu prierais les soirs auprès d'un chêne," elle dit, "ta prière pourrait être exaucée."

Ça fait, la vieille fille est allée prier, prier. Il y avait pas de réponse à sa prière. Ça fait, un soir, elle dit, "Je vas prier avec plus de ferveur!" Elle s'est mis d'à genoux, près du chêne, mis sa tête contre le chêne. "Mon Dieu!" elle crie, "fais-moi la grâce que je peux me marier!"

Il y a un vieil hibou qui fait, "Hou houou!"

"Ah," elle dit, "Grand Dieu! Partant que c'est un homme," elle dit, "envoyez-moi le tout de suite!"

There was an old maid who wanted to marry. And she was having no luck. So she went to consult her grandmother. So the grandmother told her, "Well, if you were to pray each night next to an oak tree," she said, "your prayer could be answered."

So the old maid went to pray, and pray. There was no answer to her prayer. So, one night, she said, "I'll pray with more fervor!" She kneeled next to the oak tree, placed her head against the oak. "My God!" she cried, "do me the favor of letting me marry!"

There was an old owl that cried, "Hoo hoooo!"

"Ah," she said, "Great God! As long as it's a man," she said, "send him along right away!"

30. "O, Fival!" (Wilson "Ben Guiné" Mitchell, Parks)

This tale, a variant of type 1705 *Talking Horse and Dog*, is well-known in the United States. Baughman found numerous references including in New York, South Carolina, and West Virginia. Parsons listed a variant from the West Indies, "All Things Talk" (I, pp. 91–92), which has a pumpkin and a piece of wood which both talk. Animal tales are based on a suspension of belief which allows the animal characters to think and act like humans. This tale, on the other hand, is based on the humans' shock at hearing an animal talk. In some versions, many animals or objects in succession scare the people who meet them. Most versions are based on an inequitable distribution of work. The complaint of the first animal

begins the flight of the man who then continues to run as he hears more animals commenting on his fine race or on the unexpected speech of the first animal.

This tale is a part of the African American John and Old Master cycle which usually expresses the symbolic revenge of an oppressed class. The revenge in this story is indirect, but nevertheless quite clear. The storyteller gives a clue concerning the underlying function of his story in his rhetorical question, "C'est manière comme l'esclavage, vous comprends?" [This was a little like slavery, do you understand?] What follows effectively reverses this image and disarms the system by means of a powerful defense mechanism: humor. Of course, Vieux Boss loses face when he runs away overwhelmed with fear when one of his mules refuses to work on Sunday, probably to pull the family buggy to church, after having worked like the rest of the mules all week long. Vieux Nèg, who is better at taking things as they come, is left alone and in control of himself on the farm in the absence of his fleeing master.

Il y avait un *boss,* un gros *boss* d'une grosse habitation, grosse habitation. Et il té travaillé tous les mulets. Il té gain à peu près cinquante et quelques *teams.* Il y avait tous des vieux bougres, des vieux nèg-là, qui labouraient tout la semaine. C'est manière comme l'esclavage, vous comprends?

Ah *well,* il té gain un vieux nèg qui té donné manger les mulets, tu comprends? Ah *well,* tous les dimanches, il té gain un vieux mulet, c'était toujours so kèn tour. C'était jamais les autres! Li té toujours apé travailler, vieux mulet a toujours travaillé. Les autres té tous assis apé *enjoy* eux-mêmes manger.

Et Vieux Nèg a vu le même. Li couri là, li couri là, li tourné *back.* Li dit, li couri au ras là, li hélé, "O, Fiva!"

Fiva dit, li dit, "Ça to lé? Mais," li dit, "mo pas aller aujourd'hui!"

Vieux Nèg a couté ça. Té gain un de ces grosses chiques tabac. Li coupé paquet de tabac en deux. En deux! Li va. Li retourné *back.* Li dit ça à so *boss,* li dit, "Maître," li dit, "ça to crois c'est? Mo couri pour hélé à Fiva. Fiva dit moi li pas aller couri beau matin. Li travaille pas. C'est jamais so kèn tour."

"O," Boss a dit, "Va donc, toi. To fou, toi!"

There was once a boss, a big boss on a big farm, big farm. And he worked all the mules. He had about fifty odd teams. There were lots of old guys, old black men who worked all week long. This was a little like slavery, do you understand?

Ah well, he had one old black man who fed the mules, do you understand? Ah well, every Sunday, there was one old mule, and it was always his turn. Never the others! He was always working, the old mule always worked. The others were all sitting around enjoying themselves and eating.

And Vieux Nèg saw the same one. He went there, went there, he turned around. He said, he went up to him, and yelled, "Oh, Fiva!"

Fiva said, "What do you want? Well," he said, "I'm not going today!"

Vieux Nèg heard this. He had one of those big chews of tobacco. He cut that pack of tobacco in two. In two! He went. He went back. He told this to his boss, he said, "Master," he said, "what do you think happened? I went to call Fiva. Fiva said to me that he wasn't going this morning. He's not working. It's never his turn [to rest]."

"Oh," Boss said, "go on, you. You're crazy!"

"Mais," li dit, *"All right!"*

Boss-là part. Li parti, Vieux Boss-là. Li parti ayoù tous les autres-là dînaient. Li hélé. Et li dit à so ti chien [Âsifflementsê]. Li pélé ti chien-là Gyp. Li dit, "O, Fiva!"

Li dit, "Si mo vas, to vas mourir à soir, toi!"

Tonnerre m'écrase! Boss a parti galoper comme ça-là, c'était un assassin. Et li va arrêter en bas un ti n'arbre, à force li té gain chaud. Li té apé venter à so chapeau. Ti chien té accroupi au ras li.

Li dit, *"Hot dog,* c'est première fois mo vois une bêtaille causer."

Ti chien a dit, comme ça-là, "Moi aussi!" Tonnerre! Ça a parti, et ça a parti. Yé té parti chacun ses côtés.

"Well," he said, "All right!"

Boss leaves. Vieux Boss left. He went to where they were all eating. He called out. And he called his little dog. [Whistles.] He called his little dog Gyp. He said, "Oh, Fiva!"

He said, "If I go, you're going to die tonight!"

May thunder crush me! Boss took off running like this was an assassin. And he stopped under a little tree, so hot was he. He was fanning himself with his hat. The little dog was crouched next to him.

He said, "Hot dog! That's the first time I see an animal talk."

The little dog said, "Me, too!" Thunder! They took off again. They left, each in his own direction.

31. Le chien qui marchait sur l'eau / The Dog Who Could Walk on Water (Revon Reed, Mamou)

This tale includes motifs X1215.13* "Remarkable dog," D2125.1 "Magic power to walk on water," J1649* "Practical retorts." The motif concerning the competition between friends is common in Louisiana French oral tradition which often features such displays of showing off, as the storyteller explains in beginning his tale. The retort by the first hunter as he sees the other's dog walking on water could be classified under motif J1530 "One absurdity rebukes another."

This story could also be read as the reflection of a Cajun cultural trait. As early as the mid-eighteenth century when they first arrived in Louisiana, the exiles refused to accept *a priori* the rich French Creole planters as their betters. Even though many were not interested in climbing the social ladder, they quickly showed themselves to be hard-working farmers, and they categorically refused second-class citizenship. They also delighted in bringing social climbers down a notch with humor and practical jokes. The *nouveau-riche* millionaire in this story gets no deference from his old hunting partner even if he does have a dog that walks on water.

Tu connais, ton Cadien, il est beaucoup menteur, et il aime brag de naturel. Et c'est naturel, dans une manière. Allons dire toi, t'as un bon chien de chasse. Moi, le mien sera tout le temps un peu meilleur. Je m'en fous pas mal comment bon ton chien est. Et je

You know, the typical Cajun is a terrible liar, and naturally likes to brag. And it's natural, in a way. Let's say you have a good hunting dog. Mine will always be a little better. I don't care how good your dog is. And there's a little story that I tell like that about two

conte une petite histoire comme ça pour deux vieux bougres qui restaient en querelle tout le temps pour les chiens, les canards. L'autre avait tout le temps un meilleur chien.

Un jour, il a frappé l'huile sur sa terre et il est venu millionaire. Il a décidé il aurait traversé le monde pour se trouver un chien meilleur que le chien à Pascal. Et il est venu en bout de trouver un chien qui avait été dressé de marcher sur l'eau, un *retriever,* mais il nageait pas; il marchait. Il courait assez vite que juste ses pattes touchaient l'eau. Ça fait, il a acheté le chien. Il a payé dix mille piastres pour. Juste pour prouver à Pascal qu'il avait un meilleur chien que lui.

Ça fait, quand il est revenu, il dit à Pascal (il lui a pas dit pas rien pour le chien), "Je m'ai trouvé un chien, mais," il dit, "t'aimerais pas aller à la chasse de canards demain?"

"O, ouais!" il dit. "T'as un chien?"

"Ouais."

"Il arrive pas au ras du mien, bien?"

Il dit, "On va voir."

Ça fait, ils ont été à la chasse. Là, Pascal a tiré le premier coup. Il y a un canard qu'a tombé à l'eau. Son chien s'est vite tiré à la nage. Il a été chercher le canard. Il a revenu largué.

Olide dit, "Guette ici! Guette bien qui mon chien peut faire!" Un autre canard. Il a tiré. Tombé à l'eau. Le chien a sauté en bas du bateau puis il a galopé sur l'eau.

Pascal a guetté ça. L'autre le guettait aussi, voir si ça l'aurait *impress.* Ça fait, il a revenu, il a ramené le canard. Il s'est proche pas trempé.

Il dit, "Qui tu crois de mon chien asteur?"

"Mais," il dit, "je vois pas qu'il est un sacré foutrement meilleur que le mien." Il dit, "Tout ça je peux dire, il connaît pas seulement nager." Il dit, "Je vois pas que c'est aussi un bon chien que ça!"

old guys who were always arguing about dogs and ducks. One always had a better dog than the other.

One day, one struck oil on his property and became a millionaire. He decided that he would travel around the world to find a dog better than Pascal's [his neighbor's] dog. And he finally found a dog which had been trained to walk on water, a retriever, but it didn't swim; it walked. It ran so fast that its feet just barely touched the water. So he bought the dog. He paid ten thousand dollars for it. Just to prove to Pascal that he had a better dog than him.

So when he came home, he said to Pascal (he told him nothing about the dog), "I found myself a dog, so," he said, "wouldn't you like to go duck hunting tomorrow?"

"Oh yeah!" he said. "You have a dog?"

"Yeah."

"He's not nearly as good as mine, eh?"

He said, "We'll see."

So they went hunting. Pascal shot first. A duck fell on the water. His dog quickly started swimming. It went to get the duck. It came back tired.

Olide said, "Look here! Watch what my dog can do!" Another duck. He shot. Fell on the water. The dog jumped out of the boat and started running on the water.

Pascal watched this. The other one watched, too, to see if this would impress him. So it came back, it brought the duck back. It was hardly wet.

He said, "What do you think of my dog now?"

"Well," he said, "I don't see that it's one bit better than mine." He said, "All I can say is that it can't even swim." He said, "I don't see where it's such a good dog!"

32. *Fido est mort / Fido Is Dead (Revon Reed, Mamou)*

This cumulative tale is related to type 2040 *The Climax of Horrors* (motif Z46). In Baughman's description of this type, the story features a talkative magpie who has died from eating the meat of a horse which was grilled in a house fire, and so on. Baughman found variants in England as well as in America (Texas, Wisconsin and Arkansas). There is an Appalachian version reported by Jones and Wheeler, "Nothing's Been Happening" (pp. 114–115). A literary version by Henri Pourrat, "Comme ça," in *A Treasury of French Tales* (pp. 322–323), includes a series of alternating good and bad news reports and ends with the wife burned in a house fire. The basic plot of this traditional tale was used as the basis for a popular French song from the 1930s which ends, *"Tout va bien, Madame la Marquise. Tout va bien, tout va très bien."* Laval's Archives de Folklore had three variants from Québec.

In the variant presented here, the principal character is Jean Sot, the Louisiana French version of Jean le Sot, the foolish hero of French tradition. The way in which Jean Sot continues to affirm to the master of the house that all is well also recalls type 1681B *Fool as Custodian of Home and Animals*. The fact that the dog in this story is named Fido (Faïdo) is a possible indication of the influence of British American tradition on Cajun culture.

Et là, le conte, moi, qui me donne envie de rire—Il avait été travailler pour un homme qu'avait une grosse plantation, un grand planteur, un éleveur de bêtes. Il est parti en vacances. Il a mis Jean Sot en charge de l'habitation, avec ses domestiques, les noirs, et d'autres, et la femme et la mère de sa femme, sa belle-mère, en autres mots, et lui, il a été en vacances.

Et au bout d'une semaine, il a décidé de foutre un *telephone call* à Jean Sot. Il l'a appelé sur le *phone*. Il dit, "Euh, Jean Sot, comment tout les affaires va là-bas?"

"O, vous! Ça va beaucoup bien, Monsieur," il dit. "Tout est correct."

"T'es sûr tout est correct?"

"Well, il y a juste Faïdo," il dit, "Faïdo est mort. Le petit chien."

Il dit, "Faïdo est mort?! Comment il est mort?"

"Mais, vous," il dit, "il est mort en mangeant de la viande de mulet, euh, brûlée."

"O, non!" il dit. "Qui il y a eu, Jean Sot? Comment ça a arrivé, ça?"

And then, the tale which makes me feel like laughing—He had gone to work for a man who had a big plantation, a big planter, a rancher. He left to go on vacation. He put Jean Sot in charge of the farm, with the servants, the blacks, and the others, and his wife and his wife's mother, his mother-in-law in other words, and he went on a vacation.

And after a week, he decided to call Jean Sot on the telephone. He called him. He said, "Uh, Jean Sot, how is everything over there?"

"Oh, sir! Everything is going very well, sir," he said. "All is well."

"Are you sure that everything is okay?"

"Well, there's just Fido," he said, "Fido is dead. The little dog."

He said, "Fido is dead?! How did he die?"

"Well, sir," he said, "he died while eating some burnt, uh, mule meat."

"Oh, no!" he said. "What happened, Jean Sot? How did this happen?"

"Mais, vous," il dit, "votre magasin a pris en feu. Les mulets a pas pu sortir des écuries. Ils ont brûlé." Il dit, "Là, le petit chien a été, il a mangé cette viande brûlée-là. Ça lui a donné mal au ventre, et puis il est mort."

Là, l'autre a attrapé la tête l'autre bout là-bas sur le téléphone. Il dit, "Comment le magasin a pris en feu, imbécile? Dis-moi vite!"

"Mais," il dit, "le magasin a pris en feu à cause de la maison qu'a pris en feu avant."

Il dit, "Comment ça a arrivé, ça, Jean Sot?"

"Mais," il dit, "tu vois, vous, votre belle-mère a eu une attaque de cœur, et elle est morte tout d'un coup et elle était ensevelie dans le cercueil et des chandelles allumées autour et," il dit, "une des chandelles a pris en feu sur les rideaux et, quand on a connu la chose, la maison était en feu et le magasin a pris en feu et le mulet a brûlé et Faïdo a mangé de la viande brûlée et il est mort. Autrement ça, tout est correct."

"Et qui c'est qui a tué la pauvre vieille femme?"

Il dit, "Mais, c'est sa fille, votre femme." Il dit, "Quand elle a connu qu'elle avait parti en cachette avec un des travaillants sur votre habitation, elle a *elope* avec un des domestiques, ça a tué la pauvre mère."

Et avec ça, l'autre aussi a tombé en crise, là-bas. Il connaissait plus qui il y avait. Ça a tout commencé à cause de Faïdo qu'avait mangé de la viande brûlée, mais Jean Sot, lui-là, il voulait pas, tu connais, il voulait pas lui dire trop à la fois.

"Well, sir," he said, "your barn caught fire. The mules couldn't get out of their stalls. They burned." He said, "Then, the little dog went and ate some of that burnt mule meat. It gave him a stomach ache, and he died."

Then, the other fellow grabbed his head on the other end of the telephone. He said, "How did the barn catch fire, imbecile? Tell me quickly!"

"Well," he said, "the barn caught fire because of the house that had caught fire before."

He said, "How did this happen, Jean Sot?"

"Well," he said, "you see, sir, your mother-in-law had a heart attack and she died suddenly and she was enshrouded with candles all around and," he said, "one of the candles ignited the curtains and, before we knew it, the house was on fire and the barn caught fire and the mule burned and Fido ate some of the burnt meat and he died. Otherwise, everything's fine."

"And what killed the poor old woman?"

He said, "Well, it's her daughter, your wife." He said, "When she found out that she had secretly run off with one of the workers on your plantation, that she had eloped with one of the servants, it killed the poor mother."

And with this, the other fellow fell into a fit. He did not know what was going on anymore. It all started with Fido who had eaten some burnt meat, but Jean Sot did not want to say too much all at once.

33. *Tu pourrais mentir / You Could Lie (Martin Latiolais, Catahoula)*

Another example of lively wit can be found in this tale, a variant of motif J1356 "The Flatterer's Retort." Martin Latiolais explained that his old friend Willie Johnson used to tell him lots of stories and jokes, many at his own expense. The old man's answer to the young girl's insulting remark is reminiscent of a story attributed to Winston Churchill who, when reproached by a woman as "repulsively drunk," reportedly replied: "Yes, Madame, and I find you to be ugly and a boor, but I shall be sober tomorrow." A similar episode was included in the W.C. Fields film "It's a Gift" from the 1930s. Motif J267 "The choice between the flattering lie and the unflattering truth" is also present here.

Un nommé Willie Johnson. Et il est mort. Sa fille reste droit là. Ma première voisine-là, c'est sa fille. Il est mort, il y a plusieurs années, mais lui, il avait une mémoire, Jack! Tu parles un vieux bougre qu'avait une mémoire! Il pouvait te raconter des contes qui duraient des heures de temps longs. Puis ça rimait, tu connais? O, lui, il aurait été bon pour ça-là, ouais! Et puis s'asseoir toute la journée, et puis te conter jamais le même.

Puis là, il racontait un tas des contes, il se mettait lui en dedans-là, mais il était tout le temps en bas, tu vois?

Il dit, une fois, il était au bal. Il dit il était après danser avec un belle fille. Ça fait, il dit à la fille-là, "Boy, t'es belle! Je te trouve belle, ouais!" il dit.

Et la fille-là dit, "Monsieur Johnson, moi, je peux pas dire autant de vous. Je vous trouve pas beau."

"Mais," il dit, "écoute! Tu pourrais faire comme moi-là, si tu voudrais, tu pourrais mentir!"

A man was named Willie Johnson. And he is dead. His daughter lives right there. My next-door neighbor is his daughter. He died several years ago, but he had a tremendous memory. You talk about a fellow with a memory! He could tell you stories that went on for hours. And they made sense, you know. Oh he would have been good at this! And he could sit down all day long and never tell the same one twice.

And then, he told lots of stories in which he used himself as a character, but always the underdog, you see.

He said, once, that he was at a dance. He said he was dancing with a pretty girl. So he said to the girl, "Boy, you're pretty! I think you're really pretty!"

And the girl said, "Mister Johnson, I can't say the same about you. I don't think you're handsome."

"Well," he said, "listen! You could do like me, if you wanted to, you could lie!"

34. *Le rat ou la souris / The Rat or the Mouse (Martin Latiolais, Catahoula)*

This tale, a variant of type 1365 *The Obstinate Wife,* and more precisely of sub-type 1365B *Cutting with the Knife or the Scissors,* without the final defiance which leads to the drowning of the wife because she continues to insist even with her last gesture that scissors

should have been used. In this text, the first separation of husband and wife is followed by another even as the couple is trying to achieve a reconciliation.

Baughman reported Anglo-American variants from New York, New Jersey, South Carolina, Wisconsin, Alberta and a literary version cited by Dorson in *Jonathan Draws the Longbow* (p. 230). Dorson also reported a version from Maine in *Buying the Wind* (p. 84), and Burrison included a version from Georgia in *Storytellers* (p. 38). Laval's Folklore Archives had only three French American versions of sub-type B, but many versions of sub-type C, which involves a woman who insists, even unto her last gesture as she drowns, that her husband has lice.

Il y avait une vieille femme et un vieux bougre qu'étaient assis en avant le foyer un soir, et il y a une souris ou un rat qu'a passé. N'importe comment, la vieille femme a dit que c'était une souris, elle.

Ça fait, le vieux bougre dit, "Vieille! C'est un rat!"

La chicane a pris. Ils se sont quittés. Une qui disait c'était une souris, l'autre disait c'était un rat. La chicane a pris. Ils se sont quittés. Ils ont resté un an délaissés.

Ça fait, ils ont décidé ils se seraient repris. Ça fait, ils s'assoient à la même place. Ça fait, le vieux bougre dit à la vieille femme, il dit, "On est bête, quand même, ouais. Se quitter une année de temps," il dit, "pour un rat."

La vieille femme dit, "Je te dis, c'est une souris!"

La chicane a repris. Ils se sont quittés encore. La vieille femme voulait pas lâcher, ni le bougre non plus.

There was an old woman and an old man who were sitting in front of the fire one night, and a mouse or a rat passed by. Anyway, the old lady said that it was a mouse.

So, the old man said, "Woman! That's a rat!"

An argument developed. They finally left each other. One insisted that it had been a mouse, the other said that it was a rat. An argument developed. They separated. They remained apart for a year.

So, they decided that they would get back together. So, they sat in the same place. So, the old man said to the old woman, "We are silly, after all. To separate for a whole year," he said, "for a rat."

The old woman said, "I tell you, it was a mouse!"

The argument flared up again. They separated again. The old woman did not want to give up, nor did the old man.

35. Jean Sot (Revon Reed, Mamou)

The hero of this tale is the traditional fool of French Louisiana, who resembles the traditional French fool Jean le Sot. Geneviève Massignon reported, in *Folktales of France* (no. 20, pp. 80–84), a tale about Jean le Sot in which the opening episode is the same as the one in this version, type 1291B *Filling Cracks with Butter*, which is also very popular in other parts of French America; there were 81 versions of this type in Laval's Folklore Archives. In the second episode, Jean Sot kills the cows instead of milking them because he confuses

tirer, to milk, with *tirer,* to shoot (motif J2259*(p), "Fool's action based on pun;" cf. J2259*(pd), "Fool worries when her husband is out shooting craps. She doesn't know how to cook them.") Compare also motif J1905, "Absurd ignorance about milking animals." In the third episode, the fool kills a mother goose instead of a young gosling. There is an analog in "Foolish John," reported by Saucier in *French Louisiana* (no. 20, pp. 69–70). Jean Sot then puts the dogs named Sel [Salt] and Persil [Parsley] into the gumbo (a variant of motif J2462.1). The preceding episodes are cast in the frame of type 1681B *Fool as Custodian of Home and Animals.* Another Louisiana French version was collected by Claudel and incorporated in his study, "Foolish John Tales from the French Folklore of Louisiana" (*Southern Folklore Quarterly* 12: 157–159). All of these massacres of farm animals have a certain black humor in the Louisiana French context, where a large part of the population still lives in the country and even much of the first and second generation urban population remains attached to the rural family homestead. Jean Sot is then wounded when he tries to attach a plow to his shirt, taking too literally his mother's instructions after he lost a pin in a haystack (motif J2460, "Literal obedience," and type 1696 *What Should I Have Said [Done]?*; motif J2129.4). For a comparable episode, see Parsons, *Antilles* II (p. 345). In the French West Indies, the tales of Jean Sot are often linked to the theme of the Master Thief (cf. 1525A). In the final episode, the fool is abandoned, one supposes, by his parents who send him off to look for a "road stretcher" (type 1296 *Fool's Errand;* motif J2346(e), "Dupe is sent to get a stretcher for a particular object when it is found to be too small"). The storyteller then gives a few possible explanations concerning the eventual destiny of such a fool. One prediction, that he goes off to the university where he becomes a professor, is based in part on a lack of regard for education within traditional Cajun society. For another French American variant, see "Jacques Pataud" in Carrière's *Missouri* (no. 63), which contains the episodes about the butter, the lost needle and a three-legged pot which is expected to walk home alone.

Jean Sot avait le cœur, on conte, beaucoup sensible. Il aimait tout le monde. Il aimait tous les bêtailles. Il aimait jusqu'à la nature, les arbres, les fleurs, la terre. Il avait un grand sentiment pour tout ce qui existait. Un jour, sa mère lui a donné un gros quart de beurre pour aller vendre à la boutique et *trade* ça pour des marchandises, des grosseries, mais en allant là-bas, Jean Sot était fier et bien associé avec la nature. Il sifflait, il chantait, mais tout d'un coup, tandis qu'il traversait un marais sec, il a vu des craques dans la terre, des grosses craques. Et il croyait que c'était des gerçures, ça. *Chapped,* on dit en anglais. Alors, il a ouvert la jarre de beurre et il a commencé à graisser les crevasses dans un effort d'essayer de les guérir. Et il pleurait.

Jean Sot had, it is said, a very sensitive heart. He loved everyone. He loved the animals. He loved even nature, the trees, the flowers, the land. He had deep feelings for everything in existence. One day, his mother gave him a big quart of butter to go and sell at the store and to trade for supplies, groceries, but on the way there, Jean Sot was proud and close to nature. He was whistling, he was singing, but all of a sudden, as he was crossing a dry swamp, he saw cracks in the ground, big cracks. And he thought they were chapped marks. So, he opened the butter jar and he started to butter the cracks in an attempt to heal them. And he wept. He thought it very sad that the land was chapped so. And when the butter ran out, he

Il trouvait beaucoup mauvais que la terre était après gercer comme ça. Et quand tout le beurre a manqué, il s'est vite retourné chez sa mère pour d'autre. Après qu'il a conté qui il y avait eu, naturellement, elle lui a pas donné d'autre beurre. Puis elle l'a bien fouetté pour ça, mais c'était trop tard.

Un jour, ses parents ont parti aussi à la ville pour acheter des nourritures, grosseries. Ils ont décidé de laisser Jean Sot en charge de l'habitation. "Tu vas tirer les vaches. Tu vas faire un gumbo avec la jeune z-oie qu'est dans la cour-là. Oublie pas aussi de mettre sel et persil dans le gumbo. Tu comprends bien?" le vieux père lui a demandé.

"Mais, puis ouais, Pap," répond l'imbécile. "Je comprends exactement qui tu veux dire."

Ça fait, aussitôt qu'ils ont parti, Jean Sot a été chercher les vaches dans le clos. Et là, il a pris le fusil et puis il les a tous tirées avec le fusil. Il a tout tué. Après ça, il a attrapé une vieille couveuse qui était après couver sur quelques œufs de z-oie. Et il lui a tordu le cou. Là, il a chauffé de l'eau après ça, puis il a appelé les deux petits chiens de maison que la mère avait, Sel et Persil. La mère a jamais jonglé à ça, qu'il aurait fait ça. Et puis, il les a coupés en petites grillades et puis, il les a tirés dans l'eau bouillante. Et là, après ça, il a bien brassé ça tout ensemble et il a mis la vieille z-oie, plumes et tripes et tout l'affaire, dans la grande chaudière d'eau bouillante.

Et quand ses parents sont revenus de la ville, ils ont trouvé quatre grosses vaches qu'étaient morts dans la cour de magasin. Et quand ils ont rentré dans la maison, Jean Sot était en train de mettre la table pour les vieux souper. Quand sa mère a vu ses chers petits chiens dans le gumbo, elle a tombé en crises, accordant l'histoire, et le vieux a essayé d'étrangler son fils. Ça, c'était Jean Sot, le sot, l'imbécile, le fou.

Un jour, la mère à Jean Sot avait besoin

went quickly home to his mother for more. After he explained what had happened, naturally, she didn't give him any more butter. And she whipped him well for that, but it was too late.

One day, his parents left to go to town to buy some food, groceries. They decided to leave Jean Sot in charge of the farm. "You will milk [tirer] the cows. You will make a gumbo with the young gosling that's in the yard. Don't forget to put salt and parsley in the gumbo. Do you understand?" the old father asked him.

"Well, of course, Pop," answered the fool. "I understand exactly what you mean."

So, as soon as they were gone, Jean Sot went to get the cows in the field. And then he took a shotgun and he shot [tiré] them all with the shotgun. He killed them all. After that, he caught one of the old laying geese that was setting on several goose eggs. And he twisted its neck. Then he boiled some water and he called the two dogs that his mother kept around the house, Salt and Parsley. The mother never thought about that, that he would have done that. And then he cut them up into little strips and then he threw them into the boiling water. And then, after that, he stirred all of that together and put in the old laying goose, feathers, guts and all, into the big pot of boiling water.

When his parents came home from town, they found four big cows that were dead in the barnyard. And when they went into the house, Jean Sot was setting the table for the old folks to eat. When his mother saw her two dear little dogs in the gumbo, she fell in a fit, according to the story, and the old man tried to choke his son. That was Jean Sot, the idiot, the imbecile, the fool.

One day, Jean Sot's mother needed a

d'une aiguille pour rapiéceter une de ses culottes. Alors, elle dit à Jean Sot, elle dit, "Attelle le wagon-là, et puis va emprunter une aiguille à coudre avec Madame Palonier, l'autre bout." C'était à peu près cinq, six miles-là. Et Jean Sot était tout le temps très obéissant. Il a parti tout de suite. Quand il a revenu, il pouvait pas trouver l'aiguille. Et quand la mère est venue investiguer, il dit, "Je l'ai tirée dans le wagon de paille ici, Mam." Il dit, "C'est drôle, je peux juste pas la trouver," il dit à sa mère.

"Mais," elle dit, "non, pauvre garçon. Il faut pas être aussi bête que ça. Il faut t'attaches ça sur ta chemise une autre fois."

"Ah, ouais, Mam. J'ai compris."

Le lendemain, son père l'a envoyé en wagon encore pour chercher une charrue qu'il avait oubliée dans le clos, une grosse charrue double. Jean Sot est revenu avec la chemise toute déchirée et le sang vidait sur sa poitrine. "Cher Dieu béni!" son père dit, "qui il y a eu?"

"Mais," il dit, "j'ai fait comme Maman m'a dit de faire hier. J'ai essayé d'attacher la charrue sur ma chemise, mais," il dit, "elle a jamais voulu rester."

Son père l'avait, accordant une autre histoire, il l'avait envoyé emprunter une raidisseuse de chemin, un *road-stretcher*, avec le *police jury* un jour, et c'était juste pour une excuse et pour voir comment fou il était. Et il a parti en sifflant comme d'habitude. Et là, ils ont mis tout le butin dans le wagon, puis ils ont déménagé en cachette de pauvre vieux Jean Sot. Ils pouvaient plus endurer ses manières. Ils ont quitté le voisinage et Jean Sot a jamais pu trouver ses parents. Et il y en a qui dit qu'il a été au collège, et il est devenu professeur. Et d'autres qui dit qu'il a embêté le roi pour sa fille, la princesse. D'autres croient qu'il est toujours en vie, dans une forme ou d'autre de fou qu'on trouve toujours dans tout les villes dans le sud-ouest de la Louisiane.

needle to mend one of his pants. So she said to Jean Sot, she said, "Hitch the wagon, and go and borrow a sewing needle from Madame Palonier, over there." It was about five or six miles away. And Jean Sot was always very obedient. He left right away. When he returned, he couldn't find the needle. When his mother came to investigate, he said, "I threw it right here in the hay wagon, Mom." He said, "It's funny, I just can't find it," he said to his mother.

"Well," she said, "no, poor child. You mustn't be so silly. You must pin it to your shirt next time."

"Oh, yes, Mom. I understand."

The next day, his father sent him again in the wagon to get a plow that he had forgotten in the field; a big, double plow. Jean Sot came back with his shirt all torn and blood flowing down his chest. "Dear holy God!" his father said, "What happened?"

"Well," he said, "I did what Mama told me to do yesterday. I tried to pin the plow onto my shirt, but," he said, "it wouldn't stay."

His father had, according to the story, sent him to borrow a road stretcher from the police jury one day, and this was just an excuse to see how foolish he was. And he left whistling as usual. And then, they loaded all their furniture in the wagon, and they moved away, unbeknownst to Jean Sot. They could no longer stand his ways. They left the neighborhood and Jean Sot was never able to find his parents. And there are some who say that he went to college, and that he became a professor. And others say that he fooled the king and won his daughter, the princess. Still others believe that he is still around, in one form or another among the fools that are found in all the towns of southwest Louisiana.

36. Jean Sot à l'école / Jean Sot at School (Clotile Richard, Carencro)

This little tale, a variant of type 1628 *The Learned Son and the Forgotten Language*, is based on a problem that is well-known in Louisiana, that of the child who is eager to abandon his native language for the English he is learning at school. This situation occurs in many societies caught between two languages. Aarne and Thompson reported variants from Lithuania, Sweden, France, Germany, Italy, Hungary, Russia and Canada. In another version from Ile Maurice, the young man asks, "What's that?" at a market to demonstrate that he has forgotten his Creole dialect. When a crab pinches his finger, he suddenly recalls his native language to curse. In a version from Québec in the collection of Luc Lacourcière (no. 475, "Maudite mardine"), the boy has forgotten his French and no longer speaks anything but English, represented in the tale by words that end in "-ine". His father finally becomes upset and exclaims, "Jat demmit! Take de *harnoi*-ine [harness], put it on the *ch'val*-ine [horse], put the *ch'val*-ine on the *tombereau*-ine [cart], and go *charrier* [haul] some *maudite mard*-ine [damn shit]!"

It is interesting to note that Baughman found no English-language variants, neither in England nor in North America.

Jean Sot avait été à l'école pour apprendre l'anglais. Ça fait, il a revenu *back* pour visiter son père et sa mère, et il faisait comme s'il comprenait plus le français.

Ça fait, il a été au jardin (son père et sa mère faisaient jardin) pour visiter. Et puis, il voit les rateaux et la pioche. Ça fait, il voulait demander à sa mère ce que c'était cet outil, pour travailler le jardin. Et puis, en même temps, il met son pied sur le rateau. Le rateau a revenu *back*, l'a frappé sur la bouche. "Ah!" il dit. "Mon fils-de-putain de rateau!"

"Ah," elle dit, "mon garçon, je vois ton français commence à te revenir!"

Jean Sot had gone to school to learn English. So he came back to visit his father and mother, and he was acting as though he no longer understood French.

So he went to the garden (his father and mother were working in the garden) to visit. And then, he saw the rake and the hoe. So he wanted to ask his mother what these tools were, to work in the garden. And at the same time, he put his foot down on the rake. The rake came back and hit him on the mouth. "Ah!" he said, "you son-of-a-bitch of a rake!"

"Ah!" she said, "my son, I see your French is coming back to you!"

37. Rover au collège / Rover in College (Évélia Boudreaux, Carencro)

Baughman reported two examples of this variant of type 1750A *Sending a Dog to be Educated*: one from Arkansas (pp. 129–130 in Vance Randolph's *The Talking Turtle*) in which the fool pays to have a crow educated, and the other from New Mexico (Baughman, unpublished manuscript), in which a dog is to be taught to speak. Mississippi comedian Jerry Clower has a version of this story in his *Stories from Home* ("Crack, W.L. and Rover," pp. 164–166), with a dog of the same name. Jones and Wheeler have an Appalachian version,

"Old Blue Learns to Read and Write" (pp. 81–82). Laval's Archives de Folklore had nine French American variants in which the dog was invariably done away with in the end because of its "indiscretion." This story is based, at least in part, on the notion that the formal educational setting was completely unfamiliar to the members of the older traditionally-oriented generation.

L'enfant a parti, il a été au collège beaucoup loin, dans un état différent que il restait. L'enfant est revenu. Son papa lui dit, "Comment l'école?"

Il dit, "Papa, c'est magnifique, l'école!" Il dit, "Tu devrais voir, Papa, quoi c'est ils faisent avec les chiens." Il dit, "Ils montront les chiens à parler. Ils montront les chiens à lire." Et il dit, "Toi qui aimes Rover si tellement, pourquoi t'envoies pas Rover au collège? Mais," il dit, "Papa, ça coûte un tas d'argent. Tu peux payer pour." Et il dit, "Comme tu aimes Rover si tellement, je serais content de l'amener."

"Mais," il dit, "mon garçon, on va faire ça!" Il dit, "Amène Rover. Mets-le à l'école." Il dit, "Je serais si content de l'entendre parler. Ça serait si une belle compagnie pour moi."

Ce fait, la semaine s'est passée. Les vacances a fini. Le garçon et le chien a parti pour aller au collège. Quand il a arrivé en chemin, il a fait quelque chose avec le chien; il l'a fait détruire. Toujours, quand il écrivait à son papa, il disait à son papa, "Papa, tu devrais voir comment Rover est après apprendre. Mais," il dit, "Papa, il y aurait besoin d'autre argent." Il dit, "J'ai pas assez d'argent. Ça prend, ça coûte beaucoup pour l'éducation à Rover."

Ce fait, le papa lui a envoyé de l'argent. Quand il écrivait, il disait, "Mon fils, comment Rover est après faire?"

"Papa, Rover est après faire si bien! Il commence à parler."

Ce fait, l'heure était arrivée pour l'enfant revient pour les vacances. Et le père était anxieux de voir les progrès que son chien aurait eu fait. Quand l'enfant a arrivé, il dit,

The child left, and went to college far away, in another state. The child returned. His father said to him, "How's school?"

He said, "Papa, school is magnificent!" He said, "You should see, Papa, what they do with dogs." He said, "they teach dogs to talk. They teach dogs to read." And he said, "You like Rover so much, why don't you send Rover to college? But," he said, "Papa, this costs lots of money. You can afford it." And he said, "Since you love Rover so much, I would be happy to take him along."

"Well," he said, "my son, we'll do just that!" He said, "Take Rover. Put him in school." He said, "I would be so happy to hear him speak. It would be such good company for me."

So the week went by. The holidays ended. The son and the dog left to go to college. When he was down the road, he did something with the dog; he had it destroyed. Always when he wrote to his father, he said to his father, "Papa, you should see how well Rover is learning. But," he said, "Papa, it'll take more money." He said, "I don't have enough money. It costs a lot for Rover's education."

So the father sent him some money. When he would write, he would say, "My son, how's Rover doing?"

"Papa, Rover is doing so well! He has started talking."

So the time arrived for the son to go home for the holidays. And the father was eager to see what progress the dog had made. When the child arrived, he said, "My son,

"Mon fils, et Rover, où est Rover?"

Il dit, "Papa, dis pas rien!" Il dit, "Je vas te dire un petit secret." Il dit, "Rover était après devenir trop *smart*. Rover était après dire quoi t'avais fait, dans le dos à Maman!" Il dit, "J'ai eu pour m'en défaire, de Rover. Je voulais pas qu'il gâte ton mariage!"

"Mais," il dit, "mon garçon, t'as bien fait!" Il dit, "Ça aurait pas été bon que ta maman connaît qu'est-ce que j'ai fait dans son dos!"

and Rover, where's Rover?"

He said, "Papa, don't say anything!" He said, "I'll tell you a little secret." He said, "Rover was getting too smart. Rover was talking about what you used to do behind Mama's back!" He said, "I had to do away with him, with Rover. I didn't want him to ruin your marriage!"

"Well," he said, "my son, you did well!" He said, "It wouldn't have been good for your mother to know what I did behind her back!"

38. La jument Verte / The Green Mare (Félix Richard, Cankton)

In this tale, the motifs J613 "Wise fear of the weak for the strong" and J814.4 "Flattering the villain to avoid being beaten or killed" are involved. Jones and Wheeler reported an Appalachian variant, "The Paint Job" (p. 115), in which a mule's tail is painted red. The clever little man who succeeds in escaping a more powerful opponent is a popular hero in the oral tradition of Louisiana, exactly in the same spirit as Compère Lapin (see the section on animal tales). In a close parallel (told by my father), two brothers go to a dance. One likes to dance, the other likes to drink. The first goes straight to the dance floor, the second to the bar. Later someone comes to tell the drinker that there has been a fight and that his brother is out cold on the floor. He runs to the musicians' table to announce that the person who hit his brother had better show himself because he wants to have a few words with him. When a huge man comes forward asking what he has to say, he says simply, "Boy, you really stung him, didn't you?" The version presented here was told by an excellent storyteller who decorates his stories with a great love for details, such as the description of the good young bachelor who listens too well to his father's advice, or that of the bully who comes forward in the end to confront the hero.

Ils m'ont dit, à Church Pointe, il y avait arrivé, des années passées, c'est comme je te dis, il y avait du monde là qui avait des cœurs. Et il y avait un bougre, un vieux garçon. Il avait jamais essayé à sortir, parce que son père, il continuait à l'écharlanter.

"Écoute, garçon. T'aurais un goût d'aller au bal, et t'aurais un goût de rencontrer des filles, peut-être te choisir une fille pour ta femme, mais," il dit, "écoute. C'est pas tout ça, non. T'as pour avoir assez de quoi, quand tu vas te rencontrer une dame, en tout cas tu

They told me, in Church Point, it happened, years ago, like I was telling you, there were people there who had heart. And there was one guy, a bachelor. He had never tried to go out because his father was always on his case.

"Listen, son. You might have a notion to go to the dance, and you might have a notion to meet some girls, maybe choose one of them for a wife, but," he said, "listen. That's not all there is to it. You have to have the means, when you meet a lady, in case you

te décides de te marier, peut-être pas longtemps après." Il dit, "Quoi c'est que tu vas soigner cette femme-là avec? T'as pour avoir de quoi pour avoir une femme. T'as pour avoir un cheval et un boghei, ça c'est sûr, et," il dit, "t'as pour avoir de l'argent. Ça fait, tu peux pas aller te marier avec les poches vides."

Ça fait, il a écouté son père et il était derrière pour se faire de l'argent. Il pouvait pas rentrer sa récolte assez vite. C'était mettre ça à la banque et puis il la comptait souvent. Et un de ces jours, il allait venir à en avoir assez, et il pourrait aller au bal.

Ça fait, il était rendu vieux garçon. Encore dans le temps, l'argent était rare. Il pouvait pas s'en trouver un tas. Il travaillait tout ça il pouvait, sur tous les côtés. Quand il avait pas d'ouvrage chez lui, il travaillait à faire des fossés, et le diable et ses cornes.

Ça fait, un bonjour, il y a quelqu'un de ses *partners* qui lui, "Écoute, voir. Moi, je crois t'es après manquer le *show*." Il dit, "Quand tu vas t'apercevoir—T'es après écouter ton papa-là, c'est bon. O, c'est une belle chose. C'est rare les enfants qui écoutent leur père, d'une certaine manière, aussi bien que ça. Mais, écoute. Il y a une limite dans cette affaire. Mais," il dit, "tout à l'heure, tu connais quoi ce qui va arriver? Tu seras rendu trop vieux, quand tu vas aller au bal, c'est des jeunes filles qui restent-là." Il dit, "Les vieilles sont toutes parties. Il y a quelqu'un qui les a pris. Ça fait, toutes celles-là qui seront là seront un tas plus jeunes que toi. Quelle c'est, tu crois, qui voudra de toi? Tu seras trop vieux. Tu pourras pas t'en trouver une. Ça fait," il dit, "écoute. Avant tu manques le bateau, tu ferais mieux venir au bal, et puis c'est comme ça que tu vas trouver une femme."

Ça fait, lui, naturellement, il était pas comme ces jeunes petits bougres-là qui allaient au bal sur un *ride* ou quelque chose comme ça. Lui, il avait son boghei neuf. Et

decide to marry, maybe not long afterwards." He said, "How will you care for that woman? You have to have means to have a wife. You have to have a horse and a buggy, that's for sure, and," he said, "you have to have money. So you can't just go and get married with empty pockets."

So he listened to his father and he was trying hard to make himself some money. He couldn't bring in the crop fast enough. It was a matter of putting it in the bank, and he counted it often. And one day, he would finally have enough, and he would be able to go to the dance.

So he became an old bachelor. In those days, money was still scarce. He couldn't find a lot of it. He worked as much as he could, in every direction. When he wasn't working at home, he worked digging ditches, and every damn thing.

So, one fine day, one of his friends said to him, "Listen, here. I think you're missing the show." He said, "One day, you'll notice— You're listening to your papa now, and that's good. Oh, it's a fine thing. It's rare to find children who listen to their father, in a way, as well as you do. But listen. There's a limit to this." He said, "Do you know what's going to happen soon? You're going to be too old, when you're going to go to the dance, there will be only young girls left there." He said, "The older ones are all gone. Someone took them all. So all the ones that will be there will be much younger than you. Which one of these do you think will want you? You'll be too old. You won't be able to find yourself one. So," he said, "listen. Before you miss the boat, you'd better go to the dance and that's how you'll find a wife."

So naturally, he wasn't like the other young guys who have to get a ride to the dance. He had a brand-new buggy. And he had a beautiful black horse. It never came

85

puis, il avait une belle bêtaille noire. Ça sortait pas de l'écurie, cette affaire. Ça fait qu'il a décidé d'aller au bal à la pointe. Il a été bonne heure, juste après le soleil couché. Ça fait, il y avait un poteau de lumière dehors qui était allumé. Et il a figuré, "*Well*, je vas mettre mon boghei là, et ma bêtaille en bas de la lumière-là. Ça fait, je suis sûr il y a rien qui va les toucher. Il y a des constables ici. Aller mettre mon boghei dans le noir là-bas, eux peut massacrer mon boghei. Quelqu'un peut couper le *top* ou. . ." tu connais.

Ça fait, pour être sûr que rien arrive, il l'amarre au poteau ayoù la lumière était. Ça fait, quelqu'un est arrivé, ils ont vu cette belle bêtaille et ce beau boghei. Ils avaient jamais vu ça, tu connais. Il y en avait, des bons bogheis, mais ça avait pas de boghei, pas comme lui. Bougre-là, un petit brin de poussière et il fallait il le lave.

Ça fait, tout à l'heure, il s'avait amené une topette, tu connais, dans le bas du boghei. Dans le temps, c'était du *moonshine* et tu pouvais pas boire ça dans la salle. Pas proche! Et il avait chaud dans la salle. Il était après avoir un bon temps. Ça fait, il décide il aurait été dehors et puis se ramasser un petit coup de ce *moonshine* il avait, et puis voir à sa bêtaille et son boghei. Il arrive là-bas. Eux avaient peint sa jument verte avec de la peinture. Non, mais, monde, monde, monde! Quand il a vu ça, ça l'a foutu en feu, tu vois.

Ça fait, il revient dans la salle. Il monte sur la table de musiciens. Il arrête la musique. Il lève ses deux mains en l'air. Il a commencé à annoncer qu'il pouvait pas voir dans le monde qui dans le tonnerre qu'avait fait ce qu'ils avaient fait avec sa bêtaille, droit là, à bic-à-blanc en bas de la lumière. Il dit que quelqu'un a venu peindre sa bêtaille vert. Il dit, "Qui-ce qui aurait fait ça?" Et puis il se cognait l'estomac, tu connais, comme s'il avait devenu un taureau tout du coup.

Tout à l'heure, il s'en vient un bougre en

out of the stall. So he decided to go to a dance at the point. He went early, just after sunset. So there was a light post outside. And he figured, "Well, I'll put my horse and buggy there under the light. That way, I'm sure that nothing will touch them. There are constables here. If I put my buggy in the dark, someone might ruin it. Someone could cut the top, or. . . ," you know.

So to be sure that nothing would happen, he tied up to the post where the light was. So as people arrived, they saw this beautiful horse and this fine buggy. They had never seen it, you know. There were some fine buggies, but not like this one. This guy, one little speck of dust and he had to wash it.

So later, he had brought along a flask, you know, on the floor of the buggy. In those days, it was moonshine and you couldn't drink in the dance hall. Not hardly! And he was hot in the hall. He was having a good time. So he decided to go outside and take a hit of the moonshine he had, and see about his horse and buggy. He arrived there. Somebody had painted his mare green. No, but, people, people, people! When he saw this, he felt on fire, you see.

So he came back in the hall. He climbed up on the musicians' table. He stopped the music. He raised his two hands in the air. He started to announce that he couldn't for the life of him imagine who in thunderation had done what had been done to his horse, right there, in plain sight, under the light. He said that someone had painted his mare green. He said, "Who would have done this?" And he was hitting himself on the chest, you know, as though he had become a bull all of a sudden.

After a while, a fellow came along across

travers de la salle qui avait la chemise déboutonnée avec le jabot grand ouvert, avec les culottes qui étaient après pendre un peu bas et il avait le mouchoir juste manière enfoncé dans sa poche. Il vient au ras de la table de musiciens-là. Il avait son estomac plein de crins, tu comprends. Il se cogne dans l'estomac comme ça. Il dit, "C'est moi le boulé qui a peint la jument." Il dit, "Quoi ce que t'as pour dire pour ça?"

"Mais," il dit, "j'ai venu pour te dire qu'elle est sec. Elle est parée pour une seconde couche."

the hall. His shirt was unbuttoned showing his chest hair, and his pants were slung low with a handkerchief just barely tucked into one pocket. He came up to the musicians' table. His chest was covered with hair, you understand. He pounded his chest and said, "I'm the bully that painted the mare." He said, "What do you have to say about it?"

"Well," he said, "I've come to tell you that she's dry. She's ready for a second coat."

39. L'enfant de soixante-quinze ans / The Seventy-five-year-old Child (Martin Latiolais, Catahoula)

Baughman lists a variant from Texas (concerning Pecos Bill) under motif X913(ea) "Hero smokes cigarettes for ninety-nine years; they finally kill him," which resembles the situation presented in this tale. Martin Latiolais's commentary at the end shows his quick wit which often focused on his own advanced years.

Il y a un vieux bougre qu'était bien malade, une fois. Il avait soixante-quinze ans. Ça fait, il était malade. Il a resté plusieurs temps malade. Ça fait, il a fini par mourir. Et son papa et sa maman étaient assis, un chaque côté de son lit, de ce vieux bougre. Ça fait, après il est mort, le vieux homme regarde la vieille femme. Il dit, "Vieille, je t'ai dit c'était un enfant on aurait pas sauvé, ça!"

Mais, il avait soixante-quinze ans. Hé! Il commençait avoir l'âge, hein?
BA: C'était l'heure?
ML: Ouais, c'était l'heure. Tu vois, moi, j'ai soixante-treize, mais je trouve pas que c'est l'heure encore!

There was an old fellow who was very ill, once. He was seventy-five years old. And he was sick. He was sick for quite a while. And he finally died. And his father and his mother were sitting, one on each side of the bed, of the old fellow's bed. So after he died, the old man looked at the old woman. He said, "Honey, I told you that this was a child we wouldn't be able to save!"

But he was seventy-five. Hey, he was starting to be old enough, eh?
BA: It was time?
ML: Yes, it was time. You see, I'm seventy-three, but I don't find that it's time yet!

40. Les jumelles / The Twins (Elby Deshotels, Reddell)

This tale is associated with motif J2234 "Is that you or your brother?" concerning the distinguishing of twins. Baughman found variants from England and Scotland. In this version, the braggart "proves" that he is able to tell one of the twin sisters from the other with the absurd affirmation that the one on the right looked more like the other one than the other one looked like her.

Il y avait ces deux vieux hommes. Ils étiont voisins et ça pêchait tout le temps ensemble. Et il y avait un, il avait la tête beaucoup, beaucoup dure. Et tu pouvais pas changer son idée. Il était tout le temps, tout le temps bien; jamais, jamais mal.

Un jour, ils estiont après pêcher dessus l'écore du bayou. Et ils se sont aperçu il y avait deux petites filles qu'étaient après jouer dans le sable. Il y en a un qui dit à l'autre, "T'as déjà vu ces petites fille-là? Les petites Hébert?"

Il dit, "Non, je les ai jamais vues."

"Mais," il dit, "c'est des jumelles." Et il dit, "Ça se ressemble autant que deux petits peut se ressembler. Ça peut pas se ressembler plus que ça se ressemble. Enfin, leur mère et leur père peut pas les distinguer. Elles sont si pareilles que leur mère et leur père peut pas dire."

"O, mais," il dit, "je te parie, moi, je peux les dire."

"O," il dit, "j'aurais bien cru que toi, tu pourrais, parce que t'es tout le temps bien; t'es jamais *wrong*. Mais," il dit, "peut-être ça va venir."

Et les deux petites filles ont marché et elles sont revenues les rejoindre. Et quand elles ont arrivé, elles se sont promenées un bout de temps. Ils ont visité avec elles autres. Ils ont charré. Et puis, ils ont parti à marcher dessus l'écore du bayou. Ça se fait, il se tourne à son ami. Il dit, "Bien mais, ça se ressemble ou ça se ressemble pas?"

"O, ouais!" il dit. "Ça se ressemble, elles autres, aussi pareilles que ça peut être."

There were these two old men. They were neighbors and they were always fishing together. And one of them was very, very hard-headed. And you couldn't change his mind. He was always, always right; never, never wrong.

One day, they were fishing on the bank of the bayou. And they noticed that there were two little girls playing in the sand. And one said to the other, "Have you ever seen those little girls? The little Hébert girls?"

He said, "No, I've never seen them."

"Well," he said, "they are twins." And he said, "They look as much alike as two children can. They couldn't look more alike than they do. In fact, their mother and father can't tell them apart. They are so alike that their mother and father can't tell them apart."

"Oh, but," he said, "I'll bet you that I can tell them apart."

"Oh," he said, "I should have known that you could, because you're always right; you're never wrong. But," he said, "maybe the day will come."

And the two little girls walked and came up to them. And when they arrived, they walked around a little. They visited with them. They chatted. And then, they left walking along the bank of the bayou. So, one turned to his friend. He said, "Well, then, do they look alike or not?"

"Oh, yes!" he said. "They look as much alike as possible."

"Ah," il dit, "je t'ai dit tu pouvais pas les distinguer."

"Ah," il dit, "j'ai pas dit ça. J'ai dit ça se ressemble, mais," il dit, "je peux les distinguer."

"Mais," il dit, "comment tu vas faire?"

"Mais," il dit, "celle-là à la droite, elle ressemble un peu plus à l'autre."

"Ah," he said, "didn't I tell you that you couldn't tell them apart?"

"Ah," he said, "I didn't say I couldn't. I said they look alike, but," he said, "I can tell them apart."

"Well," he said, "how are you going to do this?"

"Well," he said, "the one on the right, she looks a little more like the other one."

41. D'autre tabac! / More Tobacco! (Elizabeth Landreneau, Mamou)

This is a version of the rarely reported type 1173A *The Devil Is to Fulfill Three Wishes*, although in this case, there is no deal with the devil, only a bewildered simple man. (Compare also to type 1337 *Peasant Visits the City* and to motif J1742 "The countryman in the wide world.") Mistaking the nature of the good fortune his neighbors try to bestow upon him, the poor countryman chooses only the provisions he is used to buying. When asked what more he would like, he starts over on his limited list. Dorson (*Buying the Wind*, pp. 88–89) presented a Maine version in which a stereotypical drunken Indian asked first for rum, then for sugar, and finally for more rum. Parsons described a similar situation in "Boys Goes to Town" (*Antilles*, no. 86), also without the devil motif.

Ouais, un jour, il y avait un voisinage, et il y a un vieux homme qu'était beaucoup pauvre. Vieux Gabriel. Et ses voisins ont décidé ça l'aurait amené à la boutique pour lui donner des affaires, acheter des affaires pour lui manger, ça il avait de besoin. Et ils l'ont pris. Ils l'ont amené. Il était surpris de ça et il se comprenait pas bien. Ça fait, ça dit, "Qui tu veux, Gabriel? Achête ça tu veux, ouais. Ça t'as de besoin."

"Bien, mais," il dit, "je vas prendre du tabac."

Et ça dit, "Quoi d'autre?"

"Je vas prendre du sucre."

"Et encore d'autre?"

"Je vas prendre du café."

Et là, il avait fini. Il a arrêté. "Mais," ça dit, "tu peux avoir d'autre chose. Tu peux avoir plus."

Yes, one day, there was this neighborhood, and there was an old man who was very poor. Old Gabriel. And his neighbors decided that they would take him to the store to give him a few things, buy a few things for him to eat, things that he needed. And they came to pick him up. They took him. He was surprised about all this and didn't understand exactly what was happening. So they said, "What do you want, Gabriel? Buy what you want, what you need."

"Well, then," he said, "I'll take some tobacco."

And they said, "What else?"

"I'll take some sugar."

"And what else?"

"I'll take some coffee."

And then he was finished. He stopped. "But," they said, "you can have something else. You can have more."

"Je peux avoir d'autre chose?" il dit. "Je peux avoir plus?"

"O, ouais!"

"Bien, mais," il dit, "je vas prendre d'autre tabac."

"I can have something else?" he said. "I can have more?"

"Oh, yes!"

"Well, then," he said, "I'll take some more tobacco."

42. Marquer la place / Marking the Place (Elmo Ancelet, Lafayette)

This tale is common among fishermen. It is based on both of the absurd responses associated with type 1278A *Marking a Good Fishing Spot,* according to Baughman who found variants from Texas, Missouri, Indiana, and Colorado. In the version presented here, the storyteller localizes the tale, casting his own fishing buddies as the dupes who are trying to mark their great bream [bluegill perch] spot.

C. J. puis Bennett Guilbeau étaient à la pêche. Et puis eux étaient dans le bateau après attraper des patassas, et puis un tas de patassas. Et quand eux a eu fini remplir la glacière, Bennett dit à C. J., "T'as marqué la place?"

"O, ouais!" il dit.

"Mais," il dit, "ayoù tu l'as marqué?"

"Mais," il dit, "je l'ai marqué dessous le bateau."

"Mais," il dit, "C. J., sacré couillon! Comment tu crois, comment tu fais pour dire on va avoir le même bateau une autre fois?"

C. J. and Bennett Guilbeau were out fishing. And they were in a boat catching bream, a lot of bream. And when they finished filling their ice chest, Bennett said to C. J., "Did you mark the place?"

"Oh, yes!" he said.

"Well," he said, "where did you mark it?"

"Well," he said, "I made a mark on the bottom of the boat."

"Well," he said, "C. J., you damned fool! How do you know, how can you be sure that we'll get the same boat next time?"

43. Frapper la main / Hitting the Hand (Elmo Ancelet, Lafayette)

Aarne and Thompson noted only Hungarian variants for type 1349D* *What is the Joke?* Baughman did not include the type number, but did describe a similar motif J2131.1(a) "Stranger puts hand on a stone, lets numskull hit it as hard as he likes. Man removes his hand; numskull shows another the trick. He has no stone; so he puts his hand in front of his face." He noted variants only from Ontario. Dorson reported a Maine version in *Buying the Wind* (pp. 93–94). There are nevertheless countless versions of this story which typically casts the traditional fool as the dupe: in France, it is the Belgian; in Québec, it is the bloke [Englishman]; in Nova Scotia, it's the Québecois; in British American tradition, it can be the

"Aggie," the "Polack," the white man (for blacks), the black man (for whites), and so on. The gestural humor of this story makes it difficult to render effectively in transcription.

Il y avait un bougre qu'était après marcher, puis il a rencontré un de ses amis. Il dit, "Je te parie, si je mets ma main devant le poteau-là," il dit, "je te parie cinq piastres que tu peux pas la frapper."

"O, mais," le bougre dit, "ça, c'est un pari."

Ça fait, il a mis sa main, et puis quand l'autre bougre a tiré après, il a halé sa main. L'autre bougre a sacré ça à le poteau. Il a manqué de casser sa main.

Ça fait, il a continué plus loin, il a rencontré un de ses autres amis. Mais il dit entre lui-même, "Ça, c'est une chance pour rattraper mes cinq piastres." Il dit ça à le bougre-là, "Je te parie je mets ma main et tu peux pas la frapper."

Bougre dit, "Mais ça, c'est un pari."

Il regarde pour un poteau. Il regarde pour un arbre, quelque chose. Il y avait pas rien. Ça fait [le conteur met sa main devant son propre visage], il dit, *"Okay,"* il dit, "tire!"

There was a fellow who was walking along and he met one of his friends. He said, "I'll bet you, if I put my hand in front of that post," he said, "I'll bet you five bucks that you can't hit it."

"Oh, well," the fellow said, "that's a bet."

So he put his hand up, and when the other fellow tried to hit it, he pulled his hand away. The other fellow smacked the post. He almost broke his hand.

So he walked along a little farther, he met another of his friends. And he said to himself, "There's a chance to win back my five dollars." He said to the other fellow, "I'll bet you that you can't hit my hand."

The fellow said, "Well, that's a bet."

He looked for a post. He looked for a tree, something. There was nothing. So [the storyteller places his hand in front of his own face], he said, "Okay," he said, "shoot!"

44. La vache de l'homme qu'entendait dur / The Cow Owned by the Man Who Was Hard of Hearing (Burke Guillory, Mamou)

This tale belongs to type 1698G *Misunderstood Words Lead to Comic Results*. Baughman described a remarkably similar variant from Arkansas collected by Vance Randolph (*The Talking Turtle*, pp. 39–41). A deaf man has asked the preacher to announce the loss of his cow; he thinks the preacher is doing so when he is actually extolling a woman who will be married on the following Sunday. The deaf man interrupts the announcement, just as in the present text, to say, "Her rump's caved in, folks, and she's got one spoiled tit." Laval's Archives de Folklore had 26 versions of this type, without specifying the episodes. Compare also type 1832L* *A Woman Orders Mass to be Said for her Stolen Ox*, which features another confusion due to a similar misunderstanding in church.

Un vieux homme entendait dur. Ça fait, avant la messe commence, il a été le dimanche. Il allait tous les dimanches à la

An old man was hard of hearing. So before mass started one Sunday, he went to church. He went to Mass every Sunday. He

messe. Il fait dire au prêtre, "Je voudrais tu fais un annonce pour moi." Il dit, "J'ai perdu une vache." Et il dépeint la vache, à qui elle ressemblait. Il dit, "Annonce au monde, si ça voit cette vache-là, c'est pour moi."

Prêtre dit, "C'est bien." Et le vieux s'a assis dans le banc en avant. Il entendait beaucoup dur. Mais avant de faire les annoncements pour la vache, il a annoncé les bans d'un mariage, "Mademoiselle Telle-une-telle."

Et le vieux bougre écoutait-là. Et il dit, il a arrêté le prêtre, il dit, "Oublie pas de les dire, aussi, elle a une corne creuse et un téton gâté!"

sent a message to the priest, "I would like you to make an announcement for me." He said, "I've lost a cow." And he described the cow, what it looked like. He said, "Announce to the people that, if they should see such a cow, it's mine."

The priest said, "All right." And the old man sat in the front pew. He was very hard of hearing. But before making the announcement about the cow, the priest announced the banns of marriage, "Miss So-and-so. . . ."

And the old fellow was listening. And he said, he stopped the priest and said, "Don't forget to tell them, also, that she's got one hollow horn and a spoiled teat!"

45. Dans le lit ou sur la table / On the Bed or on the Table (Stanislaus "Tanisse" Faul, Cankton)

This tale is a variant of type 1379* False Members, with only a Spanish American (Cuban) reference in Thompson and none in Baughman. Burrison has a variant, "The Synthetic Bride" (p. 183), in which the husband runs away in the end, without a clever remark, complaining only that he was fooled by his bride.

Une fois, il y avait une fille, un garçon qu'a rencontré une fille. Il la trouvait belle. Elle était belle. Ça fait, ils prétendent que il l'aimait assez, il a demandé pour la marier. "Mais," elle dit, "Okay." Il se sont mariés. Elle restait joliment loin, tu sais. Il fallait il va la marier là-bas chez son père à elle.

Le soir, ils ont fait la veillée. Ils ont été pour se coucher. Elle avait une petite table auprès de son lit. Ça se fait, elle s'a assis sur le bord du lit. Premièrement, elle a ôté ses dents. Elle les a mis sur la petite table. Elle a ôté un bras. Elle l'a mis sur la petite table. Elle a ôté une jambe. Elle l'a mis sur la petite table. C'était du liège, ça. Là, elle avait un œil en crystal. Elle l'a ôté. Elle l'a mis sur la petite table. Là, elle s'a quitté aller dans le lit, tu

Once, there was a girl, a boy who met a girl. He found her beautiful. She was beautiful. So they say that he loved so much that he asked to her to marry him. "Well," she said, "Okay." They got married. She lived pretty far away, you know. He had to go to her father's house to marry her.

That night, they stayed up late. They went to bed. She had a little night table next to the bed. So she sat on the edge of the bed. First, she took out her teeth. She put them on the little table. She took off an arm. She put it on the little table. She took off a leg. She put it on the little table. This was all made of cork. Then, she had a glass eye. She took it out. She put it on the little table. Then she let herself fall into bed, you see. She lay

vois. Elle s'a couchée. Lui, il a resté là à la petite table. Il disait pas rien. Elle dit, "Quoi? Tu te couches pas?"

"Mais," il dit, "je connais pas. Il y en a autant sur la petite table comme il y a dans le lit. Je connais pas ayoù il faut je me couche."

down. He stayed by the little table. He said nothing. She said, "What? Aren't you coming to bed?"

"Well," he said, "I don't know. There's just as much of you on the little table as there is in the bed. I don't know where I should lie."

46. La vache à cinq veaux / The Cow with Five Calves (Stanislaus "Tanisse" Faul, Cankton)

This tale is a variant of type 1567F *Hungry Shepherd Attracts Attention,* in which the principal character earns an invitation to join his neglectful hosts at table by telling a story about a fifth calf who had to wait its turn to eat. Aarne and Thompson listed Spanish, Spanish American, German and French variants. Dorson presented an English-language translation of a Mexican American version in *Buying the Wind* (pp. 445–446). See Delarue, *Bulletin folklorique de l'Ile de France,* XII [1950], pp. 130 ff. for a discussion of French variants. In another Louisiana French variant, reported by Alfred Dupérier in "A Narrative of Events," *New Iberia* (compiled by Glenn R. Conrad, p. 60), the story is attributed to a certain Athanase Hébert who was renowned for his quick wit. Like the character in this story, he brought up the story about the five calves when he was not invited to sit at the dinner table upon his arrival from the cattle range.

Il y avait un bougre, une fois, un étranger. Il est venu par ici, et il était tard, et lui, il était las. Il était à cheval. Il était las. Il a arrivé à une place. Un homme était après tirer sa vache pour faire à souper, tu connais.

Là, il a dit ça, il dit, "Moi, je suis trop tard pour trouver les personnes que je cherche." Il dit, "Est-ce que je pourrais pas rester icitte à soir? Il y aurait pas une place pour moi coucher?"

Il dit, "Ouais."

Il a descendu. Il a désellé son cheval. Il a rentré. C'était frais. La cheminée était allumée dans la maison. La cuisine se trouvait bord là. Ça fait, ils ont arrivé; ils étiont après charrer. Ça fait, c'était temps pour souper et la femme a fait signe il fallait il va souper. Et le vieux a été souper et l'homme a resté là.

There was a fellow, once, a stranger. He came by this way, and he was late and he was tired. He was on horseback. He was tired. He arrived in a certain place. A man was milking his cow for supper, you know.

So he said, "It's too late for me to find the people I need to find." He said, "Couldn't I stay here tonight? Would there be a place for me to sleep?"

He said, "Yes."

He dismounted. He unsaddled his horse. He went inside. It was cool. The fireplace was lit in the house. The kitchen was on this side. So they arrived; they were chatting. So it was time for supper and the woman of the house indicated that he should come and eat. And the old man went to eat and the stranger stayed there.

Là, en étant après souper, il dit à l'homme, à l'étranger, "Qu'est-ce que vous avez vu des plus fort dans votre route?"

"Well," il dit, "j'ai vu une vache avec cinq veaux."

"O! O! Mais," il dit, "quoi ce que ça fait? Il y a un veau qui avait pas de tété?"

Il dit, "Non."

Il dit, "Mais quoi il faisait?"

"Mais," il dit, "il faisait comme moi, il guettait."

Then, while having his supper, he said to the man, to the stranger, "What is the strangest thing that you've seen in your travels?"

"Well," he said, "I saw a cow with five calves."

"Oh! Oh! But," he said, "what did it do? There was one calf that didn't have a teat?"

He said, "No."

He said, "Well, what did it do?"

"Well," he said, "it did what I am doing. It watched."

47. Les rêves des Indiens / The Dreams of Indians (Stanislaus "Tanisse" Faul, Cankton)

This tale is built upon motif K66(a) "Dream contest between Indian and white man." Baughman described a sub-variant K66(aa) in which the Indian announces after the exchange of gifts "that they will dream no more," that the white man "dreams too hard for him," with variants from New York, South Carolina and Georgia. This story is also popular in the John and Old Master cycle of African American oral tradition. Compare, for example, "Dreaming Contest," in Dorson's *American Negro Folktales* (no. 207). Burrison reports a similar story, "Uncle Billy and the Vision of the Corn," a variant of motif K66(ca), in which Uncle Billy counters a divine revelation concerning his donating a wagon load of corn with a "revelation" of his own that he should not.

Il y avait des Indiens droite ici pendant un temps. C'était leur territoire. Et ils ont réussi à les chasser, mais pendant un temps, il y avait du monde qui les avaient adoucis alentour. Ça causait bien. C'était du monde *smart*, mais c'était des chasseurs. Il y en a quelques uns qui ont resté qui étaient vaillants et doux.

Ça eux autres rèvent là, il faut ça s'efface. Si eux autres ont rêvé que tu leur as donné quelque chose, il faut tu leur donnes. Hâlaille pas avec ça!

Ça fait, il y a un homme, il avait une belle carabine, une carabine de guerre, une grosse carabine. Et l'Indien avait un goût pour. Et l'Indien avait un beau cheval de

There were Indians right here at one time. This was their land. And they were eventually run off, but at one time, there were people who had civilized them around here. They spoke well. They were smart people, but they were hunters. There were a few kind and gentle ones who remained.

Whatever they dreamed had to come true. If they dreamed that you gave them something, you had to give it to them. You couldn't fool around with that!

So there was a man who had a fine rifle, a military rifle, a big rifle. And an Indian wanted it. And the Indian had a beautiful saddle horse. The next morning, the Indian

selle. Le lendemain matin, l'Indien arrive. Il dit, "J'ai rêvé que tu m'avais donné ta carabine." Il a été, il a attrapé la carabine. Il lui a donné.

Quelque semaines après ça, l'homme a été au sauvage. Il dit, "J'ai rêvé que tu m'avais donné ton cheval." Puis il avait le cheval avec un cable dessus. Il dit, "J'ai rêvé hier au soir que tu m'avais donné ton cheval."

Il dit, "Tiens, mais," il dit, "allons plus rêver!"

arrived. He said, "I dreamed that you gave me your rifle." He went and got his rifle. He gave it to him.

Several weeks later, the white man went to the Indian. He said, "I dreamed that you gave me your horse." And he had the horse on a lead rope. He said, "I dreamed last night that you gave me your horse."

He said, "Here, take it, but," he said, "let's not dream anymore!"

48. Un prêtre à l'envers / A Backwards Priest (Claude Landry, Bayou Pigeon)

The motifs involved in this tale include J1910 "Fatal disregard of anatomy," and J1942 "Inappropriate care due to ignorance." Luc Lacourcière reported in an interview that he had collected variants of this story in the Beauce region of Québec in which people tried to straighten an injured man's club foot. Lacourcère also explained that the tale was locally understood to be thinly-veiled reference to a well-known judge from the region.

Il y avait un prêtre, ça lui donnait loin à marcher pour aller. Il faisait l'église, la messe, dedans deux différentes campagnes. Ça lui donnait un bon bout à marcher d'une à l'autre.

Ça fait, un matin, il faisait froid. Même ça glaçait. Ça fait qu'il a pris à s'en aller à pied. Il a donné la messe dans une place, mais là, il était parti pour l'autre chapelle. Et voilà qu'il s'en allait, il était proche glacé. Il y a un jeune bougre qui s'en vient sur son *motorcycle.*

"Père," il dit, "vous voulez un *ride?*"

"O!" il dit, "garçon, moi je sais pas *about ride* dessus ces affaires-là."

Il dit, "Écoute, Père. C'est loin d'aller à l'autre chapelle là-bas, et il fait froid." Il dit, "Ça serait mieux que marcher, ça serait plus vite."

"Ouais," il dit, "garçon, je vas te dire quoi, ça va être froid aussi."

"Non, mais," il dit, "Père, tourne ce col et puis ton capot, vire-le devant derrière. Là

There was a priest who had far to go on foot. He said Mass in two different areas. He had far to walk to get from one to the other.

So one morning, it was cold. In fact, it was freezing. So he left walking. He said Mass in one place, but then he was leaving for the other chapel. And he was on his way, he was almost freezing. A young man showed up on a motorcycle.

"Father," he said, "do you want a ride?"

"Oh!" he said, "Son, I don't know about riding on one of those things."

He said, "Listen, Father. It's a long way to the other chapel and it's cold." He said, "It would be better than walking, it would be faster."

"Yes," he said, "Son, I'll tell you what, it would be colder, too."

"No, but," he said, "Father, turn that collar around and turn your coat backwards.

où ce que le vent peut pas passer en travers. Ça va pas être trop froid."

"Mais," il dit, "tu connais, garçon, c'est peut-être pas une mauvaise idée, ça." Il a attrapé son capot, il l'a fourré l'autre manière. Ils allont à peu près à un mile. Ils ont manqué le détour dans le bois.

Le *policeman* a arrivé en arrière du *wreck*. Ils ont trainé le jeune bougre de dedans le fossé. Il y avait d'autre monde qui avait arrivé là avant le *policeman*. Le *policeman* dit ça, "Quoi ce qui a arrivé ici?"

Il y en a un qui a dit ça, "Mais, il y en avait deux dessus ce *motorcycle*. Celui-là, on l'a trainé de dans le fossé, ça a l'air comme si qu'il va le faire. Mais l'autre bougre là-bas, *by the time* qu'on lui a redroiti la tête dessus les épaules, il était mort."

So that the wind can't pass through it. I won't be too cold."

"Well," he said, "you know, Son, that might not be such a bad idea." He took his coat, and put it on the other way. They went about a mile. They missed a turn in the woods.

The policeman arrived after the wreck. They dragged the young man from the ditch. There were other people who had arrived before the policeman. The policeman said, "What happened here?"

One person said, "Well, there were two on the motorcycle. This one we dragged out of the ditch, it looks like he might make it. But the other fellow over there, by the time we put his head back straight on his shoulders, he was dead."

49. Les oeufs craqués / Cracked Eggs (Adley Gaudet, Bayou Pigeon)

This unclassified story is representative of the quick-witted Cajuns who find humor in everyday life. Compare the section "Les Originaux" [The Eccentrics] in Catherine Jolicœur's *Les plus belles légendes acadiennes* (pp.197–203), for similar examples of clever comments. W. K. McNeil reported a related story in *Ozark Mountain Humor* (no. 138). A customer asks the price of cigars and is told "two for a quarter." He buys one cigar for fifteen cents instead. A second customer immediately steps up and says, "Here's a dime; I want the second one."

Il y avait une femme dans Lafayette. Elle a été à la grosserie. Elle dit à Monsieur Viator, elle lui a demandé voir combien est-ce qu'il vendait ses œufs. Il dit, "Trente-cinq sous la douzaine pour les bons, mais," il dit, "les massacrés, ceux-là qui sont craqués, c'est vingt-cinq sous la douzaine."

Elle dit, "Comment ça serait de m'en craquer trois ou quatre douzaines?"

There was a lady in Lafayette. She went to the grocery store. She said to Mr. Viator, she asked him the price of his eggs. He said, "Thirty-five cents a dozen for the good ones, but," he said, "the damaged ones, those that are cracked are twenty-five cents a dozen."

She said, "How would you like to crack me three or four dozen?"

50. L'homme coursé par le gros chat / The Man Chased by a Panther (Lazard Daigle, Pointe Noire)

This tale is related to motif J1495.1 "Man runs from actual or supposed ghost. The ghost runs beside him. The man stops to rest; the ghost stops, says 'That was a good run we had!' The man says, 'Yes, and as soon as I get my breath, I'm going to run some more.'" Baughman reported variants from New Jersey, South Carolina, Indiana, Florida, Iowa and Wisconsin. This tale is enormously popular among both black and white Southerners. W. K. McNeil included a Tennessee variant in *Ghost Stories of the American South* (pp. 131–132), and an Arkansas variant in *Ozark Mountain Humor*. Carl Lindahl has found several unpublished versions in the Mary Parlor Randolph collection at the University of Arkansas. In this Louisiana version, it is not a question of a ghost, but a panther which speaks. Compare also type 1705 *Talking Horse and Dog* ("Oh, Fiva!" no. 28, this collection) in which one animal's speech starts the man's flight and the words of a second animal, which has run with him, send him on a second lap.

Il y avait un homme qui était après voyager à pied dans le bois et il y a un gros, gros chat, terrible gros chat qui a tombé derrière lui. Il a pris à se sauver, sauver, sauver. Quand il a cru qu'il était assez loin, il était largué, il s'a assis sur un *log*. Quand il s'a assis, le chat a venu. Il s'a tiré sur le *log*.

Le chat lui dit, "On a pris une grande course!"

"Ouais, mais," il dit, "pas comme on va reprendre!"

Ça, ils ont parti à la course, mais là, je connais pas combien longtemps ils ont couru.

There was a man who was traveling on foot in the woods and a great big cat, terribly big cat started chasing him. He took off running, running, running. When he thought he was far enough, he was tired, he sat on a log. When he sat, the cat came along. It jumped onto the log.

The cat said to him, "We had a fine race!"

"Yes, but," he said, "not like the one we're going to have now!"

They took off running, but I don't know how long they ran.

51. Quoi-ce qui bouche le trou? / What's Blocking the Hole? (Lazard Daigle, Pointe Noire)

This is a version of type 1229 *If the Wolf's Tail Breaks*, in this case featuring a bear instead of a wolf, with references to Sweden and the West Indies (Flowers, p. 585). Baughman listed variants of this story under motif X1133.3.2(a) "If the bear's tail breaks," with variants reported from Scotland, Nova Scotia (formerly Acadia) among the Micmac Indians, and from several American states. Brandon found a parallel from Louisiana in the 1940s, "Deux hommes et l'ours" [Two men and the bear] (II, no. 37). Compare also type 1900 *How the*

Man Came out of a Tree Stump, in which the man escapes from a trap by holding onto the bear's tail.

Il y avait une femelle ours qui avait des petits ours. Et deux hommes qui étaient dans le bois, ils ont trouvé ça, dans un bois creux, dans un arbre par terre qui était creux. Il y en a un qui dit, "Je vas me fourrer après. Guette autour."

Ça fait, il s'a fourré pour attraper les petits ours et leur mère a venu. Ça fait, l'autre a rentré en dedans. Et la mère voulait rentrer. L'homme s'a battu avec et il l'a attrapée par la queue. Il la tenait.

"Hé!" l'autre crie. "Quoi c'est qu'il y a? Comment ça se fait qu'il fait noir? Quoi-ce qui bouche le trou?"

Il dit, "Si la queue casse, tu vas voir quoi ce qui bouche le trou!"

There was a female bear that had some little bears. And two men who were in the woods found them in a hollow tree that had fallen. One of them said, "I'll go in there. You look out."

So he got in there to catch the baby bears and the mother arrived. So the other one went in, too. And the mother bear wanted to come in. The man fought with her and managed to catch her by the tail. He held on.

"Hey!" the other one yelled. "What's wrong? Why is it dark? What's blocking the hole?"

He said, "If this tail breaks, you'll see what's blocking the hole!"

52. *Attraper des chaouis / Catching Raccoons (Lazard Daigle, Pointe Noire)*

For a parallel to this story, compare it to type 1630B* *The Bear Thought to be a Log:* "A man, thinking he sees a log in the river, swims out and seizes it. It is a bear which seizes him. Friends on shore shout 'Let go of the log.' He answers, 'The log won't let go of me.'" Compare also "Tiens bien, Bouki!" (no. 6, this collection), in which Bouki can't let go of the awakened bear's tail which Lapin tricked him into grabbing while the bear was sleeping. Raccoons are well-known for their aggressiveness, especially when wounded. Another comparison, also involving a raccoon, can be found in "He Talked Kind of Slow" (pp. 115–116 of Randolph's *The Talking Turtle*). Jerry Clower has a Mississippi variant, "A Coon Hunting Story" (*Stories from Home*, p. 141–144), in which John climbs up a sweet gum tree to dislodge a coon only to find that it is actually a lynx. A terrrible fight ensues and John pleads for his friends to "shoot this thing." They explain that they can't for fear of hitting him, to which he answers, "Well, just shoot up in here amongst us. One of us has got to have some relief."

Il y avait deux chasseurs. Là, il y en a un qui avait monté après un chaoui et l'autre était en bas. Il l'a attrapé.

L'autre lui dit, "Tu l'as attrapé?"

There were two hunters. And one of them had climbed after a raccoon and the other was on the ground. The climber caught it.

The other one said, "Did you catch it?"

"Ouais," il dit, "monte vite m'aider à le lâcher!"

"Yes," he said, "now come up here and help me let him go!"

53. "On a tué le cheval à Pépère!" / "We Killed Pépère's Horse!" (Edward Morin, Pointe Bleue)

This tale belongs under motif Baughman X584.2* "Man without gun accompanies a hunter." In this version, both hunters are armed. There is a similar tale, "Hunting Partners," in Dorson's *American Negro Folktales* (no. 208, p. 354). Laval's Archives de Folklore had some French American variants, but they were not classified.

Tu connais pour le cheval à Pépère? Mais John et Pierre a été à la chasse. Et ça s'en allait jusqu'à au bord du bayou. Tout d'un coup, John a tiré l'autre bord. Pierre dit, "On a tué un chevreuil!"

"O, non," il dit, "j'ai tué un chevreuil!"

"Non," il dit, "on a tué un chevreuil!"

Et il fallait ça fait un tour pour croiser le bayou pour aller voir l'autre bord. Quand ils ont arrivé, Pierre a dit, "T'as tué le cheval à Pépère!"

"Oooo, non!" il dit, "On a tué le cheval à Pépère!"

You know about Pépère's horse? Well John and Pierre went hunting. And they went up to the bayou's edge. All of a sudden, John shot on the other side. Pierre said, "We killed a deer!"

"Oh no," he said, "*I* killed a deer!"

"No," he said, "*we* killed a deer!"

And they had to go around to cross the bayou to go and see on the other side. When they got there, Pierre said, "You shot Pépère's horse!"

"Oh, no!" he said. "*We* shot Pépère's horse!"

54. Les deux hobos / The Two Hobos (Andrew Chautin, Gillis)

There is a parallel to this story in type 1671* *To Buy an Island*, in which a drunk man goes to the king to buy an island or a city. There is a variant in Jones and Wheeler's *Laughter in Appalachia* (pp. 64–65) about three poor tenant farmers with a jug of white lightning. After a few swigs, the first decides to buy his wife a new sewing maching and the second will buy his wife a new washing machine. The third exclaims, "Pass me that jug again; I ain't out of debt yet!" Brandon included a Louisiana variant in her study, "Riches pour seulement un moment" [Rich for only a moment] (II, no. 32), also based on vagabonds who want to buy the railroad. There is an expression in French Louisiana: "La saoulerie enrichit" [Drunkenness makes one feel rich]. It can also make characters fearless, as in "La souris" [The mouse] (Archives de Folklore, coll. Jolicœur, no. 494), from New Brunswick, in which a mouse drinks wine in the presbytery. It hears a noise, runs off, then stops and says, "Where's that cat so I can catch it?"

Il y avait deux *hobos* qui étaient après marcher sur le chemin de fer. Ils étaient pauvres et ils étaient après penser comment ils étaient malpris. Il y avait un qui avait pas de souliers, et l'autre avait des vieux souliers. Ses orteils étaient après sortir. L'autre avait la chemise toute déchirée. Ils avaient faim et ils avaient soif. Ils étaient après dire comment pauvres ils étaient. Il y en a un qui dit, "On a seulement pas d'argent."

"*Well,*" il y en a un qui dit, "j'ai vingt-cinq sous ici."

Il dit, "Moi, j'ai quinze sous. Tu peux juste croire comment pauvre on est. On peut pas s'acheter à manger."

"Mais," l'autre dit, "on peut s'acheter un *drink*, donc. Allons s'acheter un *drink* de vin."

Ils avaient quarante sous dans leurs poches entre eux autres deux. Ils ont acheté un demi gallon de vin. Ils ont pris à boire et à marcher. Quand ils avaient bu à peu près la moitié du vin-là, il y en a un qui dit, "Arrête. Je veux te dire quelque chose. Tu connais, je veux acheter le chemin de fer et la compagnie et tout ça qui va avec."

L'autre dit, "Tu peux pas faire ça. Tu peux pas acheter ça!"

Il dit, "Comment ça se fait je peux pas acheter ça?"

"Mais," il dit, "je vas pas te les vendre!"

There were two hobos who were walking along the railroad tracks. They were poor and they were pondering how bad off they were. One had no shoes, and the other had old shoes. His toes were sticking out. One's shirt was all torn up. They were hungry and thirsty. There were talking about how poor they were. One said, "We don't even have any money."

"Well," one said, "I have twenty-five cents here."

The other said, "I have fifteen cents. Can you believe how poor we are? We can't even buy something to eat."

"But," the other said, "we can buy ourselves a drink, though. Let's go and buy ourselves a drink of wine."

They had forty cents in their pockets between the two of them. They bought a half-gallon of wine. They started drinking and walking. When they had drunk about half the wine, one of them said, "Stop. I want to tell you something. You know, I want to buy this railroad track and the company and everything that goes with it."

The other one said, "You can't do that. You can't buy that!"

He said, "Why can't I buy that?"

"Well," he said, "I'm not going to sell them to you!"

55. *Le hobo catholique* / The Catholic Hobo (*Lazard Daigle, Pointe Noire*)

This is a tale about beggars (motif X530) which involves a variant of motif J2461.2 "Literal following of instructions about greetings." The second beggar, coached by the first, undoubtedly ruins his chances of receiving an offering with his overly enthusiastic answer to the anticipated question about his religion.

Il y avait un *hobo* qui avait pour de-mander à manger en quelque part et ils ont pas voulu lui donner à manger parce qu'il

There was a hobo who had to ask for something to eat somewhere and they didn't want to give him anything because he wasn't

était pas Catholique. Ça fait, il a rejoint un autre *hobo*. Il lui dit, "Si tu vas demander à manger là, dis t'es un Catholique, parce qu'ils vont pas te donner à manger si t'es pas un Catholique."

Il a arrivé, et il a demandé à manger. Ils lui ont demandé s'il était Catholique. "O, ouais!" il dit. "Mon père était un prêtre et ma mère était une sœur!"

Catholic. So he met another hobo. He told him, "If you're going to ask for something to eat there, say that you're Catholic, because they won't give you anything if you're not Catholic."

He arrived and he asked for something to eat. They asked him if he was Catholic. "Oh, yes!" he said. "My father was a priest and my mother was a nun!"

56. *Le commis-voyageur / The Traveling Salesman* (Évélia Boudreaux, Carencro)

This joke can be classified under motif J1819 "Physical phenomena misunderstood." This is also one of the many possible episodes of type 1544 *The Man who Got a Night's Lodging.* Louisiana oral tradition includes many stories built upon the adventures and misadventures of traveling salesmen who must spend the night in a country household. Compare also type 1363* *The Second Cat,* which plays upon a similar confusion, though the motives are very different. The story presented here doesn't play on the usual problem concerning the farmer's daughter, but quite a different one concerning the farmer's son. Like the beggar in the previous story, this traveling salesman errs in pretending to be more religious than he is, mistaking praying for a much more natural function.

Les automobiles avaient commencé sortir et il y avait bien peu. Et le commis-voyageur avait une automobile, et il connaissait pas grand'chose pour entretenir l'automobile. Et toujours, sur sa route, l'après-midi était après s'avancer. Il a eu du tracas.

Il dit, "Qu'est-ce que je vas faire? Personne autour d'ici pour moi aller chez eux pour coucher que je vois, et," il dit, "personne alentour connaît arranger le char."

Il a parti. Il a marché un bout sur le chemin. Il a vu une petite maison beaucoup loin. Il dit, "Je vas marcher à la maison." Il a marché. C'était la maison d'un habitant, et l'habitant avait un jeune garçon, et sa femme et lui qui restaient là.

Ce fait, là, il a conté l'histoire qu'il était en tracas et il connaissait pas comment, où il aurait couché et mangé, que personne autour

Automobiles had just started coming out and there were very few around. And this traveling salesman had a car, and he didn't know much about its maintenance. In any case, on his way, it was getting late in the afternoon. He had some trouble.

He said, "What will I do? There's no one around here for me to ask for lodging and," he said, "no one around here knows how to fix cars."

He left. He walked for a way on the road. He saw a little house far away. He said, "I'll walk to that house." He walked. It was the home of a farmer, and the farmer had a young boy who lived with him and his wife there.

So he told the story of how he had trouble and he didn't know how, where he would sleep or eat, and that no one around

connaissait arranger les chars.

"Mais," il dit, "on peut te garder coucher à soir, mais," il dit, "il faudra tu couches avec le jeune garçon. On a pas une chambre extra pour toi."

"O, mais," il dit, "ça, ça va me faire bien!" Il dit, "Je peux coucher avec le jeune garçon. Ça me fait pas rien."

Le soir, la femme a préparé un bon souper pour leurs moyens. Elle avait cuit plein. Quand ils ont eu fini souper, l'habitant dit, "Ici on va au lit bonne heure. Il faut se lever bonne heure, et on travaille dur." Et il dit, "Le petit garçon va te montrer où la chambre. La femme a préparé le lit."

L'enfant et l'homme a parti pour aller à leur chambre, et tout naturellement, l'enfant s'est déshabillé et mis son linge de nuit plus vite que l'homme. La dame avait mis un change de linge de nuit pour l'homme sur le lit. Il s'est habillé pour la nuit, et il a vu le petit garçon se mettre à genoux sur l'autre bord du lit, et appuyer sa tête sur le bord du lit comme si qu'il était après prier avec beaucoup de piété.

L'homme dit, "Moi, je suis pas un Catholique, mais il faudra je fais comme l'enfant." Il dit, "Je peux pas risquer d'offenser ce bon monde. Ils sont trop bons pour moi."

Quand il avait eu fini s'habiller, il s'est mis à genoux sur le côté du lit où lui, il était. Et le petit garçon s'est mis à rire. Et il riait, il riait. L'homme a levé sa tête. Il a dit a l'enfant, "Qu'est-ce que j'ai fait de mal?"

Et l'enfant continuissait à rire. Ça tracassait l'homme beaucoup. Il dit, "Dis-moi, donc, s'il vous plaît, quoi j'ai fait de mal?"

L'enfant riait toujours. "O!" il dit. "Le pot de chambre est ici, bord-là et," il dit, "Maman sera fâchée après toi!"

knew how to work on cars.

"Well," he said, "we can put you up for the night, but," he said, "you'll have to sleep with the boy. We don't have an extra room for you."

"Oh, well," he said, "that will do me just fine!" He said, "I can sleep with the boy. I don't mind at all."

That night, the wife prepared a good supper according to their means. She had cooked a lot. When they finished eating supper, the farmer said, "Here we go to bed early. We have to get up early and we work hard." And he said, "The boy will show you to the bedroom. My wife has made the bed."

The child and the man left to go to the bedroom, and naturally, the child got undressed and put on his night clothes faster than the man. The woman had placed a change of night clothes for the man on the bed. He got dressed for the night, and he saw the little boy get down on his knees on the other side of the bed, and put his head down on the side of the bed as though he were praying with great piety.

The man said, "I'm not Catholic, but I'll have to do just like the boy." He said, "I can't risk offending these good people. They've been too good to me."

When he finished dressing, he got down on his knees on the side of the bed where he was. And the little boy started laughing. And he laughed, he laughed. The man raised his head. He said to the boy, "What have I done wrong?"

And the child continued laughing. This worried the man very much. He said, "Tell me, please, what have I done wrong?"

The child was still laughing. "Oh!" he said. "The chamber pot is on this side and," he said, "Mama will be very angry with you!"

57. *La jarre de cornichons / The Jar of Pickles* (Revon Reed, Mamou)

Another traveling salesman joke, this tale falls under the catch tale motif Z13.4*(m) "Young man stays overnight with hill couple. He cannot eat enough greens at supper. That night when husband goes to see about disturbance among the horses, the woman says, 'Young man, now's your chance.' He gets up, goes to the kitchen, eats the rest of the greens." Baughman listed one version from Arkansas. Here, the farmer's wife shows an interest which goes beyond turnip pickles (K1514 "Adulteress gets rid of husband while she entertains lover"), but she is frustrated in her attempt. Vance Randolph included a version of this story entitled "The Stranger and the Beans" in his collection *Who Blowed Up the Church House?* Burrison has a variant, "A Rough Night on the Farm" (p. 187–188), which develops another punch line based on the sleeping husband's reaction in the morning after being covered with peas (the food in question) and hit on the head with the bowl. Compare also type 1775 *The Hungry Parson,* which also describes a late-night search for food, but with different results.

On conte l'histoire d'un vendeur, en premier les *Model T Fords* avaient sorti, ils étaient appelés des *drummers*. Ça allait habitation à habitation, et ça vendait des balais, des grandes affaires que le monde avait de besoin.

Alors ce jeune homme, un joli jeune homme, il a embourbé droit là dans une petite manche, pas loin d'un vieux bougre-là qui restait dans une habitation. Il a descendu de son char. C'était presqu'à la nuit. Il a demandé de l'aide. Et le vieux dit, "O, on pourra pas t'aider jusqu'à demain matin. Les mulets sont tous dans le clos et," il dit, "t'es invité de rester à la veille si tu veux." Il dit, "Moi, je suis un vieux homme. Je m'ai juste marié avec une jeune dame. Une jeune femme, une bonne cuiserine, cuiseuse." Il dit, "Tu peux rester coucher avec nous autres."

"Mais," il dit, "j'apprécierais ça beaucoup, Monsieur."

Alors, ils ont eu un bon souper, et durant le souper, la petite femme s'est élevée, elle a été attraper une jarre de cornichons de navets. Ça aimait les navets, ce monde-là, et particulièrement quand ils étiont en cornichons avec du vinaigre. Et lui, il avait jamais goûté ça. Il a trouvé ça tellement bon,

The story is told about a salesman, in the first days of the Model T Fords, they were called drummers. They would go from farm to farm, and they would sell brooms, all sorts of things that people needed.

So this young man, a handsome young man, bogged down right there in a little clearing, not far from the home of an old man. He got out of his car. It was almost night. He asked for help. And the old man said, "Oh, we won't be able to help you until tomorrow morning. The mules are all out in the fields and," he said, "you're invited to stay the night if you like." He said, "I'm an old man. I've just married a young woman. A young woman, a good cook." He said, "you can stay and sleep with us."

"Well," he said, "I would appreciate that very much, Sir."

So they had a good supper, and during supper, the little woman got up and went to get a jar of turnip pickles. They liked turnips, those people, and especially when they were pickled with vinegar. And he had never tasted them. He found them to be very good, he ate two or three. After a while, the old

103

il a mangé deux ou trois-là. Tout à l'heure, le vieux homme, ça l'a manière choqué.

Il dit, "C'est assez, on dirait. On a juste une—On a pas de trop. Si ça fait pas rien, on va arrêter de manger ça." Ça fait, il a serré ça dans le buffet. Mais le vieux dit, "Moi, je travaille dur. Faudra je vas me coucher. Une chose, mon garçon, il y en a juste un lit ici. Faudra on couche les trois dans le même lit. Si ça te fait rien, je vas me coucher dans le milieu."

"O, non," le jeune bougre dit. "Non."

Et il dit, "Moi, je travaille dur. Allons se coucher d'abord. On va se lever beau matin. On va aller sortir ta voiture, et puis là, tu pourras t'en aller."

Ça se fait, ils se sont couchés, et le vieux-là, ça a pas été cinq minutes avant il a commencé à ronfler. Mais la femme, elle, elle se tordait. Elle avait l'œil sec. Et le jeune homme aussi, l'autre bord, là-bas, il pouvait pas dormir. Il était nerveux.

Tout d'un coup, la femme s'est levée assis dans le lit, puis elle a commencé à crier. Elle a réveillé le vieux bougre à coup de tapes, et puis elle lui dit, "Vieux, vieux, attrape vite le fusil et va vite au magasin là-bas." Elle dit, "Il y a un voleur de poules qu'est après voler les poules. Va faire quelque chose vite!"

Ça se fait, lui, il s'est réveillé tout à moitié endormi. Il a buté sur le pot de chambre. Il a attrapé le fusil, puis il a parti pour tout ça il y avait moyen à la cour de magasin. Elle a levé la lampe un peu, la mèche de la lampe, et puis elle a regardé le bougre l'autre bord là-bas. Elle dit, "Asteur, c'est ta chance! T'auras jamais une chance comme ça de ta vie, garçon!"

Il dit, "Tu crois?"

"O, ouais," elle dit, "le magasin est loin. Ça va lui prendre un bon bout de temps."

"Tu crois j'ai le temps?"

"Ouais!" elle dit. "Je te dis t'as le temps!"

man was a bit put out.

He said, "That's enough, one might say. We have only a—We don't have much. If it's all right, we'll stop eating these." So he put them away in the buffet. And the old man said, "I work hard. I'll have to go to bed. There's just one thing, my boy, there's only one bed here. All three of us will have to sleep in the same bed. If you don't mind, I'm going to sleep in the middle."

"Oh, no," the young man said. "No."

And he said, "I work hard. Let's go to bed then. We'll get up early. We'll go and get your car out, and then you'll be able to go on your way."

So they went to bed, and the old man— was sleeping before five minutes had passed, he was snoring. But the woman was twisting. She had a roving eye. And the young man as well, on the other side, he couldn't sleep. He was nervous.

All of a sudden. the woman sat up in bed, and she started yelling. She woke up the old fellow with slaps, and she told him, "Old man, old man, get the shotgun and go quickly over to the barn." She said, "There's a chicken thief stealing the chickens. Go and do something quickly!"

So he got up still half asleep. He tripped over the chamber pot. He got the shotgun, and he took off as fast as possible for the barnyard. She raised the lamplight a little, the wick of the lamp, and she looked at the fellow across the way. She said, "Now's your chance! You'll never have another chance like this in your life, son!"

He said, "Do you think so?"

"Oh, yes," she said, "the barn is far away. It'll take him a good while."

"Do you think I have time?"

"Yes!" she said, "I tell you you have time!"

Alors, il a sauté en bas du lit, et puis il a foncé à la cuisine, puis il a ouvert le buffet, et puis il a mangé tous les cornichons de navets qu'il a pu tandis que le vieux était au magasin.

So he jumped out of bed, and he ran to the kitchen, and he opened the buffet, and he ate all the turnip pickles he could while the old man was at the barn.

58. Les hot dogs / The Hot Dogs (Elizabeth Landreneau, Mamou)

This tale is a bawdy version of type 1339A *The Fool Is Unacquainted with Sausages*. In the collection of Jacques Michaud in Laval's Archives de Folklore, two stories present a similar situation involving bananas (a bawdy version of type 1339B *Fool Is Unacquainted with Bananas*). In the first (I, no. 30), two old maids want to buy two of them. When they are told that bananas are only sold in threes, one says to the other, "We could eat the third one, eh?" In the second story, an old maid hears three girls talking about bananas "as long as this," and she asks, "Was that fellow a Canadian?"

In this Louisiana version, the nun is profoundly concerned about the nature of her wiener. Obviously, this tale is also part of the cycle of anticlerical humor which paradoxically is quite popular among the otherwise religious Cajuns.

Il y avait deux nonnes qu'étaient venues d'Europe. Ça voulait venir dans l'Amérique parce qu'elles étaient jamais venues. Elles estiont curieux de voir et elles avaient jamais vu des *hamburgers*. Ça voulait venir pour manger des *hamburgers*. Elles ont arrivé à un *hamburger stand*, et ils étaient *out*. Ça dit, "Ça nous reste juste des *hot dogs*."

Ça fait, elles se sont regardées une à l'autre. *Well*, elles ont décidé elles auront pris des *hot dogs*. Et il y une que, naturellement, il y a une qu'a été servie avant l'autre. Et elle a élevé son *bun*. Quand elle l'a élevé, elle l'a vite rebaissé.

Ça fait, l'autre est venue, la deuxième est venue. Elle dit, "Quoi ce il y a? Tu manges pas ton *hot dog*?"

Elle dit, "J'ai espéré voir quelle partie du chien toi, t'as eue!"

There were two nuns who came from Europe. They wanted to come to America because they had never come. They were curious to see it and they had never seen hamburgers. They wanted to eat hamburgers. They arrived at a hamburger stand, and they were out. They said, "We only have hot dogs left."

So they looked at one another. Well, they decided to get some hot dogs. And one, of course, was served before the other. And she raised her bun. As soon as she raised it, she quickly put it back down.

So the other one came, the second one came. She said, "What's the matter? You're not eating your hot dog?"

She said, "I was waiting to see what part of the dog you would get!"

59. Le fer dans le lit / The Iron [To Do It] in Bed (Évélia Boudreaux, Carencro)

The humor in this tale is based on the French homonyms "le fer" [the iron] and "le faire" [to do it]. The exploitation of this available confusion would seem obvious. In fact, this is one of the most popular traditional stories in French Louisiana. I have also heard variants in France, Belgium, Québec, and among the Acadians in New Brunswick. In one French version (from Lille), the mother cries out in the end, "Do it on the sofa! It's all the same!" In Louisiana, the popularity of this joke is based in part on the fact that it is naughty without being obscene. Most of the variants I've heard were told by little old ladies who were delighted to wander so close to forbidden territory. (Cf. type 1345* *Stupid Stories Depending on Puns* and motif J1805.5.1 "Words understood only in their sexual connotation," as described by Hoffman in *Traditional Erotica*.)

Une fois, il y avait une vieille fille et elle avait fini par trouver à se marier. Et c'était une excitation beaucoup dans la maison! La vieille maman était veuve et elle voulait sa fille trouve à se marier, mais ça prenait du temps.

Ça fait, finalement, le jour a arrivé pour le mariage. Après le mariage, ils ont eu la célébration. L'heure était arrivée pour les mariés aller à leur chambre. La maman savait que sa fille avait tout le temps les pieds froids. Et elle avait l'habitude de chauffer un fer à repasser et le mettre dans son lit, pour réchauffer ses pieds le soir. Ça fait, la maman voulait d'être vaillante et bonne pour la fille. Elle a chauffé le fer, et elle l'a mis dans le lit. Mais le marié s'est aperçu du fer dans le lit. Et il connaissait pas quoi c'était. Il a levé les couvertes, et il a trouvé le fer. Et il a demandé à la mariée pourquoi le fer était dans le lit. Elle a dit, "Pour réchauffer mes pieds." Elle dit, "Mes pieds sont tout le temps si froids."

Mais la maman, tellement elle était excitée, avait l'oreille à la porte pour écouter quoi qu'allait dans la chambre des mariés. Et tout d'un coup, le marié a jeté le fer par terre, en disant à la mariée, "Tu as plus besoin le fer pour réchauffer tes pieds!"

Once, there was an old maid and she had finally found herself a husband. And there was much excitement in the house! Her old mother was a widow and wanted her daughter to find a husband, but it had taken long.

So finally, the day arrived for the wedding. After the wedding, they had a celebration. The time arrived for the newlyweds to go up to their room. The mother knew that her daughter always had cold feet. And she used to heat an iron to put in her bed, to heat her feet at night. So the mother wanted to be nice and good for her daughter. She heated the iron, and she put it in the bed. But the groom noticed the iron in the bed. And he didn't know what it was. He raised the covers and he found the iron. And he asked the bride why the iron was in the bed. She said, "To heat my feet." She said, "My feet are always so cold."

But the mother was so excited that she had an ear against the door to listen to what was going on in the newlyweds' bedroom. And all of a sudden, the groom threw the iron down on the floor, saying to the bride, "You don't need an iron to heat your feet anymore!"

La maman dit, "Qu'est-ce que c'est ce train?"

Elle dit, "Maman, il veut pas le fer dans le lit!"

"Mais," elle dit, "mais, chère, si il veut pas le faire dans le lit, fais par terre!"

The mother said, "What's that noise?"

She said, "Mama, he doesn't want the iron [le fer] in the bed!"

"Well," she said, "well, dear, if he doesn't want to do it [le faire] in the bed, then do it on the floor!"

60. *Prosper et Lilly Mae et Petit Lou et Clodice (Elby Deshotels, Reddell)*

This tale is a sort of Louisiana French *schwank*, a story which is funny throughout and doesn't depend on a punch line for its humor. The humor builds almost until the end, but the story ends on a relatively calm note when the two friends decide to go fishing together after all. The general motifs of this story about the double cuckolds include K1500 "Deception connected with adultery," Hoffman's X725.3.1 "When husband is absent, wife invites adulterous relationship" and X735.9 "Limits to sexual performance." In this version, all the characters commit adultery, a double case of K1510.2 "Wife of philanderer gets revenge by having an affair herself." Stories about cuckolds abound in literature based on oral tradition from Jehan Bodel and Chaucer to Rabelais and La Fontaine. In the end, these two men put aside their anger, each understanding not only what the other has done, but also what he has just done himself. The one wife we meet also seems to find a comfortable place for the experience in her life. This euphemism-laden story about "getting even" concludes with the timely reaction of a spent man faced with a seemingly insatiable woman.

Une fois, il y avait deux amis, c'était des pêcheurs. Et il y en a un, son nom, c'était Petit Lou, et l'autre, Prosper. Et Petit Lou était marié avec Clodice, et la femme à Prosper, c'était Lilly Mae.

Ça se fait, un jour, Prosper venait dedans le bayou et il avait une *net* d'étendue droit devant la maison à Petit Lou. Ça se fait, il a arrêté pour *check* sa *net*, et Clodice l'a appelé. Elle dit, "Prosper, viens. Je veux parler avec toi. J'ai besoin de parler avec toi."

Il dit, "Clodice, je veux pas venir, parce que," il dit, "Petit Lou est pas là."

"Mais," elle dit, "c'est ça qui fait faut tu viens." Elle dit, "Petit Lou est pas là. Je veux parler avec toi."

Ça se fait, il a rentré. Quand il a rentré dans la maison, elle dit, "Prosper, t'aurais pas

Once there were two men who were fishing buddies. And one was named Petit Lou, and the other, Prosper. And Petit Lou was married to Clodice, and Prosper's wife was Lilly Mae.

So one day, Prosper was going to the bayou and he had a net stretched out just in front of Petit Lou's house. So he stopped to check his net, and Clodice called out to him. She said, "Prosper, come here. I want to talk to you. I need to talk to you."

He said, "Clodice, I don't want to come, because," he said, "Petit Lou isn't there."

"Well," she said, "that's precisely why you must come." She said, "Petit Lou is not home. I want to talk to you."

So he went in. When he was inside the house, she said, "Prosper, wouldn't you like

envie d'une tasse de café?" Ça se fait, elle lui a donné une tasse de café. Elle dit, "Viens avec moi dans la chambre à coucher." Elle dit, "On va boire du café." Elle dit, "Tu t'aperçois, le lit est pas fait."

Il dit, "Ouais, Clodice, je m'aperçois le lit est pas fait."

Elle dit, "Tu connais quoi faire le lit est pas fait?"

"Ah," il dit, "je connais pas."

Elle dit, "Parce que j'ai des faiblesses quand je me fâche." Et elle dit, "Des fois, je tombe par terre et je me fais mal à ma tête." Elle dit, "Ça fait des bosses sur ma tête quand je cogne ma tête sur le plancher et," elle dit, "je suis fâchée."

"Mais," il dit, "Clodice, quoi faire t'es fâchée?"

Elle dit, "Parce que droit asteur-là, Prosper," elle dit, "Petit Lou est après faire l'amour à Lilly Mae."

"Mais," il dit, "jamais de la vie! Petit Lou ferait pas ça."

Elle dit, "Les voisins m'a dit." Elle dit, "Quand t'es *gone* de chez toi, Lilly Mae met une essuie-mains blanche dessus la porte." Et elle dit, "Il va, et puis il fait l'amour à Lilly Mae." Elle dit, "Prosper, je suis bonne pour Petit Lou, ouais. Je suis une bonne femme, ouais, mais," elle dit, "il devrait pas faire comme ça parce que—Et là, quand je jongle à Lilly Mae, comment gros ça me fâche!" Elle dit, "Ça me donne des faiblesses. Je voudrais pas tomber par terre, ça fait, j'ai pas arrangé le lit." Elle dit, "Si je tombe, je veux tomber dans le lit."

Elle dit, "Prosper, c'est pas bien, non, ça. Je suis une bonne femme, et puis, je travaille dur pour Petit Lou." Elle dit, "J'arrange les *nets* et je piécetage son linge et je fais tout ça et c'est pas—" Elle dit, "Tu connais, ça me fâche assez," elle dit, "j'ai envie de me revenger. C'est ça on devrait faire, c'est se revenger!"

some coffee?" So she gave him a cup of coffee. She said, "Come with me in the bedroom." She said, "We'll drink some coffee." She said, "You will notice that the bed is not made."

He said, "Yes, Clodice, I notice that the bed is not made."

She said, "Do you know why the bed is not made?"

"Ah," he said, "I don't know."

She said, "Because I get faint when I get mad." And she said, "Sometimes I fall down and I hurt my head." She said, "This gives me knots on my head when I hit my head on the floor and," she said, "I'm mad."

"Well," he said, "Clodice, why are so mad?"

She said, "Because right this very minute, Prosper," she said, "Petit Lou is making love to Lilly Mae."

"Well," he said, "I can't believe it! Petit Lou wouldn't do that."

She said, "The neighbors told me." She said, "When you're away from home, Lilly Mae hangs a white handkerchief on the door." And she said, "He goes and makes love to Lilly Mae." She said, "Prosper, I'm good to Petit Lou, yes. I'm a good wife, yes, but," she said, "he shouldn't do this to me because—and then, when I think of Lilly Mae, it makes me so mad!" She said, "It makes me faint. I wouldn't want to fall on the floor, so I haven't made the bed." She said, "If I fall, I want to fall on the bed."

She said, "Prosper, it's not right, you know. I'm a good wife and I work hard for Petit Lou." She said, "I fix the nets and I patch his clothes and I do all that and it's not—" She said, "You know, it makes me so mad," she said, "I feel like getting even. That's what we should do, get even!"

Ça fait, quand Prosper a dit, "Allons se revenger," la camisole à Clodice a frappé le plancher (elle avait une camisole neuve elle avait fait avec des sacs de *feed* peinturés), et les *overalls* à Prosper a tombé dessus la camisole à Clodice. Ça fait, ils se sont revengés.

Et ils aviont juste fini de se revenger-là, elle dit, "Prosper, je suis plus fâchée que jamais. Plus que ça va, plus je me fâche." Elle dit, "On devrait se revenger encore." Ça se fait, il se sont revengés encore.

Ça a resté un bout de temps. Elle dit, "Je suis toujours pas contente. Je suis toujours manière fâchée."

"Mais," il dit, "Clodice, moi, je suis pas proche content, moi, non plus." Il dit, "Quand je jongle à Petit Lou avec Lilly Mae!" Il dit, "T'es sûre?"

Elle dit, "Ecoute. Je suis une bonne femme, ouais, Prosper." Elle dit, "C'est pas bien, non, ça Petit Lou est après faire, faire l'amour à Lilly Mae." Elle dit, "Tu connais, c'est pas que je suis une mauvaise femme. La seule raison je fais ça je suis après faire-là, c'est pour me revenger." Et elle dit, "Je connais que Petit Lou est après me maltraiter." Ça se fait, il se sont revengés encore.

Ça a resté quelques minutes-là. Elle dit, "Prosper, je suis après me refâcher tout à nouveau encore."

Il dit, "Lilly Mae," il dit, "Clodice, j'ai commencé à jongler. C'est peut-être juste des charades." Il dit, "Je suis plus aussi fâché que j'étais tout à l'heure!" Il dit, "J'ai commencé à croire, c'est des charades."

En même temps, ils ont entendu quelqu'un qu'a cogné dessus la galerie. Mais pour ce temps-là, Prosper avait mis ses *overalls* et Clodice avait mis sa camisole. Petit Lou dit, "Clodice, ouvre la porte. C'est moi qu'es là." Ça se fait, elle lui a ouvert la porte. Il dit, "Prosper, qui toi tu fais icitte?"

So when Prosper said, "Let's get even," Clodice's nightgown hit the floor (she had a new nightgown that she had made with painted feed sacks), and Prosper's overalls fell on top of Clodice's gown. So they got even.

And they were just finished getting even when she said, "Prosper, I'm madder than ever. The more it goes, the madder I get." She said, "We should get even again." So they got even again.

They stayed for a while. She said, "I'm still not happy. I'm still a little mad."

"Well," he said, "Clodice, I'm not nearly happy either." He said, "When I think of Petit Lou with Lilly Mae!" He said, "Are you sure?"

She said, "Listen. I'm a good wife, yes, Prosper." She said, "It's not right, what Petit Lou is doing, making love to Lilly Mae." She said, "You know, it's not that I'm a bad wife. The only reason I'm doing what I'm doing now is to get even." And she said, "I know that Petit Lou is mistreating me." So they got even again.

They stayed for a few minutes. She said, "Prosper, I'm getting mad all over again."

He said, "Lilly Mae," he said, "Clodice, I started thinking. This may be all just a misunderstanding." He said, "I'm not nearly as mad as I was a while ago!" He said, "I started thinking, this is a misunderstanding."

At the same time, they heard someone knocking on the front porch. But in the meanwhile, Prosper had put his overalls back on, and Clodice had put her gown back on. Petit Lou said, "Clodice, open the door. I'm home." So she opened the door for him. He said, "Prosper, what are you doing here?"

Il dit, "Petit Lou, j'étais après t'espérer."
Il dit, "J'ai entendu dire ayoù il y avait du
poisson à vendre. Je voulais tu viens avec
moi. On aurait été l'acheter."

Petit Lou dit, "Comment tu crois les
choses sont forts? Comment tu crois?" Il dit,
"Toi, t'es icitte. Toi, t'es icitte à ma maison
après m'espérer et moi, j'étais à ta maison à
toi, après t'espérer toi!"

Ça se fait, ils se sont mis ensemble. Ils
ont monté dedans le chaland et puis ils ont
été s'acheter du poisson.

He said, "Petit Lou, I was waiting for
you." He said, "I heard where there was some
fish to sell. I wanted you to come with me.
We'll go to buy some."

Petit Lou said, "Don't you think it's
funny? Don't you know?" He said, "You're
here. You're here at my house waiting for me
and I was at your house waiting for you!"

So they got together. They got into the
boat and they went to buy some fish.

61. Mange une balle de foin / Eat a Bale of Hay (Burke Guillory, Mamou)

This tale belongs to the general category 1800–1809 *Jokes Concerning the Confessional*. It is interesting to note that jokes about priests are as popular in Louisiana as they are in Québec and France, where a spirit of anti-clericalism has existed for many years. Here, the priest exposes a side more in tune with the flesh than with the faith in his confessional. When a young penitent confesses that he has caressed his fiancée intimately but only to a point, the worldly priest demonstrates his disdain with a cynical penance.

Un homme va confesser au prêtre. Il dit,
"Père, je veux confesser mes péchés."

"C'est bon, mon garçon, comment. . .?"

Il dit, "J'ai joué avec les mains de ma
fille. J'ai touché les mains de ma prétendue."

"O, mais," il dit, "ça, c'est pas un péché,
jouer avec les mains de ta prétendue. Pas de
péché là. C'est tout ça t'as fait?"

"Non, mais," il dit, "je l'ai caressée un
peu."

"Ah, mais," il dit, "ça même, c'est pas un
péché. Si t'aimes ta prétendue. Tu dois la
marier. Il y a pas de péché." Il dit, "C'est tout
t'as fait avec ta prétendue?"

"Non," il dit, "Père, j'ai joué avec ses
tétons."

Il dit, "Ah, ça, c'est un peu plus sérieux.
Ça commence à être dans la ligne d'être un
péché, mais," il dit, "même, à bien jongler,

A man goes to confess to a priest. He
says, "Father, I want to confess my sins."

"That's good, my son, how. . .?"

He says, "I caressed the hands of my
girlfriend. I touched the hands of my
fiancée."

"Oh, well," he says, "that's not a sin,
caressing the hands of your fiancée. No sin
there. Is that all you did?"

"No, well," he says, "I caressed her a
little."

"Ah, well," he says, "even that is no sin.
If you love your fiancée. You're going to
marry her. There's no sin there." He says, "Is
that all you did?"

"No," he says, "Father, I played with her
breasts."

He says, "Ah, now, that is a little more
serious. That's starting to be in the line of a
sin, but," he says, "even so, after thinking

JOKES

c'est peut-être pas un péché." Il dit, "C'est tout ça t'as fait?"

Il dit, "Ah, oui! C'est tout, mon Père."

Il dit, "T'as arrêté? C'est tout ça t'as fait? T'es sûr?"

Il dit, "Ah, ouais! C'est tout. Je te promets."

"Bien, mais," il dit, "pour ta pénitence, tu vas aller chez toi, tu vas manger une balle de foin."

Il dit, "Manger une balle de foin? Père," il dit, "tu crois que je suis un cheval?"

Il dit, "Non, mais t'es grandement aussi couillon!"

about it, that's maybe not a sin." He says, "Is that all you did?"

He says, "Ah, yes! That's all, Father."

He says, "You stopped there? That's all you did? Are you sure?"

He says, "Ah, yes! That's all. I promise."

"Fine, well," he says, "for your penance, you will go home and you will eat a bale of hay."

He says, "Eat a bale of hay? Father," he says, "do you think I'm a horse?"

He says, "No, but you're every bit as stupid!"

62. *Un cochon entre les jambes / A Pig between the Legs* (Elizabeth Landreneau, with Revon Reed)

This tale was told as true, but its attribution is second-hand, at best. It is, in fact, a slightly off-color variant of an international tale type 1838 *The Hog in Church*. Thompson listed variants from many countries including France, England, Spain, Germany, Finland, Sweden, Romania, Hungary, Yugoslavia, and Russia. Laval's Archives de Folklore had nine French American variants. Instead of being in church, the pig in this version is locked in a stable during an outdoor wedding. The unsuspecting bridegroom is carried away by the pig, which runs through the outdoor banquet with the groom in a most embarrassing position. The function of this story seems to include the demystification of the formal wedding ritual by means of a little Rabelaisian humor. Traditional Cajun wedding receptions typically included songs and stories which poked fun at the institution of marriage, partly out of irreverence, but partly also out of a desire to remind the newlyweds of the dangers which awaited inattentive or careless couples.

Un gros mariage, tu connais, des autres fois passées, ça faisait le dessert dehors sous les arbres, l'été. Et c'était le seul temps le monde mangeait des gâteaux, quand il y avait des noces. Ça fait, c'était des grosses noces. Et ils aviont toutes les tables de gâteaux, tout ça dehors. Le marié et la mariée étaient à la table et ils ont mangé. L'homme, il a mangé des gâteaux, il a mangé des gâteaux. Et là, son beau-père-là, il avait un gros cochon il

At a big wedding, you know, a long time ago, dessert was served outdoors under the trees, in the summertime. And this was the only time people ate cake, when there was a wedding. So there was a big wedding. And they had the cake tables and everything outside. The bridegroom and the bride were sitting at a table and they ate. The man ate some cake, he ate lots of cake. And his father-in-law had a big pig that he had locked up in

111

avait renfermé dans une écurie pour pas qu'il tracasse le monde.

Ça fait, le bougre, lui, tout à l'heure, le mal au ventre l'a pris, le marié. Ça fait, il a baissé à la course. Et puis il a pris à déboutonner ses culottes avant d'arriver bien. Quand il a ouvert, il a ouvert l'écurie comme ça-là, le cochon a fait, "Ouff!" Il a sorti-là, et puis il a passé entre ses jambes, et puis il a parti. Il courait tout parmi tout le monde, les tables de gâteaux et de manger, et le bougre était couché sur le dos du cochon, avec les culottes en bas!

RR: Ça, c'était un joli portrait. Ça a dû causer un divorce.

ÉL: Mais il paraît c'était un conte vrai, ça.

RR: Supposé.

ÉL: Supposé vrai.

RR: Ça nomme le bougre et tout. Défunt Philippe LaHaye avait conté ça une fois chez Fred, et le bougre pouvait pas descendre.

ÉL: Il était pris.

RR: Le cochon avait passé son nez dans son fond de culottes!

one of the stalls so that it wouldn't bother the people.

So the fellow, the bridegroom, after a while, he got a stomach ache. So he took off running. And he started unbuttoning his pants before he quite got where he was going. When he opened, he opened the stall door, the pig went, "Ouff!" It came out of there, and it passed between his legs and took off. It ran around among all the people, the tables full of cake and food, and the fellow was laying on the back of the pig, with his pants down!

RR: That was a fine picture. It must have caused a divorce.

EL: But it seems that this was a true story.

RR: Supposedly.

EL: Supposed to be true.

RR: They name the fellow and everything. The late Philippe LaHaye told this story once at Fred's, and the fellow couldn't get off.

EL: He was stuck.

RR: The pig had run its nose in the seat of his pants!

63. La truie dans la berouette / The Sow in the Wheelbarrow (Claude Landry, Bayou Pigeon)

This tale is deftly told to be suggestive without being vulgar. It's hard to keep from laughing throughout at the notion of a huge sow in a wheelbarrow, surprised during the first trip, a little less surprised during the second and third, and ready ahead of time for the fourth. Legman gave a variant in the "Monkeys and Elephants" section of *Rationale of the Dirty Joke* (I, p. 197), in which he treated the cycle of jokes which focuses on the human-like sexual appetite of female animals.

T'as entendu cil-là pour le Cadien. Il s'avait marié. Il restait loin, loin, loin dans la campagne. Son premier voisin était deux miles, sûr. Et il avait quelques volailles. Il avait une truie. Il avait un mulet et un cheval. C'était juste lui et sa femme, tu sais? Ça fait, ils ont convenu qu'ils auraient élevé des petits cochons.

You heard the one about the Cajun. He had gotten married. He lived way, way, way out in the country. His first neighbor lived two miles away, at least. And he had a few chickens. He had a sow. He had a mule and a horse. He lived along with his wife, you know? So they agreed that they would raise pigs.

Ça fait, sa femme dit, "Mais, Bèbe, t'as pas de verrat."

"Non, mais," il dit, "notre voisin là-bas, lui, il élève des cochons. Lui, il a un verrat là-bas." Il dit, "Je vas emmener la truie là-bas et puis la *breed*.

Ça fait, *sure enough*, l'homme, à matin, il a parlé avec son voisin. Son voisin dit ça, "Mais sûr, emmène la truie là-bas dans ton char."

"Mais," il dit, "j'ai pas de char."

"Mais," il dit, "comment est-ce que tu vas l'emmener?"

"Mais," il dit, "tout ce que j'ai, c'est une berouette."

"Mais," il dit, "mets-la dans la berouette et puis emmène-la là-bas dans la berouette."

Ça fait, *sure enough,* le lendemain matin, il se lève bien de bonne heure. Il met la truie dans la berouette. Elle pesait à peu près deux cents livres, tu sais? Il s'en a été sur le fond du *gravel road* à peu près deux miles, à pousser cette berouette avec cette truie là-dedans.

Il arrive là-bas. Ils la mettont dans le parc avec le mâle. Le mâle l'a grimpée. Le bougre lui dit ça, *"Well*, ça devrait être bon." Il rentre *back* la truie sur la berouette. *Back* deux miles là-bas chez lui.

Le lendemain matin, il se lève. Il va là-bas au parc regarder. Il vient *back* dans la maison. Sa femme dit ça, "Quoi il y a, Bèbe?"

"God dog!" il dit, "je connais pas quoi ce qu'il y a, mais on a pas de petits cochons encore."

Elle dit, "Mais peut-être que ça a pas pris."

"Peut-être pas," il dit. "Demain matin, je vas faire la même chose."

Back en haut du chemin. *Breed* la truie encore. Il va. Il regarde dans le parc. Pas de petits cochons encore. Il dit à sa femme, "Moi, je connais pas quoi ça il y a de *wrong.*"

So his wife said, "But Baby, you don't have a boar."

"No, but, " he said, "our neighbor over there, he raises pigs. He has a boar over there." He said, "I'll take my sow over there and have her bred."

So sure enough, the man, the next morning, he talked to his neighbor. His neighbor said, "Well, sure, bring your sow over in your car."

"Well," he said, "I don't have a car."

"Well," he said, "how are you going to bring it?"

"Well," he said, "all I have is a wheelbarrow."

"Well," he said, "put her in the wheelbarrow and bring her over in the wheelbarrow."

So sure enough, the next morning, he woke up real early. He put the sow in the wheelbarrow. She weighed about two hundred pounds, you know? He went down to the end of the gravel road about two miles, pushing that wheelbarrow with that sow in it.

He arrived there. They put it in the pen with the male. The male mounted her. The fellow said, "Well, that ought to be good." He put the sow back in the wheelbarrow. Back two miles to his house.

The next morning, he got up. He went to the pen to look. He came back in the house. His wife said, "What's the matter, Baby?"

"God dog!" he said, "I don't know what's the matter, but there are no little pigs yet."

She said, "Well, maybe it didn't take."

"Maybe not," he said. "Tomorrow morning, I'll do the same thing."

Back on the road. Bred the sow again. He went. He looked in the pen. Still no little pigs. He said to his wife, "I don't know what's wrong." So he loaded the pig back in the

Ça fait, il embarque la truie dans la berouette. Pousser *back* pour les deux miles. Il revient *back*.

Le lendemain matin, il se lève de bonne heure. Il dit à sa femme, "Bèbe, écoute. Moi, je vas te dire la franche vérité. Moi, je suis fatigué." Il dit, "Comment ça serait que tu irais voir au parc là-bas, voir si on a pas de petits cochons à ce matin."

"Mais," elle dit, *"okay,* Bèbe." Ça fait, elle va là-bas. Lui, il était toujours couché dans le lit. Elle revient *back."*

"Well," il dit, "Quoi ce que—on a des petits cochons?"

Elle dit, "Non, Bèbe, mais la truie est après t'espérer dans la berouette!"

wheelbarrow. Pushed it back for two miles. He came back.

The next morning, he got up early. He said to his wife, "Baby, listen. I'll tell you the honest truth. I'm tired." He said, "How would you like to go to the pen and see if we don't have some little pigs this morning?"

"Well," she said, "okay, Baby." So she went out there. He was still in bed. She came back.

"Well," he said, "What's—do we have any little pigs?"

She said, "No, Baby, but the sow is waiting for you in the wheelbarrow!"

Menteries et Contes Forts /
Lies and Tall Tales

64. *Le grand poisson et la chaudière pour le cuire / The Great Fish and the Pot to Cook It (Burke Guillory, Mamou)*

Types 1960B *The Great Fish* and 1960F *The Great Kettle* are two of the episodes found together under type 1920A, the first: "The Sea Barons"; the other: "Many Fried Fish." Baughman lists thirteen American variants, all of which feature a great vegetable and a great pot. (See the next tale in this collection.) In this Louisiana variant, the storyteller uses the two episodes without placing the lies in the context of a contest. Giant fish stories are among the most common Louisiana tall tales; English-language versions from Lonnie Gray and Sara Kent are included in *Folktales of Louisiana*.

T'as conté à Ancelet pour l'homme qu'avait attrapé le gros poisson, un goujon caille qu'avait douze manches de hache entre les deux yeux? Et pour le cuire, ils ont battu une chaudière. À force la chaudière était grande, les deux hommes qu'étaient après mettre les anses chaque bord s'entendaient pas, leurs coups de marteau sur la chaudière.

Did you tell Ancelet about the man who had caught the big fish, a spotted catfish which had a span of twelve ax handles between its eyes? And to cook it, they built a pot. This pot was so big that the two men hammering the handles in place one on each side couldn't hear each other's blows, their hammer blows on the pot.

65. *La grosse pomme de chou et la chaudière pour le cuire / The Big Head of Cabbage and the Pot to Cook It (Stanislaus "Tanisse" Faul, Cankton)*

In this variant of the preceding story, featuring a great cabbage (type 1960D), the storyteller does use the context of type 1920 *Contest in Lying*. The second liar returns the favor with an even more incredible story, more to get a little peace than to win the informal

competition. This story also is indicative of a renewed Cajun spirit after the brutal Americanization process of the early part of this century. The local farmer returns fire on Texas, the source of the original lie in this story. Cajuns grew up having to live with the notion that everything that was bigger and better about America was just across the Sabine River. But this time, the nouveau-Texan doesn't get the last word. Burrison has a variant, "Big Kettle for a Big Turnip" (pp. 174–175), in which the host tells the first lie and the traveler, the second. The theme of "outlying Texans" is also popular among many of that state's English-speaking neighbors. See particularly the tall tale of Arkansawyer Hubert Wilkes who recounts a visit to Arkansas by some Texans bragging about the sixty-pound watermelons grown in their home state. Wilkes countered by describing an Arkansas watermelon that "busted and the juice of it drownded two men before they could get out of the way of it" (W.K. McNeil, *Ozark Mountain Humor*, p. 43). Burrison also presents a tall tale, "Another Joke on Outsiders," in which a Georgian gets the better of visiting Texans by pretending that a turtle weighing "four or five pounds" is "just a common-size Georgia bedbug" (p. 121).

Une fois, il y avait deux camarades, mais il y en a un, il était menteur, menteur, menteur, mais ça s'adonnait bien. Ça fait, le grand menteur, il a été au Texas, lui. Et il s'avait convenu il aurait été rester au Texas. Ça fait, il dit à l'autre, il dit, "Viens avec moi. Allons rester au Texas. Il y a de la bonne terre là-bas. Il y a moyen de faire des récoltes, ça fait drôle."

"O," l'autre dit, "non, moi, je fais ma vie ici. Moi, je veux pas aller là-bas. Je vas m'ennuyer." Il dit, "Je pourras pas rester."

"O, non!" Il dit, "Tu t'ennuyeras pas." Il dit, "C'est des belles places." Enfin, il dit, "Moi, je suis *gone* rester."

"Mais," il dit, "va. Si c'est bon, plus tard, je vas peut-être aller."

Ça fait, le bougre a été. Il a déménagé là-bas. Dans l'année d'après, il a revenu faire une promenade par ici. Il a emprunté un cheval pour lui *ride*. Il a passé en avant de chez l'autre bougre, et son camarade était après rabourer.

Il arrive. Il dit, "Pourquoi t'es après graffigner toujours la vieille terre?"

"Ah, bien," il dit, "je suis après faire ma vie."

Il dit, "Tu viens là-bas au Texas, c'est là il y a de la bonne terre."

Once, there were two friends; one was a terrible liar, but they got along well. So the great liar went to Texas. He had decided that he would go to live in Texas. So he told the other guy, "Come with me. Let's go to live in Texas. There is good land there. We could make great crops there."

"Oh," the other said, "no, I make a living here. I don't want to go over there. I'll be lonesome." He said, "I won't be able to stay."

"Oh, no!" He said, "You won't be lonesome." He said, "It's a beautiful place." Finally, he said, "I'm going to live there."

"Well," he said, "go. If it's good, later, I might go."

So the fellow went. He moved there. The next year, he came back on a trip here. He borrowed a horse to ride. He went by the other fellow's house, and his friend was plowing.

He arrived. He said, "Why are you still scratching the same same old dirt?"

"Ah, well," he said, "I'm making a living."

He said, "You should come to Texas,

"Mais," il dit, "comment, quoi c'est vous autres fais?"

Il dit, "Écoute. Je vas te dire une chose." Il dit, "Il y a un homme, il a fait une pomme de chou." Il dit, "Il a cent têtes de moutons, et les cent moutons vont se coucher à l'ombre en bas de cette grosse pomme de chou."

L'homme lui dit, "Mais, c'est sûr une belle pomme, j'imagine."

Ça fait, le bougre a continué à raconter toutes sortes des affaires, tu connais, comment il avait vu, quoi il avait entendu. Un bout de temps, mais là, c'est que c'était rendu à midi. L'homme voulait s'en aller dîner, lâcher pour aller dîner. Le bougre lui dit, "Moi, depuis je suis *gone*," il dit, "quoi t'as vu de nouveau?"

"Mais," il dit, "j'ai vu cinquante z-hommes après faire une chaudière." Il fallait—Dans ce temps-là, tu connais, il fallait ça cogne, ça visse ça. Il dit, "Avec chacun un marteau assez loin à loin qu'un entendait pas l'autre cogner."

"O, mais," il dit, "quoi ils vouliont foutre avec une pareille grosse chaudière?"

"Mais," il dit, "cuire ta pomme de chou!" Ça lui a donné la chance d'aller dîner.

that's where the good land is."

"Well," he said, "why, what do you plant?"

He said, "Listen. I'll tell you something." He said, "There's a man who made a head of cabbage." He said, "He has one hundred sheep, and the hundred sheep can sleep in the shade of that one head of cabbage."

The man told him, "Well, that's surely a fine cabbage, I guess."

So the fellow continued telling all sorts of stories about things, you know, what he had seen, what he had heard. For a while, but then it was almost noon. The man wanted to go home to eat, knock off to eat. The fellow told him, "Since I've been gone," he said, "what new things have you seen?"

"Well," he said, "I saw fifty men making a pot." They had to—In those days, you know, they had to hammer to attach the parts. He said, "Each man had a hammer and they were so far apart that they couldn't hear each other's blows."

"Oh, well," he said, "what in the world did they want to do with such a big pot?"

"Well," he said, "cook your cabbage!" That gave him the chance to go and eat.

66. *Laurent et Télismar à la pêche / Laurent and Télismar Fishing (Edward Morin, Pointe Bleue)*

Baughman described a similar motif X1215.8(ba) "Man tosses a half-dollar into river; the dog dives, comes up with eight-pound catfish and fifteen cents in change," with variants from New Jersey and Kentucky. The opening of this Louisiana version provides an interesting illustration of a Cajun cultural trait: the tracing of family ties before engaging in a conversation. Here the teller knew full well that I was not from the area and had no way of knowing who these people were. It was simply part of an elaborate opening formula he was using to launch his lie, giving it a semblance of veracity by giving his characters a genealogy.

EM: Tu connais Télismar et Laurent?
BA: Non.

EM: Do you know Télismar and Laurent?
BA: No.

EM: Mais Laurent, c'est un garçon à Tréville, et Télismar, c'est un garçon à vieux Josien. Tu les connais?

BA: Non.

EM: Mais Josien et Tréville, c'est les garçons à Hilaire. Tu connais qui c'est, Hilaire?

BA: Hmmm, non.

EM: Mais, Hilaire, c'est un frère à Dom Luis. Mais, Laurent et Télismar, c'étaient des grands pêcheurs. Et ça aimait beaucoup aller à la pêche. Ça fait, ils ont été à la pêche aux carpes à la rivière Mentau. Naturellement, Laurent a amené son chien qu'il appelait Délai. Et ils estiont après pêcher, et ça mordait pas, et ça mordait pas. Ils aviont chacun un grand manche des lignes, avec des appâts de bouillie. Et pas rien.

Jusqu'à Télismar s'est choqué. "Tonnerre des dieux!" Il dit, "'Regarde ça là qui saute. Moi, je lui tire une piastre."

Délai, il a escoué la queue-là, il a *dive*. Il est revenu avec une carpe de seize livres, et trente-cinq sous en échange!

EM: Well, Laurent is one of Tréville's sons and Télismar is one of old Josien's boys. Do you know them?

BA: No.

EM: Well, Josien and Tréville were sons of Hilaire. Do you know who Hilaire is?

BA: Hmmm, no.

EM: Well, Hilaire, is Dom Luis's brother. Well, Laurent and Télismar were great fishermen. And they liked very much to go fishing. So they went carp fishing in the Mermentau River. Naturally, Laurent brought along his dog named Délai [Delay]. They were fishing and the fish weren't biting. They each had a rack of lines, with dough for bait. And nothing.

Until Télismar got mad. "Thunder of the gods!" He said, "Look at what's jumping there. Here, I'll give it a dollar."

Délai shook his tail and dived. He came back with a sixteen-pound carp and thirty-five cents in change.

67. Le tourbillon / The Twister (Mme Edward Morin, Pointe Bleue)

Motifs X1611.1.16* "Remarkable wind does work for man" and X1611.1.8*(g) "Tornado sucks up all the water in its path" are part of this version of type 1960C *The Great Catch of Fish* (well known in many forms in the United States; see W.K. McNeil, *Ozark Mountain Humor*, no. 22). The storyteller attributes this tale to his grandfather, a man known for his unbridled imagination.

Une fois, ils étaient assis dessus la galerie. Il y a pris un de ces petits tourbillons qui montent en haut-là. Il a passé dans le petit Lac de Bois, eux appelaient, ayoù les nègres restaient l'autre bout de Lac Alleman. Puis il dit ça ramassait toute l'eau et toute l'affaire-là. Et il dit, force c'était haut et gros! Il a attelé. Il a été voir et il dit quand il a arrivé, "Un bébé tas de poissons!" Il dit, "C'était plus haut que mon cheval!"

Once they were sitting on the porch. There came along one of those little twisters which go up in the sky. It passed in Lac de Bois, as they used to call it, where the black people lived on the other side of Lac Alleman. And he said, it picked up all the water and everything. And he said, it was so high and big! He hitched the horse. He went to see and he said when he arrived, "There was a hell of a pile of fish." He said, "It was higher than my horse."

68. La hache à August / August's Ax (Edward Morin, Pointe Bleue)

This tale is related to motif X1622.3.3.2*(a) "Man trapped in a burning hotel pours pitcherful of water out the window, slides to safety on the icicle which forms," described by Baughman, with variants from Pennsylvania and Missouri. In the second variant, the icicle is formed from the man's own urine. In this one from Louisiana, a hunter uses the same means to retrieve his ax which has fallen to the ground. (See also number 74 in this section.)

Auguste a été à la chasse et il a tiré un écureuil et l'écureuil a tombé dans un trou. Et le trou était pas assez grand pour lui passer sa main. Ça fait, il avait une petite hache. Il a égrandit le trou. Bon, mais, en égrandissant le trou, il a échappé la hache par terre. Et il faisait frais, frais, frais! Il avait pas envie de redecendre ramasser sa hache. Ça fait, il a arraché l'affaire, il a *wee-wee* dessus le manche de sa hache. Là, il a pris la chandelle, et il l'a halé en haut. Il a égrandit son trou, et il a attrapé son écureuil.

Auguste went hunting and he shot a squirrel and the squirrel fell into a hole. And the hole wasn't big enough for him to put his hand in it. So he had a little ax. He enlarged the hole. But while enlarging the hole, he dropped the ax on the ground. And it was very, very cold. He didn't feel like going back down to retrieve his ax. So he took out his thing, he wee-weed on the ax handle. Then he took the icicle and pulled it up. He enlarged his hole and he caught his squirrel.

69. Vieux Narcisse Mayeux / Old Narcisse Mayeux (Edward Morin, Pointe Bleue, with Revon Reed)

In this cycle of lies featuring Narcisse Mayeux, a half-real, half-imaginary character, several motifs come into play: X1241.1 "The great horse," which here has hooves so deep that it can walk on an egg without breaking it; X1767.2*(a) "Draft draws wood out of stove, up chimney," but instead of the wood, here the draft draws a cat; X1611.1.5.1*(a) "Man who is gawking at the doings of the wind is turned inside out," but here it is a screaming pig that is victimized. All of these are described by Baughman, with variants from various parts of the United States. Jerry Clower has a version in *Stories from Home* ("My New House," p. 191) in which a brickmason claims that the homeowner's little dog will have to be kept chained to keep it from being "sucked up this chimney." Québecois folklorist Luc Lacourcière reported hearing a tale in New Brunswick in which neighbors were invited to come and see a chimney with a supposedly great draft. They found themselves in a smoky room and remarked that it wasn't very effective after all. The owner retorted, "If it doesn't draw smoke, it sure does draw curious folks!"

All right, tu connais, il y a vieux Narcisse Mayeux. C'était un homme qu'avait un tas de *trades.* Il avait un moulin à maïs. Il tournait

All right, you know, there's old Narcisse Mayeux. He was a man who had lots of trades. He had a corn mill which operated by

ça à chevaux. Et c'était un chasseur. C'était ça tu voulais: un pêcheur, un homme à cochons. Et il avait un cheval il appelait Balle, et qui tournait le moulin à maïs. Et un jour, il y a une poule qu'a monté dans la cabane en haut. Elle a lâché un œuf par terre. Et Balle avait le sabot si creux, il a marché sur l'œuf. Il a pas cassé l'œuf.

Et c'était un bon metteur de briques, vieux Mayeux. Il s'est fait une cheminée. Et quand il l'a finie, elle était finie-là, son chat a passé en avant la cheminée-là. Ça l'a halé en haut!

RR: Le *draft!*

EM: Le *draft!*

RR: Levée de cheminée.

EM: Et il avait une truie qu'était beaucoup avare. Et il la soignait avec son maïs de moulin. Et un jour, il y avait un gros, gros vent du nord. Il a sorti avec son baquet-là pour aller *feed* sa truie. Elle s'est plantée là. Elle criait et le vent a rentré dedans. Ça lui a tournée à l'envers.

RR: Un gros vent!

horse power. And he was a hunter. He was anything you please: he fished, he raised pigs. And he had a horse named Balle [Bullet] and he used it to turn the corn mill. And one day, a hen went up into the shack up above the mill. She laid an egg on the ground. And Balle had hooves so deep that he walked on the egg and didn't break it.

And he was a good bricklayer, old Mayeux. He made himself a chimney. And when he finished it, the cat walked in front of the fireplace. It hauled the cat up the chimney!

RR: The draft!

EM: The draft!

RR: Chimney draw.

EM: And he had a sow which was very greedy. And he fed it with the corn from his mill. And one day, there was a very strong north wind. He went out with his bucket to feed the sow. She was there. She was yelling and the wind went inside her. It turned her inside out.

RR: A big wind!

70. La bataille de chats / The Cat Fight (Clence Ancelet, Lafayette)

This tale, told as true, or "for cash," as the storyteller put it, is set during the youth of the storyteller and in his native rural community of Ossun, in the northwestern corner of Lafayette Parish. Although the story contains factual information concerning cock and dog fights in the area, the essential element, the cat fight, is told as a joke. This is a variant of motif X1212(a) "Wildcats fight; they climb each other until they are out of sight. Their squalling is heard for two hours; fur drifts down for two days." Baughman found variants in Arkansas and Kentucky. See also "The Cats that Clawed to Heaven" in Leonard Roberts's *South from Hell-fer-Sartin.* This tale was recognized by the staff of Laval's Archives de Folklore, but no examples were found in the collection.

Barry, Monsieur Royer au ras de la maison m'a demandé pour je te raconte ce conte-là. Il a été né et élevé dans le petit village de Mire.

Barry, Mister Royer who lives nearby asked me to tell you this tale. He was born and raised in the little town of Mire.

Il dit, il y avait deux hommes dans le vieux temps qu'étaient riches, bien riches les deux, mais entêtés comme t'as jamais vu de ta vie. Il y en a un qu'avait un gaïme, et l'autre, pour se foutre de lui, s'a acheté un meilleur gaïme, et il a tué son gaïme.

Ça fait, quand la bataille de chiens a venu quelques années après, l'autre bougre s'a acheté un bon chien pour battre. Eux appelaient ça un *pit dog*. Et eux battaient ces chiens-là chez Monsieur Norbert Lormand à Ossun, trois miles dans le nord de Scott, trois miles au nord de le Triangle Club. Et là, l'autre bougre s'a acheté un chien et puis, ils ont battu les chiens. Ça fait, un a gagné une bataille de chiens. L'autre a gagné une bataille de gaïmes. Ils ont resté annulés, mais ça s'aimait pas.

Quelque temps après ça, ils ont commencé dire comment ils avaient des bons chats. Il y en a un qu'avait un chat blanc et un qu'avait un chat noir. Mais c'était les deux plus gros chats qu'il y avait eu dans le voisinage.

Ça fait, ils ont amarré une bataille pour cent piastres. Et cent piastres dans le vieux temps, c'était pareil comme cent mille à présent. Et ils ont lâché ces deux chats-là, et le noir s'a tiré sur le blanc premier. Là, le blanc s'a tiré sur le noir. Là, ça a continué comme ça-là jusqu'à ça a été assez haut qu'eux pouvaient plus les voir du tout. Mais eux savaient la bataille était après aller toujours donc, parce que le duvet noir et le duvet blanc tombaient par terre, sur la terre.
BA: Ça, c'est beaucoup fort!
CA: C'est fort, ouais. C'est Monsieur Royer qui m'a dit fallait je dis ça.
BA: Ça, c'était dans le voisinage de Ossun?
CA: Dans le voisinage de Ossun, mais lui, il venait du petit village. Il a été élevé à Mire, lui. Mais ça battait les chiens à Ossun, chez Monsieur Norbert Lormand. Ça battait des gaïmes aussi là. Il y avait des batailles de gaïmes aux gaffes et de batailles de gaïmes à

He said that there were two men in the old days who were rich, very rich both, but as hard-headed as you've ever seen in your life. One had a fighting cock, and the other, to make fun of him, bought a better one, and killed his friend's cock.

So when the dog fights came around a few years later, the other fellow bought a good fighting dog. They called it a pit dog. And they fought dogs at Mister Norbert Lormand's place in Ossun, three miles north of Scott, three miles north of the Triangle Club. And then, the other fellow bought himself a dog and they had a dog fight. So one won the dog fight. The other won the cock fight. They remained tied, but they didn't like each other.

A little while later, they started talking about how they had good cats. One had a white cat and the other had a black cat. And these were the two biggest cats in the neighborhood.

So they arranged a fight for one hundred dollars. And one hundred dollars in those old days was just like one hundred thousand now. And they released those two cats and the black one jumped on the white first. Then the white one jumped on the black one. And they continued like that until they were so high that no one could see them anymore at all. But they knew the fight was still raging because the black fur and the white fur were falling to the ground.
BA: That's pretty hard to believe!
CA: It's hard to believe, all right. It's Mister Royer who told me I had to tell it.
BA: That was in the neighborhood of Ossun?
CA: In the neighborhood of Ossun, but he comes from the town. He was raised in Mire. But the dog fights were in Ossun, at Mister Norbert Lormand's place. They fought cocks there too. There were gaffe cock fights and spur cock fights. Uncle Evon Ancelet and

l'éperon. N-oncle Évon Ancelet et puis n-oncle Ansbé Ancelet, un élevait des gaïmes à l'éperon, et l'autre élevait des gaïmes aux gaffes. Ils se sont élevés beaucoup des bons gaïmes. Et Monsieur McGee Arceneaux, et puis eux battaient contre Gilbert Cortois de Jeanerette, et puis du monde de Nouvelle Ibérie, puis Possum de Lafayette. Charles Broussard était dans les batailles de gaïmes. Il y avait un tas de batailles de gaïmes, tous les dimanches. Là, les batailles de gaïmes étaient dans l'été. Dans l'automne, quand ça faisait frais, c'était là les batailles de chiens commençaient.

BA: Et la bataille de chats?

CA: La bataille de chats! Ah, là, je connais pas. Ça, c'est Monsieur Royer qui m'a raconté ça. Le crédit va à Monsieur Royer.

Uncle Ansbé Ancelet, one raised spur cocks and the other raised gaffe cocks. They raised many great cocks. And Mister McGee Arceneaux, and they fought against Gilbert Cortois from Jeanerette, and people from New Iberia, and Possum from Lafayette. Charles Broussard was in the cock fights. There were lots of cock fights, every Sunday. Then, in the fall, when it turned colder, the dog fights started.

BA: And the cat fight?

CA: The cat fight! Ah, now, I don't know. It's Mister Royer who told me that one. The credit goes to Mister Royer.

71. *La belle chasse sans fusil / The Great Hunt without a Gun (Adley Gaudet, Bayou Pigeon)*

This tale is a variant of the great hunt stories often listed under type 1890 *The Lucky Shot*. In this case, however, the hunt is without a gun. A man out for a walk to check on his holdings remarks that he will not take along a shotgun, either to placate his wife who doesn't want him to come home too late or to demonstrate his hunting prowess. Nevertheless, the call of the hunt overwhelms him when he sees a deer in the woods. He attracts the deer with a handful of salt and then catches it by the tongue. Baughman described motif X1124(a) "Hunter catches deer by putting salt on top rail of rail fence," in which the deer are caught by the tongue when they lick a frozen metal rail substituted for the wood rail, as well as motif X951 "Lie: Remarkable Squeezer." This first episode leads to a series of fortuitous accidents of the sort often associated with stories about the great hunt or the great fishing trip (cf. type 1895 *A Man Wading in Water Catches Many Fish in his Boots*), including type 1893 *The Man Lays a Bag by the Fence Hole*, with which he catches rabbits, also without a gun. If a type were to be created for this plot outline, it might be titled, "The Hunter in Spite of Himself." Burrison has similar strings of lucky accidents in "The Wonderful Hunt" (p. 169), and in "Lucky Shots" (p. 170), both of which include the boots full of fish.

Une fois, il y avait un homme, il restait en haut du Petit Pierre Part. Et il a été voir à ses animaux à la coulée Adeline, qu'ils

Once there was a man who lived upstream on Bayou Pierre Part. And he went to see about his animals along what people

l'appelaient. Et il a dit à sa femme, il dit, "Je vas aller voir à mes animaux, et je vas pas m'amener un fusil. Je vas m'amener du sel. Il a mis ça dans sa carnassière. Il a été là-bas dans le bois.

Il a vu quelques uns de ses animaux, et là, il a vu un gros chevreuil. Il s'a collé contre un bois, et puis il a mis du sel dans sa main. Il a attrapé une poignée de sel. Le chevreuil a venu. Et ça dit quand il mettait sa main dessus quelque chose, c'était pareil comme un étau. Ça se barrait! Le chevreuil a venu. Il a mis sa langue dedans sa main qu'il a barrée dessus sa langue. Et le chevreuil s'a tiré par en arrière et la langue lui a resté dans sa main. Il a été à la coulée. Il a commencé à laver la langue de chevreuil dans la coulée et il y a une grosse barbue de neuf livres qui a venu attraper la langue du chevreuil. Il l'a tirée dedans une bouillée d'éronces. Et quand la barbue a tombé, elle a tapé un lapin. Et avant que le lapin peuve crever, il a *kick,* et il a *kick* si dur avec ses pattes, il a tué six jeunes perdrix. Il a tout mis ça dans sa carnassière. Et il avait ses deux chiens avec lui. Et les chiens étaient après courser un lapin. Et il a été puis il a vu le lapin s'en venir. Il avait des bottes en gomme qui lui arrivaient aux genoux. Il a ôté une des ses bottes et le lapin a venu se fourrer droit dedans sa botte. Il avait son lapin. Il l'a tué. Il l'a mis dans sa carnassière. Et il y avait une autre coulée qu'il fallait qu'il traverse. Et il croyait pas que c'était aussi creux que ça, mais quand il a pris à aller en travers de la coulée, l'eau a été par dessus les genoux. Et quand qu'il a arrivé l'autre bord de la coulée, ça commençait à le piquer dans les jambes, tout partout. Il s'a arraché les bottes et il avait deux douzaines de patassas dans ses bottes.

Et quand qu'il a arrivé chez lui, sa femme voyait pas comment ce qu'il pouvait avoir autant de quoi avec pas un fusil en seulement. Pas de fusil du tout. Ça, c'est fort.

call Coulée Adeline. And he told his wife, he said, "I'm going to check on my animals, and I won't take along a shotgun. I'll take along some salt." And he put some in his hunting bag. He went into the woods.

He saw a few of his animals, and then he saw a big deer. He got next to a tree, and he put some salt in his hand. He took a handful of salt. The deer came. And it was said that when he put his hand on something, it was just like a vise. His grip locked! The deer came along. It put its tongue in his hand which locked onto it. And the deer drew back and its tongue stayed in his hand. He went to the stream. He began to wash the deer tongue in the stream and a big nine-pound catfish came and latched onto the deer tongue. He threw it into a patch of briars. And when the catfish fell, it hit a rabbit. And before the rabbit died, it kicked and kicked so hard with its paws that it killed six young quail. He put all this into his hunting bag. And he had his two dogs with him. And the dogs were trailing another rabbit. He went and saw the rabbit coming. He had on knee-high rubber boots. He took off one of the boots and the rabbit came and ran right in to his boot. He had his rabbit. He killed it. He put it into his hunting bag. And there was another stream that he had to cross. And he didn't think it was as deep as it was, but when he started to cross the stream, the water went over his knees. And when he arrived on the other side of the stream, something started pricking his legs all over. He took off his boots and he had two dozen bream in his boots.

And when he arrived home, his wife couldn't see how he had gotten all that he had without even a shotgun. No gun at all. That's hard to believe.

72. Le traceur de chevreuil / The Deer Tracker (Lazard Daigle, Pointe Noire)

Hunting stories abound in Louisiana French oral tradition, especially among the many avid hunters in the area. Often the stories focus less on the great hunt (type 1890) than on the hunter himself. In this tale, there is a variant of motif X1124.5* "Hunter trails animal in reverse, ends up at animal's birthplace," described by Baughman.

J'ai entendu parler de ce bougre qui avait tracé un chevreuil. Il était beaucoup bon traceur, beaucoup, beaucoup bon. Il traçait n'importe quoi. Et de quelque manière, il a pris à tracer un chevreuil. Mais il a fait une petite erreur. Il a pris à le retracer en regrichant la trace, ayoù ce qu'il devenait. Au lieu de descendre, il a pris à monter. Il a tracé le chevreuil et il a suit la trace jusqu'au jour où il est né. Quand il a arrivé, l'essence du chevreuil était juste après commencer.

I heard tell of this fellow who had tracked a deer. He was a very good tracker, very good. He could track anything. And somehow, he started tracking a deer. But he made a little mistake. He began following a trail backwards, going towards where the animal had come from. Instead of going with the trail, he went against it. He tracked the deer and he followed the trail up to its birth place. When he arrived, the scent of the deer was just getting started.

73. Le fusil crochi / The Bent Shotgun (Lazard Daigle, Pointe Noire)

Here is another tale of the great hunter, a variant of type 1890E *Gun Barrel Bent*. In the collection of Conrad Laforte in Laval's Archives de Folklore, there is a version from Québec, "Le canon crochi de carabine" [the crooked rifle barrel] (motif L1045) classified under type 1894 *Man Shoots a Ramrod Full of Ducks* (X1111). Calvin Claudel recorded a Spanish variant in Louisiana (*JAF* 58 [1945], pp. 221–222) in which the ducks are along the curved shore of a lake. Pierre Daigle's "All His Ducks in a Row" (in *Folktales of Louisiana*) is an English-language version from Cajun tradition.

Il y a un homme qui avait été à la chasse aux canards. Et c'était un marais rond et les canards étaient posés tout le tour au ras de l'écore. Il aurait voulu tuer tous les canards. Il savait pas comment faire. Ça fait, il a crochi son fusil pareil comme le marais était rond. Il a tiré, et le plomb a fait le tour, tué tous les canards.

There's a man who had gone duck hunting. And it was a round pond and the ducks had lighted all around next to the bank. He wanted to kill all the ducks. He didn't know what to do. So he bent the barrel of his shotgun according to the lines of the pond, and the pellets went all around and killed the ducks.

74. La chandelle de glace / The Icicle (Adley Gaudet, Bayou Pigeon)

Number 67 of this collection is also about a hunter who makes an icicle by urinating in order to retrieve his ax without coming down out of the tree he is in. Baughman described a similar motif X1622.3.3.2(a)* "Man trapped in burning hotel pours pitcherful of water out the window, slides to safety on the icicle which forms," with variants from Pennsylvania and Missouri. In Québec, this episode is often associated with type 852 *The Hero Forces the Princess to Say, "That is a Lie."* There is also in the first part of this story a variant of type 1890A *Shot Splits Tree Limb.* Burrison has a limb-splitting shot in "The Unlucky Hunt" (p. 171–172).

Il y avait un homme, il a été à la chasse. N-oncle Ellis, ils l'appelaient. Il a parti, *boy,* c'était froid le matin. Il dit qu'il y avait de la glace, tu sais, ça glaçait à mesure. Il y avait sept bec-croche dessus une branche de cypre. Et *boy,* ils disent qu'il pouvait tirer de la carabine. O, *man,* ils disent qu'il était un *crack shot.* Il pouvait en tuer un avec la balle mais il a pensé que, il avait tant de chance à essayer d'avoir les sept. Il voulait les sept bec-croche qui étaient sur la branche. Il dit, "Well, la meilleure chose que moi, je peux faire asteur, c'est fendre la branche. Là, les bec-croche vont rester pris pareil comme un piège." Il dit qu'il a craqué une balle, il avait un .38. Il dit que la branche a fendu et que les bec-croche ont tombé, tout coincé les pattes.

"Mais, là," il dit, "comment ce que je vas arriver en haut-là?" C'était assez froid qu'il dit qu'il a monté en l'air mais avant qu'il a arrivé à la branche en l'air, il dit qu'il a échappé son casse-tête. Il avait son casse-tête dans sa ceinture. Le casse-tête tombe en bas. "Mais," il dit, "il faudra que je redescends encore en bas." Il dit qu'il a regardé bien comme ça. Il avait une bonne envie de pisser. Il dit qu'il a pissé dessus son casse-tête et là, il l'a élevé avec la chandelle de glace. Ça avait glacé. Et là, il a coupé la branche et il a eu ses sept bec-croche. Mais, *boy,* il dit qu'un peu plus et il l'avait pas, non!

There was a man who was out hunting. He was called Uncle Ellis. He left and, boy, it was cold that morning. He said that there was ice, you know, ice was forming as he went. There were seven *bec-croche* [ibis] on a cypress tree branch. And boy, they say that he could really shoot a rifle. Oh, man, they say he was a crack shot. He could kill one with one bullet but, he thought, he had just as much chance to try to get all seven. He wanted the seven *bec-croche* that were on the branch. He said, "Well, the best thing I can do now is to split the branch. Then the *bec-croche* will get caught just like in a trap." He said that he shot, he had a .38. He said that the branch split and the *bec-croche* fell, catching them all by the feet.

"Well, now," he said, "how am I going to get up there?" It was so cold that he said he went up, but when he got up to the branch, he said that he dropped his hatchet. He had his hatchet in his belt. The hatchet fell to the ground. "Well," he said, "I'll have to go back down." He said that he looked carefully. He needed to pee. He said that he peed on the hatchet and then he picked it up with the icicle. It had iced. And then, he cut the branch and he had his seven *bec-croche.* But boy, he said just a little more and he wouldn't have gotten them!

75. *Une plus fort / A More Unbelievable One (Adley Gaudet, Bayou Pigeon)*

This tale can be classified under type 1920 *Contest in Lying,* including motif X981*(d) "Unusual occurrences in shooting," and featuring especially motif X907.1 "Second liar corroborates the lie of the first." In this case, the second liar complains afterwards that the first lie was very difficult to confirm. This storyteller was born east of the Atchafalaya Basin and had virtually no contact with the black Creole population while growing up. Consequently, all of his characters speak Cajun French, both blacks and whites.

C'était dans le temps de l'esclavage. Il y avait un homme et il avait son nègre, et puis il y avait un autre homme qui voulait tout le temps dire une histoire plus fort que l'autre. Mais ce jour-là, il a dit à son noir, il dit, "Regarde ce bougre qui vient là-bas-là. Lui, il veut tout le temps dire une plus fort que moi, mais guette, je vas lui en dire une à ce matin qui est plus fort." Il dit, "Il faudra que tu sermentes. Et quand je vas lui dire ça, toi, tu dis que t'as vu ça. Guette quoi ce que je vas lui dire."

Ça fait qu'ils ont arrivé. Ils se sont rencontrés les deux. Il dit, "Hé, quoi ça dit à ce matin?"

"O, *well,*" il dit, "ça dit *all right.*"

Il dit, "Je vas te dire quelque chose tandis que j'y pense là. Tu me dis tout le temps des affaires que toi, tu fais qu'est fort, mais moi, je vas t'en dire une à ce matin qui est fort. Et," il dit, "c'est correct. Tu pourras demander à mon noir-là. Lui, il l'a vu." Il dit, "J'ai été à la chasse hier et j'ai tiré un chevreuil et je lui ai foutu une balle dans l'oreille et dans la patte d'en arrière."

"O, Lord," il dit, "tu peux pas me dire ça. Ça, c'est trop loin à part, la patte d'en arrière et puis l'oreille."

"Mais," il dit, "demande à mon noir. Il peut te dire."

"O, oui, monsieur," il dit "ça, c'est correct. J'étais droit-là quand qu'il l'a tiré. Le chevreuil était après se gratter l'oreille avec la patte d'en arrière, et il lui a passé la balle dans l'oreille et dans la patte."

This happened during the time of slavery. There was a man and he had his black man, and there was another man who always wanted to tell a bigger lie than the other. But on this day, he said to his black man, he said, "Look at that fellow coming over there. He always wants to tell a bigger lie than me, but watch, I'll tell him one this morning that's bigger." He said, "You'll have to swear. When I tell him, you say that you saw it, too. Watch what I'll tell him."

So they arrived. They met. He said, "Hey, how's it going this morning?"

"Oh, well," he said, "it's going all right."

He said, "I'll tell you something while I'm thinking about it. You're always telling me unbelievable things that you've done. And," he said, "this is true. You can ask my black man, here. He saw it." He said, "I went hunting yesterday and I shot a deer and the bullet hit its ear and its back hoof."

"Oh Lord," he said, "you can't tell me that. That's too far apart, the back hoof and the ear."

"Well," he said, "ask my black man. He can tell you."

"Oh, yes, Sir," he said, "that's right. I was right there when he shot it. The deer was scratching its ear with its back hoof, and he shot it in the ear and the back hoof."

Une fois qu'ils ont parti, c'est là qu'il a dit à son *boss,* il dit, *"Boss,* disons pas des forts comme ça parce que, *boy,* l'oreille d'un chevreuil et puis sa patte d'en arrière, c'est loin à part, oui, ça!"

Once they had left, he told his boss, he said, "Boss, let's not tell lies like that because, boy, a deer's ear and its back hoof sure are far apart to put together!"

76. *Le menteur et son nègre / The Liar and his Black Man (Witness Dugas, Lafayette)*

This tale is a variant of type 1920D *The Liar Reduces the Size of his Lie,* in this case when his partner tugs at his coat. Laval's Archives de Folklore had three versions, including "Le conteur de menteries" [The teller of lies] in the collection of Jacques Michaud (MIC 102) in which the liar says that he has seen a mile-long church. His brother signals him by stomping on his foot, and he blurts out an attempted retraction, "et dix-huit pouces de large" [and eighteen inches wide]. Burrison has a variant of what is probably the most common version of a closely related story concerning the fisherman who offers to blow out the lighted lantern he says he caught if his friend will reduce the size of his fish (Baughman type 1920H* *Will Blow Out Lantern).* In this Louisiana tale, the liar is forced to reduce his lie perilously close to the truth and he eventually rebels.

Il y avait un bougre qui allait à la chasse. Et il avait tout le temps un nègre avec lui pour approuver ça il tuait. Quand il mentissait, il fallait tout le temps lui haler sur sa queue de capot. Ça fait, il a tiré un chaoui. Et il avait dix pieds de queue. Le nègre hale sur sa queue de capot. Il dit, "Pas aussi long que ça, *boss."*

Ça fait, il tourne de bord. "Mais," il dit, "peut-être pas dix pieds, mais," il dit, "sûr sept pieds."

Le nègre lui hale sa queue de capot encore. Il dit, "Peut-être pas sept pieds, mais," il dit, "sûr cinq pieds."

Il le hale encore. "Mais," il dit, "quoi? Tu veux je le laisse avec pas de queue?"

There was a fellow who used to go hunting. And he always had a black man with him to confirm what he had killed. When he lied, the black man had to pull on his coattail. So he shot a raccoon. And it had a tail ten feet long. The black man pulled on his coattail. He said, "Not that long, boss."

So he turned around. "Well," he said, "maybe not ten feet, but," he said, "surely seven feet."

The black man pulled on his coattail again. He said, "Maybe not seven feet, but," he said, "surely five feet."

He pulled again. "Well," he said, "what? Do you expect me to leave it with no tail at all?"

77. Le cochon de seize mille livres / The Sixteen-Thousand-Pound Pig (Burke Guillory, Mamou)

This tale is another variant of type 1920D (see number 76 earlier in this collection). In this case, the size of a pig is in question and the liar's friend forces him to reduce his claim. When he is pushed too far, he rebels and insults his doubters. In a similar story, "Histoire de menteries" [Story of lying] (no. 103, collection of Jacques Michaud, in Laval's Archives de Folklore), a liar announces that he saw two thousand cats fighting in the street. His friend tells him to eliminate a few if he wants him to believe the story. "Ben," il dit, "i n'a deux." [Well, he says, there were two.] His friend, still not satisfied, says, "Tâ menti, m'en vas r'ôter un." [You're lying, I'm going to take out another one.] In this Louisiana version, the liar has the last word.

Un contait à son ami, à mon père, il dit lui, il avait vu un cochon qu'avait pesé seize mille livres.

"O, mais," il dit, "Rousse," il dit, "euh, un cochon de seize mille livres, tu fais erreur. Peut pas être. Il y a pas de chevaux, il y a pas de bêtailles qui pèsent seize mille livres. C'est huit tonnes, ça! Il y a pas de cochon gros comme ça."

"*Well,*" il dit, "peut-être je fais erreur. C'est seize cent livres, mais," il dit, "il y avait un six dedans toujours."

Il dit, "Même seize cents livres. C'est un gros cochon un tas, ça! Mais," il dit, "j'ai jamais connu un cochon de seize cents livres."

"Bien, mais," il dit, "peut-être six cents livres." Il dit, "Je vas dire une chose. Il était un tas plus gros que toi, mais il était pas presqu'aussi cochon que toi!"

One man was telling his friend, my father, he said that he had seen a pig that weighed sixteen thousand pounds.

"O, but," he said, "Rousse," he said, "uh, a sixteen-thousand-pound pig, you're making a mistake. Can't be. There isn't a horse, no animal that weighs sixteen thousand pounds. That's eight tons! There are no pigs as big as that."

"Well," he said, "maybe I'm wrong. It's sixteen hundred pounds, but," he said, "there's a six in there anyway."

He said, "But sixteen hundred pounds. That's an awfully big pig! Well," he said, "I've never known of a sixteen-hundred-pound pig."

"All right, well," he said, "maybe six hundred pounds." He said, "I'll tell you one thing. It was a lot bigger than you, but it wasn't nearly as big a pig as you!"

78. La bande de canards / The Flock of Ducks (Hube Reed, Mamou)

This tale belongs to the general motif category X1700, "Lies based on absurd logic or lack of it." One must think twice before catching the surprise ending.

La première année je m'ai marié, j'étais sur le bord de la coulée Duralde et j'élevais des canards. Et j'ouvrais le parc le matin. Ça

The first year I was married, I lived on Duralde Creek, and I raised ducks. And I would open the gate in the morning. They

prenait la coulée. J'avais une bande de canards. Et l'après-midi, proche au soleil-couché, ça revenait à la brune. Ça rentrait dans le parc. Mais il y en manquait un et deux. Il y a tout le temps un rat-de-bois ou un chaoui ou un cocodril qui en mangeait trois ou quatre dans ma bande de canards. Et tous les jours, ça revenait, ça rentrait dans le parc, la bande rapetissait. Un jour, la bande est revenue, il y en avait plus un. Il y avait plus un canard dans la bande. Les cocodrils, les chaouis et les rats-de-bois les avaient tous mangés.

would go out on the creek. I had a flock of ducks. And in the afternoon, around sun-down, they would come back around dusk. They returned to the yard. But one or two would be missing. There was always a possum or a raccoon or an alligator that would eat three or four of my flock of ducks. And every day, they would come back, go back in the yard, and the flock was getting smaller. One day the flock returned and there wasn't one duck left. Not one duck left in the flock. The alligators, the raccoons and the possums had eaten them all.

Contes de Pascal / Pascal Tales

79. Pascal et son bicycle / Pascal and His Bicycle (Elvin Fontenot, Hube Reed and Alexandre Manuel, Mamou)

This brief tale gives a description of Pascal's fabulous bicycle. It is with this same bicycle that he rides on high-power electrical lines jumping over the crossbars when he gets to a pole. The ongoing theme of Pascal's great speed on a bicycle (motif X1796.5 "Fast vehicle") is developed in this story about his crossing of the Atlantic ahead of Lindbergh, avoiding the whales for fear of a getting a flat tire. Jim takes a similar trip across the Pacific, arriving in Japan so quickly that he was able to answer his own telephone call from California. (Compare type 1887* *Cattle Merchant's Voyage Across the Sea*, with variants only from Russian sources in the Aarne-Thompson index.)

EF: Pascal, c'est pas lui qu'avait rentré dans la mer en bicycle:?
HR: Il allait vite, mais ouais. Il a été à l'Angleterre, là-bas. Quand Lindbergh a monté l'aéroplane: pour aller, il était après espérer Lindbergh là-bas. Lui, il allait, il allait assez vite, c'était—Il allait sur la mer!
BA: Sur son bicycle?
HR: Sur son bicycle. Il a jamais eu un *flat*. Il cognait trois ou quatre baleines, des petites baleines. Il y en avait une, elle était à peu près un mile de long.
AM: Jim a été à Tokyo, lui.
HR: Jim a été avec Tojo et Tokyo Rose.
AM: Il avait appelé là-bas au téléphone de la Californie et ça a *ring*: deux ou trois fois et il s'a répond.

EF: Pascal, wasn't he the one who went out on the ocean on a bicycle?
HR: He was fast, yes indeed. He went over to England. When Lindbergh got in his airplane to go. He was waiting on Lindbergh there. He was fast, so fast. He rode on the ocean!
BA: On his bicycle?
HR: On his bicycle. He never had a flat. He would hit three or four whales, little whales. One of them was about a mile long.
AM: Jim went to Tokyo.
HR: Jim went with Tojo and Tokyo Rose.
AM: He had called there on the telephone from California and it rang two or three times and he answered his own call.

HR: O, ouais! Faut ça *ring* trois fois.
AM: Il a descendu de son bicycle et il s'est répondu lui-même, quand il a arrivé au téléphone.
HR: Quand il a appelé là-bas, avant ça peut élever le téléphone, il s'est répond lui-même.

AM: Ouais. Il était rendu de la Californie.
HR: Et là, c'était pas un bébé, mais il avait le vent avec lui, tu connais? Là le courant, toute l'affaire. Mais, écoute! Il pagotait, ouais, cher! Ses jambes étaient sûr grosses comme mon cigare, mais il mettait du quatorze dans les souliers.

HR: Oh yeah! It has to ring three times.
AM: He got off his bicycle and he answered his own call when he got to a telephone.

HR: When he called there, before anyone else could pick up the telephone, he answered it himself.
AM: He was already there from California.
HR: And then, he was really something, but he had the wind at his back, you know? And the current and everything, but listen! He really pedaled, buddy! His legs were surely as big as my cigar, but he wore a size fourteen shoe.

80. Mayo sur la lune / Mayo on the Moon (Irving and Revon Reed, Mamou)

In this story, Irving Reed presents Mayo as guardian of the moon. Compare this notion with Antoine de St. Exupéry's *Le petit prince,* in which the main character is guardian of an imaginary planet. Mayo is in charge of producing water to create rivers and lakes there, which he accomplishes by spitting on the rocks. Compare this with motifs F635 "Remarkable spitter" and D921.1 "Lake (pond) produced by magic," as well as the well-known Biblical story in which Moses furnishes water in the desert by striking the rocks with his staff. The humor of this tale is based, in part, on the fact that the real Mayo, on whom this character is loosely based, worked for Mamou Water Works before he died. In the cosmology of these Pascal stories, he must also extinguish the sun in one of his great lakes. Compare motif X1753*(c) "Man is given job of breaking day every morning."

IR: Il y avait pas d'eau là-bas sur la lune, quand ils ont arrivé, mais Mayo a fait de l'eau! Mayo travaillait pour l'affaire d'eau.

RR: Il travaillait pour *Mamou Waterworks.* Il a trouvé de l'eau sur la lune?
IR: Mayo va prendre une qualité de pierre il y a dessus la lune et il reste peut-être cinq gallons d'eau. Ça connaît pas comment longtemps, mais il boit peut-être deux gorgées par jour. Et il va cracher sur une de ces pierres-là, ça fait une rivière, une rivière que l'eau coule partout, il paraît. Il a fait un gros *pond:* l'autre jour, le dernier gros crachat il a fait-là, quand il a fait la rivière. Ça tombe

IR: There was no water there on the moon, when they arrived, but Mayo made water! Mayo had worked for the waterworks company.
RR: He worked for Mamou Waterworks. He found water on the moon?
IR: Mayo takes a certain kind of stone that is found on the moon and when there are about five gallons left. No one knows how long, but he drinks about two swallows [of water] a day. And he'll spit on one of the stones, and it makes a river, a river of water flowing everywhere, it seems. He made a great pond the other day, the last big spit he spit, when he made the river. It flows into the lake. It's

là-dedans. C'est tout de l'eau fraîche. Et à tout moment, il éteint le soleil là-dedans. Il l'éteint le soir. C'est pour ça tu le vois pas.

all fresh water. And now and then, he puts out the sun in it. He puts it out at night. That's why you don't see it.

81. La mer plantée en riz / The Ocean Turned Ricefield (Irving and Revon Reed, Mamou)

In this series of exchanges, Revon tries to push his brother Irving to tell a well-known Pascal story in which the hero and his friends go whale fishing, but Irving rejects the idea. Instead, he develops the second idea Revon proposes concerning the time a few of Pascal's friends and neighbors dried the Pacific Ocean to plant rice on the ocean floor. Despite their hard work, Pascal and Jim pierced the huge rain cloud which loomed overhead with a railroad spike, causing the rain to fall for thirty-nine days and thirty-nine nights (conspicuously one day and night shy of the Biblical forty, which God said would never happen again). When asked about the salt that should be missing from the ocean recently refilled with rainwater, Irving explained that Jim had gotten some salt from Avery Island (a local salt mine) to restore the ocean to its original salinity [motif X956*(a) "Hero responsible for salt in Pacific Ocean"].

BA: Ce bougre, Pascal-là, Revon m'a dit qu'il allait à la pêche de baleine.
RR: Ouais, ils avaient été à la pêche une fois. C'était la vieille qu'avait attrapé une baleine, hein? Tu m'avais conté ça une fois. Elle était après pêcher sur la côte de la mer. Elle a attrapé un *bite;* c'était une baleine. Elle a commencé à caler, mais elle a jamais voulu lâcher la ligne. J'oublie quelle qualité d'appât elle avait, mais je crois c'était des marsouins, je crois, qu'étaient autour de deux ou trois mille livres. Elle avait beaucoup des appâts, mais c'est une grosse, grosse baleine, tu m'avais conté, elle avait attrapée. Et il y a un bout, ils la halent à terre, mais j'oublie comment ça finit, ça. Tou-tout connaît le conte. Elle et Jim, quand ils avaient été au— et là, quand ils ont planté le *Atlantic. . . .le Pacific Ocean* en riz. Tu te rappelles de l'année-là?
IR: O! Quand ils ont chessé la mer-là?
RR: Ils ont chessé la mer. Ils l'ont tout

BA: This fellow, Pascal, Revon has told me that he went whale fishing.
RR: Yeah, they had gone fishing one time. It was the old lady who caught a whale, wasn't it? You told me that about that once. She was fishing on the coast of the ocean. She got a bite; it was a whale. She started sinking, but she would never let go of the line. I forget what kind of bait she was using, but I think it was dolphins, I believe, that weighed about two or three thousand pounds. She had lots of baits, but it was a very big whale, according to your story, that she had caught. And at one point, they were hauling it on shore, but I forget how it ends. Tou-Tout knows the tale. She and Jim, when they had gone to— And then, when they planted rice in the Atlantic . . . the Pacific Ocean. Do you remember that year?

IR: Oh! When they dried the ocean?
RR: They dried the ocean. They planted the

plantée en riz en dedans.

IR: Ils ont chessé la mer et tout ça qui voulait des droits de liés, ça voulait des droits de *soybeans*. Il y en a qu'a planté des patates. Et les pauvres petites baleines, ça sautait dans la poussière. Quand ils l'ont chessée, il y avait des *porpoises*, et tout ça que tu pouvais demander, et ils l'ont chessée.

BA: Pourquoi ils avaient chessé l'affaire?

IR: Mais, ça voulait planter du riz et des *soybeans* et des affaires. La terre était rendue à court.

BA: O, ouais.

IR: Tu connais, il y avait des enfants qu'avaient faim, et il y a pété une avalasse. Il a mouillé trente-neuf jours. Ça mouillé dix pouces d'épais tous les demie-heure. Ça a tout rempli la mer.

BA: Mais, ils ont perdu toute leur récolte?

IR: C'est Jim qu'avait percé le fils-de-putain de gros nué. Il l'avait percé avec une aiguille, mais pas une petite aiguille, non. Une de ces grosses *spikes* de chemin-de-fer-là. Et il est venu là, "Tiaupe!"

RR: Et ils ont pas manqué leur récolte à cause de ça?

IR: Mais tout l'affaire était perdue!

RR: *Except* le riz, je pense.

IR: Le riz est venu, il avait dix-neuf pieds de long.

BA: Le riz?

IR: Et il arrivait, juste il pouvait faire une petite grappe en haut, pauvre petite bête. Et ça passait en bateau, ça coupait leurs petites grappes-là, pour eux-autres manger pour pas ça crève de faim. Les fraises, elles avaient resté au fond là-bas-là. Défunt Mayo, il plongeait, puis il les cassait, puis il les lâchait-là, "Ploupe!" Ça sortait-là, ça flottait en haut.

RR: Et Jim les ramassait.

IR: Et Pascal était fourré dans l'affaire. C'est Pascal qu'a tout fait l'affaire. *Boy*, c'est un fils-de-putain, ouais, ce Pascal.

BA: Quoi c'est qu'il a fait?

whole thing in rice.

IR: They dried up the ocean and all those who wanted to claim land rights wanted to plant soybeans. And some planted sweet potatoes. And the poor little whales would jump in the dust. When they dried it all up, there were porpoises and everything you could ask for, and they dried it all up.

BA: Why had they dried it all up?

IR: Well, they wanted to plant rice and soybeans and other things. There was a shortage of land.

BA: Oh yeah.

IR: You know, there were children who were hungry, and then it poured down raining. It rained for thirty-nine days. It rained ten inches every half-hour. The ocean was refilled.

BA: But they must have lost all their crops.

IR: Jim's the one who pierced the son-of-a-bitch of a cloud. He pierced it with a needle, but not a little needle. One of those big railroad spikes. And he came along, "Tiaupe!"

RR: And this didn't ruin their crop that year?

IR: Well, everything was lost.

RR: Except the rice, I guess.

IR: The rice came along, it was nineteen feet high.

BA: The rice?

IR: It grew, just able to form a small bunch above the surface, poor little thing. And they came along in boats, cutting the little bunches so that they would have something to eat and not starve to death. The strawberries had stayed down on the bottom. The late Mayo would dive down and break them loose and then let them go. "Ploop!" They came up and floated on the surface.

RR: And Jim would pick them up.

IR: And Pascal was involved in the affair. It was Pascal who caused it all. Boy, he's a son-of-a-bitch, that Pascal.

BA: What did he do?

IR: Mais c'est lui, c'est lui qu'a tout fait l'affaire. C'est lui qu'a fait Jim—Ça il disait à Jim-là, Jim l'écoutait.

RR: C'est lui qu'a cassé le nué?

IR: Il a fait Jim aller casser les nués. Jim a tout percé ces gros nués-là. En dernier, il avait une grosse *cross-tie*. Il les perçait-là, "Ouah!" Et la mer était sec, mais il l'a remplie dans, dans, o, avant trente jours, mais ces chères grosses baleines et les *porpoises* et toute qualité de poissons, ça battait. Et ils ont gonflé dessus l'eau, et puis ça faisait signe avec leur queues comme ça. [geste indiquant un salut]

BA: Ils disaient merci?

IR: Ils disaient merci.

BA: Mais, c'était pas l'eau fraîche qu'a tombé en dedans-là?

IR: Ouais. Non, non, mais là, Jim est venu avec son emballeuse et il a salé la mer. Tu te rappelles de ça, Revon?

RR: Quand il avait salé la mer, ouais.

IR: Quand la grosse pluie a pris, les poissons d'eau salée pouvaient pas vivre dans l'eau douce. Pascal a percé les nués. Et Jim est venu-là avec des tonnes de sel. Il est venu droit là à *Avery's Island* après le sel.

BA: O, ouais!

RR: C'est là où il dit, "Comment t'aimes la mer?" Et l'autre a goûté, "Mais," il dit, "elle est juste bonne, juste assez de salée."

IR: Well, it's him, he's the one who did it all. He's the one who made Jim—Whatever he told Jim, Jim listened to him.

RR: He's the one who pierced the cloud.

IR: He made Jim go and pierce the clouds. Jim pierced those big clouds. In the end, he had a cross tie. He would pierce them, "Wah!" And the sea was dry, but he filled it in, in, oh, before thirty days, but those big old whales and the porpoises and all the other kinds of fish, were flapping. And they would swell up on the water and they would wave with their tails like this. [gesture indicating a wave]

BA: They were saying thank you?

IR: They were saying thank you.

BA: But wasn't it fresh water that fell in there?

IR: Yes. No, no, but then Jim came along with his flying haybaler and he salted the sea. Don't you remember that, Revon?

RR: When he salted the sea, yes.

IR: When the rains started, the saltwater fish couldn't live in the fresh water. Pascal pierced the clouds. And Jim came along with tons of salt. He went to Avery's Island for the salt.

BA: Oh yes!

RR: That's when he said, "How do you like the sea?" And the other one tasted, "Well," he said, "it's just right, just salty enough."

82. *Boulé Sévenne se fouille un trou / Boulé Sévenne Digs a Hole for Himself* (Hube Reed, Alexandre Manuel and Elvin Fontenot, Mamou)

In this conversation Hube and Alexandre discuss Alexandre's remarkable bull, Boulé Sévenne (motif B871.1.1.1 "Giant ox"), which has obvious similarities with Babe, Paul Bunyan's giant blue ox. Boulé Sévenne buries itself in a hole in a fit of anger and must be unearthed. This story resembles type 75 *The Help of the Weak*, perhaps best known as an animal tale about a mouse that helps a lion escape from a trap after having been spared earlier by the lion, though this version lacks the reversal of the ending. Klipple described an African variant in which the elephant is pulled from a deep hole by helpful rats and parrots

which throw dirt and leaves into the hole until it is filled. Boulé Sévenne is described later as being so large that the bell around its neck is a church bell (motif X1235.1.1 "Cow of Paul Bunyan wears a church bell for cowbell;" this motif about the church bell around the animal's neck is found in Rabelais's *Gargantua et Pantagruel*). The storytellers proceed to describe Boulé Sévenne as being so large than it eats pine trees and whole briar patches in a single bite (cf. motif X1237.2.5*[1], "Babe eats up fifty hectares of Douglas fir"). Its picture alone weighs fifteen pounds (cf. motif X1237.2.3*[c] "Weight of blue ox"), and has remarkably long horns (cf. motif X1237.2.3*[fa] "Eagle wears out seventeen sets of feathers flying from one of Babe's horns to the other").

AM: Mon vieux bœuf peut faire l'ouvrage.
HR: O, mais lui, il va sentir, il va gratter avec ses grandes cornes. Ça prend quinze minutes, un petit yinquis, pour voler dessus le bout pour arriver à l'autre bout.
AM: Quand mon vieux bœuf est fâché . . .
HR: Cher Bon Dieu!
AM: . . . c'est comme dans le *Wild West.*
HR: Il gratte-là. Il peut gratter, cher Bon Dieu! Dans vingt minutes, il sera vingt pieds de creux.
AM: Il a commencé à gratter dessus une montagne, il a fait un *valley.*
HR: Tu te rappelles?
BA: Il a fait un *valley* de ça?
AM: Ouais, *sure!* Il a fait un *valley.*
HR: Tu te rappelles? Tu te rappelles l'année passée, quand, comment il s'appelle, Boulé?
AM: Boulé.
HR: Boulé a fouillé un trou neuf par quatorze.
AM: O, ouais!
HR: Et cent pieds de creux. Là, tu crois pas il tournait? Là, on connaissait pas comment le faire revenir. On l'a—L'autre était *gone* avec la raidisseuse, ça Tante Coque met son— Comment t'appelles ça? Son—ses cheveux-là?

AM: Ouais, sa chevelure.
HR: Ouais. Bien mais, Alexandre dit, "Moi, je connais comment le faire revenir." Mais il pèse sept tonnes. On a commencé a jeté de la terre. À chaque fois on jetait de la terre, il s'escouait, il s'escouait. Mais la terre montait

AM: My old bull can do the job.
HR: Oh yeah, he'll sniff, he'll scratch with his long horns. It takes a sparrow fifteen minutes to fly from one end of his horns to the other.
AM: When my old bull is mad . . .
HR: Dear God!
AM: . . . it's like the Wild West.
HR: He paws the ground. He can really paw, dear God! In twenty minutes, he'll be twenty feet deep.
AM: He started pawing on a mountain and made a valley.
HR: Do you remember?
BA: He made a valley out of it?
AM: Yeah, sure! He made a valley.
HR: Do you remember? Do you remember last year, when, what's his name? Boulé?
AM: Boulé.
HR: Boulé dug a hole nine by fourteen.

AM: Oh yeah!
HR: And a hundred feet deep. Then don't you think he was turning? Then we didn't know how to bring him back. We—The other guy was gone to get a tightener, the thing that Tante Coque puts in—What do you call that? Her—for her hair?
AM: Yeah, her hairdo.
HR: Well, anyway, Alexandre said, "I know how to get him back." But he weighs seven tons. We started throwing dirt. Each time we'd throw some dirt, he'd shake, he'd shake. But the dirt would come up a bit, a little bit

un petit brin plus haut, un petit brin plus haut. On a jeté de la terre. Il y en avait, mais cher Bon Dieu! C'était comme le *waterworks tank*. On défouillait la terre comme ça, dessus Boulé. Boulé s'escouait. Mais ça lui mettait à peu près six pouces.

AM: Ouais, il l'a *pack and pack and pack*.

HR: À peu près six pouces à la fois. Il l'a *pack*. Il l'a *pack*. Il l'a *pack*. Quand on a jeté le dernier caillou de terre-là, Boulé a sauté à côté.

AM: Ouais, il était en haut. Il lui restait juste trois pattes, ouais, à Boulé dans ce temps-là.
HR: Ouais!
AM: Mais, Jack, il était *tough*.
HR: C'était pas un bébé! Mais sa cloche-là, le prêtre t'avait donné la vieille cloche. C'était à toi qu'il a donné la cloche? *Boy*, on peut l'attendre de loin, ouais, quand il se perd. Il a une cloche d'église pendue dans le cou. "Badingue, badangue!" Nous autres, on connaît ayoù il est. Mais ça résonne dans les quatre coins. On le trouve. Il revient.
AM: C'est lui qu'avait les grandes cornes.
HR: Combien il pesait? Combien de tonnes il pesait à peu près? Si tu l'aurais bien—Mais il vit toujours, hein? Tu l'as dans la savanne toujours?
AM: O, ouais! Il est toujours dans la savanne.
HR: Il mange des petits pins d'une bouchée, des petits pins haut comme ça-là. [geste pour indiquer environ un mètre et demi]
AM: Ouais.
HR: Ça lui fait une bouchée. Mais Alex est content. Les arbres, c'est rendu trop. Tant qu'à les talles d'éronces, cher Bon Dieu! Il mange ça d'une bouchée.
EF: Tu l'as à la place là-bas? À Duralde?
HR: Ouais, il est là-bas.
AM: Ouais.
HR: On va aller. On va aller le voir après-midi. Je vas amener mon Kodak. On va prendre des portraits, mais t'avais un portrait

higher. We threw dirt. There was a lot of it. Dear Lord! It was as high as the waterworks tank. We threw dirt onto Boulé Sévenne. He'd shake. And he'd rise about six inches.

AM: Yeah, he packed and packed and packed it.
HR: About six inches at a time. He packed it. He packed it. He packed it. When we threw down the last clump of dirt, Boulé just jumped out.
AM: Yeah, he had reached the top. Boulé only had three feet left, in those days.
HR: Yeah!
AM: But, Jack, he was tough.
HR: He was no baby! But his bell, the priest had given him an old bell. Was it to you he gave that bell? Boy, we can hear him from far away when he's lost. He has a church bell hung around his neck. "Bading, badang!" We know where he is. Why, it resounds to the four corners. We find him. He comes back.

AM: He's the one with the long horns.
HR: How much did he weigh? About how many tons did he weigh? If you had—But he's still living, isn't he? Do you still have him in your pasture?
AM: Oh, yeah! He's still in the pasture.
HR: He eats little pine trees in one bite, little pine trees about this high [gesture to indicate about four or five feet].
AM: Yeah.
HR: They're gone in a bite. But Alex is happy. The trees have gotten too thick. As for the briars, dear Lord! He eats them in a single bite.
EF: You have him at your farm out there? In Duralde?
HR: Yeah, he's there.
AM: Yeah.
HR: We'll go. We'll go to see him this afternoon. I'm going to take my camera. We'll take pictures, but you had a picture the other

l'autre jour. Rien que le portrait pesait quinze livres.

AM: O, il était gros!

day. The picture alone weighed fifteen pounds.

AM: Oh, it was big!

83. *Jim rencontre une femelle seal au North Pole / Jim Meets a Female Seal at the North Pole* (Irving and Revon Reed, Mamou)

Here, Irving tells about the time the old witch aunt (motif G200) captures Pascal. The poor hero is thrown out of an airplane (a rather mundane variant of motif G242.5 "Other objects that bear witches aloft") over the North Pole where he falls like an arrow due to his incredible thinness (motif X924 "Lie: remarkably thin persons") into the snow. He is cared for by a female seal which falls in love with him. Later they have children that share the characteristics of both Pascal and the seal (cf. motif A2382 "Why certain animals are hybrid") which explains the origins of penguins (cf. the section A1900–1999 in the motif index concerning the origin myths of various birds). But they later divorce, unable to resolve the difference in their size.

IR: La vieille tante faisait ça elle voulait.

RR: C'était une *witch*.

IR: C'était manière—C'était la cousine de la vieille *king* des *witches*.

RR: Une diablesse!

IR: Une diablessot! C'est le plus dans les *witches* il y avait. La diablesse-là, ça, c'est en bas. C'est un prince et un roi. Elle voulait tuer pauvre vieux Pascal. Elle a pété Pascal dans son aéroplane-là. Pascal était aussi content-là. Elle l'avait saoulé à moitié.

RR: . . . pris dans un *ride*.

IR: Elle voulait lui donner un *ride*, puis pas de parachute, pas rien, non! Pascal faisait—Il avait six pieds quatre pouces, et il pesait quatre-vingt-neuf livres.

RR: Il était maigre!

IR: Il était fin comme une aiguille. Elle l'a amené au-dessus du *North Pole*. Elle avait un aéroplane, il y avait pas rien. Elle a arrivé au-dessus du *North Pole*-là, elle a halé le petit *hatch*-là, "Ploupe!" *Good-bye,* Pascal! Pascal s'en venait-là. Il s'en allait droit comme une flèche de sauvage. Il est venu, il est tombé

IR: The old aunt did whatever she wanted to do.

RR: She was a witch.

IR: She was kind of—She was the cousin of the old king of witches.

RR: A she-devil!

IR: A she-devil-er! That's the highest there is among the witches. The she-devil is lower. Like a prince and a king. She wanted to kill poor old Pascal. She threw Pascal in her airplane. Pascal was so happy. She had gotten him half-drunk.

RR: . . . took him for a ride.

IR: She wanted to give him a ride, and without a parachute or anything! Pascal was going. He was six feet four inches tall and he weighed eighty-nine pounds.

RR: He was skinny!

IR: He was a thin as a needle. She took him over the North Pole. She had an airplane, and there was nothing [for him]. She arrived over the North Pole and she pulled the little hatch, "Ploop!" Good-bye, Pascal! Pascal was coming down. He was going as straight as an Indian's arrow. He came down, he fell in the

dans cette neige-là. Force il venait vite, il a fait un trou gros comme un chas d'aiguille. Il a passé à travers de la neige.

RR: Il avait un grand nez aussi.

IR: Ouais, il a passé à travers. Il a nagé en dessous de la neige-là, en dessous la glace et la neige en bas. Tonnerre! Il s'est rejoint une femelle *seal*.

BA: Une femelle quoi?

IR: Une *seal*. Ces grosses—Ils ont fait l'amour un bout de temps. Elle avait envie de le manger, mais elle a vu qu'elle était amoureuse. Elle était en course! Pascal lui a calé, là. Une *seal*, ça porte trois jours. Trois jours après, il y a eu des petits pascals qu'a sorti dessus la neige. C'était des pingouins. C'était tous des petites affaires minces. C'était tous des petits pascals, tous des mâles. Et ils ont pas pu *breed*. C'était tous des mâles.

BA: Ça fait, ils sont perdus?

IR: Hein? Elle a divorcé Pascal. Elle pesait à peu près neuf cent vingt livres et Pascal pesait quatre-vingt-neuf livres.

snow. He came down so hard that he made a hole as big as the eye of a needle. He went through the snow.

RR: He had a big nose, too.

IR: Yeah, he went right through it. He swam under the snow, under the ice and the snow down there. Thunderation! He met a female seal.

BA: A female what?

IR: A seal. Those big—They courted for a while. She felt like eating him, but she saw that she was falling in love. She was in heat! Pascal sank it to her. A seal gestates for three days. Three days later, there were little Pascals coming out onto the snow. They were penguins. They were all little skinny things. They were all little Pascals, all little males. They couldn't breed. They were all males.

BA: So they have been lost?

IR: What? She divorced Pascal. She weighed about nine hundred twenty pounds and Pascal weighed eighty-nine pounds.

84. *Les gros maringouins du Texas / The Big Mosquitoes from Texas (Hube Reed, Mamou)*

This story is an example of a special case in tradition of Pascal stories in which the storyteller casts himself as the hero of his own story. This tale suggests several types and motifs: type 1960M *The Giant Insect*, of which there is a Mexican variant that describes mosquitoes as big as cows; type 1881 *Man Carried Away by Geese*, which includes an episode that parallels this one; type 1960M$_2$ *Large Mosquitoes Carry Off Men or Animals*, with variants from Alberta and sixteen American states as described by Baughman. Baughman also described motif X1286.1 "Lie: the large mosquito," which has numerous subdivisions bearing on the supposed activities of these imaginary creatures: for example, motif X1286.1.2(c) "Mosquitoes weigh ten pounds," in a variant from Kansas, which is far-surpassed by Hube Reed's mosquitoes that weigh in at two hundred pounds. Also X1286.1.(a) "Men get under steel building without floor to escape mosquitoes; the mosquitoes drill through the roof; the men clinch the bills and the mosquitoes fly away with the building," as described in a variant from Indiana. Dorson presented another version in *American Negro Folktales*, "The Gallinipper" (no. 227, pp. 361–62): a mosquito pierces through a tree to get to a man hiding on the other side; its beak is caught and it dies leaving bones covering five

hectares! This version is different in that the mosquito does not escape. I have heard a similar tale from Marius Babineaux from Robert's Cove, Louisiana. Tall tales featuring mosquitoes are extremely common in the South; W.K. McNeil has published seven Ozark versions (*Ozark Mountain Humor*, pp. 25–30), including one (25a) set in Louisiana. Hube ends his tale with a description of his return trip from the shores of Lake Pontchartrain where he finally succeeded in landing his mosquito-borne shack, then with a description of Texas, which would have been a much worse landing place.

BA: *Okay*-là, l'affaire pour les marigouins.
HR: Quand le tonnerre a arrêté hier, cet ouragan de tonnerre, il y en avait un drôle de train. J'ai halé ma fenêtre; j'ai vu il y avait deux maringouins de Texas qu'étaient après se brosser les dents avec des lattes de mon jardin.
BA: C'est gros ça, ces maringouins?
HR: Ouais, c'est des maringouins de Texas. Ils sont à peu près six pieds de haut, à peu près deux cents livres. Ça, c'est des jeunes. Il y en a qui vient un petit brin plus gros, mais ils ont peur de venir par ici. Le monde va croire c'est des aéroplanes communistes. Ça va les *shoot down*. J'ai ramassé cinq piastres des *toothpicks*, un sac plein. J'ai vendu pour cinq piastres des *toothpicks* au Mamou Wholesale. Là, c'est à force les bouts de bois volaient. Tu vois, c'était fait en bois, les lattes de jardin. C'est fait en bois, ça, comme des *picket fences*. Mais là, les deux mêmes-là, ils m'ont reconnu quand j'étais à la Grande Chenière pour *gauge*, dans une petite maison de six pieds carrés.
BA: Quoi, tu travaillais là-bas?
HR: Ils m'ont attaqué. Moi, j'ai fermé la porte, mais les dards allaient en travers. Mais je les pliais les becs avec mon *wrench*. Là, t-à l'heure, quand j'ai ouvert la porte à peu près dix minutes juste après, j'étais dans les nués. Ils sont allés à la vole avec moi et la cabane.
BA: Ils sont forts!
HR: J'ai fait une petite craque et je les cognais sur la tête. Là, quand il y en restait trois, elle a commencé à *lose altitude*. On était dans les nués! Mais j'ai *land* au ras d'en ville-là, sur l'écore de Pontchartrain Beach.

BA: Okay, the one about the mosquitoes.
HR: When the thunder stopped yesterday, that thunderstorm, there was a strange noise. I opened my window; I saw that there were two mosquitoes from Texas that were brushing their teeth with the fence pickets from my garden.
BA: Were they big, these mosquitoes?
HR: Yeah, they were Texan mosquitoes. They were about six feet tall, about two hundred pounds. Those were the young ones. There are some that get a little bigger, but they are afraid of coming out this way. People will think they are communist aircraft. They'll shoot them down. I picked up five dollars worth of toothpicks, a full bag. I sold five dollars worth of toothpicks at Mamou Wholesale. There were so many bits of wood flying. You see, they were made of wood, my garden pickets. They're made of wood, like picket fences. But then, the same two [mosquitoes] recognized me when I was in Grande Chenière as a gauger, in a little six-foot-square house.
BA: What, you worked out there?
HR: They attacked me. I closed the door, but their beaks went through. I bent their beaks with my wrench. Then later, when I opened the door about ten minutes later, I was in the clouds. They flew away with me and the shack.
BA: They were strong!
HR: I opened a crack in the door and I hit them on the head. Then when there were three left, we started losing altitude. We were up in the clouds! But I landed near New Orleans, on the shore of Pontchartrain Beach.

BA: O, ouais? Là, ça s'a posé doucement?

HR: O, ouais, tout doucement. Il y en restait rien que deux. Rien que deux qui—Pareil comme un *helicopter.*

BA: O, ouais?

HR: O, ouais. Ils ont *feather their props.* Il a fallu que je *hitchhick back.* Ça m'a pris deux mois. Le monde avait peur de moi. Ça croyait que j'étais un sauvage et un nègre et un dégo et un Chinois et un Japonais. Ça me prendait pour toutes sortes d'affaires.

BA: Pourquoi?

HR: Moi, je ressemble à toutes sortes d'affaires. J'ai le sang mêlé. J'ai sept qualités de sang. Je suis comme une tortue; elle a sept qualités de viandes. Mais j'ai quitté mon *job;* j'avais peur de ces bêtailles. Ils auront pu venir un petit brin plus, et là, *gone* avec moi dans le Texas. Moi, j'aime pas aller au Texas.

BA: Pourquoi?

HR: Mais l'état de Texas et trop gros. Il y a trop de sable là. C'est gros, mais c'est rien que du sable. Ils ont des gros melons et n'importe qui est gros là-bas. Mais les maringouins, ça, c'est l'affaire plus grosse ils ont. Ils ont des *cowboys* asteur, ça avaient l'habitude avoir des *ten gallon hats.* Ça fait, les Cadiens ont copié dessus eux-autres. Asteur, ils ont des *eleven gallon hats.* Ça veut plus gros que n'importe qui. Tu connais, quand tu mets onze gallons d'eau dans ton chapeau, puis tu le mets sur ta tête, mais ça tient la tête froide, tu connais, mais l'eau coule des fois, s'il est pas bien serré.

BA: Ça coule dans les oreilles?

HR: Tu peux te noyer avec ça, mais ça te lave les oreilles quand même. Ça ôte le sable. C'est rien que du sable il y a dans le Texas quand même.

BA: Comment ça se fait t'as peur d'aller là-bas?

HR: Mais, j'ai peur que ces maringouins m'attaquent encore!

BA: O!

HR: Ils ont des becs croches! Ça peut pas

BA: Oh yeah? Then it landed softly?

HR: Oh yeah, very softly. There were only two left [flying]. Only two who—Just like a helicopter.

BA: Oh yeah?

HR: Oh yeah. They feathered their props. I had to hitchhike back. It took me two months. People were afraid of me. They thought I was Indian and black and Italian and Chinese and Japanese. They mistook me for all sorts of things.

BA: Why?

HR: I look like all sorts of things. I have mixed blood. I have seven kinds of blood. I'm like a turtle; they have seven kinds of meat. But I quit my job; I was afraid of those animals. They could have gone a little farther and left for Texas with me. I don't like going to Texas.

BA: Why?

HR: Well, Texas is too big. There's too much sand there. It's big, but it's nothing but sand. They have big watermelons and everything is big there. But the mosquitoes are the biggest things they have. There are cowboys now, they used to have ten gallon hats. So the Cajuns copied them. Now, they have eleven gallon hats. They want to be bigger than anyone else. You know, when you put eleven gallons of water in your hat, and you put it on your head, it keeps your head cool, you know, but the water leaks sometimes, if it's not tight.

BA: It leaks in your ears?

HR: You can drown that way, but it washes your ears anyway. It takes out the sand. There's nothing but sand in Texas anyway.

BA: Why are you afraid to go there?

HR: Well, I'm afraid those mosquitoes will attack me again.

BA: Oh!

HR: They have crooked beaks! They can't

béquer. Ceux-là que j'ai plié le bec-là, ils se sont tous dépris. Leurs *partners* ont tout défoncé la petite office.

kiss anymore. Those whose beaks I bent, they all got away. Their friends broke up the little shack.

85. L'opération à Hube / Hube's Operation (Hube Reed and Alexandre Manuel, Mamou)

Beginning with a discussion about his death, Hube warns Alexandre not to steal the coins which cover his eyes during his wake. In Greek mythology, it was important to place an offering in the mouth of the dead so they might pay Charon who carried the souls of the dead across the Acheron River. The subject of death led Hube to a discussion of immortality which then led him to describe his plan to avoid death and acquire an excellent memory at the same time: a double operation replacing his brain with that of an elephant and adding the heart of a sea turtle on the right side. (Compare type 1911A *Horse's New Backbone,* with a variant from Kentucky described by Baughman.) This new heart will permit Hube to live three hundred more years, during which time he swears that he will not shave. Compare also motif X1721.2 "Skillful surgeon removes and replaces vital organs," especially sub-division (b), with variants from Michigan and Illinois which cast a man who has received an organ transplant from an Angora goat and begins acquiring its characteristics. Compare also type 660 *The Three Doctors,* in which surgeons take out their own organs to replace them later as proof of their talents. The maid unknowingly throws the organs out and then replaces them later with animal organs when the doctors ask for them. When the surgeons transplant the animal organs into their bodies, they begin to take on characteristics of the animals. English-language variants of this tale are reported from Kentucky (Marie Campbell, *Tales from the Cloudwalking Country,* pp. 187–188), as well as Maine and the American West (J.H. Brunvand, *The Study of Folklore,* p. 142). For a study of this type, see Luc Lacourcière's "Les transplantations fabuleuses," in *Cahiers d'histoire* (no. 22).

HR: Quand je vas mourir (j'ai fait mon *will* l'autre jour), je veux ça prend rien que ma tête. Et les côtes, que ça donne ça aux chiens. Je vas aller chez Simon-là, je veux il me donne une de ces petites boîtes à souliers-là. Je vas mettre ma coyoche en dedans-là, rien qu'avec assez pour une petite cravate. Fermer les n-œils. Si il met des *four bits,* Alex, prends-les pas, non! Quitte-moi monter avec mes taxes en haut-là.
AM: Je te garantie, si je suis cassé, je vas les prendre les deux.
HR: C'est comme ça je veux aller. Et je parie

HR: When I die (I made out my will the other day), I want them to take nothing but my head. And the ribs, they can give them to the dogs. I'm going to go to Simon's, I want him to give me one of those little shoeboxes. I'll put my old bean in there, with only enough room for a little tie. Close my eyes. If they put fifty-cent pieces, Alex, don't take them! Let me go up with my taxes.

AM: I guarantee you, if I'm broke, I'll take both of them.
HR: That's how I want to go. And I'll bet

Shorty croit pas ça, non. Tu me crois ou tu me crois pas?

S: Je te crois pas.

HR: C'est dur à croire qu'il me croit pas. Mais je vas me faire opérer la semaine qui vient. Je vas me mettre une cervelle d'éléphant. Là, tu oublies jamais. J'auras pas besoin de mon petit livre pour écrire ces *notes*-là.

AM: Un éléphant?!

HR: Tu vois, hier, je voulais dire quelqu'un pour il vient souper. J'ai oublié. Et là, je veux me faire mettre un cœur de caouane bord-là. [geste désignant le côté droit] Tu connais ces caouanes de mer-là, ça vit trois cents années, ça. Ça fait, quand ce maudit va arrêter de battre comme ça-là, j'aurais un petit bouton-là, "Proupe!" Et ce cœur de caouane va commencer, ces caouanes de mer-là qu'a des ailes, manière. Là, je veux pas me raser. Comment tu crois, j'aurais un bébé de barbe, trois cents années.

Shorty doesn't believe that. Do you believe me or not?

S: I don't believe you.

HR: It's hard to believe that he doesn't believe me. But I'm going to have an operation next week. I'm going to have them put an elephant brain in my head. That way, you never forget. I won't need my little book to write my notes.

AM: An elephant?

HR: You see, yesterday, I wanted to tell someone to come and have supper. I forgot. And then, I want to have them put a sea turtle heart on this side [gesture indicating right]. You know those sea turtles live three hundred years. So when this damned thing stops beating, I'll have a little button, "Proop!" And that sea turtle heart will start up, those sea turtles that have what looks like wings. Then, I won't shave. Don't you think I'll have a fine beard, after three hundred years?

86. *Les oreilles à Hube sonnent / Hube's Ears Ring (Hube Reed and Elvin Fontenot, Mamou)*

During a lull in the conversation, the noon siren happened to ring and Hube immediately launched into the following story about the time he ate some pork at a supper raising his blood pressure and causing his ears to ring so loudly in the middle of the night that it woke up all the old ladies in town who went to church thinking that it was the church bell they heard. Compare motif X1767.1*(b) "Loud snoring causes people to complain of church bell's ringing at night." This story includes an imitation of the Latin chants of the Roman Catholic liturgy, sometimes called "la messe noire" (the black Mass) in the Louisiana tradition, this time attributed to a groggy priest. See also type 1824 *Parody Sermon* and motif G243 "Witches' sabbath" which also feature a burlesque imitation of liturgical Latin.

HR: Il y en a un là-bas qu'est toujours après larguer. [référence au responsable de la sirène de midi qui s'endort habituellement] L'autre jour, il s'a endormi, quelque chose.

EF: O! O!

HR: There are those there who are always getting tired. [reference to the person responsible for sounding the noon siren who regularly falls asleep and misses his cue.] The other day, he fell asleep, or something.

EF: Oh! Oh!

143

HR: Il a sonné l'affaire à deux heures, à deux heures de l'après-midi.

EF: Ça pourrait tout réveiller les *firemen*.

HR: Pareil comme moi, quand je restais au bout-là-là, à la grosse hôtel, icitte chez Dartez-là. Tu connais, quand je mange de la viande de cochon, je suis *allergic* de ça. Ça me fait ma tête, mes oreilles me faire, "Bingue, bingue, bangue, bingue." À quatre heures du matin (j'avais été chez Shorty et j'avais mangé des *pork chops*) et mes oreilles ont commencé à sonner. Toutes les vieilles femmes, elles sont beaucoup religieuses, elles se sont tout préparées. Elles ont arrivé à l'église à quatre heures et demie. Elles ont réveillé le prêtre. Ça croyait c'était la cloche de l'église qui sonnait. Tout ce temps-là, c'était mes oreilles. "Bingue, bingue, bangue!" Là, elles sont pas contentes avec moi, non. Mais le prêtre s'a mis à les croiser. Il les a croisées, puis là, il les a . . .

EF: Il les a confessées.

HR: [chanté] Vobiscum. Aussi qu'a petit marteau. Cache ton sucre en arrière de la cheminée.

EF: [chanté] Viens encore . . .

HR: [chanté] Viens encore quand tu peux, quand tu pourras. [parlé] Maudites vieilles oreilles!

HR: He sounded the thing at two o'clock, two o'clock in the afternoon.

EF: That could wake up the firemen.

HR: Just like me, when I lived on the other end of town, in the big hotel, right there with the Dartez family. You know, when I eat pork, I'm allergic to it. It makes my head, my ears go, "Bing, bing, bang, bing." At four in the morning—I had gone to Shorty's and I had eaten some pork chops and my ears began to ring. All the old ladies, they are very religious, they all got dressed. They arrived at church at four-thirty. They woke the priest. They thought it was the church bell that was ringing. All that time, it was my ears. "Bing, bing, bang!" Then they were not at all happy with me. But the priest began blessing them. He blessed them and then, he . . .

EF: He confessed them.

HR: [chanted] *Vobiscum. Also unto little hammer. Hide your sugar behind the chimney.*

EF: [chanted] *Come again . . .*

HR: [chanted] *Come again when you can, when you will be able . . .* [spoken] Damned old ears!

87. L'emballeuse à Jim / Jim's Haybaler (Irving and Revon Reed, Mamou)

When Revon Reed tried to suggest a previous storyline to his brother, Irving was not interested and instead launched into the following original story about an unusual voyage to the moon (F16) taken by Jim. Compare it to the story in which Pascal and Olide try to reach the moon in a used washing machine, elsewhere in this section. The idea of voyaging to the moon is certainly not original. Cleator meticulously describes human fascination with getting to the moon in "Some Imaginary Voyages," which appears in *To the Moon*. According to this study, the Ancient Greeks decribed how Menippus tried to fly to Zeus with a vulture's wing and an eagle's wing; equipped with these wings, he arrived on the moon where he met the philospher Empedocles, who had already arrived there by leaning too far over and falling into Mount Etna which exploded and propelled him to the moon.

There is an interesting literary variant from seventeenth-century France in Cyrano de Bergerac's *Voyage dans la lune,*which features a similar accidental voyage. After an unsuccessful attempt powered by bottles filled with dew, the hero finally gets to the moon by means of a rocket which has been accidentally launched and is affected by a change in gravity as it approaches the moon where the hero eventually lands on the "tree of life." Gabriel Daniel's *Le voyage du monde de Descartes* (Amsterdam, 1706) parodies the famous philosopher's concept concerning the dissociation between the body and the spirit. A special tobacco causes a sneeze and a subsequent fainting spell, resulting in a separation of the body and the spirit which gives the person the power to travel to the moon. Science fiction writers have long fantasized about getting to the moon. An early example is Jules Verne's *From the Earth to the Moon.* Burrison has a remarkably similar story from Georgia ("A Trip to the Moon," p. 175), in which the storyteller says she got to the moon by reaching up and grabbing it from a tall bluff. Once there, she found that the moon was indeed made of cheese, and that it was so old, it was full of skitters (insects). She eventually tied the skins of these skitters together to make a rope to come back to Earth. All this fantasy was surpassed, of course, on July 20, 1969, when the American space mission Apollo 11 did indeed land on the heavenly body which had so long attracted humans, and astronaut Neil Armstrong fulfilled dreams that had lasted for centuries by stepping out onto the moon.

In this Louisiana version, Jim gets to the moon by accident on a runaway haybaler (cf. motifs F66.1 "Voyage to upper world in chariot," F16 "Visit to land of moon," and X1004.3.1* "Lie: man rides exploding boiler") and there he meets some little green men (cf. F233.1 "Green fairy") who speak no less than fourteen languages.

IR: Tu connais ces vieilles emballeuses à foin-là? C'était emmené avec un cheval. Et pauvre défunt Jim, il est mort, mais il est sur la lune asteur. Raleigh est mort. C'était une grosse mule, ça l'appelait Raleigh. Pauvre vieille Raleigh est morte et Jim a pris à jongler qui il aurait fait avec cette emballeuse-là. Ça fait, il l'a *convert* avec un vieux petit *gas motor* . . .

RR: Je croyais c'était une laveuse.

IR: . . . fait avec une de ces *lawn-mowers*-là, manière. Il l'a *crank*, la fouleuse a parti. Tu connais, ça qui foulait la balle? Elle a parti, elle a parti, elle a parti. Pauvre vieille cousine —Comment elle s'appelait? La maman à Mémé-là? Tante Nat! Tante Nat était après guetter dans la fenêtre. Tante Nat, elle guettait. *"Good-bye! Good-bye!"* elle dit à Jim. "Reviens!" Et Jim pouvait plus haler le *clutch*, et le *clutch* était accroché. Il a été-là dessus la lune.

IR: You know those old haybalers? They were pulled by horses. And poor old Jim. He's dead, but he's on the moon now. Raleigh died. There was a great big mule they called Raleigh. Poor old Raleigh died and Jim started thinking about what he would do with that haybaler. So he converted it with a little gas motor . . .

RR: I thought it was a washing machine.

IR: . . . taken from one of those lawnmowers, sort of. He cranked it, the packer started up. You know, the thing that packs the bale? It started, and started and started. Poor old cousin—What was her name? Mémé's mother? Aunt Nat! Aunt Nat was looking out her window. Aunt Nat was watching. "Good-bye! Good-bye!" she said to Jim. "Come back!" And Jim could no longer pull the clutch, the clutch was stuck. He went all the way to the moon.

145

BA: O!

IR: Il a été. Il s'est posé là. Il a fait son *duty*-là. Il a rejoint deux ou trois petits bougres verts. Ils avaient la peau verte. Ça parlait français.

BA/RR: O, ouais!

IR: Ça parlait quatorze langages! Il dit, "Tu peux me donner le chemin *back to* Mamou?

"Hmmm," ça dit, "on a été à peu près vingt fois à Mamou. Tout ça on voit, c'est des *saloons*. Il y a une église. Il y a un et deux qui va à la messe." Il dit, "Nous autres, on est tous des Catholiques ici." Là, il a pété un petit coup de sifflet-là. Il en a vu à peu près cinq cents de ces petits diables verts-là qu'a sorti. Ils se sont tous mis accroupis à Jim. Ils disent, "Ça, c'est Saint Jim."

Et l'emballeuse courait toujours. Il dit, "Écoute! Je vas manquer de gaz. Il faudra je me hâte m'en rentourner. Et *sure enough,* il a manqué de gaz. Et elle s'est éteint.

"Mais," il dit, "comment je vas faire?" Mais sur la lune, ils ont un tas de gaz dessus leur estomac. Ça rôte un tas. Et il a pris à les faire rôter dans le *tank* de gaz. Et rôte que je te rôte! Tout à l'heure, l'aiguille a montré *full.* Il a halé la petite corde-là. "Craque!" Ça a reparti-là, "Titicourabungdabungdabungda!" Il est venu là, et il est tombé droit là, au ras de chez les LaHaye là-bas. C'est Aubry LaHaye qui a été à son secours.

BA: Oh!

IR: He went. He landed there. He did his duty. He met two or three little green men. They had green skin. They spoke French.

BA/RR: Oh, sure!

IR: They spoke fourteen languages! He said, "Can you show me the way back to Mamou?

"Hmmm," they said, "we went about twenty times to Mamou. All we see are saloons. There's one church. One or two people go to Mass." He said, "Here, we are all Catholics." Then he whistled sharply. And about five hundred of those little green devils came out. They all prostrated themselves before Jim. They said, "This is St. Jim."

And the haybaler was still running. He said, "Listen! I'm going to run out of gas. I'm going to have to hurry to get back. And sure enough, he ran out of gas. The machine stopped running.

"Well," he said, "what am I going to do?" But on the moon, they have lots of gas in their stomachs. They burp a lot. And he started getting them to burp in the gas tank. And burp after burp! Soon enough, the needle reached full. He pulled on the little rope. "Crack!" It started back up again, "Titicourabungdabungdabungda!" He came back and fell right over there next to the LaHaye's house. Aubry LaHaye's the one who went to help him.

Contes Légendaires / Legends

88. Le contrôleur d'esprits et le bœuf / The Spirit Controller and the Bull
(Samuel Gautreaux, Cecilia)

Legends about buried treasure are among the most abundant and important in Louisiana French oral tradition. There is said to be a considerable amount of treasure buried at one time or another in Louisiana. A significant part of this treasure is alleged to have belonged to the pirate (or corsaire) Jean Lafitte, but the majority of it is due to less romantic origins. During the Civil War, some (including the Cajuns, who traditionally placed little stock in formal banks) actually buried their money and valuables to protect them from pillaging Yankee (and Confederate) soldiers. Some of these people died before retrieving their money and, supposedly, a certain amount of this "treasure" is still buried in the area. Samuel Gautreaux and his brother Leonard searched for buried treasure throughout south Louisiana with a variety of means including metal detectors. They also acquired a treasure of stories about the subject along the way.

This treasure story features a fire-breathing bull (motif N553.5 "Tabu: fear of threatening animals while treasure is being raised") and a "spirit controller" who is supposed to help the treasure hunters dig up the treasure. In this variant they succeed in retrieving the treasure in spite of the supernatural spirits that were protecting it. Compare this story to "Buried Treasure and Hants" reported by Dorson in *American Negro Folktales* (no. 115, pp. 229–231) in which a "jackleg preacher" tries to find a coffer with the help of his wife, but she becomes afraid and they lose it. Burrison has a story, "The Grateful Headless Ghost" (p. 209–210), in which a restless soul promises money to someone in exchange for revealing his grave to the local authorities. There is a similar account in *Folktales of Louisiana* of a spirit controller foiled in his attempt to recover a slave owner's treasure.

À Charenton, dans le nord du lac Charenton, il y avait ce vieux Indien qui s'appelait Jim. Et ils ont demandé à vieux Jim ayoù un certain chêne avec une marque au nord du lac. Et vieux Jim a dit il connaissait.

In Charenton, north of Lake Charenton, there was an old Indian named Jim. And they asked old Jim where there might be a certain marked oak tree north of the lake. And old Jim said he knew.

147

Ça fait, ils ont été. Ils ont commencé à fouiller. Et dès qu'ils ont fouillé un bout, il y avait un gros bœuf qui s'en venait en travers de le bois avec la flamme qui lui sortait du nez.

Ça fait, ça a passé. Et ça a juste touché la pelle de le bougre qu'était après fouiller, et tout la bande a échappé. Ça fait, dès que le bougre a regardé, tous les autres étaient *gone*. Ça fait, il a *gone* aussi.

Et le bougre dit à l'Indien, *"Well,"* il dit, "faudra je retourne en ville après un contrôleur d'esprits." Ça fait, il dit, "Je vas revenir *back.*"

Ça fait, quelque temps après, il a revenu *back,* mais c'était dans le temps qu'il y avait ces vigilants-là, tu connais, les Ku Klux Klan. Et sa femme croyait que c'était ça le monde qui voulait causer avec lui. Ça fait, sa femme a pas voulu il va avec eux. Ça fait, le contrôleur d'esprits-là, il dit à l'Indien, "Est-ce que tu nous livres ta part?"

Et l'Indien dit, "Ouais, *go ahead,* vous autres peux l'avoir."

Ça fait, ils ont été. Ça fait, quelque temps après, l'Indien dit à pauvre Pap—Il était après passer dans le bois pas loin de là. Ça fait, il a décidé il aurait été dans le nord du lac pour voir, tu connais. Le trou était là, et la caisse, et les marques de piastres étaient dessus les bois qu'ils ont cassé de la caisse. Ça fait, ils l'ont trouvé. Le contrôleur d'esprits l'avait fait. Faut croire il a contrôlé le bœuf-là, le bœuf avec la flamme. Mais ça dit la flamme sortait dans le nez et ça pouvait l'entendre s'en venir dans le bois. Ça entendait le bois craquer, tu connais, dès qu'il sautait. Plus ça craquait fort, plus près il venait, jusqu'à il arrivait côté d'eux.

So they went. They started digging. And as soon as they had dug a ways, there was a great big bull that came through the woods with flames coming out of his nose.

So it passed. And it just touched the shovel of the man who was digging, and all of them got away. So as soon as the man looked, all the others were gone. So he left, too.

And the man told the Indian, "Well," he said, "I'll have to go back to town for a spirit controller." So he said, "I'll be back."

So some time later, he came back but it was during the time of the vigilantes, you know, the Ku Klux Klan. And his wife thought they were the ones who wanted to talk to him. So his wife didn't want him to go with them. So the spirit controller said to the Indian, "Will you give us your share?"

And the Indian said, "Yes, go ahead, you all can have it."

So they went. So some time later, the Indian said to my late father—He was going through the woods not far from there. So he decided he would go north of the lake to see, you know. The hole was there, and the chest, and the markings of dollars were on the wood that they have broken off of the chest. So they had found it. The spirit controller had done it. It must be that he controlled the bull, the fire-breathing bull. But they said the flame was coming out of its nose and they could hear it coming through the woods. They heard the wood cracking, you know, when he jumped. The louder it cracked, the closer he came, until he was right next to them.

89. *Le contrôleur et sa bible / The Controller and his Bible* (*Léonard Gautreaux, Cecilia*)

The preceding story by his brother Samuel inspired Leonard to tell this one about another spirit controller who lost his nerve along with the rest of the group of treasure hunters and fled, abandoning his Bible and everything else. The use of the Bible to help control spirits, common in buried treasure legends, is found in David Allen's tale, "A Moaning Ghost and Buried Treasure" (*Folktales of Louisiana*). In "Buried Treasure and Hants" (*American Negro Folktales*, no. 115, pp. 229–231), Dorson reported a preacher who faints at the sight of an apparition. In "Waiting for Martin" in the same collection (no. 193, pp. 322–324), a similar situation exists in which a preacher cannot face a phantom, even with his Bible. He gives up and runs off. In this Louisiana version, the apparition includes motifs E581.2 "Ghost rides horse," " D141 "Transformation: man to dog," and E423.1.1(b) "Ghostly dog opaque and insubstantial" which combine to provoke the flight of the preacher along with the rest of the diggers (N576 "Ghosts prevent men from raising treasure").

J'ai été rencontrer un vieux homme à Marrero, et il m'a conté une histoire. Il a été chercher pour un trésor avec d'autres hommes. Et il y avait un contrôleur qu'avait amené une bible pour contrôler les *spirits*. Et quand ils arraivaient à la place, ils ont vu un gros cheval s'en venir à travers du bois avec un homme dessus, et quand il a descendu, c'était plus un homme qu'était sur le cheval. C'était un chien. Et il dit le chien a venu se frotter sur ses jambes. Il dit il grognait. Il dit le chien, il connaît le chien était après le toucher, mais il sentait pas à rien. C'est comme si c'était juste du vent. Et il dit ils se sont tous sauvés. Il a perdu son chapeau et ses lunettes et il a tout déchiré son linge. Et jusqu'à le contrôleur s'est sauvé et il a jamais vu sa bible après ça.

I went to meet an old man in Marrero, and he told me a story. He went to look for a treasure with some other men. And there was a controller who had brought a Bible to control the spirits. And when they arrived at the site, they saw a big horse coming through the woods with a man riding it, and when he dismounted, it was no longer a man on the horse. It was a dog. And he said the dog came and rubbed itself against his legs. He said it was growling. He said he knew the dog was touching him, but he didn't feel anything. It was like there was just a wind. And he said they all took off running. He lost his hat and his glasses and he tore all his clothes. And even the controller ran off and he never saw his Bible again after that.

90. *Une petite tombe dans le bois / A Little Tomb in the Woods* (*Inez Catalon, Kaplan*)

The woman who told this story is not in the least superstitious. In fact, she actively seeks to demystify such legends, preferring to search for a logical explanation for such phenomena. Nevertheless, she knows many legendary stories, having heard them from

friends and acquaintances. In this story, a young boy discovers a tomb in the woods, but it disappears when he attempts to show it to his mother (motifs D1148 "Magic tomb," D867 "Magic object mysteriously disappears," and C423.2 "Tabu: speaking of extraordinary sight").

Mam dit ça fouillait un tas d'argent. Un tas, un tas d'argent, le monde a sorti de dedans la terre comme ça. Et elle m'a dit son petit frère avait été dans le bois une fois chercher les bêtes. Et il avait resté plus longtemps qu'il était supposé de rester. Ça fait, sa mère l'avait parlé, puis elle voulait connaître ayoù il sortait.

Ça fait, il dit il avait vu une petite tombe dans le bois. Et il dit il y avait un tas des feuilles sur la tombe. Et il avait propreté la tombe et il avait dansé dessus. Ça fait, là, il s'avait amusé sur cette petite tombe-là dans le bois.

"Mais," elle dit, "si t'as fait ça, viens me montrer ayoù c'est." Il a été, mais ils ont jamais pu trouver la place.
BA: Mais quoi c'était, ça?
IC: Mais là, tu vois, ça, c'était que c'était pour lui, mais pas pour les autres. S'il aurait peut-être retourné lui seul, mais il était trop jeune, tu vois. Il était trop jeune.

Mom said that they used to dig a lot for money. Lots and lots of money was taken out of the ground like that. And she said that her little brother had gone in the woods to get the cows. And he stayed longer than he was supposed to stay. So his mother spoke to him, and she wanted to know where he had been.

So he said he had seen a little tomb in the woods. And he said there was a pile of leaves on the grave. And he had cleaned the tomb and he had danced on it. So he had had fun on this little tomb in the woods.

"Well," she said, "if you did this, come and show me where it is." He went, but they were never able to find the place.
BA: What was that?
IC: Well, you see, that was because it was for him, but not for anyone else. If he could have returned alone, but he was too young, you see. He was too young.

91. *Le puits enchanté / The Haunted Well (Stanislaus "Tanisse" Faul, Cankton)*

This tale is about a location that was apparently well-known to many people who lived in the Cankton area. Supernatural events associated with the same well were described by Witness Dugas, also represented in this collection. Motifs F718 "Extraordinary well," D926 "Magic well," and D1171.10 "Magic buckets" may be involved here, but the key element of the story is specifically that the buckets rose and fell unattended, spilling water on the ground around the well. Most who describe these events have indicated that they felt buried treasure was involved.

Je connais ça bien. Il y avait Jesse Venable. Ça, c'était le papa à eux autres. O ouais, eux autres ont vu ça souvent là. Il y avait deux baquets. Un chaque bout de la chaîne, tu vois. Quand tu levais un, l'autre

I know them well. There was Jesse Venable. That was their father. Oh yeah, they saw that often there. There were two buckets. One on each end of the chain, you see. When you raised one, the other one went down.

LEGENDARY TALES

câlait. Tu pouvais attraper l'eau comme ça. Et bien, ça faisait ça-là tout seul là-bas. L'eau là volait et ça frappait contre le gros puits, un puits carré là, ouais.

Il y en a qui réclame c'est le gaz dans la terre, mais non. C'est pas ça parce qu'ils ont vu d'autres des affaires. Entendu des grosses échos que la terre, on dirait, avait cassé. Ça sortait et il y avait pas rien qui paraissait.

BA: C'était pas de l'argent en terre?
SF: Supposé. C'est ça ça dit. Le chêne a été transplanté pour connaître la place, pour marquer la place. Là ayoù ce que l'argent était. Il y a un tas qu'a été chercher. Ils ont cherché un tas, mais ils ont pas pu frapper dessus, mais ils ont vu des affaires. O ouais. Ça, c'était vrai. Moi, j'ai resté voisin là des années, pour peut-être une vingtaine d'années, droit à collé de là.

You could get water that way. Well, they went all by themselves there. Water flew out and splashed against the side of the big well, a square well. Oh yeah.

There are some who claim that there was gas in the ground, but no. That wasn't it because they saw other things. Heard huge echoes as though the earth had split. They would go outside and there was nothing to see.

BA: There wasn't money buried there?
SF: Supposedly. That's what they said. The oak tree had been transplanted to indicate the place, mark the place. Where the money was. Many went to look for it. They looked often, but they couldn't find it, but they saw things. Oh yeah. This was true. I lived nearby for years, maybe twenty years, right next to that place.

92. L'homme qui demandait la pluie / The Man Who Asked for Rain (Stanislaus Faul, Cankton)

This tale is related to type 752B *The Forgotten Wind* in which a man obtains control of the weather to improve his crop, but he forgets an important part (the wind or some other weather feature), which undoes all his careful work. Laval's Archives de Folklore had three variants. In this Louisiana version, God grants to a farmer the right to make it rain on his land whenever he wants, but he isn't able to control even this single aspect of the weather. The storyteller uses the story to present a moral against pride and greed. The fact that this man seeks not only to succeed himself, but to see his neighbors fail recalls the line often attributed to Attila the Hun: "It is not enough that I win; others must lose." Motifs A1131.0.1 "Regulation of rains" and Q552.3.0.1 "Failure of crops as punishment for uncharitableness" are implied here. It may also be interesting to compare type 1830 *In Trial Sermon the Parson Promises the Laymen the Kind of Weather They Want*. They cannot agree. "Then you may have it as it was before." The tales about Petit Jean in the islands of the Indian Ocean (see *Les aventures de Petit Jean*) often tell of God coming down on Earth to meet men, as here.

Il y avait un homme, et il aurait toujours voulu avoir et que les autres aient pas. C'était une homme, tu connais, qui était glorieux, il voulait se faire accroire mieux que les autres.

There was a man, and he would have always wanted to have things that others did not have. He was a man, you know, who was proud. He wanted everyone to think more of him than of anyone else.

Il était après travailler son maïs. Le Bon Dieu passe, Il dit, "T'as du joli maïs."

"Ouais, mais," il dit, *"boy,* s'il pourrait avoir la pluie comme je voudrais, là je ferais du maïs."

Bon Dieu dit, "Mais quand t'aurais besoin de la pluie?"

"Ah, mais," il dit, "à soir, une bonne pluie, et une pluie tous les temps en temps."

"Mais," Il dit, "regarde, t'auras de la pluie à soir et à chaque fois que t'auras besoin de la pluie," il dit, "juste dis tu veux de la pluie tel temps, et tu l'auras."

"O, mais," il dit, "là, je vas faire du maïs, si je pourrais croire ça."

Il dit, "Tu l'auras. *Go ahead.*"

Ça fait, le Bon Dieu a parti. Le soir, il y a venu une bonne pluie, juste comme à peu près qu'il voulait. Droit à la barrière qui séparait l'autre clos, c'était du monde pauvre qui restait là, faire du petit maïs. Il y a pas eu de la pluie du tout.

Quelques jours après, il dit, "Là, une bonne pluie encore," il dit, "là, mon maïs viendrait." La pluie a venu, comme il voulait. Les autres, pas de pluie. Sec, leur petit maïs était jaune.

Boy, il était content. Il dit "Moi, je vas faire du maïs; les autres en fera pas."

Les autres quand ça a venu temps, le Bon Dieu a voulu, Il a donné une pluie à eux-autres, ça a fait des épis de maïs. Mais son maïs à lui a juste fait des champignons. Une petite affaire blanche à la place des épis de maïs. Il a fait pas une graine de maïs.

He was working in his corn. The Good Lord passed, and He said, "You have nice corn."

"Yes, but," he said, "boy, if it could only rain like I'd like it to, then I'd really make some corn."

The Good Lord said, "Well, when would you need rain?"

"Ah, well," he said, "tonight, a good rain, and a rain every now and then."

"Well," He said, "look, you'll have rain tonight, and every time you'll need it," he said, "just say you want rain at a specified time, and you'll have it."

"Oh, well," he said, "now I'll make some corn, if only I could believe that."

He said, "You'll have it. Go ahead."

So, the Good Lord left. That night, there was a good rain, just about as he wanted it. Right at the fence that separated his fields from those of some poor people who lived next door, who also were raising corn, there was no rain at all.

A few days later, he said, "Now, another good rain," he said, "then, my corn would come." The rain came, just as he wanted it. For the others, no rain. Dry, their little corn was yellow.

Boy, was he happy. He said, "I'm going to make some corn; and the others won't make any."

The others, when it was time, the Good Lord wanted, He gave them rain, and there were ears of corn. But his corn just made buds. A little white thing where the ear should have been. He didn't make a single kernel of corn.

93. *L'homme dans la lune,* suivi de *L'homme enraciné / The Man in the Moon,* followed by *The Rooted Man (Stanislaus "Tanisse" Faul, Cankton)*

This story is about punishments for working on Sunday (motif Q223.6). The first man finds himself condemned to the moon for cutting wood on the Sabbath (Baughman motif A751.1.1 "Man in moon is thrown there as punishment for working [burning brush or gathering sticks] on Sunday"), and the second finds himself taking root. Compare motifs Q541 "Sitting (standing) in uncomfortable position as penance" and Q551.2.2 "Miraculous adhesion of objects to human hand [feet] as punishment for working on the holy day." Coffin records a Native American tale, from the Lillouets, describing the origins of the frogs in the moon (*Indian Tales of North America,* no. 11, pp. 36–37). Jolicœur reported a version, "Face à trois mécréants" [Faced with Three Non-believers], in *Les plus belles légendes acadiennes,* in which a man is condemned to remain in place for having spoken out against a priest.

T'as entendu parler de l'homme dans la lune. Mais soi-disant, c'était une punition. Le Bon Dieu l'a puni pour quelque chose. Il était après couper du bois. Hâler du bois avec une corde. Observe. Il y en a différents. Des fois, c'est un sac de bois qu'il porte sur son dos. Tu peux le voir. D'autres fois, c'est d'autre chose. Soi-disant, c'est un homme qui est dans la lune parce qu'il a été après du bois le dimanche.

Je connais, il y a en un, il était pauvre. Ça fait, c'est ça il faisait sa vie avec, couper du bois. Il allait pas à la messe. Il avait pas le temps.

Un dimanche matin, il était parti au bois avec sa hache sur le dos. Le Bon Dieu l'a rencontré. Il dit, "Ayoù t'es *gone?*"

Il dit, "Couper du bois."

"O, mais," Il dit, "pas le dimanche."

Il dit, "O, ouais. Ça me prend tous les jours. Il faut que je travaille pour faire ma vie."

"O," Il dit, "tu vas pas à la messe?"

"Non," il dit, "j'ai plus le temps."

"O, mais," Il dit, "t'as le temps d'aller à la messe. Là, après ça, si t'as réellement besoin de couper ton bois, tu peux le couper. On peut faire sans travailler le dimanche."

You've heard tell of the man in the moon. Well, supposedly, this was a punishment. The Good Lord punished him for something. He was cutting wood. Hauling wood with a rope. Observe. There are different ones. Sometimes, it's a sack of wood that he's carrying on his back. You can see him. Other times, it's something else. Supposedly, it's a man who is in the moon because he went for some wood on a Sunday.

I know, there's one about a man who was poor. So that is how he made his living, by cutting wood. He didn't go to Mass. He didn't have the time.

One Sunday morning, he left the woods with his axe on his shoulders. The Good Lord met him. He said, "Where are you going?"

He said, "To cut wood."

"Oh, well," He said, "not on Sunday."

He said, "Oh, yeah. It takes me all the days of the week. I have to work to make a living."

"Oh," He said, "you don't go to Mass?"

"No," he said, "I don't have the time."

"Oh well," He said, "you have time to go to Mass. Then after that, if you really have to cut your wood, you can cut it. We can do without working on Sunday."

Il dit, "Non, pas moi. J'ai ma famille et je peux pas."

"Mais," Il dit, "fous tout ça par terre et va à la messe."

"O, non," il dit, "je vas pas faire ça."

"Mais," Il dit, "reste là. Tu vas rester là et tu vas chesser là. Tu dis que t'as pas le temps d'aller à la messe, t'as pour chesser là. Là, t'as le temps."

Et le monde venait, ça dit, à peu près dix pas de lui pour commencer de fouiller la terre pour essayer d'arriver à lui pour le décoller. Ça lui faisait mal pareil comme si ça coupait dessus sa viande à lui.

He said, "No, not me. I have a family and I can't."

"Well," He said, "put that down and go to Mass."

"Oh, no," he said, "I will not do that."

"Well," He said, "stay there. You will stay there and you will wither there. You said that you don't have time to go to Mass, you will have to wither there. Now, you have time."

And the people came, they said, about ten paces from him to start digging in the earth to try to reach him to free him. This hurt him just as though they were cutting on his own flesh.

94. Juif errant / Wandering Jew (Stanislaus Faul, Cankton)

The Wandering Jew (type 777; motif Q502.1), condemned to walk for all eternity for refusing something or a service to Jesus Christ, is a well-known character in the tales, legends and even songs of Europe and America. There are several studies of this cycle, including George K. Anderson's *The Legend of the Wandering Jew* and G. Paris's *Légendes du Moyen Age*.

The Wandering Jew is also popular in French American tradition. His refusal to feed Jesus is often cited as the reason for his punishment, and there is almost always a specific reference to a sighting nearby. In *Les plus belles légendes acadiennes* (pp. 183–189), Catherine Jolicœur reported accounts which placed him in Moncton and in Memramcook. In *Légendes des Iles-de-la-Madeleine* (pp. 48–49), there are similar reports from the islands and from Cape Breton. This Louisiana variant places him in Sunset in St. Landry parish, about sixty years ago with only a perpetual nickel in his pockets. (See Morel and Walter, *Dictionnaire des superstitions,* [p. 140] for a discussion of this monetary aspect of the legend.) Here he eats cakes without sitting, without even stopping. The "wandering" nature of the poor Jew seems to fascinate the French-speaking population of North America, probably because of its own history (cf. songs such as "Un Canadien errant" [A Wandering Canadian] and "Un Acadien errant" [A Wandering Acadian]).

Juif errant, c'était un homme riche dans le temps que notre Bon Dieu était sur la terre. Un homme qui avait tout ça qu'il avait de besoin. Ça se fait, le Bon Dieu a passé. Il a arrivé à la cour. Il y avait deux gros chiens et une barrière pour empêcher les chiens de sortir. Il était assis sur la galerie. Il sortait de

Wandering Jew was a rich man during the time that Our Lord was here on earth. A man who had all he needed. So, the Good Lord came by. He arrived at the yard. There were two big dogs and a fence to prevent the dogs from getting out. He was sitting on the porch. He had just finished dinner. The

finir dîner. Le Bon Dieu était là. Il a crié après ses chiens. Il dit, "Rentre."

"Mais," Il dit, "j'ai pas grand temps." Il dit, "J'ai venu voir." Ils étaient après laver la vaisselle. Il dit, "J'ai venu voir pour manger." Il dit, "J'ai faim. J'ai venu voir si t'aurais pas quelque chose pour me donner à manger," Il dit, "quand même les restants de table."

"Non," il dit, "il n'y a plus rien. Les restants de table, c'est pour mes chiens."

"Mais," il dit, "j'ai faim."

"Mais," il dit, "je vas te dire quoi. Il y en a plus, les restants, c'est pour mes chiens." Et ce Juif errant là, il avait cinq sous dans sa poche.

Le Bon Dieu dit, "Bien." Il dit, "si c'est comme ça," Il dit, "tu vas te lever et tu vas marcher jusqu'à la fin du monde. Deux mille ans, plus ou moins."

Ça fait, il s'a juste levé là et il est parti. Il a pas pu aller se chercher de l'argent, pas rien. Il avait cinq sous. Et il est après vivre avec ses cinq sous. Il rentre dans une grosserie et il peut acheter pour cinq sous. Il doit avoir de la misère, *though*. Les affaires de cinq sous, d'habitude, c'est trente sous asteur.

Mais il a été chez vieux Romain Castille. Il a acheté pour cinq sous de gâteau. Dans ce temps-là, il en avait plein. Il marchait dans la grosserie et puis il mangeait. Ça fait, ça voyait que c'était un étranger. Ça dit, "Assoyez-vous."

Il dit, "Je peux pas m'assir." Et il mangeait en marchant. Il dit, "J'ai tout le temps pour marcher." Il a sorti de la grosserie avec ses cinq sous dans la poche. Il pourrait juste se virer à une autre grosserie et acheter pour cinq sous encore.

Il a essayé de se noyer, mais il a marché sur la mer pareil comme toi, tu marches sur le *blacktop*. Et je suis sûr il est las tout le temps, tu peux croire, mais il peut pas arrêter, il peut pas s'assir, nuit et jour. Ça doit être long.

Good Lord was there. He called out to his dogs. He said, "Come in."

"Well," He said, "I don't have much time." He said, "I've come to see." They were washing the dishes. He said, "I've come to see if I might eat." He said, "I'm hungry. I've come to see if you wouldn't have something for me to eat," He said, "even the table scraps."

"No," he said, "there isn't anything left. The table scraps are for my dogs."

"But," He said, "I'm hungry."

"Well," he said, "I'll tell you what. There is nothing left, the table scraps are for my dogs." And this Jew had five cents in his pocket.

The Good Lord said, "okay." He said, "if that's the way it is," He said, "you will rise and you will walk until the end of the world. Two thousand years, more or less."

So, he just got up and left. He was not able to go to get himself some money, nothing. He had five cents. And he is living on those five cents. He goes into a grocery store and he can buy five cents worth at a time. He must be having trouble, though. Things that were a nickel once are thirty cents now.

But he went to old man Romain Castille's place. He bought five cents worth of cake. In those days, he had plenty. He was walking in the store while he was eating. So they saw that this was a stranger. They said, "Sit down."

He said, "I can't sit down." And he would eat while walking. He said, "I must always walk." He left the grocery store with his nickel in his pocket. He could only go into another grocery store and buy another nickel's worth.

He tried to drown himself, but he walked on the water just like you walk on the blacktop. And I'm sure he must be tired all the time, you know, but he can't stop, he can't sit, night or day. It must seem long.

155

Là, tu parles de cela à du jeune monde et ça veut dire c'est pas vrai, mais il a été vu par du monde que je connaissais. Et ils ont dit que c'était sûr lui. Le Bon Dieu, quand Il était sur la terre, c'est pour ça il était là, pour exempler, donner exemple au monde.

Now, you tell this to young people and they want to say that it's not true, but he was seen by people that I knew. And they said that it was surely he. The Good Lord, when He was on the earth, He was here for this reason, to be an example, to give an example to the world.

95. Feux follets [Will-o'-the-Wisps] (Inez Catalon, Kaplan)

In this account, Inez Catalon gives a Louisiana version of the legend of *feux follets* (motif F491 "Will-o'-the-Wisp. Light seen over marshy places"). According to her, *feux follets* are the souls of unbaptized babies (motif A2817 "Origin of the will-o'-the-wisp"). Compare type 330 *The Smith Outwits the Devil*, popular among cultures throughout the world as an explanation of strange nocturnal lights. The smith is admitted neither to heaven nor to hell. The devil gives him a lantern to find his way in the dark. Other motifs are evident here: F491.1 "Will-o'-the-Wisp leads people astray" and F491.3.2(a) "If a person sticks knife into ground [or in a fence post], Will-o'-the-wisp will run around and around it until he is burned up [or cut to shreds]." In *Folktales of Louisiana*, John Verret describes the *feu follet* as a "bad angel." See the section "Les feux follets" in Jolicœur's *Les plus belles légendes acadiennes* (pp. 31–41) for a comparison between this same tradition among the Acadians in the Canadian Maritimes. For a discussion concerning *feux follets* in Québec, see Jean-Claude Dupont, *Le légendaire de la Beauce* (pp. 76–78).

Tu connais, la seule manière je vas croire en dedans-là, c'est si le monde des autres fois (je parle d'à peu près cent ans passés), que peut-être le monde était assez bon, peut-être ça voyait des affaires comme ça. Mais asteur, le monde sont des hypocrites, asteur, le monde, tu connais? Ils sont pas bons parce que, tu vois, les autres fois-là, je parle du temps à peu près de ma grand'mère. T'as déjà entendu parler d'un feu follet? T'as jamais pas entendu parler d'un feu follet? Mais j'ai demandé à Mam quoi c'était un feu follet. Et elle m'a dit c'était un enfant qui mourait qu'avait jamais été baptisé. C'était un feu follet. Et ils disont le soir quand tu marches que ça faisait noir, noir-là, que le monde marchait le soir, ça voyait comme une petite lumière, pas beaucoup plus grosse qu'une chandelle. La lumière d'une chandelle.

You know, the only way I'll believe in these things is if the old folks (I'm talking about nearly a hundred years ago), maybe people were good enough, maybe they saw things like that. But now, people are hypocrites, now, everybody, you know? They're no good because, you see, in the old days, I'm talking about the time of my grandmother. Have you ever heard of a *feu follet*? You never heard of a *feu follet*? Well, I asked Mom what a *feu follet* was. And she told me that it was a child that had died before being baptized. That was a *feu follet*. And they say that at night when you walked and it was really dark, when people walked at night, they would see something like a little light, not much bigger than a candle. The light of a candle.

Et si tu observais cette lumière-là, cette petite lumière t'aurait perdu, ça. Quand même t'étais sur le chemin, après t'en aller chez toi-là. Ah bien, tu suivais cette petite lumière-là avec tes yeux, tu connais. Cette petite lumière t'aurait suit, et elle t'aurait perdu. Et quelques fois, t'étais pas avant le lendemain avant tu te trouves.

Mais ils disent si jamais le monde, ça voyait un feu follet et qu'il avait un couteau de poche, fallait il ouvre le couteau, et tu le plantes sur un poteau, si tu voyerais un feu follet, comme cette lumière-là. Mais si tu te plantes ça dessus un poteau de barrière, tu le plantes-là. Et là, cette petite lumière reste. Elle joue avec ce couteau. Là, ça te laisse tranquille.

And if you watched that light, the light would cause you to lose your way. Even though you were on the road, going home. Ah well, you would follow that little light with your eyes, you know. That little light would follow you and would get you lost. And sometimes, you wouldn't find your way until the next morning.

But they say that if ever you saw a *feu follet* and had a pocketknife, you had to open your knife, and stick it on a fence post, if you saw a *feu follet,* that little light. If you stick it on a fence post, you stick it there. And then, that little light will stay. It plays with the knife. Then it leaves you alone.

96. *La chasse-galerie* / *The Wild Hunt* (Stanislaus "Tanisse" Faul, Cankton)

The *chasse-galerie* is a widely known legend among the North American French-speaking communities. Most of the variants from Québec are based on motif M211.6 "Man sells soul to devil for visit home in boat that sails through sky," often told to explain the sound of thunder. See the chapter on the *chasse-galerie* in Dupont's *Le légendaire de la Beauce* (VII, pp. 97–99), as well as the section "La chasse-galerie" in Jolicœur's *Les plus belles légendes acadiennes* (pp. 17–29), both of which treat this French Canadian version of the legend.

In Louisiana, the legend of the *chasse-galerie* is also used to explain the sounds of thunder, but in a different way. Several motifs are involved, including E501 "The Wild Hunt" and Q223.6.2* "Person is punished for hunting on Sunday." In both, hunting is involved in the origins of the *chasse-galerie*. In *American Negro Folktales*, Dorson included three tales in which a person is punished for not having observed the sabbath. Two of these involve hunting ("Hunting Possum on Sunday," no. 139, p. 266, and "The White Quail," no. 140, pp. 226–227), the other, fishing ("Simon Fishing on Sunday," no. 141, pp. 267–268). All three feature animals which speak in one way or another. In this Louisiana tale, the irreverent hunter is condemned to hunt for the rest of time for having left church to hunt rabbits. (See also motif E501.3.8 "Wild huntsman wanders for disturbing church service.") Notice also the localizing features: rabbit hunting on the prairie and corroboration by local sighting.

La chasse-galerie, c'est un homme qui avait été à la messe dimanche matin, tu connais. Et l'église était dans la prairie. Et il y a quelqu'un avec des chiens qui les avait suit. La messe était juste bien commencée, les chiens ont sorti au ras de la porte ayoù il était assis avec un lapin, à courser un lapin. Il a sorti dehors et il a parti à la course derrière lui aussi et il est après galoper toujours.

C'est ça ils ont appelé la chasse-galerie. Pendant des années, il a galopé sur la terre, mais asteur, il peut plus. Ça va dans l'air, ça. Mon père et mon beau-frère ont resté un soir un arpent avant de rentrer dans la savane à l'écouter passer. "Hou, hou, hou," ils écoutaient, comme si c'était des cloches et des chaînes. Supposé, il passe dans chaque pays tous les sept ans.

The *chasse-galerie* is a man who had gone to Mass one Sunday morning, you know. And the church was out on the prairie. And someone's dogs had followed them there. Mass was just getting started when the dogs went by the door where he was sitting. They were after a rabbit, chasing a rabbit. He went outside and started running after them as well and he is still running to this day.

That's what they called the *chasse-galerie*. For years, he ran on earth, but now, he can no longer do this. He goes through the sky. My father and my brother-in-law stayed out one night about an acre from their pasture just listening to him pass over. "Hoo, hoo, hoo," they heard, as though there were bells and chains. Supposedly, he passes in each country every seven years.

97. La chasse-galerie / The Wild Hunt (Léonard and Samuel Gautreaux, Cecilia)

In all the descriptions of the *chasse-galerie* in Louisiana, as in France, there is the theme of the condemned hunter (E501). In this second version of the legend, the storyteller attributes the origins of the *chasse-galerie* to a local event, a man from the neighborhood who was out hunting instead of going to Mass. He was punished after his death: one could hear him crying and his dogs would bark when he passed every Sunday. This hunter, too, is said to have been hunting rabbits. This is a common feature in stories about the *chasse-galerie* in Louisiana, since rabbits are hunted with hounds that bay as they trail their quarry, thus providing the noise compared to the sound of thunder. It is interesting to note that, in this case, the hunter was not punished for eternity. People no longer heard him once his penance was fulfilled.

SG: Et la chasse-galerie, tu te rappelles de la chasse-galerie?
LG: J'ai entendu pauvre Pap parler de ça, *yeah!* C'était un homme, ses parents voulaient il va à la messe le dimanche. Il disait, "Non, faut je vas à la chasse." Il avait de bons taïaux. Ça fait, plutôt d'aller à la messe, les dimanche matins, il partait, puis il allait à la chasse de lapins.

SG: And the *chasse-galerie*, do you remember the *chasse-galerie*?
LG: I heard my late father tell about that, yeah. It was a man whose family wanted him to go to Mass on Sunday. He would say, "No, I've got to go hunting." He had good hounds. So instead of going to Mass, on Sunday mornings, he would leave and he'd go hunting rabbits.

Ça fait, après il est mort, tous les dimanches, dans l'air ils entendaient les chiens japper, puis ça entendait sa voix. Et ça a arrivé icitte à Arnaudville. J'ai un de mes beaux-frères, il était jeune, mais il se rappelle de ça. Il entendait le train. Il dit ça a été pour des années comme ça. Tous les dimanches, ils entendaient ce train-là, ces taïaux-là dans l'air et cet homme après crier après. Quelques années, ils entendaient. Ça a venu que ça—

SG: Il avait fait pénitence.
LG: *Yeah,* il a fait pénitence, je pense, mais ils entendaient plus ça.
BA: Ça a arrivé droit icitte à Arnaudville?
LG: Ouais, juste un bon mile, manière.

So, after he died, every Sunday, in the sky, they could hear dogs barking and they could hear his voice. And this happened right here in Arnaudville. One of my brothers-in-law was young but he remembers it. He could hear the noise. He said that this went on for years. Every Sunday, they would hear this noise, these dogs in the sky and this man yelling at them. For a few years, they heard this. Then it happened that—

SG: He had completed his penance.
LG: Yeah, he had made his penance, I guess, but they didn't hear this any more.
BA: This happened right here in Arnaudville?
LG: Yes, just about a mile from here.

98. Le chien étrange / The Strange Dog (Richard Guidry, Gueydan)

This legend is reminiscent of the well-known werewolf theme. There are stories about the weredog in Québec, reported by Luc Lacourcière in *Folktales Told Around the World* ("Le gros chien," p. 463). The following motifs are present in this text: B17.1.2.3 "Transformed man as hostile dog," D525 "Transformation through curse," and D712.4 "Disenchantment by drawing blood." In *Folktales of Louisiana*, another Cajun storyteller, Velma Duet, relates that a *loup garou* can also be disenchanted by bleeding. In *Missouri*, Carrière cited another French American variant (no. 12). In *Les plus belles légendes acadiennes*, Joliœur included a similar legend in which a man cleaning pork tripe next to a stream is threatened by a big dog. He throws his knife at the dog, who then is transformed into a man. The man then thanks him for disenchanting him, just as in the present text. (For a study, see Barbara Allen Wood, *The Devil in Dog Form.*) Note also the reference to known voodoo elements as part of the transformation ritual (drinking the blood of a black chicken at a crossroads at midnight) which may point to black Creole influences in this story told by a white Cajun teller.

Une fois, il y avait une femme qui était après laver des tripes de cochon au bord d'un bayou et un chien étrange s'approchait d'elle et elle dit, "Tu veux passer! Tu veux passer!" parce qu'elle en avait peur. Mais le chien ne l'écoutait pas. Il s'en allait un bout, mais il éventait les tripes de cochon puis il revenait. Et elle disait, "Tu veux passer!" Le chien s'en

Once there was a woman who was washing pig tripe next to a bayou and a strange dog came up to her and she said, "You go away! You go away!" because she was afraid of it. But the dog didn't listen to her. It would go away a certain distance, but then it smelled the pig tripe and it would come back. And she said, "You go away!" The dog

allait un bout encore, puis il revenait.

Alors la femme a dit, *"God dog!"* Puis alors, elle a lancé un couteau après le chien, puis ça lui a coupé le nez et il a saigné quelques gouttes de sang. Il a tourné en homme.

Quand il était devenu homme, il a dit à sa femme, "Merci beaucoup, Madame," il dit, "vous m'avez ôté mon gri-gri."

Elle dit, "Ton gri-gri?"

"Oui," il dit, "j'avais bu du sang de poule noire à une croix de chemin, à minuit, pour me donner l'habilité de devenir n'importe quoi ce que je voulais. Mais j'en étais fatigué! Et perdre ce sang-là, ça m'a ôté mon obligation de changer de forme. Merci beaucoup!"

would go away again and then come back.

So the woman said, "God dog!" And then she threw a knife at the dog, and it cut it on the nose and it bled a few drops of blood. It turned into a man.

When it had become a man, he said to the woman, "Thank you very much, Madame," he said, "you have released me from a curse."

She said, "A curse?"

"Yes," he said, "I had drunk the blood of a black chicken at a crossroads at midnight to give me the ability to become whatever I desired. But I was tired of this! And losing this blood has released me from my obligation to this change of form. Thank you very much!"

99. *Le pont du Nez Piqué / The Bridge over the Nez Piqué* (Edward Deshotels, Mamou)

This tale relates the legend of the old bridge over the Nez Piqué Bayou, which was supposedly a giant alligator. During the day, the giant animal rested and its body formed a bridge. At night it would leave to ravage the countryside. Lacourcière and Low created a new type for their *Catalogue raisonné*, AF 58A *The Bridge of Crocodiles*—this new version is about the rabbit who tricks lots of crocodiles into helping him cross the river: the first gathers his whole family to show that it is the biggest family among the crocodiles; they unwittingly make a bridge and the rabbit crosses by jumping from one to the other while pretending to count them. The Louisiana tale included here is, instead, a variant of type 1960 *The Great Animal*, which develops into a tall tale concerning the huge quantity of products the animal provides once it is killed and processed. There is also an "urban legend" concerning giant alligators. According to the legend, baby alligators given to children as pets are thrown out once the children lose interest. They eventually reach the sewer system where they grow unmolested to an enormous size. In *Croc*, a recent film which exploits this legend, the crocodile emerges from the sewers to menace a city.

Beaucoup des années passées, depuis les Cadiens est ici, il y a un bayou, et le nom du bayou, c'est le bayou Nez Piqué, et c'est un nom sauvage, et ça a jamais été connu qui c'est le nom même, le nom Nez Piqué, qui

Many years ago, before the Cajuns were here, there was a bayou, and the name of the bayou was the Nez Piqué, and it is an Indian name, and it was never known what the name itself, the name Nez Piqué, what it

c'est qu'il veut dire, le *meaning* du mot Nez
Piqué. Et il y a personne qu'avait jamais
connu comment le pont du Nez Piqué, il
avait été fait.

Alors, un jour, le monde s'a aperçu
qu'alentours du pont Nez Piqué, il y avait des
choses drôles qu'arrivaient. Les bêtes
qu'allaient pour manger, elles auront disparu.
Ça revenait pas chez eux-autres. Et le pont
était assez large, dans ces temps-là, il y avait
juste des wagons et des bogheis et ça, et le
monde croisait. Ils auront croisé le pont pour
aller l'autre bord, visiter, quelque chose. Là,
quand ça revenait, ils s'auront croisés sur le
pont. Alors, ils auront été, arrêté les wagons
et puis le monde visitait.

Alors, un jour, il y a un homme et son
petit garçon, son fils, a été, et le petit s'a assis
dessus le pont pour pêcher. Alors, il a dit à
son papa, "Pap, le pont est après souffler!"

Alors, ils ont étudié ça un bout de
temps, et puis c'est venu bien sérieux qu'ils
ont compris qu'il y avait quelque chose de
drôle. Alors ils ont appelé les connaisseurs,
les professeurs, et le monde qu'avaient
étudié. Et ils sont venus. Ils ont trouvé que
c'était quelque chose qu'était en vie.

Alors, ils ont fouillé, jusqu'à ils ont
aperçu que c'était un cocodril. Il avait la tête
enterrée dessus un bord, et il avait la queue
pliée dans l'autre écore, l'autre bord. Et le
soir, il sortait de là, et il prendait le bayou et
il mangeait les bêtes. Là, sur l'avant-jour, il
venait. Il se replaçait et le monde croisait.

Alors, quand ils ont trouvé pour ça, ils
ont appelé l'armée. Et ils sont venus avec un
canon. Ils l'ont tiré dix coups, dix coups de
canon pour le tuer. Et c'est dit que, quand ils
l'ont ôté, que le bayou a baissé trois pieds-là,
à force il était gros.

Alors là, ils ont appelé tout le monde et
puis ils l'ont séparé. Et il a donné cinquante
barils de graisse. Et l'armée a pris la viande,
et il y en a eu pour une année, avec cette

means, the meaning of the words Nez Piqué.
And no one knew how the bridge across the
Nez Piqué had been built.

But one day, people noticed that around
the Nez Piqué bridge, strange things were
happening. Cows that went there to eat
would disappear. They never would come
home. And the bridge was so wide, in those
days, when there were only wagons and
buggies, the people could meet while
crossing the bridge. They would cross the
bridge to go to the other side to visit, or
something. Then, when they would come
back, they would meet on the bridge. So they
would stop the wagons and the people would
visit.

So one day, there was a man and his little
boy, his son, who went and the little one sat
on the bridge to fish. So, he said to his father,
"Pop, the bridge is breathing."

So they studied this for a while, and it
got very serious and they realized that there
was something funny. So they called in
people who knew, professors and other
people who had studied this sort of thing.
They found that it was alive.

So they dug, until they found out that it
was a crocodile. It had its head buried in one
side, and its tail was folded into the other
side. And at night, it would leave and follow
the bayou and eat the cows. Then, at
daybreak, it came back. It would replace
itself and the people would cross.

So when they found out about this, they
called in the army. And they came with a
cannon. They shot it ten times, ten cannon
shots to kill it. And it is said that when they
took it out, the bayou went down three feet,
so big was it.

So then they called all the people and
they divided it. And it produced fifty barrels
of fat. And the army took the meat, and there
was enough for a year, with the meat from

161

viande de ce cocodril-là. Et ils ont vendu la peau à des *factories* qui faisaient des souliers. Ils ont fait cinquante paires de souliers et des bottes en quantité.

Et asteur, ayoù le pont du Nez Piqué, ayoù il était, asteur, c'est un pont cimenté, ils ont. Et le monde qui passe s'arrête souvent pour un bout de temps parce que, pour ceux qui veut pas le croire, ils ont publié, ils ont mis une grosse plaque et l'histoire du premier pont du Nez Piqué est là pour eux autres lire.

this one crocodile. And they sold the skin to factories that made shoes. And they made fifty pairs of shoes and untold numbers of boots.

And now, where the Nez Piqué bridge was, now there is a new cement bridge. And the people who pass on it often stop for a while because, for those who would not believe it, there is a big plaque and the story of the first bridge over the Nez Piqué is there for all to read.

100. Jody McBrown, the Indian (Elby Deshotels, Reddell)

The essential motifs in this tale are E613 "Reincarnation as bird," E423.3.5 "Revenant as owl" (a French American variant was described by Baughman), and especially G275.12 "Witch in the form of an animal is injured or killed as a result of the injury to the animal. The witch's body suffers an injury identical to that of the animal," with numerous variants described by Baughman, most of which are about cats; only one, G275.12(rc), a Hispanic version from New Mexico, involves an injured owl. The traditional concept of the werewolf (motif D113.1.1; see Dorson, *Bloodstoppers and Bearwalkers*, pp. 74–78) applies to many other were-animals, including were-owls. The storyline follows "The Witch That Was Hurt," type 3055, as described in Reidar Christiansen's *The Migratory Legends*. Compare also "The Werewolf" (no. 13 in the Grimms *German Legends*) which involved a woman in the form of a wolf. Katherine Briggs described several British variants in her *Dictionary of British Folktales* (pp. 612, 616f, 649, 672f, 704, 736f, 744ff). It is interesting to note that Jody McBrown, at least in the form of the owl, primarily speaks English, just like the "owl" in Mrs. Richard's tale (no. 28 above in this collection). It is also interesting that Jody McBrown, the protector of the deer, is an Indian (despite his name). This is perhaps due to a common perception that Native Americans are close to nature.

Une fois, il y avait un vieux sauvage, et son nom c'était Jody McBrown. Et il restait tout seul. Et la seule chose il avait, c'était un cheval, un chien, et un vieux boghei. Et il avait une savane qu'avait beaucoup, beaucoup des chevreuils dedans, et il quittait personne chasser et tuer les bêtailles dedans sa savane. Et il avait un voisin qui s'appelait Narcisse. Et il aimait beaucoup chasser les chevreuils, et il connaissait il y avait des chevreuils dans la savane à Jody McBrown.

Once there was an old Indian, and his name was Jody McBrown. And he lived alone. And the only thing he had was a horse, a dog and an old buggy. And he had a pasture in which there were many deer, and he allowed no one to hunt and kill deer in his pasture. And he had a neighbor who was called Narcisse. And he loved to hunt deer, and he knew there were deer in Jody McBrown's pasture.

Et le monde se mettait ensemble, et ça parlait pour l'âge du vieux sauvage. Il y en avait qui disaient il avait cent vingt ans. Il y en a d'autres qui disaient il avait cent trente ans. Mais ça connaissait pas pour sûr. Mais il était beaucoup, beaucoup vieux. Il avait dedans son bras un bracelet en or qui était écrit dessus, "Jody McBrown."

Un jour, le vieux sauvage a manqué. Et le monde commencé à essayer de jongler ayoù ce qu'il avait passé. Son cheval était là, et tous les soirs, son chien hurlait toute la nuit. Ça pouvait pas connaître ayoù Jody McBrown avait été. Ça pouvait pas connaître ayoù il avait passé. Il avait juste disparu. Ça fait, Narcisse a eu cette nouvelle. Bien mais, il a décidé c'était une bonne chance pour lui aller pour se *trap* des chevreuils dans la savane à Jody McBrown.

Un beau matin, il a été. Et il y avait un gros chevreuil. Il est venu pour le tirer. En même temps, il y a un gros hibou qui s'est posé. Il a effarouché le chevreuil. Le chevreuil s'est caché. Ça se fait, il été un bout plus loin. Il a vu un autre chevreuil. Il l'a approché. Quand il est venu pour le tirer, le gros hibou s'est reposé encore. Et Narcisse, c'était pas un homme qu'avait beaucoup de patience. Et il a dit à lui-même, "Si jamais tu reviens encore, ça, ça sera ton dernier coup." Et il a vu un autre chevreuil. Et quand il est venu pour le tirer-là, le hibou s'est posé. Ça se fait, il l'a tiré. Et le hibou a tombé par terre. Il était gros. Narcisse a venu, et quand il est venu au ras de lui, le hibou a voulu s'élever. Il a halé son pied pour le cogner et le gros hibou a dit, *"Don't kill me, man. I'm Jody McBrown, the Indian!"* Et Narcisse lui a dit, *"What'd you say?"* Il dit, "Moi, je suis *going home!*" Et puis, il a parti à se sauver.

Il a été chez son voisin. Il a dit à Jean-Louis, "Jean-Louis, faut tu viens avec moi. C'est pas la peine je te conte ça qu'a arrivé, tu vas pas croire." Il dit, "Faut tu viens avec moi. J'ai tué un gros hibou et il m'a parlé!" Et

And people would get together and talk about the age of the old Indian. Some said that he was one hundred twenty years old. Others said that he was one hundred thirty. But no one knew for certain. But he was very, very old. He wore a bracelet on his arm that read "Jody McBrown."

One day, the old Indian could not be found. And the people started trying to think of where he could have gone. His horse was there and every night his dog howled all night long. They couldn't understand where Jody McBrown had gone. They couldn't understand where he was. He had just disappeared. So, Narcisse heard the news. Well, he decided this was a good opportunity for him to go and trap some deer in Jody McBrown's pasture.

One fine morning, he went. And there was a big deer. He went to shoot it. At the same time, a big owl landed and scared the deer. The deer hid. So, he went a little farther. He saw another deer. He approached it. When he came to shoot it, the big owl landed again. And Narcisse was not a man with lots of patience. And he said under his breath, "If ever you come back, that'll be the last time." And he saw another deer. And when he came to shoot it, the owl landed. So he shot it. And the owl fell to the ground. It was big. Narcisse came and when got close to it, the owl tried to get up. He pulled his foot back to kick it and the big owl said, "Don't kill me, man, I'm Jody McBrown, the Indian!" And Narcisse said to him, "What'd you say?" He said, "I'm going home!" And he took off running.

He went to his neighbor. He said to Jean-Louis, " Jean-Louis, you've got to come with me. It's no use I tell you about what happened. You'd never believe it." He said, "You've got to come with me. I killed a big

il dit, "Il m'a dit son nom, c'était Jody McBrown."

Ça se fait, lui et Jean-Louis a été. Le hibou était par terre; il était mort. Et ils l'ont examiné. La première chose ils ont vu, c'était son bec, et son bec avait une grosse dent en or. Il avait deux boucles d'oreilles en or, et dans sa patte, il avait un bracelet, et c'était écrit dessus le bracelet, "Jody McBrown, *the Indian.*"

owl and it spoke to me!" And he said, "It told me its name was Jody McBrown."

So he and Jean-Louis went. The owl was on the ground; it was dead. And they examined it. The first thing they saw was its beak and the beak had a big gold tooth. It had two golden earrings, and on its foot was a bracelet, and on it was written, "Jody McBrown, the Indian."

101. Le nom de Carencro / The Name of Carencro (Évélia Boudreaux, Carencro)

This place name legend is common not only in the area around Carencro, but from one end of the French-speaking part of Louisiana to the other. Supposedly, the town was named according to a bet between two hunters who decided to name the place where they were after the first bird they noticed. The first bird turned out to be a buzzard or carrion crow which, in the local vernacular, became Carencro, and the name stuck. See motif N125.4 "Districts named from first person met in each." The town was more likely named for the the bayou Carencro which flows nearby and the bayou was in turn named for the Karancao tribe of Native Americans who once lived in the area.

Un jour, il y avait deux hommes qu'étaient à la chasse. Ils chassaient et ils trouvaient pas grand'chose à tirer. En leur route, ils ont trouvé une place et la place avait pas de nom. Ils ont dit, "Comment ça se fait qu'il pourrait pas avoir de nom pour cette place?" Ils disent, "On va la nommer le nom du premier z-oiseau on va trouver."

Ils ont continué marcher. Ils ont arrivé, il y avait une grosse animal qu'était crevée. Elle était morte sur le long d'un bayou. C'était une bêtaille qui restait dans l'eau, ils pouvaient voir, mais elle était sur terre. Elle avait crevée. Elle était morte là. Ça fait, ils ont vu qu'il y avait beaucoup de carencros là, ces gros oiseaux noirs. Et ils ont dit, "Mais c'est comme ça on va nommer la place."

Et c'est comme ça Carencro a eu son nom.

One day there were two men who were out hunting. They were hunting but they had not seen anything to shoot. Along the way, they came upon a place with no name. They said, "How is it that there is no name for this place?" They said, "We'll name it after the first bird we find."

They continued walking. They came upon a big dead animal. It was dead along the bayou. They could see that it was an animal that lived in the water, but it was out on land. It had died. It was laying dead there. So they saw that there were lots of buzzards [carencros] there, those big black birds. And they said, "Well, this is how we'll name this place."

And that's how Carencro got its name.

102. Vieux Nèg et Vieux Blanc té gain une course / Old Black Man and Old White Man Had a Race (Wilson "Ben Guiné" Mitchell, Parks)

This origin myth is based on a variant of motif A1671.1 "Why the negro works," also known in the oral tradition of black Creoles in the Caribbean. Dorson recorded a version "Colored Man, Jew and White Man" (*American Negro Folktales*, no. 70), which also features the choice of packages but without the race episode in the beginning. There are African versions in which blacks know how to do everything and whites know nothing, but this ends up being the reason that blacks do everything and the whites do nothing but supervise. In the Louisiana variant presented here, there is total chaos during the race, during which each participant tries as hard as the other to win at all costs, even cheating. This presents a rather misanthropic view of the world and its origins. The storyteller relates this metaphor for the division of labor with the weight of centuries in his tone of voice. There is the self-deprecating suggestion that the black man's lot is somehow the result of his own doing, first winning the race, but then choosing his prize unwisely.

Well, il y avait un nèg, un vieux nèg avec un vieux blanc. Yé té gain une course. Il té gain ça dans gazette. Il té affiché tout le monde. Il y avait vieux nèg-là et vieux blanc. Yé té gain une course.

Là, *well,* vieux nèg et vieux blanc-là, yé parti. Yé sorti de dans le *chute.* T'étais apé tendé les nèg et les blancs, "Hé, Monsieur Tom Jones! Hé, Monsieur Foff!"

Vieux nèg est parti la course. Li dit, "Lord, Lord!" Vieux nèg-là tourné en arrière. Vieux nèg té dit devant vieux blanc-là. Vieux blanc-là té tombé par terre. Vieux nèg-là té passé *on* li.

Quand vieux nèg arrivé au bout des sept arpents, blanc a passé, vieux nèg a passé devant blanc-là. Li fout vieux blanc une jambette, vieux n-homme-là tombé par terre.

Quand vieux nèg arrivé là-bas, li té gain un de ces gros sacs. Li té gain un gros sac. Là, li té gain un vieux petite affaire comme ça. Li té pélé ses *partners.* Li dit, "Venez aider moi." Les autres vieux macaques-là, yé té tous

Well, there was an old black man and an old white man. They had a race. They announced it in the newspapers. They announced it to everyone. There was the old black man and the old white man. They had a race.

Then, well, the old black man and the old white man took off. They left the chute. You could hear the blacks and the whites, "Hey, Mister Tom Jones! Hey Mister Foff!"

The old black man took off running. He said, "Lord, Lord!" The old black man turned around. The old black man should have been out in front of the old white man. The old white man fell down. The old black man ran over him.

When the old black man arrived at the end of seven hectares, the white man passed him, then the old black man passed the white man. He tripped the old white man, the old man fell down.

When the old black man arrived, there was one of those big sacks. There was a big sack. And there was a little old thing, like this. He called his friends. He said, "Come and help me." Those other old monkeys were

campés à côté. Yé vini là. Vieux nèg-là té gagné. Yé té hélé, "Hééé! Li gagné! Li gagné!"

Ça to crois il y avait en dedans-là? Des vieilles charrues, des vieilles pioches. Il y avait pas de vieilles affaires qu'il té pas gain!

Blanc-là vini. Li ramassé vieux petit affaire-là. Il té gain un livre avec un crayon, pour lire et écrire. Là, vieux blanc-là, li té là, mais vieux nèg-là té gain pour couri dans le clos. Li té misérable toute sa vie.

Hein? C'est pas vrai, ça?

all hanging around. They came. The old black man had won. They were yelling, "Hey! He won! He won!"

What do you think was in there? Some old plows, some old hoes. There was not one old tool that wasn't in there.

The white man came. He picked up the little sack. There was a book and a pencil to read and write. Then, the old white man was there, but the old black man had to go out into the fields. He was miserable all his life.

Eh? Is this not true?

Histoires Vraies / Historical Tales

103. Métayer Joe / Joe, the Overseer (Wilson "Ben Guiné" Mitchell, Parks)

In this story, the servant in charge of the store of corn is stealing from his boss (motif P365 "Faithless servant"). When he is caught later, no one takes pity on him. Compare motif J21.23 "Rise earlier," advice that is shown to be wise when the master catches his servants stealing, and type 1564** *The Clever Granary Watcher,* in which the master finally begins to suspect that his watcher is stealing from him. The point of this story, as told by this black Creole storyteller, seems to be the unfairness of the deception. The master gradually exposes Métayer Joe's lies by a relentless series of questions. Finally he catches the thieving overseer in a trap just after midnight and leaves him to wallow for a while in his pain and shame before firing and banishing him the next morning. In . . . *Who Blowed Up the Church House?*, Randolph included a close parallel, "The Fellow That Stole Corn," in which there is a similar lack of consideration and pity for the thief's pain when he is caught in the trap.

Et là, *well,* il y avait un vieux nèg, li té resté dans la cour d'un vieux blanc. Vieux blanc té gain confiance en vieux nèg-là. Yé té appelé vieux nèg Métayer. Vieux nèg té gain toutes les clefs à vieux blanc. Vieux blanc té pas tracassé. Yé té gain plusieurs nègs qu'apé travailler, to comprends? Quand yé té parlé pour vieux nèg, yé parlé pour quelque chose!

Li dit ça, vieux blanc, "Ah! Li tel comme ma femme, parce que vieux nèg, ça, c'était un vieux nèg qui droite. Li pas dans des bêtises. Li té gain toutes les clefs du magasin."

Li dit à vieux nèg, "Joe! O, Joe!"

Joe pas répond.

And then, well, there was an old black man who lived in the yard of an old white man. The old white man trusted the old black man. Everyone called him Metayer [Overseer]. The old black man had all the old white man's keys. The old white man was not worried. There were several black men working, you understand? When he spoke about the old black man, he had really said something important!

The old white man said, "Ah! He's just like my wife, because this old black man is a straight old black man. He's not involved in foolishness. He has all the keys to the store."

He said to the old black man, "Joe! Oh, Joe!"

Joe didn't answer.

Li dit, "Joe!"

Joe pas répond.

"O, Joe!" Li dit, "Ça semble comme mon maïs apé manquer ici, Joe."

Joe répond li, "Le maïs apé manquer dans le magasin?"

Li dit, "Oui, Joe."

Li dit, "Non. T'apé fait un *mistake*. N'a pas maïs qu'apé manquer icitte."

"Mais," li dit, "oui, magasin apé baisser."

Li dit, "Non."

Li dit, "Qui c'est ça qu'apé baisser li comme ça, Joe?"

Joe dit, "C'est les rats qu'apé baisser comme ça."

"Mais," li dit, "les rats! Mais jamais. Les rats apé manger maïs même. Ça même," li dit. Li dit, "Ça c'est une chose mo comprends pas!"

Li dit, "To peux croire ça m'apé dit toi. Mo vois gros rat à peu près haut comme ça."

"Mais," li dit, "pourquoi to pas appélé moi, Joe?"

Li dit, "Mo pas voulu réveillé toi. Mo eu peur."

Li dit, "À quelle heure to vois ça, Joe?"

Li dit, "Une heure après minuit."

"Mais," li dit, "Joe, to apé pas dormi encore?"

"Mais," Joe dit, "quand mo entend le train, mo couri guetter."

Li dit, "Ta vieille voit ça?"

Joe dit, "Non."

Li dit, "Pourquoi to pas réveillé la vieille? To sé gain témoin de ça."

Li dit, "Non, mo pas voulu réveiller ma vieille. C'est juste mo qui vois ça."

Li dit, "*Okay*, Joe." Li dit, "Mo fini avec ça, ouais, Joe." Li dit, "Laisse yé manger toujours, Joe."

Ça to crois li fait? Li té gain un ces grosses trappes-là, aussi gros qu'il y avait

He said, "Joe!"

Joe didn't answer.

"Oh, Joe!" He said, "It seems that some of my corn is missing, Joe."

Joe answered, "The corn is missing from the store?"

He said, "Yes, Joe."

He said, "No. You must be mistaken. There is no corn missing here."

"But," he said, "yes, the store is dwindling."

He said, "No."

He said, "Why is it dwindling, Joe?"

Joe said, "It must be the rats that are eating it."

"But," he said, "rats! I don't believe rats are eating that much corn. This," he said, "this is something I can't understand."

He said, "You can believe what I'm telling you. I saw a rat about this big."

"Well," he said, "why didn't you call me, Joe?"

He said, "I didn't want to wake you. I was afraid."

He said, "What time did you see this, Joe?"

He said, "One hour after midnight."

"Well," he said, "Joe, you weren't sleeping yet?"

"Well," he said, "when I heard the noise, I ran to see."

He said, "Did your wife see this?"

Joe said, "No."

He said, "Why didn't you wake your wife? You would have had a witness to all this."

He said, "No, I didn't want to wake my wife. I'm the only one who saw this."

He said, "Okay, Joe." He said, "I'm through with this, Joe." He said, "Let them go on and eat, Joe."

What do you think he did? He had one of those big traps, as big as they come. Joe

moyen. Joe té gain un trou. Quand vieux n-homme t'apé dormi, li té couri là, li té prendre tout le maïs que li té oulé. Li t'apé vendre tout le voisinage maïs. Mieux que ça, li t'apé fini vieux n-homme-là. C'est li qui té gain toutes les clefs.

Li dit à sa vieille, "Well, well, m'alé connaître ça qu'apé prendre mon maïs." Li met cette grosse trappe droite dans le trou. Une heure après minuit, Joe té là avec tous ses hommes qui té vend maïs. Joe fourré sa main dans le trou. To entends, "Kabô!" Joe commencé héler les cris.

La vieille a dit, "Hé! M'apé entendre des cris au magasin."

Li dit, "Non, non. Laisse li héler jusqu'à jour." Li dit, "N'a connaître qui c'est ça il est. Mo pas aller dans la nuit."

La vieille dit, "Vas donc voir ça qu'apé héler les cris. L'apé héler à tous les saints pour mander Bon Dieu pour aider li, qui li prit dans la trappe."

Li dit, "Non!"

Li laissé le jour ouvert sûr, pour tout le monde voir qui c'est li est. Quand li arrivé, li regardé Joe té là avec son bras pris dans le magasin, dans le trou, avec cinq maïs. Li dit, "Joe, mo té gain confiance en toi, Joe." Li dit, "Regarde ça to fais mo, Joe. Il y a longtemps t'apé ruiner moi comme ça, Joe." Li dit, "Mo crois m'alé quitter toi pour quelque temps encore."

La femme dit, "Jules, ôte donc li là, s'il toi plaît." La trappe té gain son bras près coupé.

Li dit, "Joe, c'est honteux pour toi. Mo payé toi, Joe. Regarde to gain moi." Li dit, "M'a lâcher toi. Mo pas oulé voir toi sur ma place du tout!"

had a hole. When the old man was sleeping, he would go there, and he would take all the corn he wanted. He was selling corn to the whole neighborhood. In fact, he was ruining the old man. He was the one with all the keys.

He said to his wife, "Well, well, I'm going to find out what is taking my corn." He put that big trap right in the hole. One hour after midnight, Joe went there with his men who sold the corn. Joe stuck his hand in the hole. You heard, "Kabo!" Joe started yelling.

The old woman said, "Hey! I hear cries from the store."

He said, "No, no. Let him yell until morning." He said, "We'll find out who it is. I'm not going in the night."

The old woman said, "Please go and see who is yelling so. He's crying out to all the saints to ask God to help him whoever it is who is caught in the trap."

He said, "No!"

He waited until morning so that everyone would see who it was. When he arrived, he saw Joe, who had one arm caught in the store, in the hole, with five ears of corn. He said, "Joe, I had confidence in you, Joe." He said, "Look at what you've done to me, Joe. You've been ruining me for a long time, Joe." He said, "I think I'll leave you there for a while longer."

The woman said, "Jules, take him out of there, please." The trap had nearly cut his arm off.

He said, "Joe, shame on you. I paid you, Joe. Look at what you had from me." He said, "I'm letting you go. I don't want to see you on my land ever again! "

104. La vigilance / The Vigilantes (Inez Catalon, Kaplan)

Richard Dorson included in his *American Negro Folktales* a section ("Horrors," pp. 282–299) on stories about racial injustice, especially during the years following the Civil War up to the 1890s. In Louisiana, as in most of the South, there was an effort to intimidate blacks to remain "in their place." Alexandre Barde's *Les Comités de Vigilance des Attakapas* described the early years of this ugly period. Carl Brasseaux's *Acadian to Cajun: Transformation of a People, 1803–1877* includes more recent research tracing the subject through the end of the nineteenth century. Compare also Lynwood Montell's *The Saga of Coe Ridge*, which treats similar conditions in the upland south.

In the following text, the storyteller relates two incidents from the days of the vigilantes, a local version of the Ku Klux Klan. The first is about the brutal beating of an accordion player whose only crime was to neglect the sundown curfew imposed on members of his race. The second involves the revenge of a black miller toward the end of the period in question. He succeeds with the help of his white benefactor and an ingenious homemade alarm system.

BA: Tu te rappelles la dernière fois que je suis venu ici, t'avais raconté des histoires de Mardi-Gras et ces hommes qui couraient à cheval, qui terrorisaient les—

IC: O, ça. C'était les—Comment t'appelles ça? La vigilance!

BA: La vigilance, ouais.

IC: La vigilance.

BA: Raconte-moi un petit brin de ça. Je me rappelle pas.

IC: O, mais cher, il y en avait amené un tas ici pour le temps de la vigilance. Un monde de couleur pouvait pas faire comme il voulait, tu connais. Comme il fallait il soit chez lui avant le soleil couché, et s'il était pas chez lui avant le soleil couché, et bien, ils le bûchiont. Ils le tailliont, ça appelait ça.

Mam m'a dit un soir, il y avait un homme. Il jouait de l'accordéon. Et ils ont rentré en dans là, le bal. Ils ont cassé le bal, mais pas tout le monde est parti, mais il y a quelqu'un qu'a rentré. Ils l'ont pris, puis ils l'ont ramené dans le bois-là. Ils l'ont bûché, cet homme-là, qu'il était tout marqué. Mam dit il est revenu. Il s'a assis. Il a joué de l'accordéon comme jamais il avait joué. Il a été, il s'a couché de ça-là, de cette bûcherie

BA: Do you remember the last time I came here, you told stories about Mardi Gras riders and the men who rode around on horseback terrorizing the—

IC: Oh, that. They were—How are they called? The vigilantes!

BA: The vigilantes, yes.

IC: The vigilantes.

BA: Tell me a little about that. I don't remember.

IC: Oh, well, dear, there was quite a bit going on around here during the days of the vigilantes. People of color couldn't do whatever they wanted, you know. Such as, they had to be home before sundown, and if they weren't home before sundown, well, they were beaten. They were whipped.

Mom told me that, one night, there was a man. He was playing an accordion. And they came in there, during the dance. They broke up the dance, but not everyone left, so someone came in. They got him, and they took him into the woods there. They beat him, that man, until he was covered with cuts. Mom said that he came back. He sat down. He played the accordion like he had never played before. He went home, and lay

ils l'avaient fait-là. Et ils l'ont bûché juste parce qu'il jouait de l'accordéon. Comme Clifton Chenier et puis ceux-là-là, tu connais. Et ça voulait que ça travaille pour une vie. Mais ceux qu'auraient fait bal de maison, ça engageait ce monde pour jouer bal. Là, eux, ça travaillait dans le clos. Ça faisait leur petite récolte et c'était tout. Là, si ça avait idée de travailler comme le samedi soir, mais là, ça travaillait pas samedi. Ça allait jouer leur bal. Mais il y avait du monde qui était contre ça. C'était trop aisé pour lui, poux eux, tu connais.

Ça fait, ça l'a taillé. Là, ça l'a bûché assez, d'après moi, ça lui a peut-être mâché dedans le corps. Moi, je sais pas. Mais il a rentré, il a joué, ils ont dit, Mam m'a dit, comme jamais, jamais il avait joué avant. De là-là.

BA: Tu te rappelles pas de son nom?
IC: Hmmm. Je me rappelle pas de son nom. Il y a si longtemps de ça. Il a été. Il s'a couché. De là-là, il s'a couché. Cet homme était tout raide, raide, raide, raide, raide! Et il a resté comme ça, je sais pas comment longtemps, mais il a mouru des coups.

Et tu connais quoi c'est qu'a cassé cette affaire-là? Tu parles du monde civilisé! Il y a un homme qu'avait un petit moulin à gru dans la campagne, tu connais. Ça moudait le maïs pour la farine et le gru. Ça fait, le vieux-t-homme a mouru, mais le seul qui pouvait courir le petit moulin à gru, c'était cet homme de couleur qu'avait toujours resté sur la place. Ça fait, quand le mari a mouru, la vieille femme dit à l'homme, "Mais, tu vas prendre le moulin en charge, parce que moi, je peux pas." Mais ils étaient du monde, tu connais, du monde riche. Ça fait, l'homme dit il avait manière peur de prendre ça. Elle dit, "Faut pas t'aies peur. Prends-le!"

Ça fait, il a été un jour, il dit, "*Well,*" il dit, "je vas arrêter." Il dit, "J'arrête parce que—il y a un homme." Il a nommé

down from that, from that beating that they gave him. And they beat him just because he was playing the accordion. Like Clifton Chenier and the others, you know. And they wanted him to work for a living. But those who held house dances would hire these people to play for the dance. They worked in the fields. They tended their little crops and that was all. Then, if they intended to play, let's say, Saturday night, well then, they wouldn't work on Saturday. They would go and play their dance. But there were some who were against that. That was too easy for them, you know.

So they whipped him. And they beat him so much that, the way I understand it, maybe they crushed his insides. I don't know. But he went back in, he played, they said, Mom told me, as he had never played before. From that experience.
BA: Do you remember his name?
IC: Hmm . . . I don't remember his name. It's been so long since then. He went. He lay down. After that experience, he lay down. That man was stiff, stiff, stiff, stiff, stiff! And he remained that way, I don't know how long, but he died from the blows.

And do you know what broke up this affair? You talk about civilized people! There was a man who had a little grist mill in the country, you know. They milled corn to make cornmeal and grits. So the old man died, but the only one who could run the little mill was a man of color who had always lived on the property. So, when her husband died, the old woman said to the man, "Well, you'll take over the mill, because I can't." But they were wealthy people, you know. So the man said that he was a little afraid of taking it over. She said, "You mustn't be afraid. Take it!"

So he went one day, he said, "Well," he said, "I'm quitting." He said, "I'm quitting because—there's a man." He named the man,

l'homme, mais moi, j'ai oublié ces noms-là. Et il dit, "Il a venu. Il s'a assis-là. Il m'a fait tout prendre les blancs avant, et," il dit, "fallait les noirs restent en arrière."

"Mais," elle dit, "tu vas retourner demain. Premier arrivé, premier servi." Et il a fait ça. Et là, elle lui a donné des fusils, deux fusils. Elle dit, "Si t'es jamais gêné, défends-toi!"

Et là, il a été, le soir, il s'a couché, mais il avait des poulets dans une baille. Et puis, ils ont mis les poulets à la porte, mais c'était pas barré. Il y avait des clous et des cordes, tu connais, pour arranger les portes, et tout moitié arrangées. Ça fait, tout ça le monde avait pour faire, si ça voulait rentrer, c'était haler sur la porte. Et ils ont tombé dans la baille de poulets, puis là, la poule a fait du train, et les poulets. Ça fait, la femme l'a réveillé. Elle dit, "Ils sont là!"

Ça fait, il avait le fusil près de son lit. Il a attrapé le fusil, puis il a tiré à la porte. Et cil-là qu'était à la porte, il l'a tué. Ça fait, ils l'ont prêché. Ils l'ont prêché pour la paix, pour laisser prendre cil-là qu'était mort, et ils l'auriont laissé tranquille. Ils auriont plus retourné. Ça fait, lui, il a arrêté de tirer.

O mais, ils étaient à peu près une cinquantaine, ou une centaine, quand ça allait. C'était une bande, à cheval.

but I've forgotten those names. And he said, "He came. He sat there. He made me take all the whites first, and," he said, "the blacks had to wait."

"Well," she said, "you'll go back tomorrow. First come, first served." And he did this. And then, she gave him shotguns, two shotguns. She said, "If you're ever bothered, defend yourself!"

And then, he went, that night, he went to bed, but he had put some chickens in a tub. And then, they put the chickens at the door, but it wasn't locked. There were bent nails and strings, you know, to fix doors, they rigged them as best they could. So all anyone had to do to come in was to pull on the door. And they fell into that bucket full of chickens, and the chickens made noise. So his wife woke him. She said, "They're here!"

So he had the shotgun near his bed. He grabbed the shotgun and he shot towards the door. And the one who was at the door was killed. So they pleaded with him. They pleaded with him for a truce to let them get the one that was dead, and they would then leave him alone. They wouldn't come back. So he stopped shooting.

Oh, but there were about fifty of them, or a hundred, when they would go out. They were a gang on horseback.

105. La vigilance / The Vigilantes (Westley "Kit" Dennis, Scott)

This is another story about resisting the vigilantes. The storyteller underscored the sad nature of the times and insisted that things have changed for the better. See the section, "Horrors," in Dorson's *American Negro Folktales*, which includes similar stories about the cruel treatment of black people by vigilante groups.

Moi, j'ai pas vu ça, mais ma vieille maman m'a raconté des fois et des fois pour un vieux n-oncle qu'elle avait. Je connais pas si c'était un oncle de la famille, ou si c'est

I didn't see this, but my old mother told me time and time again about an old uncle of hers. I don't know if he was a real uncle or just someone they called an uncle. But

172

juste comme ça qu'eux l'appelaient. Mais n'importe comment, elle le connaissait bien parce que c'est souvent elle allait faire des visites là. Ça l'appelait n-Oncle Rosémond. Et c'était un vieux homme. Il avait à peu près dix arpents de terre, une place pour lui-même. Et il gênait jamais personne. Il avait son affaire, et puis il la faisait.

Au village, il y avait une petite place. Il y a un petit magasin et puis là, il y avait une petite *shop* pour battre les lames de charrue. Et il allait là, lui. Mais il était tout le temps à cheval. Il avait pas de boghei. Et il a été à cheval le matin avec trois lames de charrue pour faire battre et ce monde là le connaissait bien et le bougre qui était dans le magasin le connaissait bien aussi.

Quand il a arrivé là, il dit, "Rosémond, écoute. Ils sont partis pour aller te fouetter à soir, mais dis pas à personne que je t'ai dit ça. Dis pas à personne, personne, que je te dis ça. Mais," il dit, "je vas te donner de la munition pour tu te défends, mais dévoile-moi jamais!"

C'était ces fusil à piston. Je me rappelle de ça, des fusils à piston. On mettait de la mousse noire et on la foulait, et une fois on l'avait bien foulée avec une baguette, un bâton à peu près long comme ça [geste à bras étendus], on venait et on mettait de la poudre. Là, on venait, on mettait d'autre mousse noire en haut-là. On la foulait bien. Là, on venait et on mettait nos postes ou notre plomb, n'importe quoi on voulait mettre par en dessus ça. On venait, on le mettait en haut-là. Une fois qu'on l'avait mis en haut-là, là, on mettait un autre bout, et on le foulait bien. Une fois qu'on l'avait bien foulé-là, là, il était chargé, pareil comme une cartouche.

Il s'a mis à charger les deux fourches. Une fois qu'il les a eu chargées, il s'a mis dans la maison. Il avait trois filles et puis une vieille. Et le *leader* qui avait pour aller le tailler, c'était un Judice. Il était par dessus

anyway, she knew him well because she often went to visit him. They called him Uncle Rosémond. And he was an old man. He had about ten acres of land, a place of his own. And he never bothered anyone. He had his thing, and he took care of that.

In town, there was a little place. There was a little store and then, there was a little shop to beat plow blades. And that's where he used to go. But he was also on horseback. He had no buggy. And he went on horseback in the morning with three plow blades he needed beaten and the people there knew him well and the fellow who worked in the store also knew him well.

When he arrived, he said, "Rosémond, listen. They are getting together to whip you tonight, but don't tell anyone I told you this. Don't tell anyone that I told you this. But," he said, "I'm going to give you some ammunition for you to defend yourself, but don't ever give me away! "

Those were the days of black powder rifles. I remember that, black powder rifles. We would put black moss and stuff it, and once it was well stuffed with a rod, a stick about this long [gesture indicating about five feet], we would then put in the powder. Then we'd put more black powder on top of that. We'd stuff it well. Then we would put our buckshot or our pellets, whatever we wanted to use, on top of that. We'd put it up. After we'd put it up, then we'd put in another piece and stuff it well. Once it was well stuffed, then it was loaded, just like a shell.

He set about loading both barrels. Once he had loaded them, he went into the house. He had three daughters and a wife. And the leader who was to whip him was a Judice. He was in charge of the rest of them. And the

tous les autres. Et le Judice qui avait pour aller le tailler, un de ses filles travaillait pour ce Judice-là. (Et ça, c'est la vérité, ça que je suis après vous conter.) Quand ils ont arrivé là, le soir, ils ont crié après, mais c'était tout des portes à gonds. Ça on appelle des portes à gonds, c'est des pentures qui se fourraient comme ça, un en bas, un en haut. Là, on pouvait prendre la porte et la lever.

Ils ont venu crier après, "Rosémond, ouvre la porte!"

Il dit, "Non, quoi c'est vous autres veux?"

Il dit, "Ouvre la porte!" Et deux hommes s'ont mis pour ouvrir la porte-là. Quand ils se sont mis en bas de la porte pour la lever comme ça, il a tiré, mais ils pensaient qu'il était après haler sur juste une baguette, mais avec l'excitation, il a halé sur les deux coups. Il a tué les deux hommes à la porte. Il a tué un ou deux là-bas-là. Il a tué un cheval là-bas-là aussi. Là, les autres ont été tous moitié blessés, tu connais, avec ces postes-là. Il y a pas rien pour arrêter ça. Ils ont parti pour tous se sauver. Les autres qui avaient pas été tués ou assez touchés pour empêcher, ils ont parti à se sauver, mais ils ont revenu *back* et lui a pas eu assez de temps pour charger ce fusil encore, parce que ça se chargeait à la baguette.

Il a sorti de dans la maison. Il y avait un petit marais de joncs pas loin, droit devant son magasin, droit en arrière de sa maison. Et en revenant, ils ont vu quelque chose de blanc qui a rentré dans les joncs, mais ils étiont pas sûrs si c'était lui ou quoi. Mais, n'importe comment, ils ont revenu *back* et ils ont commencé crier après. Personne répondait pas. Ses trois filles et sa femme étaient dans la maison, et ils ont rentré dans la maison fouillasser en dedans, capoter les matelas et tout quelque chose pour le découvrir, voir s'il était peut-être pas caché en dedans-là. Et celle-là qui travaillait chez les Judice, elle a crié, "Tuez pas mon papa, s'il

Judice who had to whip him, one of his daughters worked for this Judice. (And this is the truth, what I'm telling you.) When they arrived, that night, they called for him, but all the doors were on hanging hinges. They call them hanging hinge doors, on hinges that fit one part into the other, one on top, one on the bottom. One could take the door and lift it up.

They came and called out, "Rosémond, open the door!"

He said, "No, what do you want?"

He said, "Open the door!" And two men started to open the door. When they got under the door to lift it, he shot, and he thought he was pulling only one trigger, but in the excitement, he pulled both triggers. He killed both men at the door. He killed one or two farther back. He also killed a horse farther back. And many of the others were also wounded, you know, with that buckshot. Nothing can stop that stuff. They all took off running. The others who had not been killed or badly wounded took off running, but they came back and he had not had enough time to reload the shotgun, because it had to be muzzle-loaded.

He went out of the house. There was a little reedy swamp not too far away, just in front of his barn, just behind his house. And as they were returning, they saw something white going into the reeds, but they weren't sure that it was he or not. Well, anyway, they came back and they started calling out to him. No one answered. His three daughters and his wife were in the house, and they went into the house to look around in there, to turn over the mattresses and everything to find him, to see if he may have been hiding in there. And the daughter who worked for the Judice family cried out, "Don't kill my father, please! " And because she had said

vous plaît!" Et parce qu'elle avait dit ça-là (il avait mis ses trois lames de charrue battues dans le foyer), il a attrapé une lame de charrue-là, et il a coupé son cou carrément. Parce qu'elle avait demandé pour pas ils tuent son papa. Et les deux autres, ils l'ont pas fait à rien, et la vieille femme, ils l'ont pas fait à rien, mais ils ont tout bouleversé la maison.

Et là, il y a un qui dit ça, "J'ai vu quelque chose qu'a rentré dans le marais de jonc." C'est là où ils ont été là, et ils ont *shell* le marais et ils l'ont tué en dedans.

Et c'est triste, triste, triste. Et pourquoi? Cet homme avait sa petite place. Il gênait pas personne. Il gênait pas personne. Tu connais, un homme peut être jaloux ou il peut être canaille, mais s'il est jaloux et canaille, ça fait mauvais.

this (he had put his three beaten plow blades in the fireplace), he grabbed one of the plow blades, and he just cut her neck. Because she had asked that they not kill her father. And the two others, they didn't do anything to them, and the old woman, they didn't do anything to her, but they completely upset the whole house.

And then, one of them said, "I saw something go into the reed swamp." That's when they went there and shelled the swamp and they killed him in there. And that's sad, sad, sad. And why? That man had his own little place. He wasn't bothering anyone. He wasn't bothering anyone. You know, a man can be jealous or he can be wicked, but if he's jealous and wicked, it's especially bad.

106. Confrontation au village / Confrontation in Town (Westley "Kit" Dennis, Scott)

In the following story, the same narrator describes another personal experience with the vigilantes in his own neighborhood and the personal courage of his father who faced them. It is remarkable that this man has somehow preserved his sense of respect for others despite such brutal memories from his own childhood.

J'avais à peu près neuf ans. C'était tout je pouvais avoir. Et mon vieux papa allait au village tous les samedi après-midi en wagon. On avait une paire de mulets. Un s'appelait March, il était né dans mars; et l'autre s'appelait April, il était né dans avril. Et on a parti pour aller au village ce samedi après-midi-là. Il y avait un tas de ces jeunes bougres qui étaient sur l'habitation des Montgomery. Ça allait au village tous les samedi après-midi.

Ils étiont après s'en aller dans le chemin quand nous autres, on a arrivé. Mon vieux papa a arrêté son wagon et puis, ils ont tous monté dans le wagon. Il devait en avoir cinq

I was about nine years old. That's as old as I could have been. And my old father used to go to town every Saturday afternoon in a wagon. We had a pair of mules. One was named March, he was born in March; and the other was called April, he was born in April. And we left to go to town that Saturday afternoon. And there were lots of young fellows who lived on Montgomery's farm. They went to town every Saturday afternoon.

They were going down the road when we arrived. My old father stopped the wagon and then they all climbed into the wagon. There must have been five or six, at least.

ou six, sûr. Ils ont monté dans le wagon et on
a parti pour s'en aller au village.

Quand on a arrivé au village, ils ont tous
descendu chacun son bord. Là, nous autres,
on a été au magasin, chez défunt Monsieur
Léon Couvillon. Il y avait les rues étroites.
Dans ces temps-là, c'était tous des rues en
terre. C'était un peu étroit. Il y avait le
magasin bord-là, défunt Léon Couvillon
bord-là, et bord-là, c'était un Breaux. Il a
arrêté le wagon là, mais c'était deux jeunes
mulets. Ça fait, mon papa dit (ils me
donnaient tous un petit nom, Jack), il dit,
"Stay in the wagon, Jack, and hold the mules."

Ça fait, j'ai dit, *"Okay, Daddy."*

Ça fait, j'étais après tenir les mulets. Ils
étiont un peu fringants. C'était deux jeunes
mulets. Ça fait, lui, il a descendu. Il a été
dans le magasin pour acheter ses affaires. Là,
il y a un boghei qu'a arrivé un petit élan
après. Il a venu. Il s'a placé là. Mais c'était
trop étroit pour eux autres passer. Il dit fallait
j'avance les mulets.

Ça fait, mon papa a descendu à la porte,
"Non, non," il dit, "reste droit-là ayoù t'es.
On était là premier."

C'était des Bergeron, deux blancs. Il avait
un de ces *rawhides*. Il a descendu de son
boghei avec le *rawhide* comme s'il aurait
voulu cogner mon papa.

Ça fait, mon papa a dit, "Si tu te sens
comme ça, *go ahead*. Je crois je suis assez
grand pour ta baleine frapper dessus."

Mais il faut croire qu'il a compris que ça
aurait pu être plus mal ou quelque affaire.
C'est là qu'il a été, il a monté dans son
boghei. Là, l'autre Bergeron, il a rentré dans
le magasin. Je connais pas quoi ce qu'il a
acheté, mais ils sont partis carrément. Ils ont
parti s'en aller.

Et ils ont été en avant de nous autres à
peu près comme au coin là-bas et il y avait
une île de bois-de-flèche. Il y en a un qui a
rentré en dedans-là se couper des bâtons, et
l'autre a fait semblant, comme s'il était après

They climbed into the wagon and we took off
for town.

When we arrived in town, they all got
out on their respective sides. Then we went
into the store, the late Mr. Leon Couvillon's
store. The streets were narrow. In those days,
they were all dirt streets. They were quite
narrow. The store was on this side, the late
Leon Couvillon on this side, and on the other
side was a Breaux. He stopped the wagon,
but we had two young mules. So my father
said (they all called me by a nickname, Jack),
he said, "Stay in the wagon, Jack, and hold
the mules."

So I said, "Okay, Daddy."

So I was holding the mules. They were a
little frisky. They were two young mules. So
he got down. He went into the store to buy
his things. Then a buggy arrived a little later.
It came. It pulled up there. But it was too
narrow for them to pass. He said I had to
move the mules forward.

So my father came to the door, "No, no,"
he said, "stay right where you are. We were
here first."

They were Bergerons, two white men.
He had one of those rawhide whips. He got
down from his buggy with the whip as
though he wanted to whip my father.

So my father said, "If you feel that way,
go ahead. I think I'm big enough for your
whip to hit."

But it must be that he thought it might
have turned for the worse, or something.
That's when he went, he climbed up onto his
buggy. Then the other Bergeron went into the
store. I don't know what he bought, but they
came back out right away. They left.

And they went ahead of us about as far
as the corner and there was a clump of sage
orange trees. One of them went in there to
cut some sticks, and the other pretended to
be fixing something on his buggy, so that we

arranger quelque chose après son boghei, pour pas qu'on croit à rien. Et on a continué à venir. Et c'était une île qu'avait des *cherokees*. Ça bordait le chemin. Et tous les samedis tard le soir, mais les bogheis et les cavaliers, ça s'en venait, et ça allait tous au village. C'était tous des blancs, enfin. Ça quittait de Scott, puis ça allait au village. Et ils ont été en avant et puis là, chaque cavalier qui passait, ou chaque boghei qui arrivait qui était parti au village, dans ce jeune monde, ils l'ont arrêté. Et là, quand nous autres, on a arrivé à eux, ça commençait juste à faire bien, bien brun. Ils se sont mis dans le chemin avec les bâtons en l'air pour arrêter les mulets.

Ça fait, mon papa dit, "Descends par terre dans le wagon." Ils ont commencé à garrocher les bâtons. Mon père était après les séparer. Là, il m'a poussé avec son coude de bas comme ça. Et j'ai tombé dans le fond du wagon. Et en tombant dans le fond du wagon—la même après-midi, on avait trouvé une de ces tête-de-chat pour mettre sur ces grosses *gang plows*—et en tombant en dedans, j'ai tombé dessus. Je l'ai attrapé et je lui ai donné pour lui. Et quand je le lui ai donné comme ça, il l'a attrapé puis il l'a donné à un. Et là, ils ont continué à garrocher, garrocher, mais ils ont pas pu arrêter les mulets. Quand il a crié après les mulets, ils ont foncé parmi la bande, comme ça, puis là, ça a parti.

Quand on a eu dépassé la bande, nous autres, on a continué vite à aller, les mulets après galoper. Ils ont monté tous à cheval et puis là, ils ont venu et ils ont commencé à garrocher encore après le wagon, mais ils avaient pas tant de chance. Leurs chevaux à eux, ça allaient vite, et puis le wagon allait un peu vite.

On a arrêté chez un vieux bougre de couleur on appelait Jean à Madame Jacques. Son bois était à peu près un arpent de sa maison. Et ça, c'était avant on arrive à la maison. La maison était à peu près loin

wouldn't notice anything. And we kept coming. And it was a clump that had briars in it. It was growing along the road, and every Saturday afternoon, people in buggies and on horseback came by and went to town. They were all white. They left Scott, and they went to town. And they went ahead and each rider who went by or each person in a buggy who was on his way to town, among the young people, they stopped them. And then, when we arrived, it was just beginning to get dark. They got in the road with their sticks raised to stop the mules.

So my father told me, "Get down on the floor of the wagon." They started throwing sticks. My father was parrying them off. Then he pushed me down with his elbow like this. And I fell down into the wagon. And while falling down into the wagon—that afternoon we had found one of those cat's heads to use on those big gang plows—and falling down there, I fell on it. I grabbed it and gave it to him. And when I gave it to him, he grabbed it and he hit one of them with it. They kept throwing and throwing, but they couldn't stop the mules. When he called out to the mules, they rushed forward into the gang, like that, and then they took off.

When we had passed the gang, we kept going fast, the mules were galloping. They mounted up and then came and started throwing at the wagon again, but they weren't very lucky. Their horses were going fast and the wagon was going quite fast.

We stopped at the home of an old black man whom we called Jean à Madame Jacques. His woods were about an arpent from his house. And that was before we got to his house. His house was about as far as

177

comme d'ici à là-bas au *truck*-là. Bien, mon papa m'a fait descendre et puis j'ai été. J'ai rentré dans la maison. Et le bougre qui était là, lui et mon papa ont pris des bâtons et des affaires et quand ils ont passé pour s'en aller par là, c'est là où l'homme ayoù on avait arrêté-là, il en a cogné un dans le cou avec le bâton. Il a tombé par terre, mais en tombant, il s'a relevé et il a parti avec le *gang*.

Tu connais, à peu près quinze jours après ça—c'était une maison fait comme celle-là icitte, mais elle était au long du chemin et le lit est là, et l'armoire est là—ils ont passé là, et ils ont tiré après la maison. Si le monde avait été là, ils auraient tué quelqu'un dans le lit. Juste en haut du lit-là, les balles ont passé. Ils ont tiré assez, ils ont fait tomber la porte de l'armoire droite en arrière, l'autre bord. Ils ont fait tomber la porte de l'armoire à coups de balles! Et la hauteur des balles qui ont frappé la porte, ils ont pu voir que cil-là qui aurait été couché dans le lit, il aurait été tué.

Moi, j'avais à peu près neuf ans dans ce temps-là. Et avant ça, c'était une fois plus mauvais.

that old truck there. Well, my father made me get down and I went. I went into the house. And the fellow who was there and my father took sticks and things and when they passed by there to go home, that's when the man who lived there hit one of them in the neck with a stick. He fell down, but got up again just as fast and he left with the gang.

You know, about two weeks after that— it was a house made like this one, but it was along the road and the bed was there and the armoire was there—they passed by, and they shot at the house. If the people had been there, they would have killed the ones in the bed. The bullets passed right over the bed. They shot so much that they caused the armoire door to fall back. They made the armoire door fall in from the shots ! And the height of the bullets that struck the door was such that anyone who would have been sleeping in the bed would have been killed.

I was about nine years old in those days. And before that, it was twice as bad.

107. Dédé Anderson et l'argent enterré (Westley "Kit" Dennis and Norris Mitchell, Scott)

The following conversation gives a detailed description of one of the most popular stories about treasure hunting in south Louisiana, about Dédé Anderson, a gen de couleur [person of color] from near Scott in Lafayette Parish who is said to have found a large sum of money with his friends Leo Judice and Baptiste Perez. Perez is rarely mentioned now, but Anderson and Judice became community leaders and wealthy property owners.

According to the family of Dédé Anderson, he did not find any such treasure. His grandson Claude Anderson insisted that his grandfather had always regretted the stories about the treasure because they diminished the truth—that he had worked hard all his life to earn his wealth. The old man used to say, according to his grandson, that the treasure he found was his wife, who ran the house very efficiently and who helped to earn money for the family by selling eggs. The difficulty for a "black" man to earn such wealth, especially in those days, contributed perhaps to the currency of these treasure stories.

There are many local accounts of this supposed discovery. According to most, the money was found buried in a large kettle (motif N525) that had been forged to be indestructible. It is allegedly still in use as a cattle water trough.

BA: J'ai entendu parler de Dédé Anderson. Soi-disant, c'était un homme riche un tas.
WD: O, c'était un homme bien en moyen. C'était un homme bien en moyen, puis il avait un tas de la terre. Il avait deux cent et quelques arpents de terre.
NM: Si c'est pas plus.
WD: Ouais. Deux cent et quelques arpents de terre là ayoù il était.
NM: Là, il avait une autre grosse habitation dans une autre place.
BA: Comment il avait eu tout cet argent?
WD: *Well,* ce vieux monde qui nous disaiaent comme ça, ils avaient fouillé de l'argent. Ils ont trouvé de l'argent dans la terre. Avec vieux Léo Judice et puis vieux Baptiste Perez. C'était les trois.
NM: Il avait sûr la chaudière là-bas chez lui. La chaudière en fer-là.
WD: Ouais. Ils ont trouvé assez d'argent qu'ils ont pris ça et puis il s'en—Ils prétendaient dans ces temps, un bougre trouvait de l'argent, et bien, il fallait pas il garde l'argent là comme ça. Il fallait il achète de la terre avec.
NM: Pour pas ça vient après.
WD: Et ça semblait vrai parce que il avait un tas de la terre.
BA: Comment ils ont su qu'il y avait de l'argent là?
WD: *Well,* longtemps passé, c'était ça la manière. Le monde, ça parlait puis ça attrapait un et l'autre. Ça attrapait ça un et l'autre comme ça. Mais moi, ils m'ont dit, vieux Dédé-là, il a été. Il était après causer avec un bougre qu'avait demandé ayoù l'Ile Navarre était et il était après regarder sur le papier-là et quelque manière, je sais pas s'il a voulu fourré le bout de papier dans sa poche ou quoi, mais le papier-là a tombé. Il a continué à marcher. Dédé a été. Il a attrapé le

BA: I heard people talk about Dédé Anderson. Supposedly, he was a very rich man.
WD: Oh, he was a wealthy man. He was a wealthy man, and he had a lot of land. He had two hundred and some acres of land.
NM: If not more.
WD: Yeah. Two hundred and some acres of land where he lived.
NM: Then he had a big farm somewhere else.

BA: How did he get all that money?
WD: Well, the old people used to tell us he had dug up some money. They found some money buried underground. With old Leo Judice and old Baptiste Perez. There were three.
NM: He sure had the kettle over at his house. The iron kettle.
WD: Yeah. They found enough money that they took it and they—They say in those days, if a man found money, he shouldn't keep it. He should buy land with it.

NM: So they couldn't come for it.
WD: And it seems true because he had a lot of land.
BA: How did they know that there was money there?
WD: Well, long ago, this was the way. People talked and they caught what they could. They caught what they could. But they told me that old Dédé went. He was talking with a man who had asked where Ile Navarre was and he was looking on a piece of paper and somehow, I don't know if he tried to stick the piece of paper in his pocket, or what, but the paper fell. He kept walking. Dédé went. He grabbed the paper. He started looking. That's how . . .

papier. Il a commencé à regarder. C'est là
ayoù . . .

NM: C'était comme un *map*.

WD: Ouais, comme un *map*. C'est là ayoù il a
commencé . . .

NM: Il l'a donné à M. Judice. Les deux ont
été là, à la place ayoù l'argent était.

WD: Ouais, mais le bougre, c'était pas un
bougre d'ici. Il était droit dessus le map
comme nous autres, on la nommait, *all right*,
mais quand il a arrivé là, il a demandé voir si
le monde pouvait dire ayoù l'Ile Navarre
était. Et il se trouvait droit dessus l'Ile
Navarre.

NM: Il était bien près, hein? [rires]

WD: O ouais, Et là, quelque manière, je sais
pas s'il a voulu fourrer le morceau de papier
dans sa poche et puis il a tombé ou quoi.
Dédé a vu ce papier-là. Il l'a attrapé.

NM: Lui, il pouvait lire, lui.

WD: Ouais, Dédé pouvait lire.

NM: Là, il a vu quoi c'était. Là, il a été. Il a
pris ses deux autres *partners* avec lui.

WD: Ouais. Et ils ont été et puis ils ont
fouillé à la place.

BA: Quoi c'était cette affaire pour les bêtes
qui se battaient?

WD: Il y avait deux bœufs qui se battaient à
l'Ile Navarre-là tout le temps. Et là où eux se
battaient là, et bien, il y avait de l'argent là,
mais c'est pas là l'argent Dédé et eux, ils ont
trouvé. Dédé et eux, ils ont trouvé l'argent à
l'Ile Navarre, mais l'autre bord de la petite
coulée. Et c'est d'autres qu'a trouvé là ayoù
les chênes verts *twin*-là, ils sont.

NM: O, il n—avait-z-en là aussi?

WD: Ouais, ils les trouvaient là toujours.
C'était droit au ras les deux chênes verts *twin*.
Et ça montrait ça dessus le papier, mais eux,
ils ont pas été là, eux. Peut-être pour venir là
tout à l'heure, mais je pense bien peut-être ils
ont trouvé assez là-bas que . . .

NM: Ouais.

NM: It was a map.

WD: Yeah, like a map. That's when he
started . . .

NM: He gave it to Mr. Judice. The two went
there, to the place where the money was.

WD: Yeah, but the fellow, he wasn't from
here. It was all right on the map the way we
knew it, all right, but when he got here, he
asked if anyone could tell him where Ile
Navarre was. And he was right at Ile Navarre.

NM: He was close, eh? [laughter]

WD: Oh yeah. And then, somehow, I don't
know if he meant to stick the piece of paper
in his pocket and it fell or what. Dédé saw
that paper. He grabbed it.

NM: He could read.

WD: Yeah, Dédé could read.

NM: He saw what it was. Then he went. He
took his two friends with him.

WD: Yeah. And they went and they dug at
the place.

BA: What was that about the bulls that
fought there?

WD: There were two bulls that fought at Ile
Navarre all the time. And right where they
fought, there was money there, but that's not
where Dédé and his friends found the money.
Dédé and his friends found money at Ile
Navarre, but on the other side of the creek.
And someone else found some where the
twin live oaks are.

NM: Oh, there was some there, too?

WD: Yeah, they found it there. It was right
next to those twin live oaks. And this was on
the piece of paper, but they didn't go there.
Maybe meant to go later, but I think they
found enough over there, that . . .

NM: Yeah.

WD: Mais aux chênes verts là, la marque du trou est là toujours. C'est Navarre qu'a acheté ça.

NM: Là où lui, il est là, là-bas?

WD: Ouais, et il y en a qu'a été fouillé là et ils prétendent il y en a d'autre. C'est ça Navarre me dit, mais c'est connaître ayoù elle est.

WD: But at the live oak, the impression from the hole is still there. It's a Mr. Navarre who bought that land.

NM: Where he is over there?

WD: Yeah, and some went there to dig and they claim there's more. That's what Navarre told me, but it's a matter of knowing where it is.

108. Dédé et Dauterive / Dédé and Dauterive (Norris Mitchell, Scott)

This is another story about Dédé Anderson. As a prosperous farmer, he had several sharecroppers working for him according to the custom in the region. Stories about his reputation as a tough boss are due, in no small part, to the strong work ethic by which he and his own family lived. What may seem to be a violent fight, starting with a swing bar attack by Dauterive and ending with a shotgun blast from Anderson, was probably considered a fitting resolution to the problems at hand. In a discussion of the interpersonal nature of violence in the South ("Below the Smith and Wesson Line: Southern Violence," in *One South: An Ethnic Approach to Regional Culture*), John Shelton Reed explained that country folks did not always feel it necessary to invoke the law to redress a wrong between two parties. A fistfight or some other confrontation was often understood to be an adequate and appropriate way to resolve differences. William Lynwood Montell explored the extreme cases of this same notion in *Killings*. What might otherwise seem like a remarkable understatement at the end—that Dauterive took the rest of the day off—probably accurately described the results of these events. Dauterive was likely out working in Dédé Anderson's fields the next day, both satisfied that justice had been served.

Il y avait un vieux appelé Dédé Anderson. Il avait des bougres qui travaillaient pour lui. Et quand tu partais le matin pour aller dans le clos, t'avais pour demander quel bord de la pièce il fallait tu commences. Ça que t'étais après faire. Rabourer ou piocher, n'importe quoi, il fallait lui demander quel bord dans la pièce il fallait tu commences. Et là, il t'aurait dit. Et là, il aurait été dessus son cheval dans le clos voir comment le *job* était.

Et ils ont tourné en train dans le clos, lui et puis Dauterive. Ça fait, il a dételé ses mulets, il a attrapé un palonnier et il foutu quelques coups de palonnier au vieux bougre, à vieux Dédé. Ils ont eu du train

There was an old man named Dédé Anderson. There were lots of fellows who worked for him. And when you left in the morning to go out into the fields, you had to ask on what side of the field you should start. No matter what you were doing. Plowing or hoeing, anything, you had to ask on what side of the field you should start. And then he'd tell you. And then, he'd go out on his horse to see how the work was going.

And they got into a row in the fields, he and Dauterive. So he unhitched his mules, he grabbed the swing bar and he hit the old man, old Dédé, a few times with it. They had had some trouble concerning the work in the

pour le travaillage dans le clos. Il était pas après rabourer assez creux, ou quelque chose. N'importe comment, ils ont arrivé à avoir des paroles, et puis lui, il a arrêté ses mulets, et il a attrapé le palonnier et puis il a sacré Dédé à coups de palonnier.

Ça fait, Dédé a *gone*. Il a monté sur son cheval. Il s'en a été là-bas chez lui. Et un moment après, l'homme a fini ça il était après faire dans la pièce. Là, il fallait il va à la maison demander quel bord il fallait il commence dans l'autre pièce.

Ça fait, quand il est arrivé, vieux Dédé était assis dessus sa galerie. Il dit, "Monsieur Dédé, j'ai fini. Quel bord commencer dans l'autre pièce?" Vieux Dédé a jamais dit à rien. "Mais," il dit, "vous fais comme si vous parles pas, mais si j'attrape le palonnier, vous vas parler!"

Là Dédé a crié après une de ses filles pour elle amène son fusil. Et il y avait un canal qui coupait en travers de la savane. Dauterive s'a couché et il a parti à se sauver dans la savane en allant au canal. Quand il a arrivé presqu'au canal, Dédé l'a tiré. Ça fait, lui, il s'a juste tiré dans l'eau. Et l'eau ôte les plombs. Ça l'a ôté son plomb. Là, lui, il a resté là-dedans un élan. Vieux Dédé, il a rentré dans sa maison. Puis là, Dauterive a parti. Il a été chez lui pour la balance de la journée.

fields. He wasn't plowing deep enough, or something. Anyway, they finally started arguing and then he stopped his mules and he grabbed the swing bar and he got after Dédé with it.

So Dédé left. He mounted his horse. He went home. And a moment later, the man finished what he was doing in the field. Then he had to go to the house to ask on what side to start in the next field.

So when he arrived, old Dédé was sitting on his porch. He said, "Mister Dédé, I'm finished. On what side should I start in the next field?" Old Dédé never said a word. "Well," he said, "you're pretending you can't talk, but if I get that swing bar, you'll talk!"

Then Dédé yelled to one of his girls to get his shotgun. And there was a canal that cut across the pasture. Dauterive turned around and took off running across the pasture toward the canal. He had almost reached the canal when Dédé shot him. So he just jumped into the water. And the water brought out the lead pellets. It brought out the lead. So he stayed there a while. Old Dédé went back into his house. And then Dauterive left. He went home for the rest of the day.

109. *Le faiseur de pendules / The Clockmaker (Stanislaus "Tanisse" Faul, Cankton)*

Stories about the old days in Louisiana often focus on the harsh brutality of frontier life. This tale was told to illustrate that brutality. Because of the craftsman's refusal to teach his skill, he was cruelly mutilated (S165 "Mutilation: putting out eyes"; compare also motif S165.7 "Artisan who has built palace blinded so he cannot built another like it").

In the end, the storyteller discusses the options available to those who did not wish to fight in the old days. His pragmatic comments recall a popular saying, *"Mieux vaut capon vivant que défunt brave"* [Better to live a coward than die a hero].

C'était d'entendre les vieux parler des batailles. Il y avait un homme, une fois, il faisait des pendules et il vendait ça. Et il y a un homme, il voulait apprendre. Il a voulu l'homme lui montre. L'homme dit, "Non, je fais ma vie avec ça. Je peux pas te montrer. Apprends autre chose," il dit, "et moi, je vas garder ça pour moi faire ma vie."

Il lui a ôté les deux yeux. Il l'a aveuglé, l'homme, et il avait la pendule. Après il était aveuglé, l'homme dit, "Espère voir!" Il a tordu quelque chose dans la pendule. Elle a jamais remarché et il a jamais pu comprendre quoi c'était. Aveugler l'autre pauvre malheureux et puis, ça lui a servi à rien.

Le monde était criminel. C'est plus pareil. Le monde se connaît par les écoles. Le monde se rejoint. C'est pareil comme des frères et des sœurs. Habitude, quand tu rejoignais quelqu'un après que t'étais en âge, et tu l'avais vu avant, si il te faisait des grimaces, ça te choquait.

Asteur, c'est plus pareil. C'est vrai, ouais, ça. Le monde se refait au monde et c'est plus farouche comme d'habitude.
BA: Ça devait être dur a *stand* dans le temps-là. Si quelqu'un voulait se battre avec toi et toi, tu voulais pas, t'étais malpris.

SF: Mais tu connais quoi il fallait tu fais? Il fallait que tu t'en vas. C'est ça moi, je faisais!

You should have heard the old people talk of fights. There was once a man who made clocks and he sold them. And another man wanted to learn. He wanted the man to teach him. The man said, "No, I make my living this way. I can't teach you. Learn something else," he said, "and I'll keep my livelihood."

He plucked out both his eyes. He blinded the man, and he had the clock. After he was blinded, the man said, "Wait!" He twisted something in the clock. It never worked again and he was never able to understood what it was. He blinded the poor unfortunate fellow and learned nothing anyway.

People were criminal. It's not the same anymore. People know each other because of schools. People meet. It's like brothers and sisters. Once, when you met someone, after you had reached a certain age, if you had seen him before and he looked at you funny, it got you mad.

Now, it's no longer the same. This is true. People are getting along better and they're not as wild as they used to be.
BA: It must have been hard to stand all this in the old days. If someone wanted to fight you and you didn't want to fight, you were out of luck.
SF: Do you know all you had to do? You just had to walk away. That's what I did!

110. Un rendez-vous / A Duel (Stanislaus "Tanisse" Faul, Cankton)

In Louisiana, duels were a way of settling scores after arguments (P677). Generally, the choice of weapons depended on the gravity of the offense. For a major offense, the resolution could involve pistols or swords. For less serious offenses, there was usually a bareknuckle fight. At one time, in certain areas, one could find duels out in the fields nearly every Sunday after Mass, as people resolved problems that had occurred at the dance halls the night before. In this story, the teller describes an even graver situation in which one of the combatants was killed. It was clear from his tone of voice that the event had had a profound effect on the storyteller as a child.

Défunt vieux Blanco S., lui, et vieux
Pierre M., ils avaient eu plusieurs chicanes.
Le vieux papa à Monsieur Blanco voulait la
terre à vieux Pierre. Vieux Pierre avait quatre
acres de terre ayoù Freddie S. reste. Et le
vieux voulait pas s'en défaire. C'était un
forgeron. Il pouvait faire n'importe quoi avec
la forge. Et mon papa restait ici, chez les
Bohgni. Ça fait ils étiont grosse affaire. Ça se
faisait des veillées entre eux à tout moment.
Tous les dimanches, proche, ils étaient
ensemble. Eux autres aimaient beaucoup se
rencontrer. Un bon vieux homme terrible. Ça
fait, eux voulaient ça. Ça a pris en chicane.

Ça fait, il y avait un bal au ras de là, au
ras de chez Freddie. Quelqu'un avait fait un
bal de maison. Ça fait, ils s'étaient rencontrés
là. Et défunt Monsieur Blanco a pris à
picocher après le vieux bougre. Picocher
après pour le faire quitter de là et vendre la
terre à son père. Le train a pris et le vieux
avait pas peur mais pas de malice.

Ça fait, ils ont fait un rendez-vous pour
le dimanche matin. Ça, c'était le samedi soir.
Le dimanche matin à dix heures, ils se
seraient rencontrés en avant. Ils se seraient
battus aux armes. Le vieux a retourné chez
lui et il lui avait amené son fusil mais il était
dans un *sulky*. C'est comme ça qu'il se
promenait. Il avait une petite bêtaille rouge.
Bonne petite bêtaille.

Ça fait, il avait été là-bas chez lui. Il a fait
son ouvrage. Et il avait son fusil en bas dans
le *sulky*. Puis il est revenu chez défunt Pap
jusqu'à l'heure d'aller pour se battre. Mais il
avait chargé son fusil avec du coton, bouché
les deux canons de son fusil avec du coton. Il
voulait pas tuer l'homme.

Ça fait, quand ça a arrivé le temps pour
aller, défunt Pap dit ça, il dit, "Pierre, va pas."
Il dit, "Ça va réfléchir. Vous autres vas se
comprendre plus tard." Il dit, "Là, il faut
qu'un meurt." Il dit, "Rentourne-toi. Arrête
pas. *Go ahead* et dis pas rien."

The late Blanco S. and old Pierre M. had
had a few rows. The old father of Mister
Blanco wanted old Pierre's land. Old Pierre
had four acres of land where Freddie S. lived.
And the old man didn't want to get rid of it.
He was a blacksmith. He could make
anything in his smith's shop. And my father
lived here on the Bohgni's property. And they
were friends. They spent evenings together
now and then. They were together almost
every Sunday. They liked to get together. A
fine old man. So they wanted his land. And it
turned into an argument.

So there was a dance hall nearby, next to
Freddie's house. Someone had a house dance.
So they met there. And the late Mister Blanco
started to pick on the old man. Pick on him
to make him leave and sell the land to his
father. Trouble started and the old man was
without fear, but also without malice.

So they arranged a duel for Sunday
morning. It was Saturday night. Sunday
morning at ten o'clock they were to meet out
front. They would fight with firearms. The
old man went home and he brought his
shotgun, but he was in a sulky. That's how he
got around. He had a little red horse. Good
little horse.

So he had gone to his house. He did his
chores. And he had the shotgun on the floor
of his sulky. And he came back to my late
father's house until the time to go out and
fight. But he had loaded his shotgun with
cotton. He didn't want to kill the man.

So, when the time came for him to go,
my late father said, "Pierre, don't go." He
said, "They'll think this over. You'll reach an
understanding later." He said, "This way, one
must die." He said, "Go home. Don't stop. Go
ahead and don't say anything."

C'était un vieux Français. Il dit, "Au nom de Dieu, c'est ça je crois je vas faire." Il a embarqué et puis il était après s'en aller.

Quand il a passé en avant, le monde était après espérer pour. Ça fait, ils ont poigné leurs fusils. Quand ils ont vu l'homme était après s'en aller à petit train pour s'en aller chez lui, il y en a un qui dit, "Blanco, tu vas le laisser passer?" Il a tiré un coup de fusil. Il l'a frappé dans la jambe. La petite bêtaille, ça l'a frappée. Elle a juste viré de bord. Elle a revenu à la pleine course à la maison, chez mon papa.

Ça fait, ils l'ont pris. Ils l'ont mis couché et il est mort à la maison, chez mon papa. On a soigné ça. Ma maman a soigné sa jambe et tout, elle et sa vieille femme. Ils ont pas pu le sauver. Il a resté je sais pas combien de semaines malade. Il a souffert avec cette jambe! Et il est mort.

He was an old Frenchman. He said, "In God's name, that's what I think I'll do." He got in his sulky and he was going home.

When he passed in front of where they were, people were waiting for him. So they grabbed their rifles. When they saw that the man was going at a trot on his way home, one of them said, "Blanco, are you going to let him pass?" He shot once. He hit him in the leg. The little horse was hit, too. She just turned around. She came back at a gallop to our house, my father's house.

So they took him. They put him to bed, and he died there at my father's house. We took care of him. My mother took care of his leg and everything, she and his wife. They weren't able to save him. He was sick for I don't know how many weeks. He suffered terribly. And he died.

111. Victor et Arthur essaient de casser le bal / Victor and Arthur Try To Break Up the Dance (Adley Gaudet, Bayou Pigeon)

A common form of amusement for some on the Louisiana frontier was to break up a dance or take over a dance hall by causing so much trouble in the hall that everyone was forced to leave. Each neighborhood had its handful of troublemakers which regularly terrorized dance halls. A whole cycle of stories has arisen to describe their exploits. This story about counting the fighters as they are thrown out through an open window has entered oral tradition in lots of neighborhoods. The same story is also told about the legendary constable Martin Weber (see the following tale) and several other heroes and outlaws from the tough old days.

Vieux Victor Vaughn était un batailleur, tu sais, c'était un bon batailleur. Il était connu, vieux Victor Vaughn. Et un des cousins à Pap, vieux Arthur Gaudet. Ils ont été pour casser un bal un soir. Le cousin à Pap dit à vieux Victor, "Vic, allons casser le bal à soir."

Il dit, *"All right!"*

Il y avait un jeune homme et il était

Old Victor Vaughn was a fighter, you know, he was a good fighter. He was well-known, old Victor Vaughn. And one of Pop's cousins, old Arthur Gaudet, said to old Victor, "Vic, let's break up the dance tonight."

He said, "All right!"

There was a small, young man. He was

petit. Il avait juste à peu près cinq pieds, vieux Jake Mayeux. Et ça, c'est correct, ouais! C'est un *joke* dans une manière, mais c'est vrai.

Il dit, "Vic, moi, je vas rentrer en dedans-là, et toi, mets-toi à la fenêtre en dehors et comptes-les." Il dit, "Moi, je vas les passer en dehors."

Ça fait, vieux Jake s'en vient en dansant. *God damn!* Il l'attrape par le col et par la ceinture. *"Boy,"* il dit, "c'est pas rien pour passer vieux Jake en travers." Jake pesait à peu près quatre-vingt-dix livres, tu sais. Il le passe en travers la fenêtre. Il tombe en dehors.

Vic dit, "Un!"

Boy, il y a quatre ou cinq qui lui ont tombé dessus l'autre. Lui, il était grand, Arthur Gaudet. Ils l'ont sacré à travers de la fenêtre. Il tombe dehors.

Vic dit, "Deux!"

"Euh, euh, Vic!" Il dit, "Compte pas ça icitte, c'est moi!"

just about five feet tall, old Jake Mayeux. And this is true! Yeah! It's a joke, in a way, but it's true.

He says, "Vic, I'm going to go in there, and you place yourself outside by the window and count them." He says, "I'll throw them out. "

So, old Jake comes by dancing. God damn! He catches him by the collar and by the belt. "Boy," he says, "it's nothing to throw old Jake out." Jake weighed about ninety pounds, you know. He throws him out the window. He falls outside.

Vic says, "One!"

Boy, four or five guys fell upon the other one. He was pretty big, Arthur Gaudet. They threw him out the window. He fell outside.

Vic says, "Two!"

"Uh, uh, Vic!" He says, "Don't count this one. It's me!"

112. Martin Weber, Constable (Clence Ancelet, Lafayette)

This account is about a legendary constable from Ossun, a small town on the northwest corner of Lafayette Parish. He kept the peace there during the time when St. Landry Parish to the north and Acadia Parish to the west were still rather wild. Many of the residents in these parishes were frontiersmen who sometimes went to Ossun on Saturday night to attend a dance there because there were no dance halls in their region. Esta Hébert's dance hall in Ossun was the closest public meeting place on the edge of civilization. Martin Weber's reputation as a tough peacekeeper in this potentially unpeaceful place was known far and wide. There are lots of parallels from the American "Wild West," including Wyatt Earp and Wild Bill Hickok who tamed tough frontier towns such as Tombstone and Dodge City. (See Webb's *The Great Plains.*) Like them, Weber was also the toughest fellow around. He was picked to wear a badge so that his talent and energy would be channeled on the side of the law.

A typical episode in the saga of Martin Weber is related in this story. The bad guys are the infamous *Marais-bouleurs* [Marsh-bullies], well-known in the region for their rough and tumble ways, and easily identified by their tall black hats and red bandanas. In order to force the constable into a confrontation during a visit to Esta Hébert's dance hall, one of the

members of the gang began parading around the dance floor with all of his friends' hats on his head, in defiance of Weber's strict no-hats-in-the-hall policy. After an uncharacteristic second warning, the constable fell upon the imprudent outlaw, knocking the hats off with his stick and sending them flying around the room. He held the rest of the gang at bay and eventually threw them all out rather unceremoniously.

Monsieur Martin Weber, c'était mon oncle, ça. Il a marié la sœur de ma mère. Il était constable, là-bas chez Esta Hébert. Il soignait des différents de bals. Et c'était un homme qui tenait beaucoup la paix. C'était un homme qu'avait pas peur. C'était un homme basset, un gros basset. Il était *bald-headed*. Il avait pas peur d'à rien.

Et un soir, chez Esta Hébert, il y avait venu des hommes de Marais-bouleur, des bogheis avec des *tops* baissés. Puis moi et Monsieur Francis Guilbeau, on était assis en haut-là après les guetter faire, et puis eux avaient venu pour prendre le bal pour eux, éteindre les lumières, puis prendre le bal, eux. C'est ça ils ont dit.

Ça fait, défunt Martin s'avait compris avec plusieurs hommes, et puis ils s'avaient caché des affaires pour si ça venait plus mal. Mais défunt Martin dit, "Vous autres as pas besoin de vous tracasser. Je vas les tenir en bas."

Il y en avait un qu'a venu ayoù le monde danse pas-là. C'était entre les musiciens et puis les bancs-là. Il avait plusieurs chapeaux sur sa tête. Ça fait, défunt Martin a été, puis il a dit, bien poliment, "Jeune homme, ici, on marche pas avec des chapeaux sur la tête. Tu vas aller les faire *check*." (Tu donnais ton chapeau, puis tu donnais cinq sous, je crois ou dix sous, puis là, eux donnaient ton chapeaux après le bal.) Mais il a continué à marcher. Défunt Martin a été l'avertir. La deuxième fois, il a dit, "Quand je vas revenir la troisième fois, ça sera pas joli!" Ça fait, la troisième fois, il a venu avec un bâton, puis il a pris a cogner et puis les chapeaux a pris à voler, puis là, il a arrivé à cette tête-là. Et puis il l'a arrêté. Ça fait, les autres a foncé. Et

Mister Martin Weber was my uncle. He had married my mother's sister. He was a constable at Esta Hébert's place. He took care of several different dance halls. And he was a man who kept the peace particularly well. He was a man who wasn't afraid. He was a short man, a heavy short man. He was bald-headed. He was afraid of nothing.

And one night, at Esta Hébert's place, there came some of those men from the Marais-bouleur, in buggies with the tops down. And I and Mister Francis Guilbeau were sitting up high watching the whole affair. And they had come to take over the dance, turn out the lights, and take over the dance. That's what they said.

So the late Martin Weber had set up a plan with several men, and they had hid things in case things got worse. But old Martin said, "You all don't need to worry. I'll keep them under control."

There was one who came where people weren't dancing. This was between the musicians and the benches. He had several hats on his head. So old Martin went and said, very politely, "Young man, around here, we don't walk around with hats on. You will go and check them." (You would give your hat and pay five cents, or ten cents, and then they would give you your hat after the dance was over.) But he continued walking. Old Martin went to warn him. The second time, he said, "When I come back the third time, things will get ugly!" So the third time he came with a stick, and he started hitting and the hats started flying, and then he got to his head. And so he stopped him. So the others rushed him. And when they rushed forward,

quand ils ont foncé, il a sorti son pistolet, puis il a crié, "Grand rond!" Et ils se sont grand rond, aussi.

C'était un homme que jamais, jamais personne a pu prendre le dessus de lui. Si ça arrivait à là, il attrapait une main au fond de culotte, et puis une main dans ton cou, et puis il te tirait en travers la porte. Puis là, la citerne t'arrêtait souvent des fois. Ça, c'était comme c'était. Il était un homme, aussi bon constable comme la terre a jamais fait. Mais il avait pas peur de rien, et puis il coupait le train avant ça commence.

BA: Et puis, ces Marais-bouleurs, comment tu faisais pour connaître que c'était des Marais-bouleurs?

CA: *Well*, eux avaient tous des grands chapeaux, des grands chapeaux proche tout noir. Et puis, eux avaient un mouchoir dans le cou. Ça, c'était la manière. Mais ils ont jamais pris la place ce soir-là. C'est comme ça eux se distinguaient, avec un grand chapeau puis un mouchoir rouge dans le cou.

BA: Ça venait d'une certaine place?

CA: Ouais, ça venait d'une certaine place. Ça venait de dans le nord de nous autres. Ça venait—Je peux pas dire ayoù ça devenait, autre que alentour du clos d'huile. C'était des vaillants bougres, *but....*

BA: Ça aimait se battre?

CA: Ça aimait se battre, *that's right!* C'est ça, c'était. C'est comme ça, c'était. Mais c'est plus comme ça asteur. C'est du vaillant monde asteur. Depuis le clos d'huile de Bosco a venu, et puis ce monde-là, ça a mêlé.

C'est comme ça, c'était dans le vieux temps. Un homme pouvait pas aller dans un endroit d'un autre. Et quand il allait dans un endroit d'un autre, eux le faisaient partir, ou fallait il batte. C'était une manière de vivre dans ce temps-là.

BA: Et dans ce temps-là, c'était quand Martin Weber était constable, c'était dur dans ce temps-là?

CA: O ouais! C'était dur. Ça, o ouais! C'était

he drew his pistol, and he yelled, "Circle!" and they made a circle.

No one ever, ever got the jump on this man. If things got bad, he would catch you by the seat of your pants with one hand and by the neck with the other, and he'd throw you right out the door. And often enough, you didn't stop until you reached the cistern. That's how it was. He was a man, as good a constable as ever walked the earth. And he wasn't afraid of anything, and he would stop trouble before it started.

BA: And the Marais-bouleurs, how did one know who they were?

CA: Well, they all had tall hats, big hats almost always black. And they had bandanas around their necks. That was their way. But they never took over the dance that night. That's what distinguished them, the tall black hats and the red bandanas around their necks.

BA: Did they come from a certain place?

CA: Yes, they came from a certain place. They came from north of where we lived. They came—I can't say where they came from, other than from around the oil fields. They were nice fellows, but....

BA: They liked to fight?

CA: They liked to fight, that's right! That's what it was. That's how it was. But it's not that way any more. They're nice people now. Since the Bosco oil field was developed, and those people met other people.

That's how it was in the old days. A man couldn't easily go from one place to another. And when he went from one place to another, they would make him leave, or he had to fight. That was a way of life in the those days.

BA: And in those days when Martin Weber was constable, things were tough ?

CA: Oh yes! Things were tough. Oh, as for

des temps durs. C'était dans le mauvais temps, ça.

BA: Ça se battait souvent?

CA: Ouais! Ça se battait, ça se battait souvent. C'était possible d'avoir plus que trois ou quatre batailles par soir. C'était souvent des fois, c'était proche tout le temps comme ça.

that, yes! Those were tough times. Those were bad times.

BA: People fought often?

CA: Yes! They'd fight, and fight often. It was possible to have more than three fights a night. Many times, it was almost all the time like that.

113. Romain Weber et son rendez-vous / Romain Weber and His Duel (Clence Ancelet, Lafayette)

Martin Weber, the fearless constable featured in the previous story, was from a family filled with extraordinary men. (See the section "Les originaux," in Jolicœur's *Les plus belles legendes acadiennes*.) The bravery of one of his brothers, Romain, rivaled that of Martin himself. In this story, he has arranged a duel, but his rival does not show up at the appointed time, so he goes to find him. When his reluctant adversary finally shows up at his own home, he finds Romain still waiting there for him.

BA: Tandis qu'on est après parler, juste vite-là, c'est pas toi qui m'avais conté pour le frère à Martin Weber qu'avait eu un rendez-vous avec l'autre bougre?

CA: O *yeah!* Ça, c'était Monsieur Romain Weber, ça. Monsieur Romain Weber avait amarré un rendez-vous pour se battre à l'arme. Et il avait demandé à sa femme pour cuire la meilleure grosse poule il y avait dans la cour, par rapport il était parti se battre aux armes. Et elle lui a cuit la poule et il a mangé. Et il a parti bonne heure. Et quand il a arrivé à la place ayoù eux devaient se battre-là, il a demandé si son camarade était là, mais eux lui a dit non. Il avait pas venu, il avait pas rapporté.

Ça fait, il l'a espéré jusqu'à tard le matin. Et là, eux lui a demandé quoi c'est il aurait fait. "Mais," il dit, "je vas aller voir quoi c'est il y a avec le bougre." Il a arrivé chez la femme, et il a demandé à la femme, "Madame, je suis Monsieur Romain Weber et j'avais détaillé une bataille à l'arme avec votre

BA: While we're discussing it, very quickly, wasn't it you who told me about Martin Weber's brother who arranged a duel with another fellow?

CA: Oh yeah! That was Mr. Romain Weber. Mr. Romain Weber had arranged a duel to be fought with pistols. And he had asked his wife to cook the best and biggest chicken in the yard because he was going to duel with pistols. And she cooked the chicken for him and he ate it. And he left early. And when he arrived at the place where they were to fight, he asked if his comrade was there, but they said no. He had not arrived, he had not come through.

So he waited until late in the morning. And then, they asked what he would do. "Well," he said, "I'm going to go to see what's wrong with the fellow." He arrived there and asked the fellow's wife, "Madame, I'm Mr. Romain Weber and I had arranged a pistol duel with your husband, and I have my rifle

mari, et j'ai mon fusil asteur-là." Il dit, "Je veux savoir ayoù votre mari."

"Mais," elle dit, "il est pas là. Il va pas revenir." Elle dit, "Je suis sûre il va pas revenir parce qu'il a dit il aurait pas revenu."

Et il a espéré. Et quand il a revenu, il a causé avec. Et il a dit à Monsieur Romain que c'était mieux quitter toute l'affaire tranquille. Il a espéré dessus les escaliers du bougre. Et puis, quand le bougre a arrivé, il a dit qu'il voulait pas se battre et qu'il voulait des arrangements. Et là, défunt Romain Weber a été. "Mais," il dit, "mon ami, on est aussi amis asteur comme on a jamais été." Il dit, "Quand tu vas passer à la maison, si tu veux coucher dans mon lit, ou tu veux manger à ma table, ça, c'est *fine*. Si tu veux pas te battre, si tu veux passer pour capon," il dit, "ça, c'est *all right*! Mais," il dit, "j'avais venu pour finir avec toi, ou toi, t'aurais fini avec moi."

O ouais! C'était aussi raide comme tu peux trouver, mais c'était aussi vaillant comme il y en a sur la terre.

here and now." He said, "I'd like to know where your husband is."

"Well," she said, "he's not here. He's not coming home." She said, "I'm sure he's not going to come back, because he said he wasn't coming back."

And he waited. And when he came back, he spoke with him. And he said to Mister Romain that it would be better to leave the thing alone. He waited on the fellow's front steps. And then, when the fellow arrived, he said he didn't want to fight and that he wanted to make an arrangement. And then, the late Romain Weber went. "But," he said, "my friend, we're just as close now as we have ever been." He said, "When you come by my house, if you want to sleep in my bed, or if you want to eat at my table, that's fine. If you don't want to fight, if you are willing to pass for a coward," he said, "that's all right! But," he said, "I had come to finish you, or you would have finished me. "

Oh yes! He was as unrelenting as you could find, but he was also as nice as anyone on earth.

114. Adam Weber (Clence Ancelet, Lafayette)

Another of Martin Weber's brothers was Adam, who was known for his love not of fighting, but of fishing. He wasn't very fond of working and it took virtually no effort to convince him to leave his fields for the bayous. Often enough, his wife found herself alone on the farm. Compare motif W111.4 "Lazy husband." "The Lazy Farmer" and "The Well Digger" in Vance Randolph's *The Talking Turtle* offer other examples of lazy men.

N-Oncle Adam Weber, c'était un frère à Martin Weber. Il a marié Tante Choute. Choute c'était une fille à Monsieur Louis Ancelet, ça. Et il travaillait pas dur. On l'a connu dans le vieux temps.

Moi et Sidney Sonnier et défunt Louis Sonnier (c'est des garçons à défunt Bèbe Sonnier), un jour on a passé pour aller

Uncle Adam Weber was one of Martin Weber's brothers. He married Aunt Choute. Choute was one of Louis Ancelet's daughters. And he didn't work very hard. We knew him in the old days.

Sidney Sonnier, the late Louis Sonnier (sons of the late Bèbe Sonnier) and I were going out to catch some fish one day. And he

attraper du poisson. Et il avait son Moline. Il était après entourer la récolte. Il a arrêté dans le milieu des rangs et il a crié, *"Whoa!"* Et puis là, il a descendu et puis il a envoyé les mulets chez lui et puis il dit à Tante Choute, *"Dételle-les!"* Il dit, *"Moi, je suis parti à la pêche!"*

was working his Moline [farm implement]. He was ringing his fields. He stopped in the middle of the rows and he yelled, "Whoa!" And then he dismounted and he sent his mules home and he yelled to Aunt Choute, "Unhitch them!" He said, "I'm going fishing!"

115. *Le whisky volé / The Stolen Whiskey (Stanislaus "Tanisse" Faul, Cankton)*

The Cajuns have a long history as contraband runners, from the earliest days of the Acadian colony at the turn of the seventeenth century, when they traded with the English despite French prohibitions and with the French despite English prohibitions. Antonine Maillet treated this subject in several of her historical novels (cf. *Les cordes de bois*). Once resettled in Louisiana, some preserved these old habits. During Prohibition, many illegally made and sold alcohol. The key to survival in this risky business included the development of ingenious precautions against getting caught by the revenue men, federal agents assigned to control this activity. Complete discretion, such as that displayed by the neighbor in the following tale, was common and expected. Compare motifs J1563 "Treatment of difficult guests" and K335.0.4 "Owner frightened away from goods by a bluff." See also "You Ain't Coming Back," in Randolph's *The Talking Turtle,* for a similar intimidation story from the Ozarks.

Il y avait vieux Ab Venable et un homme, défunt Mélan Faul. Il avait volé du whisky. Il avait du *white mule*. Et ça a arrêté pour le chercher l'avant-midi. L'homme était après labourer ou planter du maïs, je crois. Il avait été au chemin. Il dit ça, il demande comment voir, s'il connaissait Mélan Faul. Il dit, "Mélan Faul m'a volé un baril de whisky. Je veux savoir ayoù il reste directement."

"Hmmm," vieux Ab dit, "je connais pas au juste ayoù il reste, mais il reste pas bien loin."

Il dit, "Je suis parti asteur mettre une charge contre lui." Et l'homme a continué à charrer, charrer, charrer. À tout moment, la femme à vieux Ab venait à la porte regarder s'il était pas après lâcher. Il était proche midi. Ça fait, l'homme, quelque sorte de manière, il

There was old Ab Venable and another man, the late Mélan Faul. He [Mélan Faul] had stolen some whiskey. He had some white mule. And they stopped to look for him in the morning. The man was plowing or planting corn, I think. He had gone to the road. He said, he asked if he knew Mélan Faul. He said, "Mélan Faul stole a barrel of whiskey from me. I want to know where he lives right now."

"Hmm," old Ab said, "I don't know exactly where he lives, but he doesn't live that far from here."

He said, "I going right now to bring a charge against him." And the man kept on talking, talking, talking. Every once in while, old Ab's wife came to the door to see if he wasn't about to knock off. It was almost noon. So the man, somehow, came around to

191

s'a échappé de demander voir comment il connaissait Mélan Faul.

Il dit, "Ouais, c'est mon frère!"

L'homme a *gone*. Ça l'a fait honte, il a parti. Et là, il a pu aller dîner. Et c'était pas parent du tout.

asking how he knew Mélan Faul.

He said, "Yes, he's my brother!"

The man left. He was ashamed, and left. And then, he was able to go and eat. And they weren't related at all.

116. Le vieux garçon et les chiens / The Bachelor and the Dogs (Stanislaus "Tanisse" Faul, Cankton)

This story, told as true, is actually a variant type 1530* *The Man and his Two Dogs:* "The Shepherd" and "Get the Sticks," in which a visitor is frightened away when he misunderstands the names of the two dogs for commands to the dogs. A variant of the treatment of difficult guests (J1563) is also involved here, this time in the context of courtship as a young man tries to visit an overprotected girl. Sunday afternoon was the time traditionally set aside for courting and fathers could sometimes find themselves tied up for hours at a time supervising the couple. This father found a way of screening potential suitors at the gate by simply calling the names of his aggressive-looking dogs.

J'en ai une que défunt Joe Faul contait. Il était vieux garçon. Il était tout le temps après venir tracasser. On appelait ça tracasser. Ça voyageait tout le temps. Il faisait des veillées à l'une et l'autre maison.

Ça fait, il allait voir une fille. Enfin, il avait sorti avec une fille et il a demandé pour aller la voir un dimanche après-midi. Elle lui avait dit oui. Il dit qu'il s'est fait expliquer ayoù elle restait. Il a été à cheval. Il a arrivé à cheval. Là, il dit il y a deux gros chiens *bulldog* qui ont venu. Il dit ça montait sur la barrière et ça jappait mauvais. Et le vieux homme était assis sur la galerie avec sa jambe croisée.

Il dit ça, il dit, "Les chiens sont mauvais?"

Il dit, "Non. [aux chiens] Laisse faire et Garde aux dents!"

"Mais," il dit, "c'est une sacrée affaire si je les laisse faire garder leurs dents."

Il dit, "Il a fallu que je m'en vas. Il a pas arrêté ses chiens."

I know a story that the late Joe Faul used to tell. He was a bachelor. He was always coming around and bothering folks. It was called bothering. He was always on the road. He went from one house to another to spend his evenings.

So he was going to see a girl. Anyway, he had gone out with a girl and he had asked to see her one Sunday afternoon. She had said yes. He said that he got directions to her house. He went on horseback. He arrived on horseback. Then, he said, two big bulldogs came. He said they were up against the fence and they were barking fiercely. And the old man was sitting on the porch with his legs crossed .

He said, "Are the dogs vicious?"

He said, "No. [to the dogs] Let Things Be and Watch for their Teeth!"

"Well," he said, "that's a fine situation if I'm to let things be and watch for their teeth." He said, "I had to go away. He wouldn't call his dogs."

117. Les deux nicheurs / The Two Practical Jokers (Félix Richard, Cankton)

This tale is a variant of motif J1169.5 "The laughing ass," as described by Baughman, with variants mostly from the South (Virginia, Kentucky and North Carolina) as well as from Connecticut. The storyteller insisted that this story really happened in his neighborhood where there is indeed a strong tradition of practical joking. (See "La jument verte / The Green Mare," no. 38, this collection.) Most times, the pranks are relatively innocent. One might send a new worker to get a tool which does not exist, such as a log-stretcher or a left-handed wrench. A family might return home after an outing to find their furniture on the roof or their wagon hanging from a tree. Nevertheless, this tradition was not without a darker side, such as the example given in this story. For other practical jokes involving horses, see "Roclore" (p. 51), in Saucier's *Folk Tales from French Louisiana*. The wide distribution of this storyline indicates that it is probably fictitious despite the protests of the storyteller that it was absolutely true. Even if this is not the case, the fact that the storyteller felt so strongly that it was true gives the story at least a psychological credence which preserves its chilling effect.

On dirait, c'est manière drôle de dire ça, *but* supposé ça a arrivé. C'est une histoire vraie. Dans le temps, le monde était canaille. On dirait asteur, t'entends plus autant parler des affaires qui arrivent parce que le monde est civilisé un peu et le monde a peur de la loi. Et il faut ça.

Il y avait deux garçons qui courtisaient la même fille, et c'était deux hommes qui étaient grosse affaire. Ça restait un chaque bord du chemin et ça allait au bal ensemble et chacun avait un joli cheval.

Ça fait, un soir, ils allaient au bal. Ils ont amarré les deux chevaux sur deux poteaux côte à côte et ils ont commencé à danser au bal, mais eux étaient en contrepointe. Quand un dansait avec la fille, l'autre dansait avec quelqu'un d'autre, et lui demandait l'autre danse. Ça fait, eux s'échangeaient ça toute la nuit. Ils ont dansé chacun son tour avec la même fille. Eux aimaient la fille et la fille aimaient les deux, mais elle connaissait pas quel choisir, et ces deux homme étaient trop grosse affaire pour se chercher du train l'un à l'autre. Les parents auraient pas aimé ça, tu connais.

One might think that it is odd to say this, but this is supposed to have happened. It is a true story. In the old days, people were naughty. Now, it seems that one hears less about such things happening because people are civilized a little and people respect the law. And this is important.

There were two boys who were courting the same girl, and they were very friendly. They lived just across the road from each other, and they went to the dance together and each had a beautiful horse.

So, one night, they were going to the dance. They tied up their horses to side-by-side posts, and they started dancing, but they were in counterpoint. When one danced with the girl, the other danced with someone else, and reserved the next dance. So they went back and forth like this all evening. They each danced in turn with the same girl. They loved the girl and the girl liked both of them, but she didn't know which of them to choose, and these two men were such good friends that they were not going to fight amongst themselves. Their families would not have liked that, you know.

Ça fait, il y a un qui dit à l'autre, je pense, "Tant qu'à toi, je vas te faire payer quelque chose pour ça." Et tout quelqu'un avait des bons couteaux. Il a sorti dehors. Il a été joindre le cheval de son *partner*, l'autre bougre qui était après danser avec la fille, et il lui a coupé la queue en balai, au moyeu même. Il lui a tout coupé. Puis dans le temps, le bougre avait un beau cheval. Il avait une belle queue et il brossait ce crin et puis c'était soigné comme tu soignes ton char aujourd'hui. C'est ça les chars ils avaient.

Ça fait que, tout à l'heure, c'est que lui, il a rentré dans la salle et lui, il a commencé à danser avec la fille. Son *partner* sort dehors voir si personne avait coupé sa selle, ou tu connais. Ça fait, lui, il va dehors. Il découvre quelqu'un avait coupé la queue de son cheval. Il s'a imaginé que c'était son *partner* qui lui avait fait ça. Ça fait, lui, il a fait quelque chose sur le cheval à l'autre bougre.

Ça fait, en s'en allant, il y avait un beau clair de lune. C'est que cil-là qui avait coupé la queue du cheval, il était après rire et tout les temps en temps, il se faisait une petite farce. Ça fait, tout à l'heure, son camarade lui dit, "Mais quoi c'est qui te fait rire comme ça?"

"Mais," il dit, "je connais pas. Il y a quelqu'un qui t'a joué une niche. Je vois ils ont coupé la queue de ton cheval en balai."

"O mais," il dit, "ça m'étonne pas que ton cheval est après rire depuis quand on est parti de la salle." Lui, quoi tu crois il avait fait? Il avait coupé la babine d'en bas de son cheval. Tu voyais toutes les dents. Il faisait comme si il était après rire. Il avait plus de babine.

Ça fait, eux s'avaient rendu joliment une mauvaise échange. Seulement, cil-là qui avait la babine coupée était un tas plus mauvais. Là, c'est manière cru, mais c'est une histoire vraie.

So one said to the other, I guess, "As for you, I'll make you pay for this." And everyone had a good knife. He went outside. He went out to his partner's horse, that of the other fellow who was dancing with the girl, and he cut its tail hairs off, leaving just the stump. He cut it all off. And in those days, the fellow had a beautiful horse. It had a beautiful tail and he brushed the tail, and he cared for it just like you care for your car today. Horses were their cars.

So, later, he went back into the dance hall and started dancing with the girl. His partner went outside to see if anyone had cut his saddle, or, you know. He went outside. He discovered that someone had cut his horse's tail. He imagined that it was his partner who had done this to him. So he did something to the other fellow's horse .

So while going home, it was a beautiful moonlit night. The one who cut the other horse's tail would laugh every now and then. He would amuse himself with what seemed a joke. So after a while, his friend said to him, "What in the world is making you laugh like that?"

"Well," he said, "I don't know. Someone played a trick on you. I see that someone has cut your horse's tail down to the nub."

"Well," he said, "it's no wonder then that your horse has been laughing since we left the dance hall." What do you think he had done?" He had cut the lower lip of the other horse. You could see all its teeth. It looked as though it was laughing. It had no more lower lip.

So they had given each other a bad exchange. The only thing is that the one whose horse's lip was cut had the worst of it. Now, that's pretty raw, but it's a true story.

118. La femme avec sa compagnie / The Woman and Her Company (Stanislaus "Tanisse" Faul, Cankton)

In Louisiana French oral tradition, there are lots of little stories in which hosts and hostesses make their guests understand that it is time to leave. In type 1449* *The Stingy Hostess at the Inn,* the woman explains to her guests that she cannot feed them because she has no spoons. Here, the reference to the foul weather for those who are not already home has the same goal for this hostess who is not stingy, but simply poor.

Similar stories are told to signal visitors that it is time to leave at the end of an evening visit. For example, a man may tell his wife, "Well, if I weren't home, I'd go there!" or "Wife, let's go to bed so that these good people can go home! "

Une femme, une fois, avait une pleine maison de compagnie et ça a pris à mouiller, mouiller, mouiller. Puis elle était pauvre. Elle avait pas rien pour donner à manger à tout le monde le soir. Ça fait, tout d'un escousse, elle dit, *"Boy, boy!* Ça, c'est un vilain temps pour le monde qu'est pas chez eux!"

A woman, once, had a houseful of visitors and it started raining, and raining, and raining. And she was poor. She had nothing to feed them all that night. So, suddenly, she exclaimed, "Boy, boy! What a terrible storm for those who are not yet home! "

119. Régile Reed (Fred Tate, Mamou)

According to motif K455.4 "The other man will pay the bill," three rascals eating in an inn each convince the innkeeper in turn that one of the others will pay for the meal, and they all eventually escape without paying. This variant features a sole rascal who plays a similar trick worthy of Compère Lapin himself, under the pretext of thanking his two benefactors. The storyteller insisted that this was one of many such exploits by the infamous Régile Reed, a renowned practical joker from Mamou. The storyteller's remark toward the end is the perfect justification of oral tradition: that the facts are not as important as the story itself.

Il était parti dans l'ouest. Il y a deux bougres qui l'ont ramassé. Ils lui ont donné un *ride* jusqu'à Houston qui était à peu près cent miles. Ça fait, quand ils ont arrivé à Houston, il dit aux bougres, il dit, "Vous autres étais assez bons de m'avoir donné un *ride,* je veux vous acheter chacun un bon *steak.*"

Ils ont été dans un restaurant et ils ont acheté trois *steaks.* Naturellement, il a pris le

He was headed out west. Two fellows picked him up. They gave him a ride to Houston which was about one hundred miles away. So when they arrived in Houston, he said to the fellows, he said, "You've been so nice to give me a ride, I want to buy each of you a steak."

They went into a restaurant and they bought three steaks. Naturally, he ordered his

sien *rare*, tu connais. Et le sien a été paré avant. Ça fait, quand ils ont donné son *steak*, il s'est dépêché à manger vite. Il dit, "Moi, je suis pressé. J'ai des affaires à faire, mais je vas passer au *cashier* et je vas payer pour vous autres." Il dit, "Quand je vas vous pointer, vous autres vas élever vos mains pour elle connaître c'est pour vous autres j'ai payé."

Ça fait, il a été, il a pris un cigare. Il a pris à charrer avec la *cashier* un bout de temps. Là, tout à l'heure, il dit, "Écoute, les deux bougres là-bas vont payer." Et c'était trop loin pour eux autres entendre quoi c'est il disait. Et puis, il les a pointés au doigt. Eux, ils ont levé leurs mains comme si c'était *okay*. Et il a parti.

Régile était bon pour avoir des affaires comme ça. Je connais pas si c'était tout vrai, mais c'était bien composé quand ça sortait. C'était un bougre qui roulait un tas.

rare, you know. And his was done first. So when he was given his steak, he hurried and ate it quickly. He said, "I'm in a hurry. I have a few things to take care of, but I'll go to the cashier and I'll pay for you both." He said, "When I point to you, you raise your hands so that she'll know that you are the ones I'm paying for.

So he went, he got a cigar. He started talking to the cashier. Then, after a while, he said, "Listen, the two fellows over there are paying for me." And it was too far for them to hear what he was saying. And then he pointed to them. They raised their hands as though it were okay. And he left.

Régile was good at that kind of thing. I don't know if it's all true, but it sure was well-composed when it was told. He was a fellow who travelled a lot.

120. Valery Mayer (Maude Ancelet, Lafayette)

This conversation describes another clever rascal, my own grandfather, who had a reputation among family and friends as a great storyteller and practical joker. As American comedian George Carlin once explained in a piece about his occupation, it is the job of some people to notice the funny stuff and report on it regularly to audiences. In the Pacanière region between Leonville and Arnaudville, the job was Valery Mayer's. His aptitude for clever retorts served him well as a traveling bread salesman in the first episode. In the second, for a laugh, he irreverently "treats" a slaughtered pig to stop its bleeding. A *traiteur* is the Louisiana French equivalent of a faith healer. In another episode, he even finds humor in a skimpy lunch. The last episode is about a prank he liked to play on Easter Sunday. Pâquer refers to the practice of striking two decorated boiled Easter eggs against each other to see which is the stronger. One holds his egg while the other strikes it with his own from above. The one whose egg breaks loses; traditionally he gives up his egg to be eaten by the winner. Pop Mayer found a way to win a laugh with a broken egg.

BA: J'ai entendu plusieurs histoires pour comment Pop Mayer était paillasse. Il faisait toutes sortes d'affaires, comme il vendait du pain pour la petite boulangerie et Mom Mayer était après me dire comment il arrivait

BA: I've heard several stories about how Pop Mayer was funny. He would do all sorts of things, for example, he sold bread for the little bakery and Mom Mayer told me how he arrived one afternoon with eggs, oranges,

un après-midi, il avait des œufs, des oranges et des pommes de terre, tout quelque chose autre que de l'argent pour son pain.

MA: Il jouait des niches jusqu'à avec le pain. Il avait perdu contrôle de son camion quand il était après délivrer le pain et eux lui donnaient des œufs pour payer le pain. Ça fait, il avait beaucoup des œufs et quand il a perdu contrôle, les œufs ont cassé, le pain tombait, et les papiers rouvraient. Ça fait il avait des tranches de pain pleines de z-œufs. Quand il a arrivé à un de les voisins que il connaissait bien, il lui a donné le pain tout trempe avec les œufs. Elle dit, "Quoi c'est tu veux je fais avec ça?" Elle dit, "Le pain est tout trempe avec des œufs."

"Mais," il dit, "fais de la poutine!"

Il était très farce. Il jouait des niches, et tout quelqu'un l'aimait, parce qu'il les faisait rire. Eux espéraient pour il vient.

BA: Mom Mayer pouvait pas rester fâchée avec lui.

MA: Non, elle pouvait pas rester fâchée. Elle me disait tout le temps elle pouvait pas rester fâchée parce que, quand même si elle avait le cœur cassé, il pouvait la faire rire.

BA: Et là il était un traiteur aussi.

MA: Il était un traiteur, et il jouait des niches jusqu'à avec ça.

BA: Quoi c'est il traitait pour?

MA: Le sang. Arrêter le sang. Et un jour—tout les familles se mettaient ensemble pour faire des boucherie tout les semaines—et quand c'était le tour de son père, et eux a attrapé le cochon, eux avaient commencé pour le faire saigner. Pop Mayer était caché après dire la prière pour faire le sang arrêter. Et tout d'une escousse, eux s'a aperçu le cochon saignait plus. Eux savaient carrément quoi c'est qu'avait arrivé. Son père a tourné de bord, il a dit, "*Boy*, c'est toi qu'es après faire ça en arrière-là!" Et il riait.

Il riait avec ses joies à lui-même. Il y a des fois il contait des contes, et il commençait à rire avant il finissait. Et c'était

potatoes, everything but money for his bread.

MA: He'd play tricks even with the bread. He lost control of his truck after he had delivered bread and they'd given him eggs to pay for the bread. So he had lots of eggs and when he lost control, the eggs broke, the bread fell, the paper wrapping opened. So he had slices of bread full of eggs. When he arrived at one of the neighbors, someone he knew well, he gave her the bread that was wet with eggs. She said, "What do expect me to do with this?" She said, "The bread is all wet with eggs."

"Well," he said, "make bread pudding!"

He was very funny. He'd play tricks, and everyone liked him because he made them laugh. Everyone waited for him to arrive.

BA: Mom Mayer couldn't stay mad at him.

MA: No, she couldn't stay mad. She always told me that she couldn't stay mad because, even if she had a broken heart, he could make her laugh.

BA: And wasn't he a treater, too?

MA: He was a treater, and he played tricks even with that.

BA: What did he treat?

MA: For bleeding. To stop bleeding. And one day—families would get together to slaughter [a pig or a calf] every week—and when it was his father's turn, and they caught the pig, they had started to bleed it. Pop Mayer was hiding and saying the prayer to stop bleeding. And all of a sudden, they noticed that the pig had stopped bleeding. They knew right away what was happening. His father turned around and said, "Boy, you're the one doing that back there!" And he laughed.

He laughed with his own joy. There were times he'd be telling stories and he'd start laughing before he reached the end. And

197

tout des choses que il . . . C'était pas des *jokes* il entendait. Ça venait de lui. Ça venait de lui. Il faisait des jokes avec ça qui venait dans sa tête. Ça qu'arrivait le jour-ça.

Une fois, moi et Daddy, on avait été chercher Pop Mayer à l'ouvrage. Et je dis, "T'as dîné?"

Il dit, "Ouais."

Je dis, "Quoi t'as mangé?"

Il dit, "Des petits pois bourrés." Il pouvait faire jusqu'à des *jokes* avec sa misère, parce que eux étaient pauvres et il en avait un tas de la misère. Mais il contait des contes. Tout quelqu'un l'admirait. Eux espéraient il arrive toute différente place, des soirées de familles ou dans des magasins, tout quelque chose.

BA: Moi, je me rappelle de lui, à Pâques, il se mettait un pot-de-chambre à l'envers. Il s'assisait dessus et puis il commençait à raconter des contes. Puis là tout quelqu'un commençait à venir.

MA: Eux venaient avec leurs œufs, pour pâquer les œufs. Mais son œuf à lui était tout le temps cru. Il s'arrangeait pour aller en haut. Puis là quand c'était son heure de pâquer avec quelqu'un d'autre, il commençait à rire avant il cogne l'œuf. Là l'œuf coulait sur ta main, et puis lui, il riait.

these were all stories that he . . . They were not jokes that he'd heard. They came from him. They came from him. He made jokes with what came into his head. Whatever happened that very day.

Once, Daddy and I were going to pick up Pop Mayer at work. And I said, "Did you eat?"

He said, "Yeah."

I said, "What did you eat?"

He said, "Stuffed peas." He could even make jokes about his own suffering, because they were very poor and he had lots of suffering. But he told stories. Everyone admired him. Lots of people could hardly wait for him to arrive, at family suppers, in stores, everywhere.

BA: I remember him at Easter time. He'd put a chamber pot upside down. He'd sit on it and start telling stories. And everyone came around.

MA: They came with their eggs, to *pâquer* eggs. But his egg was always raw. He would arrange to be on top. Then when he'd *pâquer* with someone, he'd start laughing before he hit the egg. Then the egg would drip all over your hand, and he'd laugh.

121. *Moonshining (Ida Mayer, Lafayette)*

Here, my grandmother gives a first-hand account drawn from her family's many adventures in moonshining. Her brothers, including Andrew Chautin, made great moonshine whiskey, but sometimes got caught selling it. Her husband, Valery Mayer, was good at selling it without getting caught, but couldn't make it himself. When Valery and Ida married, it was a match made in heaven, as well as in the Pacanière woods where the family stills were hidden. To protect themselves from the Revenue agents, the moonshiners devised early warning systems, such as the one described here. Bootleggers also came up with clever ways to stretch their profits and avoid detection. And they had to watch diligently in both directions at once. A family story tells of my grandfather carrying whiskey in a shoebox. He was approached by a suspicious character who claimed he wanted to buy some whiskey.

He said he didn't have access to the illegal stuff, but the man insisted. So my grandfather said he'd see what he could do, but he needed ten dollars. The fellow gave him the money, but demanded collateral. My grandfather said, "Here, then, hold my shoes until I get back." He, of course, did not return, but he also did not cheat the man, who discovered the whiskey when he opened the shoebox.

Here his wife tells about a client who was disappointed in his plan to water down the whiskey he was buying so that he could resell it because my grandfather beat him to the punch, and then about a foolish supplier who accidentally set fire to the whiskey barrel in their house while checking it. The nerves of the tender young housewife were understandably rattled, though not so much that she did not think of warning her neighbor not to create a scene as she was running out of the house with children under each arm. Through experiences such as this, she quickly developed nerves of steel and became an able partner in the family enterprise. Nevertheless, the code of secrecy which once characterized such clandestine activities continues to influence her. Even after all these years and the long-expired statute of limitations, it took a while for these stories to emerge even in conversations with members of her own family.

BA: La boisson était défendu dans ce temps-là?

IM: D'après moi, ouais.

BA: Mais tout le monde faisait leur boisson eux-mêmes?

IM: Pas tout, mais il y en a qui faisaient leur boisson eux-même.

BA: Et ça le vendait?

IM: Ha, mais là je connais pas si ça le vendait. Ça faisait un peu pour eux-autres boire. J'ai pas idée ça le vendait. Que moi, je connais pas.

Hé mais, boy, quand ça voyait les Revenues après venir quand ça faisait un petit peu-là, ça partait sur tout les bords. Tu connais, ils avaient pas grand argent pour acheter de la boisson, tu connais, et là ça faisait un petit peu pour eux-autres boire comme ça. Boy, quand ça voyait les détectifs, les Revenues. *God dog*, ça épaillait partout.

Quand eux étaient après faire le whisky dans le bois, quand ça commençait à donner la nouvelle que les Revenues étaient sur le chemin pour voir quoi qu'était quoi, si c'était-il vrai eux étaient après faire du whisky, ça les mettait la cache à l'oreille. Ça mettait un jeune bougre sur un cheval et puis

BA: Was liquor outlawed in those days?

IM: Probably so, yes.

BA: But everybody made their own liquor themselves?

IM: Not everybody, but there were some who made their own liquor.

BA: And they sold it?

IM: Ah, well, now I don't know if they sold it. They made a little for them to drink. I don't think they sold it. Not that I know about.

Hey, but boy, when they saw the Revenuers coming when they were making a little, they took off in all directions. You know, they didn't have much money to buy liquor, you know, and they made a little for them to drink like that. Boy, when they saw the detectives, the Revenuers, God dog, they scattered everywhere.

When they were making whiskey in the woods, when they started getting the news that the Revenuers were on the road to see what was what, if it was true that they were making whiskey, they spread the word. They had a young fellow go around on horseback from camp to camp to tell them that a

199

le bougre-là passait place en place à ces *camps* leur dire il y avait un Revenue qu'était après investiguer, tu connais, voir si eux étaient après faire le whisky. *Boy*, tu les voyais épailler partout. Ça laissait l'affaire telle comme c'était et puis ça épaillait sur tout les bords. Tout quelque chose restait droit là. Eux disent quand ça voyait l'affaire était calme, mais là ça prenait à avancer à les *camps* encore. C'était réellement farce pour les voir faire.

Une fois Mayer était après vendre du whisky à Lafayette. Il vendait un petit peu de whisky à Lafayette. Quand il y avait un gros *depression*. Et bien là, il amenait quelques galons pour vendre. Un gros *depression*. Il y avait proche pas rien d'autre chose à faire. Ça fait, un jour, il avait amené un petit peu du whiskey. Ça fait là, il y a un nommé René T. qu'avait venu chercher un peu pour vendre, pour vendre lui aussi, tu connais, por faire un petit peu. Ça fait là, quand René T. a arrivé chez lui, il a voulu couper le whisky por en faire un peu plus, tu connais. Ça fait, il parlait un peu croche. Il a goûté le whisky por voir comment fort il était por le couper avec un peu de l'eau. Ça fait, quand il a vu il était pas assez fort. Il dit, "Mo pas coupé li," il dit, "M. Valery Mayer avait coupé en avant de moi. Ça fait," il dit, "mo pas pu coupé."

Tu connais, une autre fois, il s'avait fait un petit robinet. Il avait mis un barril et puis il avait fait manière comme un petit cabinet, dans son cabinet, il avait mis un barril, et puis il avait mis un petit robinet après. Ça fait, il y a un bougre qui venait délivrer un peu du whisky, du *moonshine*. Et là, ça vidait ça en dedans, tu connais. Ça fait là, quelque temps après, à peu près une semaine après— Quand quelqu'un voulait quelque chose, ça dévissait le petit comme un robinet, tu connais. Ça mettait son quart ou son *pint*, et puis il l'avissait.

Ça fait, un jour, le bougre est venu—cil-

Revenuer was investigating, you know, to see if they were making whiskey. Boy, you'd see them scattering everywhere. They'd leave everything just as it was, and they took off in all directions. Everything stayed behind. They say when they saw that things had cooled off, they'd head out to the camps again. It was funny to see them do this.

Once, Mayer was selling whiskey in Lafayette. He was selling a little whiskey in Lafayette. When there was a great depression. Well, he would bring home a few gallons to sell. A big depression. There was almost nothing else to do. So, one day, he had brought a little whiskey. So, a fellow named René T. came by to get a little to sell himself, you know, to make a little money. So, when René T. arrived home, he wanted to cut the whiskey to make a little more, you know. So, he talked funny. He tasted the whiskey to see how strong it was to cut it with a little water. So when he saw that it wasn't strong enough, he said, "I didn't cut it," he said, "M. Valery Mayer had already cut it before me. So," he said, "I wasn't able to cut it at all."

You know, another time, he had made a little spiggot. He had a barrel and he had made a little cabinet, in his cabinet he had put a barrel and he had put a little spiggot on it. So there was this fellow who came around to deliver whiskey, moonshine. And he'd pour that in there, you know. So, some time later, about a week later—When someone wanted something, they'd open the spiggot, you know. They'd place their quart or pint and then they'd close it.

So one day, the fellow came—the one

là qui vendait le whisky—il est venu lui apporter le whisky, et puis il voulait—Il a mis sa main manière comme ça dans le barril pour voir s'il y en avait assez qui restait ou s'il fallait il en met d'autre. Ça fait, le couillon, il prend une allumette et puis il la gratte, tu connais, pour voir combien qui restait dans le barril. La flamme a pris dans le barril. Il connaissait pas ça aurait fait ça. Ça a pris en flamme enfin. La voisine, Eva B., elle restait justement l'autre voisine. Elle gâtait Maudry—et puis ça, c'est vrai, ouais—elle gâtait Maudry et Bobby. Quand elle a vu la flamme comme ça-là—Elle avait rentré. Mais elle dit, *"Ida, what's going on?"* elle dit.

"Mais," je dis, "l'imbécil," je dis, "il a craqué une allumette," je dis, "le feu a pris dans le barril."

"Mais," elle dit, "Ida!" Ça fait, elle a attrapé Bobby et Maudry, *your mama, you know, both sides and she ran in the street to bring them at her house.* "Mais," je dis, "Eva, fais attention!" J'étais jeune, tu connais. Je dis, "C'est un peu contre la loi," je dis. "Va pas crier partout sur le chemin avec les deux petits. Ils vont croire c'est une affaire abominable." Je pouvais pas l'empêcher. Elle a parti quand même.

Là il y avait une vieille négresse après *wax* le plancher. Elle dit, "Madame, quoi qu'est après aller *on?*"

Mais je dis, enfin, j'ai dit la même affaire encore. Je dis le bougre a *scratch* une allumette et puis il l'a mis trop près du whisky et je dis la flamme a pris.

Elle dit, "Prends une serviette et puis, "elle dit, "trempe-la, puis tords-la, puis envoie-la dans le whisky." Et elle dit, "Prends une autre et puis couvre-la, toujours trempe."

Moi, j'étais assez nerveuse, j'ai pris une petite couverte sec, et puis j'ai juste couvert le whisky comme ça. Et là, j'ai mis une autre moyenne serviette en dedans. Le feu a pris après les deux serviettes. J'étais jeune, tu connais. Et puis ça m'avait fait nerveuse.

who sold the whiskey—he came to deliver some whiskey, and he wanted—He put his hand sort of like this in the barrel to see if there was any left or if he should put some more in. So, the fool, he takes a match and he scratches it, you know, to see how much was left in the barrel. The barrel caught fire. He didn't know it would do this. The inside of the barrel was in flames. A neighbor, Eva B., who lived just next door. She was close to Maudry—and this is true—she was very close to Maudry and Bobby. When she saw the flame—She had come in. She said, "Ida, what's going on?" she said.

"Well," I said, "the fool," I said, "he lit a match," I said, "and the barrel caught fire."

"Well," she said, "Ida!" So she grabbed Bobby and Maudry, your mama, you know, both sides and she ran in the street to bring them at her house. "Well," I said, "Eva, be careful!" I was young, you know. I said, "It's kind of against the law," I said. "Don't go yelling everywhere in the streets with the two kids. Everybody will think that something horrible has happened." I couldn't keep her. She went out anyway.

Then there was an old black woman waxing the floor. She said, "Madame, what's going on?"

I said, well, I told her the same thing. I said the fellow scratched a match and put it too close to the whiskey and it caught fire.

She said, "Take a towel and," she said, "wet it and wring it and throw it in the whiskey." And she said, "Take another one and cover it, another wet one."

I was so nervous, that I took a dry little blanket and I just covered the whiskey like that. And I put another little towel in there. The two caught fire. I was young, you know. And I was nervous.

Elle dit, *"Mrs. Mayer,"* elle dit, "pas sec!" Elle dit, "Ça va brûler." Là enfin, ça allait, la pauvre vieille négresse et puis elle a trempé une serviette et elle l'a tordue manière. Elle l'a envoyé dans le whisky. Elle a trempé une autre couverte, tu sais. Elle a tout couvert le whisky, mais là ça a éteint la flamme.

BA: C'était dans la maison?

IM: Mais ouais. Ça fait, quand Pop Mayer a arrivé, il dit, "Mais quoi qu'a arrivé?" Il a arrivé un petit peu après. "Mais," il dit, "quoi qu'a arrivé?" Je lui ai conté l'affaire. Il dit, "Ce fils de putain!" Il dit, "Tu veux me dire," il dit, "il connaissait pas mieux que ça." Boy, il était chaud!

BA: Ça a tout brûlé le whisky?

IM: Ça a proche tout brûlé le whisky. Ça l'avait tout brûlé, ouais. Mais il dit, "Il faudra il prend la perte." Il dit, "Je vas sûr pas aller payer du whisky il a brûlé."

She said, "Mrs. Mayer," she said, "not dry!" She said, "It'll burn." So finally, the poor old black woman went and wet a towel and wrung it a little. She threw it into the whiskey. She wet another blanket, you know. She covered the whiskey and this put out the fire.

BA: This was in the house?

IM: Well, yes. So when Pop Mayer arrived, he said, "Well, what happened?" He arrived a little later. "Well," he said, "what happened?" I told him. He said, "That son-of-a-bitch!" He said, "Do you mean to tell me," he said, "he didn't know any better than that?" Boy, he was really mad!

BA: Was the whiskey burned?

IM: It almost burned up all the whiskey. It was burned, yes. So he said, "He'll have to take the loss." He said, "I'm surely not going to pay for whiskey that he burned."

122. Les Revenues / The Revenuers (Andrew Chautin, Gillis)

Tales of bootleggers who succeed in escaping from federal revenue agents abound in Louisiana French oral tradition. They are based on the same principle as many animal tales, glorifying the trickery of the clever bootlegger and ridiculing the efforts of the bumbling government men who represent the higher authority Cajuns seem so delighted in deflating. Here my great-uncle tells of a great escape that was facilitated because of the ridiculousness of the situation. The Revenue agents apparently found it hard to shoot someone who made them laugh so hard. Burrison has a related story, "Doody's Escape from the Revenuers" (pp. 204–205), in which a bootlegger gets away by running and walking across the bottom of the river (he couldn't swim). Once back in his cabin, he denies he was in the woods, and his wife provides an alibi.

Un jour, j'arrivais au camp, et je m'étais aperçu qu'il y avait quelque chose qui était *wrong.* J'ai vu des pistes dans la boue que j'étais pas accoutumé de voir. Ça fait, j'étais à cheval et il y avait pas de selle, pas rien sur le cheval. J'avais justement mis la bride en haut et puis j'avais amarré après la barrière du

One day, after arriving at my camp, I noticed there was something wrong. I saw tracks in the mud that I was not used to seeing. So, I was on horseback, and I had no saddle, nothing on the horse. I had just passed the bridle over and tied up to the fence that ran around the camp. And the

camp. Et les *revenue men* étaient cachés depuis l'avant-jour pour m'espérer.

Ça fait, j'ai arrivé là. J'ai descendu. J'ai amarré le cheval avec la corde après la barrière. Quand j'ai descendu, il y a deux des *revenues* qui ont galopé en allant à moi avec deux pistolets qui ressemblaient longs comme ça. [geste pour indiquer environ trois pieds]

J'ai sauté sur ce cheval. Et c'est un cheval qui était nerveux puis vite. Et le cheval s'a aperçu qu'il y avait quelque chose qui était *wrong*. Quand j'ai monté en haut de lui, j'ai pas eu le temps pour démarrer la corde après la bride. Et les *revenues* ont pris à galoper en allant à moi et ils m'auraient attrapé. Quand j'ai vu ça, j'ai jonglé le plus court je peux faire, c'est ôter la bride du cheval et rester en haut. Ça fait, j'ai poussé la bride et j'ai ôté ça de dans sa tête. Le cheval a tourné et puis ça a parti. Il passait en travers des éronces et il sautait avec moi monté sur son dos. Il avait la queue de collée en arrière de mon épaule après se sauver.

Et ils nous ont pas attrapés. Hé, j'avais peur, donc.

revenue men were hidden in there since before dawn waiting for me.

So I got there. I dismounted. I tied the horse with the rope reins to the fence. When I was down, two reveneurs came running toward me with two pistols that seemed as long as this. [gesture indicating about three feet]

I jumped onto the horse. And this was a frisky and fast horse. And the horse had noticed that something was wrong. When I mounted it, I had not had time to untie the rope reins. And the reveneurs started running toward me and they would have caught me. When I saw this, I thought the fastest thing I could do was to take the bridle off and stay on. So I pushed the bridle and took it off its head. The horse turned and took off. It went through briars and jumped with me on its back. It had its tail raised high, right up against my shoulder, running away.

And they didn't catch us. Hey, but I was scared, though.

123. Du whisky dans les fossés / Whiskey in the Ditches (Andrew Chautin, Gillis)

Not everyone was always able to escape from the government agents, but even in those cases when someone was caught, there was a story to tell. In this tale, the neighbors are so horrified to see good whiskey wasted that they salvage what they can. Compare motif F162.2.2 "Rivers of wine in otherworld." There is a parallel story from the more recent drug traffic. When federal agents burn confiscated marijuana, neighbors gather at the fence line to breathe deeply.

Il y a du monde qui faisait le *bootleg whiskey* et là d'autres le serraient en haut de leurs greniers, dans leurs maisons, dans leurs magasins. Et il y en un qui avait un magasin plein avec des barils de whisky et les *revenues* ont été. Ils ont pris à casser les barils. Le

There were people who made bootleg whiskey and others stored it up in their attics, in their houses, in their bars. And one fellow had a barn full of whiskey barrels and the reveneurs went. They started to break the barrels. The whiskey was flowing everywhere

whisky coulait partout dans la cour, dans les fossés. Les *boozeheads* ont été se chercher chacun une tasse et puis ils allaient dans les fossés. Eux s'attrapaient des *drinks* et ça se saoulaient. Ça a arrivé au platin. Ça allait chercher du whisky dedans les fossés.

in the yard, in the ditches. The boozeheads went to get cups and they went into the ditches. They would collect drinks and get drunk. This happened in the flats. They would go and collect the whiskey in the ditches.

Bibliography

Underlined portions of titles indicate the shortened forms used to identify these works in the headnotes to the individual tales.

Classification References

Aarne, Antti, and Stith Thompson. 1961. *The Types of the Folktale: A Classification and Bibliography.* Folklore Fellows Communications 184. Helsinki: Academia Scientiarum Fennica.

Bascom, William. 1992. *African Folktales in the New World.* Bloomington and Indianapolis: Indiana University Press.

Baughman, Ernest W. 1966. *Type and Motif-Index of the Folktales of England and North America.* Indiana University Folklore Series 20. The Hague: Mouton.

Bolte, Johannes, and Georg Polívka. 1913–32. *Anmerkungen zu den Kinder- und Hausmärchen der Brüder Grimm.* Leipzig: Dieterich'sche Verlag.

Christiansen, Reidar Thoralf. 1958. *The Migratory Legends.* Folklore Fellows Communications 175. Helsinki: Academia Scientiarum Fennica.

Delarue, Paul, and Marie-Louise Tenèze. 1957–85. *Le conte populaire français.* vols. 1–3. Paris: Maisonneuve et Larose.

Flowers, Helen L. 1952. "A Classification of the Folktales of the West Indies by Types and Motifs." Diss. Indiana University.

Hoffman, Frank. 1973. *Analytical Survey of Anglo-American Traditional Erotica.* Bowling Green, OH: Bowling Green University Popular Press.

Klipple, May A. 1938. "African Folk-Tales with Foreign Analogues." Diss. Indiana University.

Lacourcière, Luc, and Margaret Low. n.d. "Catalogue raisonné du conte populaire français en Amérique du nord." Unpublished manuscript.

Legman, Gershon. 1968 (first series) and 1975 (second series). *Rationale of the Dirty Joke: An Analysis of Sexual Humor.* New York: Grove Press (first series); New York: Breaking Point (second series).

Parsons, Elsie Clews. 1933, 1936 and 1943. *Folk-Lore of the Antilles, French and English.* 3 vols. Memoirs of the American Folklore Society 26. New York: G.E. Stechert.

Robe, Stanley L. 1973. *Index of Mexican Folktales; Including Narrative Texts from Mexico, Cen-*

tral America, and the Hispanic United States. Berkeley, Los Angeles, and London: University of California Press.

Thompson, Stith. 1955–58. *Motif-Index* of Folk-Literature: A Classification of Narrative Elements in Folktales, Ballads, Myths, Fables, Mediaeval Romances, Exempla, Fabliaux, Jest-Books, and Local Legends. 6 vols. Bloomington: Indiana University Press.

Woods, Barbara Allen. 1959. *The Devil in Dog Form: A Partial Type Index of Devil Legends*. Berkeley: University of California Press.

Linguistic, Historical and Cultural References

Allain, Mathé, and Barry Jean Ancelet. 1981. *Anthologie: Littérature française de la Louisiane*. Bedford, NH: National Materials Development Center for French.

Ancelet, Barry Jean, Jay Edwards, and Glen Pitre. 1991. *Cajun Country*. Jackson: University Press of Mississippi.

Ancelet, Barry Jean. 1980a. "Talking Pascal in Mamou: A Study in Folkloric Competence." *Journal of the Folklore Institute* 17: 1–24.

———. 1982. "Elements of Folklore, History, and Literature in Longfellow's *Evangeline*." *Revue de Louisiane/Louisiana Review* 11: 118–26.

———. 1983. "And This Is No Damn Lie: Oral History in Story Form." *International Journal of Oral History* 4: 99–111.

———. 1984. *The Makers of Cajun Music/Musiciens cadiens et créoles*. Austin: University of Texas Press.

———. 1985. "Ôte voir ta sacrée soutane: Anti-clerical Humor in Louisiana French Oral Tradition." *Louisiana Folklore Miscellany* 6, 1: 26–33.

———. 1988. "A Perspective on Teaching the Problem Language in Louisiana." *French Review* 61: 345–56.

———. 1989. "The Cajun Who Went to Harvard: Identity in the Oral Tradition of South Louisiana." *Journal of Popular Culture* 23, 1: 101–14.

Anderson, George K. 1965. *The Legend of the Wandering Jew*. Providence: Brown University Press.

Arsenault, Bona. 1965. *Histoire et généologie des Acadiens*. Québec: Le Conseil de la Vie Française en Amérique.

Barde, Alexandre. 1861. *Histoire des comités de vigiliance aux Attakapas*. St. Jean Baptiste: 1861. Impr. du Meschacébé et de l'Avant-coureur.

Bascom, William. 1977. "African Folktales in America: The Talking Skull Refuses to Talk." *Research in African Literatures* 8: 266–91.

Bouvier, Jean-Claude, ed. 1980. *Tradition orale et identité culturelle: Problèmes et méthodes*. Paris: Éditions du Centre National de la Recherche Scientifique.

Brasseaux, Carl A. 1987. *The Founding of New Acadia: The Beginnings of Acadian Life in Louisiana, 1765–1803*. Baton Rouge: Louisiana State University Press.

————. 1992. *Acadian to Cajun: Transformation of a People, 1803–1877.* Jackson: University Press of Mississippi.

Broussard, James. 1942. *Louisiana Creole Dialect.* Baton Rouge: Louisiana State University Press.

Brown, Becky. 1988. "Pronominal Equivalence in a Variable Syntax." Diss. University of Texas, Austin.

Brunvand, Jan Harold. 1972. "The Study of Contemporary Folklore: Jokes." *Fabula* 13,2: 1–19.

de Cerisier, René. 1638. *L'innocence reconnue, ou Vie de Ste Geneviève de Brabant.* Paris.

Chaudenson, Robert. 1974. *Le léxique du parler créole de la Réunion.* 2 vols. Paris: Librairie Honoré Champion.

Conrad, Glenn R., ed. 1978. *The Cajuns: Essays on Their History and Culture.* Lafayette: University of Southwestern Louisiana, Center for Louisiana Studies Publications.

————. ed. 1979; rev. 1986. *New Iberia.* Lafayette: University of Southwestern Louisiana Center for Louisiana Studies Publications.

Conwell, Marilyn J., and Alphonse Juilland. 1963. *Louisiana French Grammar I: Phonology, Morphology and Syntax.* The Hague: Mouton.

Cyrano de Bergerac, Savinien. n.d. *L'autre monde, ou Les états et empires de la lune et du soleil.* Paris and New York: Cercle du livre de France.

Dégh, Linda. 1969. <u>*Folktales and Society*</u>: *Story-telling in a Hungarian Peasant Community.* Bloomington: Indiana University Press, 1969.

Ditchy, J[ay] K[arl], ed. 1932. *Les Acadiens louisianais et leur parler.* Baltimore: The Johns Hopkins University Press; and Paris: Librairie E. Droz.

Dorman, James H. 1983. *The People Called Cajuns.* Lafayette: University of Southwestern Louisiana, Center for Louisiana Studies Publications.

Dorson, Richard M. 1964. <u>*Buying the Wind*</u>: *Regional Folklore in the United States.* Chicago and London: University of Chicago Press.

————., ed. 1972. *Folklore and Folklife: An Introduction.* Chicago and London: University of Chicago Press.

————. 1976. *Folklore and Fakelore.* Cambridge, MA, and London: Harvard University Press.

Dupont, Jean-Claude, ed. 1978. *Folklore français d'Amérique: Mélanges en l'honneur de Luc Lacourcière.* Ottawa: Éditions Leméac.

Fine, Elizabeth. 1983. "In Defense of Literary Dialect: A Response to Dennis R. Preston." *Journal of American Folklore* 96: 321–330.

————. 1984. *The Folklore Text: From Performance to Print.* Bloomington: Indiana University Press.

Gerber, A. 1893. "Uncle Remus Traced to the Old World." *Journal of American Folklore* 6: 245–57.

Goldstein, Kenneth S. 1964. *A Guide for Field Workers in Folklore.* Hatboro, PA: Folklore Associates.

Gould, Philip. 1981. *Les Cadiens d'asteur / Today's Cajuns.* Lafayette: Left Coast Press.

Griffiths, Naomi E. 1973. *The Acadians: Creation of a People.* New York: McGraw-Hill Ryerson.

Guidry, Richard. 1982a. *C'est p'us pareil*. Lafayette: University of Southwestern Louisiana, Éditions de la Nouvelle Acadie.

———. 1982b. *Les jeunes Louisianais*. Baton Rouge: Louisiana State Department of Education.

———. 1983. *La famille Richard*. Baton Rouge: Louisiana State Department of Education.

Guilbeau, John. 1950. "The Spoken French of Lafourche Parish." Diss. University of North Carolina, Chapel Hill.

Hallowell, Christopher. 1979. *People of the Bayou: Cajun Life in Lost America*. New York: Hastings.

Hand, Wayland D., ed. 1971. *American Folk Legend: A Symposium*. Berkeley, Los Angeles, and London: University of California Press.

Harley, Timothy. 1885; rpt. 1970. *Moon Lore*. Rutland, VT: C. E. Tuttle.

Jamison, Mrs. C. V. 1905. ["A Louisiana Legend Concerning Will o' the Wisp."] *Journal of American Folklore* 18: 250–51.

Jolicœur, Catherine. 1970. *Le vaisseau fantôme: Légende étiologique*. Québec: Presses de l'Université Laval.

Kniffen, Fred. 1963. "The Physiognomy of Rural Louisiana." *Louisiana History* 4: 291–99.

Lacourcière, Luc. 1970. *Les transplantations fabuleuses: Conte-type 660*. Québec: Archives de Folklore.

Lindahl, Carl. 1988. "Who is Jack?: A Study in Isolation." *Fabula* 29: 373–82.

———. 1994. "Jack, My Father, and Uncle Ray: Frank Proffitt, Jr.'" In *Jack in Two Worlds*, ed. William B. McCarthy. Chapel Hill: University of North Carolina Press.

Maillet, Antonine. 1971. *Rabelais et les traditions populaires en Acadie*. Québec: Presses de l'Université Laval.

———. 1974. *La Sagouine*. Ottawa: Éditions Leméac.

———. 1977. *Les Cordes-de-bois*. Ottawa: Éditions Leméac.

Montell, William Lynwood. 1970. *The Saga of Coe Ridge: A Study in Oral History*. Knoxville: University of Tennessee Press.

———. 1986. *Killings: Folk Justice in the Upper South*. Lexington: University Press of Kentucky.

Morel, Robert, and Suzanne Walter. 1967. *Dictionnaire des superstitions*. Verviers, Belgium: Marabout.

Morgan, Raleigh, Jr. 1959. "Structural Sketch of St. Martin Creole." *Anthropological Linguistics* 1,8: 20–24.

———. 1960. "The Lexicon of Saint Martin Creole." *Anthropological Linguistics* 2,1: 7–29.

Paris, Gaston. 1903. *Légendes du Moyen âge*. Amsterdam: Rodopi.

Parr, Una M. 1940. "A Glossary of the Variants from Standard French in Terrebonne Parish, with an Appendix of Popular Beliefs, Superstitions, Medicines, and Cooking Recipes." M.A. thesis, Louisiana State University, Baton Rouge.

Phillips, Hosea. 1936. *Étude du parler de la paroisse Evangéline (Louisiane)*. Paris: Librairie E. Droz.

Poirier, Pascal. 1964 and 1977. *Glossaire Acadien*. Moncton: Université de Moncton.

Post, Lauren C. 1962. *Cajun Sketches from the Prairies of Southwest Louisiana.* Baton Rouge: Louisiana State University Press.

Preston, Dennis R. 1982. "'Ritin' Fowklower Daun 'Rong." *Journal of American Folklore* 95: 304–26.

―――. 1983. "Mowr Bayud Spellin': A Reply to Fine." *Journal of American Folklore* 96: 330–39.

Propp, Vladimir. 1968. *Morphology of the Folktale.* Austin and London: University of Texas Press.

Read, William A. 1931. *Louisiana-French.* Louisiana State University Studies, no. 5; gen. ed., Charles W. Pipkin. Baton Rouge.

Reed, John Shelton. 1982. *One South: An Ethnic Approach to Regional Culture.* Baton Rouge: Louisiana State University Press.

Reed, Revon. 1976. *Lâche pas la patate: Portrait des Acadiens de la Louisiane.* Ottawa: Éditions Parti Pris.

Rushton, William Faulkner. 1979. *The Cajuns: From Acadia to Louisiana.* New York: Farrar, Straus and Giroux.

Saint-Exupéry, Antoine. 1943. *Le petit prince.* New York: Reynal and Hitchcock.

Schmitz, Nancy. 1972. *La mensongère (conte-type 710).* Québec: Presses de l'Université Laval.

Taylor, Joe Gray. 1976. *Louisiana: A Bicentennial History.* The States and the Nation series, ed. James Morton Smith. New York: W. W. Norton & Company.

Tedlock, Dennis. 1983. *The Spoken Word and the Work of Interpretation.* Philadelphia: University of Pennsylvania Press.

Thompson, Stith. 1946. *The Folktale.* New York: Holt, Rinehart and Winston.

Valdman, Albert, ed. 1981. *Haitian Creole-English-French Dictionary.* Bloomington: Indiana University, Creole Institute.

Voorhies, Edward T. 1949. "A Glossary of Variants from Standard French in St. Martin Parish, Louisiana, followed by some of the Folklore of the Parish." M.A. thesis, Louisiana State University, Baton Rouge.

Webb, Walter Prescott. 1931. *The Great Plains.* Boston: Ginn and Company.

Whitfield [Holmes], Irene Thérèse. 1939. *Louisiana French Folk Songs.* Baton Rouge: Louisiana State University Press.

Wilson, Justin, and Howard Jacobs. 1974. *Justin Wilson's Cajun Humor.* Gretna: Pelican Publishing.

Winzerling, Oscar William. 1955. *Acadian Odyssey.* Baton Rouge: Louisiana State University Press.

Wright, Hamilton, Helen Wright, and Samuel Rapport, ed. 1968. *To the Moon!* New York: Meredith Press.

Collections

Abernethy, Francis E., ed. 1966. *Tales from the Big Thicket.* Austin and London: University of Texas Press.

Abrahams, Roger D. 1964; rev. 1970. _Deep Down In the Jungle_: Negro Narrative Folklore from the Streets of Philadelphia. Chicago: Aldine Publishing.

Æsop. 1949. _Æsop's Fables_. Trans. James and George Tyler Townsend. Philadelphia: J. B. Lippincott Company.

Ancelet, Barry Jean. 1977. "Je suis surement pas un conteur de contes, mais . . . : Oral Literature of French Louisiana," M.A. thesis, Indiana University.

———. 1980b. "Creole Tales from Louisiana." _Revue de Louisiane / Louisiana Review,_ 9: 61–68.

Barat, Christian, Michel Carayol, and Claude Vogel, eds. 1977. _Kriké Kraké_: Recueil de contes créoles réunionais. Travaux de l'Institut d'Anthropologie Sociale et Culturelle de l'Océan Indien, no. 1.

Bødker, Laurits, Christina Hole, and G. D'aronco, eds. 1963. _European Folk Tales_. Hatboro, Pennsylvania: Folklore Associates; and Copenhagen: Rosenkilde and Bagger.

Botkin, B. A., ed. 1945. _Lay My Burden Down_; A Folk History of Slavery. Chicago: University of Chicago Press.

Brandon, Elisabeth. 1955. "La paroisse de Vermillon: Moeurs, dictons, contes et légendes." Diss. Université Laval.

Brewer, J. Mason. 1958. _Dog Ghosts and Other Texas Negro Folktales_. Austin: University of Texas Press.

———. 1968. _American Negro Folklore_. New York: Quandrangle / The New York Times Book Company.

Briggs, Katharine, M. 1960. British Folktales. Hirts. Bloomington: Indiana University Press.

Burrison, John A., ed. 1989. _Storytellers:_ Folktales & Legends from the South. Athens: University of Georgia Press.

Carrière, Joseph Médard. 1937. _Tales from the French Folklore of Missouri_. Evanston and Chicago: Northwestern University Press.

Carayol, Michel and Robert Chaudenson, eds. 1978a. _Lièvre Grand diable_ et autres: Contes créoles de l'Océan Indien. Conseil International de la Langue Française. Paris: Edicef.

———. and ———. eds. 1978b. _Les aventures de Petit Jean: Contes créoles de l'Océan Indien._ Conseil International de la Langue Française. Paris: Edicef.

Chase, Richard. 1943. _The Jack Tales_. Boston: Houghton Mifflin Company.

———. 1948. _Grandfather Tales_. Boston: Houghton Mifflin Company.

Claudel, Calvin. 1944. "Louisiana Tales of Jean Sot and Bouqui and Lapin." _Southern Folklore Quarterly_ 8: 287–99.

———. 1945. "Spanish Folktales from Delacroix, Lousiana." _Journal of American Folklore_ 58: 208-224.

———. 1948. "A Study of Louisiana French Folktales in Avoyelles Parish." Diss. University of North Carolina: Chapel Hill.

——— 1955. "The Folktales of Louisiana and Their Background." _Southern Folklore Quarterly_ 19: 164–70.

———. 1978. _Fools and Rascals_: Louisiana Folktales. Baton Rouge: Legacy Publishing Com-

pany.

Claudel, Calvin, and Joseph Médard Carrière. 1943. "Three Tales from the French Folklore of Louisiana." *Journal of American Folklore* 56: 38–44.

Clower, Jerry. 1992. *Stories from Home.* Jackson: University Press of Mississippi.

Coffin, Tristram P., ed. 1961. *Indian Tales of North America: An Anthology for the Adult Reader.* Austin: University of Texas Press.

Contes créoles illustrés: Textes bilingues créoles français. 1976. Paris: Agence de Coopération Culturelle et Technique.

Delarue, Paul, ed. 1956. *The Borzoi Book of French Folk Tales.* New York: Alfred A. Knopf.

Dorrance, Ward Allison. 1935. *The Survival of French in the Old District of Sainte Genevieve.* Columbia: University of Missouri Press.

Dorson, Richard M. 1946. *Jonathan Draws the Long Bow.* Cambridge, Massachusetts: Harvard University Press.

———. 1967. *American Negro Folktales.* Greenwich, CT: Fawcett Publications.

———., ed. 1975. *Folktales Told Around the World.* Chicago and London: University of Chicago Press.

Dubose, Louise Jones, ed. 1941. *South Carolina Folk Tales.* Columbia, SC: Bulletin of the University of South Carolina.

Dupont, Jean-Claude. 1978. *Le légendaire de la Beauce.* Montréal: Leméac.

Equilbecq, F.-V. 1972. *Contes populaires d'Afrique occidentale.* Paris: Maisonneuve et Larose.

Fauset, Arthur Huff. 1931. *Folklore from Nova Scotia.* Memoirs of the American Folklore Society 24. Boston and New York: Houghton Mifflin Company.

———. 1927. "Negro Folk Tales from the South (Alabama, Mississippi, Louisiana)." *Journal of American Folklore* 40: 213–303.

Fortier, Alcée. 1887. "Bits of Louisiana Folk-Lore." *Transactions and Proceedings of the Modern Language Association* 3: 101–68.

———. 1895. *Louisiana Folktales* in French Dialect and English Translation. Memoirs of the American Folklore Society 2. Boston and New York: Houghton Mifflin Company.

Glassie, Henry. 1982. *Irish Folk History: Texts from the North.* Philadelphia: University of Pennsylvania Press.

Grimm, Jacob and Wilhelm. 1972. *The Complete Grimm's Fairy Tales.* Trans. [Margaret] Hunt. 2nd ed. New York: Pantheon Books.

———. 1981. *The German Legends of the Brothers Grimm.* Trans. and ed. Donald Ward. Philadelphia: Institute for the Study of Human Issues.

Halpert, Herbert N. 1947. "Folktales and Legends from the New Jersey Pines: A Collection and Study." Diss. Indiana University.

Harris, Joel Chandler. 1955. *The Complete Tales of Uncle Remus.* Boston: Houghton Mifflin Company.

Harvison, C. Renée, Carl Lindahl, and Maida Owens, eds. n.d. *Swapping Stories: Folktales of Louisiana,* forthcoming.

Jackson, Bruce. 1974. *Get Your Ass in the Water And Swim Like Me: Narrative Poetry from*

Jansen, William Hugh. 1949. "Abraham 'Oregon' Smith: Pioneer, Folk Hero and Tale-Teller." Diss. Indiana University.

Jones, Loyal, and Billy Edd Wheeler, eds. 1987. *Laughter in Appalachia: A Festival of Southern Mountain Humor.* Little Rock: August House.

Jolicœur, Catherine. 1981. *Les plus belles légendes acadiennes.* Montréal and Paris: Stanké.

La Fontaine, Jean de. 1923. *Les fables.* Paris: Garnier.

Laforte, Conrad, ed. 1980. *Menteries drôles et merveilleuses: Contes traditionnels du Saguenay.* Montréal: Éditions Quinze / Mémoires d'Homme.

Legaré, Clément, ed. 1980. *La bête à sept têtes et autres contes de la Mauricie.* Montréal: Editions Quinze / Mémoires d'Homme.

Lemieux, Germain, ed. 1973–91 *Les vieux m'ont conté: contes franco-ontariens.* 32 vols. Montréal: Éditions Bellarmin; and Paris: Maisonneuve et Larose.

McNeil, W. K., ed. 1985. *Ghost Stories from the American South.* Little Rock: August House.

———. 1989. *Ozark Mountain Humor.* Little Rock: August House.

Massignon, Geneviève, ed. 1968. *Folktales of France.* Folktales of the World series; gen. ed. Richard M. Dorson. Chicago and London: University of Chicago Press.

Munchausen, Baron. 1944. *The Adventures of Baron Munchausen.* New York: Pantheon.

Perrault, Charles. 1946. *Contes.* Montréal: Les Editions Variétés.

Randolph, Vance. 1951. *We Always Lie to Strangers: Tall Tales from the Ozarks.* New York: Columbia University Press.

———. 1952. *Who Blowed Up the Church House? and Other Ozark Folktales.* New York: Columbia University Press.

———. 1957. *The Talking Turtle and Other Ozark Folktales.* New York: Columbia University Press.

———. 1958. *Sticks in the Knapsack and Other Ozark Folktales.* New York: Columbia University Press.

———. 1976. *Pissing in the Snow and Other Ozark Folktales.* Urbana, Chicago and London: University of Illinois Press.

Ranke, Kurt, ed. 1966. *Folktales of Germany.* Folktales of the World series; gen. ed. Richard M. Dorson. Chicago and London: University of Chicago Press.

Saucier, Corinne. 1972. *Folk Tales from French Louisiana.* Baton Rouge: Claitor's Publishing Division.

Saucier, Corinne. 1949. "Histoire et traditions de la paroisse des Avoyelles en Louisiane." Diss. Université Laval.

Saxon, Lyle, Edward Dreyer, and Robert Tallant, eds. 1945. *Gumbo Ya-Ya.* Boston: Houghton Mifflin Company.

Serpas, Paul F. 1967. *Tales of Louisiana Treasure.* Baton Rouge: Claitor's Publishing Division.

Thomas, Rosemary Hyde, trans. 1981. *It's Good to Tell You: French Folktales from Missouri.* Columbia: University of Missouri Press. Translation and re-edition of Carrière 1937.

Thompson, Stith. 1966. *Tales of the North American Indians.* Bloomington: Indiana University Press.

25 Best Lies of 1933. 1934. Burlington, WI: Burlington Liars Club.

Index of Tale Types

The following table lists the Cajun and Creole folktales according to the international classification developed by Antti Aarne and Stith Thompson in *The Types of the Folktale*. Entries followed by [AF] are listed according to the supplemental numbers developed by Luc Lacourcière and Margaret Low in their "Catalogue raisonné du conte populaire français en Amérique du Nord." The designation [B] refers to Ernest Baughman's *Type and Motif-Index of the Folktales of England and North America*.

277A. *Frog Tries in Vain to Be as Big as the Ox.*

280A. *Ant and the Lazy Cricket.*

301A. *Quest for a Vanished Princess.*

303. *Twins or Blood-Brothers.*

315A.*Cannibal Sister.*

327B. *Dwarf and the Giant.*

513B. *Land and Water Ship.*

565. *Magic Mill.*

660. *Three Doctors.*

706. *Maiden Without Hands.*

712. *Crescentia.*

713.* *Warrior and Faithful Wife.*

726. *Oldest on the Farm.*

752B. *Forgotten Wind.*

769. *Dead Child's Friendly Return to Parents.*

777. *Wandering Jew.*

883A. *Innocent Slandered Maiden.*

1030. *Crop Division.*

1049. *Heavy Axe.*

1115. *Attempted Murder with Hatchet.*

1119. *Ogre Kills His Own Children.*

1173A. *Devil Is To Fulfill Three Wishes.*

1229. *If the Wolf's Tail Breaks.*

1278A [B]. *Marking a Good Fishing Spot.*

1291B. *Filling Cracks with Butter.*

1296. *Fool's Errand.*

1319. *Pumpkin Sold as an Ass's Egg.*

1337. *Peasant Visits the City.*

1339A. *Fool Is Unacquainted with Sausages.*

1345.* *Stupid Stories Depending on Puns.*

1349D.* *What Is the Joke?*

1363.* *Second Cat.*

1365B. *Cutting with the Knife or the Scissors.*

1379.* *False Members.*

1449.* *Stingy Hostess at the Inn.*

1476. *Prayer for a Husband.*

1525A. *Theft of Dog, Horse, Sheet or Ring.*

1530.* *Man and His Two Dogs.*

1544. *Man Who Got a Night's Lodging.*

1564.** *Clever Granary Watcher.*

1567F. *Hungry Shepherd Attracts Attention.*

14. *Les petits ouaouarons.*

15. *Froumi et Grasshopper.*

26. *Barbe-bleue et Barbe-rouge.*

19. *Petit Pouce.*

19. *Petit Pouce.*

18. *Petit Poucet.*

20. *Jean l'Ours et la fille de roi.*

24. *Cendrillonne.*

85. *L'opération à Hube.*

21. *L'histoire de Sainte Geneviève.*

21. *L'histoire de Sainte Geneviève.*

21. *L'histoire de Sainte Geneviève.*

23. *Le voyageur.*

92. *L'homme qui demandait la pluie.*

27. *La famille qu'avait perdu la petite fille.*

94. *Juif errant.*

21. *L'histoire de Sainte Geneviève.*

5. *En haut la terre ou en bas la terre.*

25. *Petit Jean et le diable.*

25. *Petit Jean et le diable.*

18. *Petit Poucet.*

41. *D'autre tabac!*

51. *Quoi-ce qui bouche le trou?*

42. *Marquer la place.*

35. *Jean Sot.*

35. *Jean Sot.*

8. *Les oeufs de lument.*

41. *D'autre tabac!*

58. *Les hot dogs.*

59. *Le fer dans le lit!*

43. *Frapper la main.*

56. *Le commis-voyageur.*

34. *Le rat ou la souris.*

45. *Dans le lit ou sur la table.*

118. *La femme avec sa compagnie.*

29. *La vieille fille qui voulait se marier.*

22. *Fin Voleur.*

116. *Le vieux garçon et les chiens.*

56. *Le commis-voyageur.*

103. *Métayer Joe.*

46. *La vache à cinq veaux.*

1960M$_2$. *Large Mosquitoes Carry Off Men or Animals.*

2015. *Goat Who Would Not Go Home.*

2031. *Stronger and Strongest.*

2040. *Climax of Horrors.*

84. *Les gros maringouins du Texas.*

17. *Bicoin et les choux.*

16. *Neige casse la patte de la froumi.*

32. *Fido est mort.*

Index of Motifs

The following table catalogues the motifs found in *Cajun and Creole Folktales*. Unless otherwise noted, all numbers cited are from Stith Thompson's *Motif-Index of Folk-Literature*. Entries followed by **[B]** are from Ernest Baughman's *Type and Motif-Index of the Folktales of England and North America*. Entries followed by **[H]** are from Frank Hoffman's *Analytical Survey of Anglo-American Traditional Erotica*.

Motif Number and International Title	Story Number and Cajun or Creole Title
A751.1.1. [B] *Man in moon is thrown there as a punishment for working (burning brush or gathering sticks) on Sunday.*	93. *L'homme dans la lune.*
A1131.0.1. *Regulation of rains.*	92. *L'homme qui demandait la pluie.*
A1671.1. *Why the Negro works.*	102.*Vieux Nèg et Vieux Blanc té gain une course.*
A1974. *Creation of penguins.*	83. *Jim rencontre une femelle seal au North Pole.*
A2382. *Why animal is a hybrid.*	83. *Jim rencontre une femelle seal au North Pole.*
A2494.4.4. *Enmity between dog and rabbit.*	10. *Le chien et le lapin.*
A2817. *Origin of the will-o'-the wisp.*	95. *Feux follets.*
B17.1.2.3. *Transformed man as hostile dog.*	89. *La contrôleur et sa bible.*
	98. *Le chien étrange.*
	21. *L'histoire de Sainte Geneviève.*
B301.1. *Faithful animal at master's grave dies of hunger.*	
B524.1.2. *Dogs rescue master from tree refuge.*	19. *Petit Pouce.*
B535. Animal Nurse.	21. *L'histoire de Sainte Geneviève.*
B871.1.1.1. *Giant ox.*	82. *Boulé Sévenne se fouille un trou.*
C423.2. *Tabu: speaking of extraordinary sight.*	90. *Une petit tombe dans le bois.*

X1124.5.* [B] *Hunter trails animal in reverse, ends up at animal's birthplace.*   72. *Le traceur du chevreuil.*

X1133.3.2(a). [B] *If the bear's tail breaks.*   51. *Quoi-ce qui bouche le trou?*

X1212(a). [B] *Wildcats fight: they climb each other until they are out of sight.*   70. *Le bataille de chats.*

X1215.8(ba). [B] *Man tosses a half-dollar into river. . .*   66. *Laurent et Télismar à la pêche.*

X1215.13.* [B] *Remarkable dog.*   31. *Le chien qui marchait sur l'eau.*

X1235.1.1. *Cow wears church bell for cowbell.*   82. *Boulé Sévenne se fouille un trou.*

X1237.2.3(c).* [B] *Weight of blue ox.*   82. *Boulé Sévenne se fouille un trou.*

X1237.2.3(fa).* [B] *Eagle wears out seventeen sets of feathers flying from one of Babe's horns to the other.*   82. *Boulé Sévenne se fouille un trou.*

X1237.2.5(l).* [B] *Babe eats up fifty acres of Douglas fir.*   82. *Boulé Sévenne se fouille un trou.*

X1241.1. *The great horse.*   69. *Vieux Narcisse Mayeux.*

X1286.1. *Lie: the large mosquito.*   84. *Les gros maringouins du Texas.*

X1286.1.2(a). [B] *Mosquitoes weigh ten pounds.*   84. *Les gros maringouins du Texas.*

X1286.1.4(a). [B] *. . . Mosquitoes drill through the roof; the men clinch the bills and the mosquitoes fly away with the building.*   84. *Les gros maringouins du Texas.*

X1611.1.5.1(a).* [B] *Man who is gawking at the doings of the wind is turned inside out.*   69. *Vieux Narcisse Mayeux.*

X1611.1.8(g).* [B] *Tornado sucks all water in its path.*   67. *Le tourbillon.*

X1611.1.16.* [B] *Remarkable wind does work for man.*   67. *Le tourbillon.*

X1622.3.3.2.(a).* [B] *Man trapped in burning hotel pours pitcherful of water out the window, slides to safety on the icicle which forms.*   68. *La hache à August.*   74. *La chandelle de glace.*

X1700. *Lies: logical absurdities.*   78. *La bande de canards.*

X1721.2. [B] *Skillful surgeon removes and replaces vital organs.*   85. *L'opération à Hube.*

X1753(c).* [B] *Man is given job of breaking day every morning.*   80. *Mayo sur la lune.*

X1767.1(b).* [B] *Loud snoring causes people to complain of church bells ringing at night.* 86. *Les oreilles à Hube sonnent.*

X1767.2(a).* [B] *Draft draws wood out of stove, up chimney.* 69. *Vieux Narcisse Mayeux.*

X1796.5.* [B] *Fast vehicle.* 79. *Pascal et son bicycle.*

X1812(a). [B]. *Cook bakes enormous pudding.* 24. *Cendrillonne.*

Z13.4(m).* [B] *Young man stays overnight with hill couple . . . eats the rest of the greens.* 57. *La jarre de cornichons.*

Z42. *Stronger and strongest.* 16. *Neige casse la patte de la froumi.*

Z46. *Climax of horrors.* 32. *Fido est mort.*

Index of Narrators

Unless specifically described as Creole, all the following narrators are Cajun. After the name of each storyteller, the number(s) of the tale(s) told by that individual appear in boldface. A few tales that appear in the Jokes section of the Introduction are unnumbered; these tales are listed by page numbers, in parentheses.